I0881949

AI Literacy in Early Childhood and Primary Education

Muhammad Usman Tariq
https://orcid.org/0000-0002-7605-3040
Abu Dhabi University, UAE & University College Cork, Ireland

IGI Global
Scientific Publishing
Publishing Tomorrow's Research Today

Vice President of Editorial	Melissa Wagner
Director of Acquisitions	Mikaela Felty
Director of Book Development	Jocelynn Hessler
Production Manager	Mike Brehm
Cover Design	Jose Rosado

Published in the United States of America by
IGI Global Scientific Publishing
701 East Chocolate Avenue
Hershey, PA, 17033, USA
Tel: 717-533-8845 | Fax: 717-533-7115
Website: https://www.igi-global.com E-mail: cust@igi-global.com

Copyright © 2027 by IGI Global Scientific Publishing. All rights reserved. No part of this publication may be reproduced, stored or distributed in any form or by any means, electronic or mechanical, including photocopying, without written permission from the publisher. Use of this publication to train generative artificial intelligence (AI) technologies is expressly prohibited. The publisher reserves all rights to license its use for generative AI training and machine learning model development.

Product or company names used in this set are for identification purposes only. Inclusion of the names of the products or companies does not indicate a claim of ownership by IGI Global Scientific Publishing of the trademark or registered trademark.

Library of Congress Cataloging-in-Publication Data

LCCN: 2025031520 (CIP Data Pending)
ISBN13: 979-8-3373-4893-3
Isbn13Softcover: 979-8-3373-4894-0
EISBN13: 979-8-3373-4895-7
British Cataloguing in Publication Data
A Cataloguing in Publication record for this book is available from the British Library.

All work contributed to this book is new, previously-unpublished material.
The views expressed in this book are those of the authors, but not necessarily of the publisher.
This book contains information sourced from authentic and highly regarded references, with reasonable efforts made to ensure the reliability of the data and information presented. The authors, editors, and publisher believe the information in this book to be accurate and true as of the date of publication. Every effort has been made to trace and credit the copyright holders of all materials included. However, the authors, editors, and publisher cannot assume responsibility for the validity of all materials or the consequences of their use. Should any copyright material be found unacknowledged, please inform the publisher so that corrections may be made in future reprints.

Table of Contents

Detailed Table of Contents

This chapter presents a comprehensive AI Literacy Continuum model that emphasizes a developmental, human-centred approach to AI education spanning early childhood to university. It critiques fragmented, late-stage AI instruction and advocates for integrated, ethical, and inclusive learning pathways. Drawing on global case studies and rigorous pedagogical frameworks, the chapter highlights how curiosity, empathy, and critical reflection serve as foundational pillars of AI literacy. It underscores the vital role of teachers and institutions in fostering readiness, cultural sensitivity, and ethical responsibility. Policy recommendations call for systemic alignment, lifelong learning ecosystems, and collaborative international efforts to ensure equitable access and sustained impact. Ultimately, the chapter redefines AI literacy as an extension of human literacy—nurturing reflective, empowered citizens capable of shaping AI's role in society with wisdom and conscience.

As affective AI (emotion AI) becomes embedded in children's lives, a critical educational gap has emerged. Current AI literacy initiatives focus on computational thinking, neglecting the socio-emotional competencies needed to navigate complex interactions with machines that simulate emotion. This chapter introduces the Socio-Emotional AI Literacy (SEAL) framework, a pedagogical model for early education (ages 6–12). Based on a conceptual synthesis of developmental psychology, emotional intelligence, and critical technology studies, the SEAL framework has four pillars: Algorithmic Awareness (deconstructing AI "emotion"), Empathetic Interpretation (centering the child's feelings), Critical Discernment (questioning bias and authenticity), and Ethical Interaction (promoting responsible use and data privacy). By providing a structured approach to this neglected domain, the SEAL framework offers a crucial contribution toward empowering children to become critical, ethical, and emotionally intelligent architects of their technological future.

Understanding how young children make sense of complex systems such as social interactions, ecosystems, and technological environments has become central to cognitive and educational research. Grounded in theories by Piaget, Vygotsky, and information processing scholars, this chapter explores how children develop systems thinking and causal reasoning skills from early childhood. It highlights how developmental mechanisms such as abstraction, analogy, and feedback recognition form the foundation for understanding interdependence and change. The chapter integrates perspectives from cognitive science and social constructivism, emphasizing how sociocultural and contextual factors including culture, language, and educational settings shape children's cognitive growth. Using examples from Malaysia and Southeast Asia, it connects theoretical foundations to educational practice and policy, advocating for early education that cultivates systems reasoning, curiosity, and reflective awareness of complexity.

This chapter explores the use of artificial intelligence (AI) in early childhood language education, focusing on its potential to enhance vocabulary, grammar, and social-emotional communication skills. It discusses the role of AI tools like voice assistants and chatbots in enhancing these skills. The chapter also discusses the importance of equity, inclusivity, and ethical design in AI-based learning tools. It calls for teacher training, interdisciplinary collaboration, and ongoing research to ensure AI supports safe, effective, and meaningful language learning for young learners.

This chapter proposes a hands-on approach to AI education for children aged 6-12, focusing on building simple AI projects without the need for coding, a barrier I've seen firsthand in my work with technology integration. Leveraging my experience in system design, I aim to create activities that allow young learners to interact with AI concepts through tangible, code-free methods. For instance, children could design a basic AI-driven sorting game using physical objects like colored blocks, where they define rules for an AI to follow, such as grouping by color or size, using pre-built tools like Google Teachable Machine's image recognition features. Another activity might involve creating an AI-assisted storyboard, where children input ideas into a drag-and-drop interface to generate a narrative, then refine it based on their creative vision. These projects are grounded in experiential learning principles, ensuring children actively engage with AI processes while bypassing technical hurdles.

The systematic literature review looks into how AI literacy is integrated into primary education through different curriculum frameworks, pedagogical approaches, and policy initiatives across the global arena. Pulling from studies between 2000 and 2025, the review synthesizes research done in advanced and developing countries alike to arrive at overarching trends, challenges, and interesting pedagogies in early AI education: In some countries, AI is placed under computational thinking and digital skills curricula, while in others, isolated modules or interdisciplinary approaches are trialled. Pedagogical approaches range from experiential learning and gamification to project- and inquiry-based learning. While promisingly moving ahead, remaining gaps include teacher readiness, equitable access, and adequately supportive contextualised policies. We call for the evolution of AI literacy initiatives that subscribe to inclusivity, cultural responsiveness, and age-appropriateness, anchored by strong educational frameworks.

As artificial intelligence (AI) becomes increasingly embedded in early and primary education through apps, virtual assistants, and adaptive learning tools, fostering critical thinking in children (ages 3–11) is vital for responsible interaction with AI. This chapter, "Developing Critical Thinking: Helping Children Question AI Outputs," explores ways to help young learners evaluate AI-generated content with curiosity and discernment. It introduces AI in the context of children's daily lives and cognitive development, covering bias, reliability, and errors. The chapter offers age-appropriate teaching strategies, classroom activities such as analyzing AI stories, and discussions on fairness. It highlights collaboration with parents and communities to support learning beyond school. By nurturing critical thinking as

Preface

The integration of artificial intelligence (AI) into everyday life is no longer a distant vision of the future; it is a defining reality of the present. From voice assistants and recommendation systems to autonomous vehicles, intelligent healthcare, and personalized digital platforms, AI technologies increasingly shape how we live, learn, work, and interact. As these systems become deeply embedded within society, the need for AI literacy has emerged as an essential educational priority. Yet, despite the rapid advancement of AI across industries and communities, education systems around the world have been comparatively slow to adapt.

While tertiary institutions and, increasingly, secondary schools have begun introducing AI-related subjects and computational thinking initiatives, a significant gap remains in preparing younger learners for an AI-driven world. Primary and early years education continue to focus largely on traditional literacies, often overlooking the foundational knowledge and critical thinking skills required to understand and responsibly engage with intelligent technologies. This gap presents both a challenge and an opportunity: if AI influences the future of every child, then AI education should not be reserved for specialists or introduced only at advanced levels of schooling.

Recognizing this urgency, several leading nations, including China and the United States, have formally acknowledged the importance of embedding AI education from as early as six years of age. These policy developments reflect a broader global understanding that AI literacy is becoming a new form of basic literacy one that sits alongside reading, writing, and numeracy as an essential competency for the twenty-first century. Importantly, introducing AI education in early childhood is not primarily about coding or technical mastery. Rather, it is about cultivating curiosity, creativity, pattern recognition, ethical reasoning, problem-solving, and critical thinking through developmentally appropriate learning experiences.

This book was conceived in response to the growing need for practical, inclusive, and research-informed approaches to AI education for young learners. Its purpose is to establish a foundational framework for integrating AI education into early childhood and primary school curricula beginning at age six. By bridging the gap between national AI policy ambitions and practical classroom implementation, the book seeks to provide educators, curriculum developers, policymakers, and educational technology innovators with actionable strategies for introducing AI concepts in meaningful and age-appropriate ways.

Throughout this book, readers will explore key themes related to AI literacy, curriculum design, pedagogy, ethics, teacher preparation, and global best practices. Particular attention is given to the developmental needs of young children, ensuring that AI education is accessible, engaging, and aligned with broader educational goals. The book also examines the cultural and societal dimensions of AI education, recognizing that approaches to curriculum implementation may differ across educational systems and communities. In doing so, it contributes to the growing interdisciplinary field of AI and education by advancing discussions on age-specific AI pedagogy, cross-cultural curriculum design, and scalable implementation models.

CHAPTER OVERVIEW

Chapter 1

The opening chapter examines the growing need to equip early-grade teachers with the pedagogical competencies required to teach AI literacy in foundational education. Drawing on global competency frameworks such as UNESCO's CARE-KNOW-DO and DigCompEdu, the chapter highlights the challenges faced by many education systems, particularly in developing contexts, including inadequate infrastructure, insufficient teacher preparation, and fragmented implementation strategies. It emphasizes the importance of ethical awareness, reflective practice, and context-responsive professional development in preparing educators for AI-integrated classrooms. Recommendations are offered for embedding AI literacy into teacher education and strengthening institutional and cross-sector collaboration.

Chapter 2

This chapter explores curriculum design principles for introducing AI literacy in junior primary education. Using key educational theories including Bruner's spiral curriculum, Piaget's cognitive development theory, Vygotsky's sociocultural theory, and Tyler's objectives model, the chapter proposes developmentally appropriate approaches to AI curriculum implementation. It also reviews AI education initiatives in countries such as the United States, Britain, and China, providing comparative insights into emerging global practices. The chapter concludes with a proposed model for implementing AI curricula in primary schools alongside practical recommendations for policymakers and educators.

Chapter 3

This chapter introduces an AI Literacy Continuum model that presents AI education as a developmental journey extending from early childhood to university-level learning. The chapter critiques fragmented and late-stage approaches to AI education, advocating instead for integrated, ethical, and human-centred learning pathways. Through international case studies and pedagogical frameworks, it highlights the importance of curiosity, empathy, critical reflection, and ethical responsibility as core components of AI literacy. Policy recommendations focus on equitable access, institutional readiness, and the development of lifelong learning ecosystems that position AI literacy as an extension of human literacy itself.

Chapter 4

Addressing the emotional and ethical dimensions of AI, this chapter presents the Socio-Emotional AI Literacy (SEAL) framework for children aged 6–12. The framework responds to the increasing presence of affective AI technologies that simulate emotional interactions with users. Built upon developmental psychology, emotional intelligence, and critical technology studies, the chapter introduces four pillars: Algorithmic Awareness, Empathetic Interpretation, Critical Discernment, and Ethical Interaction. The chapter argues that socio-emotional competencies are essential for helping children critically and responsibly navigate AI systems that increasingly shape communication and social experiences.

Chapter 5

This chapter explores the cognitive foundations underpinning AI literacy in early childhood and primary education. Drawing on the theories of Piaget, Vygotsky, and information processing scholars, it examines how children develop systems thinking, causal reasoning, abstraction, and feedback recognition. The chapter highlights how sociocultural factors such as language, culture, and educational context influence cognitive development and children's understanding of complex systems. Using examples from Malaysia and Southeast Asia, the discussion connects cognitive theory with educational policy and classroom practice, advocating for learning environments that nurture curiosity, systems reasoning, and reflective awareness.

Chapter 6

Focusing on language development, this chapter investigates the role of AI technologies in supporting young learners' communication skills. It discusses how tools such as voice assistants and chatbots can enhance vocabulary acquisition, grammar learning, and social-emotional communication. At the same time, the chapter addresses concerns related to inclusivity, ethics, and equitable access to AI-supported learning environments. Emphasis is placed on teacher preparation, interdisciplinary collaboration, and ongoing research to ensure that AI technologies contribute positively and safely to children's language learning experiences.

Chapter 7

This chapter presents a hands-on, experiential approach to AI literacy through simple, code-free projects designed for children aged 6–12. By removing technical barriers such as programming complexity, the chapter demonstrates how children can engage meaningfully with AI concepts through interactive activities using physical objects and user-friendly digital tools. Examples include AI-assisted sorting games and storyboard creation activities that encourage creativity, experimentation, and problem-solving. Grounded in experiential learning principles, the chapter highlights how practical engagement can foster foundational AI understanding while maintaining accessibility for young learners.

Chapter 8

Through a systematic literature review, this chapter provides a global comparative analysis of AI literacy initiatives in primary education from 2000 to 2025. It examines curriculum frameworks, pedagogical strategies, and policy developments across both developed and developing nations. The chapter identifies emerging trends, including the integration of AI into digital skills and computational thinking curricula, as well as the use of experiential, inquiry-based, and gamified learning approaches. Persistent challenges such as teacher readiness, equitable access, and policy alignment are also explored. The chapter concludes by advocating for inclusive, culturally responsive, and age-appropriate AI literacy frameworks supported by strong educational policies.

Chapter 9

The final chapter examines the importance of developing critical thinking skills to help children question and evaluate AI-generated outputs. As AI technologies become increasingly integrated into educational tools and everyday digital experiences, the chapter emphasizes the need for children to understand concepts such as bias, reliability, fairness, and misinformation. Through age-appropriate classroom activities and reflective discussions, learners are encouraged to engage with AI thoughtfully and ethically. The chapter also highlights the role of parents, educators, and communities in supporting critical AI literacy beyond the classroom, preparing children to interact confidently and responsibly within an AI-driven society.

Ultimately, this book is guided by the belief that young learners should not simply become passive consumers of intelligent systems. Instead, they should be empowered to become informed, ethical, and active participants in shaping the intelligent society of tomorrow. By introducing AI education at the right time and in the right way, educators and policymakers have an opportunity to nurture a generation capable of engaging critically and responsibly with emerging technologies while contributing creatively to a rapidly evolving world.

It is my hope that this book will inspire collaboration among educators, researchers, governments, and technology innovators, while also encouraging continued dialogue on how AI can be taught responsibly, inclusively, and effectively from the earliest stages of learning. The future of AI is not only technological it is educational, social, and profoundly human.

Chapter 1
Empowering Early Grade Teachers With AI Pedagogical Competence for Future-Oriented Foundational Learning

Jabulisiwe Thandekile Mamba
University of KwaZulu-Natal, South Africa

Sithokozile Mamba
http://orcid.org/0009-0005-3789-4030
University of KwaZulu-Natal, South Africa

ABSTRACT

AI is transforming education in early learning. Yet, many foundational education systems, in South Africa, remain ill-equipped. This study explored the knowledge and competencies required for early-grade teachers to effectively teach AI literacy in foundational education within the rapidly evolving digital era. Using a qualitative, desk-based methodology, secondary data from Scopus, ERIC, Google Scholar, UNESCO, and OECD databases were critically synthesized. Findings showed that while frameworks such as UNESCO's CARE-KNOW-DO and DigCompEdu provide conceptual guidance, implementation remains fragmented due to poor infrastructure, inadequate training, and limited contextual adaptation. The study concluded that AI pedagogy requires ethical awareness, cognitive understanding, and reflective practice, supported by institutional reform. It recommends embedding AI literacy

DOI: 10.4018/979-8-3373-4893-3.ch001

027, IGI Global Scientific Publishing. Copying or distributing in print or electronic forms without written permission of IGI Global Scientific Publishing is prohibited. Use of this chapter to
ive artificial intelligence (AI) technologies is expressly prohibited. The publisher reserves all rights to license its use for generative AI training and machine learning model development.

in teacher education, fostering context-responsive professional development, and strengthening cross-sector collaboration to prepare foundational educators for an AI-driven future.

INTRODUCTION

AI is redefining education by demanding new forms of teacher competence that extend beyond technical skills to ethical, cognitive, and pedagogical intelligence. According to Ng et al. (2021), AI literacy equips teachers and learners to engage critically with intelligent systems rather than merely using them. Biagini (2025) asserts that for foundational education, this requires teachers who can interpret, adapt, and ethically mediate technology to suit developmental contexts. However, Van Wyk (2024) argues that teacher education institutions (TEIs) in the Global South remain underprepared for this transformation, constrained by fragmented policies, inadequate training, and limited infrastructure. Ngoveni (2025) further highlights a persistent "AI knowledge gap," where educators lack both conceptual clarity and confidence to teach AI meaningfully.

Brokensha et al. (2023) explain that AI pedagogy must also reflect local epistemologies, ensuring that technological integration aligns with indigenous knowledge and humanistic learning. Similarly, Tjano and Mphahlele (2025) emphasize the need for cognitive justice in AI education, urging frameworks that balance global innovation with cultural relevance. Therefore, as Wang et al. (2023) contend, preparing early-grade teachers for AI literacy demands a synthesis of pedagogical creativity, ethical awareness, and contextual adaptation. This study explores the knowledge and competencies required for early-grade teachers to effectively teach AI literacy in a rapidly evolving digital world, positioning educators as central agents in shaping equitable and future-ready foundational education systems.

BACKGROUND OF THE STUDY

The evolution of AI in education has heightened global attention to the competencies teachers need to support young learners in digitally mediated environments, as early exposure to AI can strengthen problem-solving and computational thinking skills essential for lifelong learning (Ng et al., 2021). AI is now a transformative force shaping classroom practice and curriculum design (Biagini, 2025); however, pedagogical frameworks and teacher training have not kept pace with technological advances (Yim, 2024), limiting the potential of AI to enhance inclusive and adaptive learning without well-prepared educators (Wang et al., 2023). In South Africa, foundational-phase implementation is hindered by TEIs' slow integration of AI literacy into teacher preparation (Van Wyk, 2024), educator uncertainty regarding AI content and ethics (Ngoveni, 2025), and persistent inequalities in digital access that deepen classroom disparities (Patel & Ragolane, 2024). A contextualized approach that aligns AI literacy with local pedagogies, ethical reasoning, and cultural responsiveness is therefore essential for meaningful AI integration in early-grade education (Brokensha et al., 2023).

PROBLEM STATEMENT

Despite the global recognition of AI as transformative in education, the preparation of teachers to translate AI concepts into meaningful early learning remains inadequate, as AI literacy is still treated as peripheral in many systems (Ng et al., 2021). The lack of coherent frameworks results in superficial, tool-focused practices (Biagini, 2025), while in South Africa, fragmented policies and weak teacher training structures further undermine readiness for AI-enhanced teaching (Van Wyk, 2024; Patel & Ragolane, 2024). Educators often lack awareness of AI's ethical, cognitive, and socio-technical dimensions, widening the gap between technological advancement and pedagogical capacity (Ngoveni, 2025), and institutional inertia and limited collaboration hinder sustainable AI pedagogy (Tarisayi, 2024). With most frameworks rooted in Western epistemologies that do not reflect local contexts (Brokensha et al., 2023), early-grade teachers face insufficient conceptual training and a lack of culturally grounded guidance, creating a critical misalignment between policy ambition, teacher competence, and classroom reality.

PURPOSE OF THE STUDY

This study explored the knowledge and competencies that early-grade teachers need to effectively teach AI literacy in foundational education within the context of the fast-changing digital era. It aimed to understand how teacher preparation, pedagogical frameworks, and institutional systems can be strengthened to enable meaningful AI integration in early learning. The insights generated from this research will benefit teacher education institutions (TEIs) by guiding curriculum redesign and capacity-building initiatives that align with digital transformation. Policymakers and education departments will benefit from evidence-based recommendations to refine strategies that link teacher development with AI readiness in schools. Early grade teachers will gain a deeper understanding of how to integrate AI concepts into their teaching practices, thereby enhancing their confidence and instructional quality. Learners will ultimately benefit from improved engagement, creativity, and preparedness for future learning environments.

OBJECTIVE OF THE STUDY

To explore the knowledge and competencies required of early-grade teachers to effectively teach AI literacy in foundational education in the context of the rapidly evolving digital world and future learning demands.

LITERATURE REVIEW

This literature review critically explores the policy and institutional frameworks shaping AI pedagogy within teacher education, focusing on how global initiatives and national systems converge to support teachers' readiness for AI integration. It examines major international frameworks, such as UNESCO's CARE-KNOW-DO model, the OECD's digital innovation agenda, and the European DigCompEdu and Substitution, Augmentation, Modification, and Redefinition (SAMR) frameworks, analyzing how these provide conceptual foundations for AI literacy among educators. The discussion further contextualizes these frameworks within national policies [including those led by South Africa's Department of Basic Education (DBE) and Department of Higher Education and Training (DHET)] and extends to comparative examples from Sub-Saharan Africa and Asia, where TEIs play pivotal roles in translating policy into practice. By linking global principles with local implementation realities, this review situates AI pedagogy within a broader discourse on equity, ethics, and digital transformation in foundational education.

Conceptualising AI Literacy in Foundational Education

Artificial intelligence (AI) has become deeply embedded in social, economic, and educational systems, compelling educators to redefine foundational learning for a technologically mediated era. AI literacy has emerged as a critical 21st-century competence that extends beyond basic digital skills to include cognitive, ethical, and sociotechnical understanding of intelligent systems (Ng et al., 2021). Scholars such as Yim (2024) and Biagini (2025) have argued that AI literacy signifies a shift from passive technology use to active engagement with and reflection on AI-driven tools. Within foundational education, this transition requires teachers to understand AI mechanisms while guiding children to interact with technology meaningfully and responsibly (MacCallum et al., 2023). Conceptualizing AI literacy involves balancing cognitive readiness, ethical awareness, and pedagogical adaptability to support lifelong learning in an increasingly automated world.

Initially, AI literacy was conflated with digital literacy and computational thinking, emphasizing learners' ability to code or operate digital devices (Ng et al., 2021). However, contemporary views broaden this understanding to encompass interpretive, critical, and sociocultural engagement with technology (Yue et al., 2024). MacCallum et al. (2023) define AI literacy as the ability to understand AI principles, interact practically with applications, and critically assess their societal impacts. Biagini (2025) adds that it combines technical fluency, ethical reasoning, and civic consciousness, skills essential for navigating the automation era. Unlike digital fluency, which focuses on functionality, AI literacy demands awareness of algorithmic bias, data ethics, and human–machine collaboration (Ngoveni, 2025). Thus, while digital fluency provides a foundation, AI literacy extends it through moral reasoning and critical reflection (Van Wyk, 2024; Patel & Ragolane, 2024).

Globally, several frameworks seek to operationalize AI literacy in education. UNESCO's AI Competency Framework outlines four pillars (knowledge, ethical use, practical engagement, and societal reflection) promoting holistic integration (Okada et al., 2025). The OECD's Learning Compass 2030 links AI literacy to transformative competencies, such as agency, responsibility, and digital citizenship, whereas ISTE emphasizes designing ethical AI-based learning environments (Black et al., 2024; Biagini, 2025; Yim, 2024). Despite shared objectives, implementation varies: UNESCO prioritizes equity in resource-limited settings, the OECD focuses on lifelong learning policy, and ISTE emphasizes classroom practice reliant on infrastructure (Pedro et al., 2019; Brokensha et al., 2023; Saal et al., 2025). This highlights the tension between global ideals and local realities, particularly in developing regions such as South Africa, where limited resources and teacher preparedness hinder adoption (Fergencs et al., 2020; Mathebula et al., 2025). Collectively, these frameworks stress that teachers must develop adaptive competence to transform abstract AI concepts into tangible learning experiences (Ng et al., 2023; Yue et al., 2024).

Introducing AI concepts early fosters cognitive readiness and aligns with developmental learning milestones. Research has shown that early exposure stimulates curiosity, creativity, and problem-solving (Yim, 2024; Qayyum et al., 2025). Ng et al. (2021) noted that young learners develop an intuitive grasp of everyday technologies when guided appropriately, whereas Druga et al. (2022) demonstrated that robotics and storytelling encourage playful digital curiosity. However, Wang et al. (2023) cautioned that without adequately trained educators, such exposure risks remaining superficial. Thus, effective implementation relies on teachers' ability to merge technological knowledge with pedagogical creativity to ensure deep and meaningful learning (Guan et al., 2025; Lucas et al., 2025).

Developmental learning theories reinforce this pedagogical need. Piaget's constructivism supports discovery-based learning through interactions with technology (Ngoveni, 2025; George, 2023), whereas Vygotsky's social constructivism emphasizes collaborative inquiry and teacher scaffolding (Tjano & Mphahlele, 2025). Holstein et al. (2020) introduce the concept of human–AI hybrid adaptivity, where AI serves as a cognitive partner enabling personalized learning. Kayal (2024) and Simuţ et al. (2024) affirmed that such environments enhance metacognitive growth and critical reasoning when developmentally appropriate. Therefore, AI should operate as a facilitator of co-constructed knowledge rather than a detached instructional tool, blending human creativity with intelligent feedback to optimize early learning.

Despite its promise, global evidence reveals significant gaps in educators' understanding of AI literacy. Ngoveni (2025) found that many teachers, especially in developing contexts, equate AI with robotics or automation, thereby neglecting its ethical and cognitive dimensions. Fundi et al. (2024) and Wiggill (2023) report that African educators often perceive AI as peripheral to their roles due to limited exposure and infrastructure. Guan et al. (2025) observed that pre-service teachers globally possess only surface-level awareness and lack pedagogical frameworks for classroom integration. Van Wyk (2024) noted that in South Africa, AI discourse remains concentrated in higher education, excluding early-grade teachers from digital transformation strategies (Patel & Ragolane, 2024; Tarisayi, 2024; Tariq, 2026). This oversight perpetuates inequality in preparing foundational learners for a data-driven future.

Ethical and cultural considerations further complicate AI literacy. Brokensha et al. (2023) caution that importing Western AI frameworks risks the digital colonization of African education. Van Wyk (2024) and Opesemowo and Adekomaya (2024) argue that many global models privilege individual cognition over collective, community-based learning central to African epistemologies. Tarisayi (2024) stresses that contextual inclusivity is crucial to prevent the alienation of local cultures. Biagini (2025) also observes that teachers' ethical awareness often stops at data privacy, neglecting deeper issues, such as algorithmic justice. Hence, contextualized AI literacy should integrate indigenous values, social realities, and humanistic ethics to promote culturally grounded and equitable education.

Institutional capacity plays a pivotal role in teacher competence. Ng et al. (2023) and Wang et al. (2023) demonstrated that access to professional development, leadership support, and infrastructure determines effective AI integration. However, in low-resource settings, training remains inconsistent and short-term (Ismail et al., 2024; Fergencs et al., 2020). Ngoveni (2025) describes this as the "AI knowledge gap," where pedagogical understanding trails technological innovation. Mathebula et al. (2025) identify weak pre-service preparation as a major barrier, producing teacher insecurity and uneven adoption. Consequently, inequities widen as better-resourced schools advance faster in developing AI competence (Sikhakhane et al., 2021; Saal et al., 2025).

Another recurring challenge is definitional ambiguity. Ng et al. (2021) argue that inconsistent definitions create fragmented curricula and assessment practices. Some systems frame AI literacy as part of STEM education, whereas others embed it in ethical or socio-emotional learning (Biagini, 2025; Yim, 2024). Qayyum et al. (2025) note that this inconsistency complicates policy and teacher training design. Holstein et al. (2020) advocate for flexible frameworks allowing local adaptation, though MacCallum et al. (2023) warn that excessive flexibility undermines clarity and accountability. Therefore, teacher education must balance conceptual precision with contextual flexibility to maintain relevance without sacrificing rigor.

Emerging scholarship underscores AI literacy's transformative role in redefining learning itself. Zou et al. (2025) describe AI pedagogical competence as combining technical skills with the design of human-centered learning experiences. This aligns with Vygotsky's principle that cognitive tools mediate higher-order thinking, positioning AI as both a medium and an amplifier of cognition (Tjano & Mphahlele, 2025; Kayal, 2024). Ng et al. (2023) argue that AI literacy nurtures essential future skills (critical thinking, adaptability, and collaboration), whereas Lucas et al. (2025) caution that without structured pedagogy, tool use risks overshadowing conceptual understanding. Therefore, fostering teacher competence requires epistemic transformation, enabling educators to rethink teaching and learning in an era in which intelligence is shared between humans and machines (Ismail et al., 2024; Van Wyk, 2024).

Conceptualizing AI literacy in foundational education reflects an evolving interdisciplinary dialogue integrating cognitive, ethical, and contextual dimensions. It challenges educators to move beyond functional digital skills toward critical, reflective, and ethical engagement with intelligent systems. While global frameworks, such as those provided by UNESCO, OECD, and ISTE, provide strategic scaffolds, their efficacy depends on local adaptation, teacher capacity, and institutional alignment. The literature affirms that successful AI literacy in early education hinges on culturally responsive pedagogy, developmental sensitivity, and sustained professional learning. Ultimately, AI literacy is less about technology itself and more about reimagining education as a human-centered process that cultivates reasoning, empathy, and cognitive agility–foundations necessary for young learners to thrive in an AI-driven future.

Pedagogical Competence and Teacher Preparedness for AI Integration

Pedagogical competence in digital and AI-enhanced learning embodies the synthesis of technological proficiency, instructional design, and adaptive cognition needed to create meaningful learning in intelligent educational environments. Ng et al. (2023) define it as the intersection of teachers' cognitive understanding, ethical awareness, and technical skills in navigating digital systems. Zou et al. (2025) further argue that it extends beyond classroom management to include the ability to co-design learning with AI systems, balancing automation with human judgment. Biagini (2025) reinforces that pedagogical competence in the AI era encompasses technological fluency, pedagogical flexibility, and ethical sensitivity, qualities that transform AI's potential into developmental learning outcomes. However, Van Wyk (2024) observes that in many Global South contexts, competence remains confined to technical skill acquisition rather than transformative practice, creating a disconnect between policy ideals and classroom realities.

The technological pedagogical and content knowledge (TPACK) framework provides a key lens for conceptualizing AI-related competence. Yue et al. (2024) describe TPACK as the integration of technological, pedagogical, and content knowledge to foster effective instruction, while Ng et al. (2021) emphasize its relevance in guiding AI-enhanced lesson design. Wang et al. (2023) extend this framework by introducing "AI Pedagogical Knowledge," reflecting teachers' understanding of machine learning, analytics, and adaptive algorithms in personalizing instruction. Simuţ et al. (2024) add that competence in AI pedagogy involves interpreting AI feedback and applying data-driven insights for formative assessment. Consequently, traditional TPACK evolves into a multidimensional model that includes AI literacy as a fourth domain critical for pedagogical transformation. Chiu et al. (2025) operationalize this concept through their Teacher Artificial Intelligence Competence Self-Efficacy (TAICS) scale, emphasizing confidence as a measurable aspect of competence development.

Empirical evidence shows persistent gaps in teachers' readiness and confidence to integrate AI. Guan et al. (2025) reveal that pre-service teachers acknowledge AI's importance but lack confidence due to limited exposure and vague curricular direction. Lucas et al. (2025) report similar trends across Europe and Asia, where teachers recognize AI's potential but remain uncertain about its ethical and conceptual implications. In Kenya, Fundi et al. (2024) found that teachers perceive AI integration as externally imposed, weakening engagement and ownership. Ismail et al. (2024) contend that readiness depends on teachers' belief in their ability to manage AI pedagogically rather than mechanically. Ngoveni (2025) adds that institutional factors (such as leadership, professional development, and infrastructure) strongly influence readiness. However, in South Africa, Wiggill (2023) observed that many teachers still view AI as abstract or irrelevant, reflecting enduring attitudinal barriers.

Teacher training and professional development remain central to addressing these challenges. Tarisayi (2024) notes that South African teacher education programs prioritize ICT literacy over AI ethics or algorithmic reasoning. Patel and Ragolane (2024) similarly highlight training that focuses on tool use rather than pedagogical innovation. Langeveldt et al. (2023) criticize outdated legal and curricular frameworks that fail to anticipate AI's implications for teaching. Conversely, Wang et al. (2023) advocate experiential and interdisciplinary learning approaches that position AI as a pedagogical collaborator, while Kayal (2024) proposes transformative pedagogy emphasizing creativity, critical thinking, and emotional engagement. Pedagogical competence, therefore, extends beyond operational ability; it requires reflective transformation and epistemological reorientation to redefine teaching for intelligent environments.

Curriculum alignment remains a major obstacle. Qayyum et al. (2025) observed that early education curricula lack explicit outcomes for AI literacy, leaving teachers uncertain about instructional goals. Pedro et al. (2019) and Saal et al. (2025) note that while global frameworks advocate AI readiness, localization for foundational education is minimal. In South Africa, digital skills are prioritized without corresponding AI pedagogical guidance, resulting in fragmented implementation and limited teacher agency (Van Wyk, 2024; Ngoveni, 2025). Mathebula et al. (2025) stress that without alignment between curriculum, training, and assessment, competence remains aspirational. Sikhakhane et al. (2021) and George (2023) further argued that this disconnect reinforces perceptions that AI belongs to advanced grades rather than early learning, stalling early adoption efforts.

Infrastructure inequities compound these challenges. Fergencs et al. (2020) find that inadequate connectivity, insufficient devices, and poor technical support continue to impede AI integration in South African schools. Fundi et al. (2024) report similar obstacles in Kenya, where AI remains largely theoretical due to lack of resources. Van Wyk (2024) attributes these disparities to systemic socio-economic inequalities that embed educational marginalization. Opesemowo and Adekomaya (2024) argued that without sustained investment in digital ecosystems, even well-trained teachers remain constrained. Ngoveni (2025) noted that skepticism and fear of job displacement among teachers stem from such systemic inadequacies. Biagini (2025) added that these anxieties reflect broader concerns about technological determinism, underscoring the need for training that addresses both technical competence and ethical confidence. Thus, readiness requires improving infrastructure while reshaping cultural attitudes toward technology.

Teachers' mindsets play a pivotal role in mediating AI adoption. Yue et al. (2024) find that younger educators show greater openness to AI, while veteran teachers often resist due to its rapid evolution. Ng et al. (2023) explained that prior experience with blended learning predicts openness to AI integration, whereas a lack of exposure breeds technophobia (Wiggill, 2023). Ismail et al. (2024) emphasize fostering growth-oriented mindsets through supportive learning environments that normalize experimentation and error. Zou et al. (2025) advocated embedding mindset development within institutional culture, arguing that system-wide support builds resilience and self-efficacy. Hence, effective readiness extends beyond technical proficiency to encompass psychological and cultural transformation that redefines teachers' professional identities in AI-enhanced education.

Comparative studies offer instructive lessons for developing teacher competence. In Hong Kong, Ng et al. (2021) describe co-design workshops that integrate AI ethics, coding, and problem-solving, thereby improving teachers' confidence. Singapore's national AI for Education program similarly employs mentorship and inquiry-based collaboration to deepen pedagogical integration (Yue et al., 2024). Kenya's Competence-Based Curriculum reform includes AI literacy workshops that foster reflective dialogue among educators (Fundi et al., 2024). In China, universities partner with schools to co-develop AI-based teaching materials under the "AI+ Education" strategy, promoting simultaneous technical and pedagogical growth (Wang et al., 2023). In Western contexts, as documented by Chiu et al. (2025), self-efficacy models and adaptive online training are leveraged to sustain long-term competence. By contrast, South Africa's donor-driven, short-term development initiatives remain poorly aligned with systemic reform, leading to superficial upskilling rather than meaningful pedagogical change (Tarisayi, 2024).

These international examples highlight the need for continuous, collaborative, and localized professional development frameworks. Ngoveni (2025) and Van Wyk (2024) emphasize that effective models treat teachers as active co-creators of innovation rather than passive recipients of training. Kayal (2024) supports this view by promoting transformative pedagogy grounded in critical engagement with AI's social and ethical implications. Okada et al. (2025) similarly propose UNESCO's CARE-KNOW-DO model, integrating ethical awareness, cognitive understanding, and participatory design; principles vital for foundational educators. Collectively, these frameworks show that AI preparedness is a process of empowerment, driven by teachers' reflective capacity and contextual insight.

Adapting these global models to resource-limited contexts, however, remains complex. Patel and Ragolane (2024) caution that many international frameworks presuppose digital maturity that African systems have yet to achieve. Brokensha et al. (2023) argue that reliance on Global North pedagogies risks epistemic dependency unless localized to reflect indigenous knowledge and relational learning. Tjano and Mphahlele (2025) introduce "cognitive justice" as a framework advocating the integration of local cultural values into AI pedagogy. In this sense, pedagogical competence becomes a sociocultural construct shaped by context, ethics, and identity. Teacher preparedness must therefore balance universal competencies, such as digital fluency and ethical reasoning, with local responsiveness that honors community epistemologies.

Pedagogical competence and teacher preparedness for AI integration encompass intertwined dimensions of knowledge, mindset, and systemic support. Competence transcends traditional teaching mastery to include design, mediation, and reflection within AI-driven ecosystems. While the TPACK framework, enriched by AI literacy, provides conceptual grounding, its success depends on infrastructure, coherent curricula, and institutional backing. Persistent readiness gaps stem from limited exposure, fragmented professional development, and inequitable access to technology. Comparative evidence reveals that countries investing in continuous, collaborative, and reflective training achieve more sustainable pedagogical transformation. However, as Van Wyk (2024), Ngoveni (2025), and Tarisayi (2024) caution, true preparedness in foundational education demands systemic reform that positions teachers as active intellectual agents shaping AI's educational future. Ultimately, pedagogical competence in the AI era signifies a shift from technological adaptation to pedagogical innovation, where teachers' reflective capacity, cultural grounding, and professional autonomy determine the depth and equity of AI integration in foundational classrooms.

Barriers to Implementing AI in Early Childhood and Primary Classrooms

The integration of AI into early childhood and primary education remains inconsistent worldwide, hindered by institutional, socioeconomic, ethical, and psychological barriers that limit its pedagogical impact. Although AI holds transformative potential for personalized learning and early cognitive development, most education systems, particularly in developing regions, struggle with systemic and human constraints. These limitations shape teachers' readiness, confidence, and competence in fostering AI literacy, thus undermining efforts to build AI-ready education systems.

Institutional and systemic barriers are among the most significant obstacles. Ngoveni (2025) notes that many schools lack the foundational capacity for AI integration, resulting in sporadic pilot projects instead of systemic implementation. Mathebula et al. (2025) argue that South African teacher training institutions remain constrained by outdated pedagogy and limited exposure to digital innovation, leaving educators ill-prepared to apply AI meaningfully. Wang et al. (2023) emphasize that institutional ecosystems, such as leadership support, infrastructure, and coherent curricula, strongly influence teacher readiness. Where such ecosystems are weak, educators perceive AI as abstract policy rhetoric rather than a practical teaching tool.

The absence of AI-focused curricula reinforces these limitations. Qayyum et al. (2025) explain that most education systems lack structured AI competencies, leaving teachers without guidance on what or how to teach. Saal et al. (2025) similarly highlight that South Africa's curriculum omits explicit AI learning outcomes, restricting teachers' ability to design relevant lessons. Without such frameworks, teachers experience anxiety about explaining complex AI concepts, such as algorithms or data ethics, to young learners (Ng et al., 2021). Pedro et al. (2019) warn that in the absence of policy coherence, AI education risks becoming a symbolic add-on rather than a substantive reform. Consequently, fragmented alignment between the curriculum, teacher training, and resource allocation perpetuates inequities, as educators rely on self-directed and uneven efforts.

Inadequate ICT infrastructure deepens these systemic issues. Fergencs et al. (2020) found that poor internet connectivity, unreliable electricity, and insufficient devices continue to hinder technology-enhanced learning in South African schools. Van Wyk (2024) links these gaps to historical underinvestment in education and technology, while Patel and Ragolane (2024) warn that short-term, donor-dependent infrastructure planning makes AI integration unsustainable. Ngoveni (2025) further explains that disparities between urban and rural schools, where the latter receive fewer resources, exacerbate educational inequality. Without equitable infrastructure, AI implementation remains fragmented and exclusionary.

Socioeconomic and policy-related inequalities compound these institutional challenges. Biagini (2025) argues that global AI education initiatives often assume access to technology, marginalizing under-resourced schools where students lack even basic computing exposure. Brokensha et al. (2023) caution that such approaches risk reinforcing digital colonialism, as imported technologies and curricula dominate local systems. Opesemowo and Adekomaya (2024) observed this trend in South Africa's higher education sector, where unadapted foreign AI tools shape learning models without cultural relevance, a dynamic that filters down to primary classrooms.

The absence of coherent policy frameworks perpetuates these disparities. Tarisayi (2024) notes that fragmented education policies and inconsistent teacher standards impede implementation, creating ambiguity around institutional accountability. Saal et al. (2025) add that digital transformation rhetoric often lacks corresponding financial investment in foundational education. The result is symbolic compliance; schools claim readiness without functional capacity. In contrast, Yue et al. (2024) and Wang et al. (2023) highlight that countries such as Singapore and Finland ensure AI integration through cohesive national competency frameworks that align teacher training, curricula, and infrastructure. Such long-term policy coordination remains largely absent in the Global South, making AI literacy both a technological and socioeconomic equity issue.

Cultural, ethical, and safety concerns present another layer of difficulty. Yim (2024) explains that educators often hesitate to introduce AI to young children, fearing their limited capacity to understand abstract concepts such as bias or privacy. Biagini (2025) adds that the use of AI in early learning raises ethical concerns about data protection and child surveillance. Ngoveni (2025) notes that the absence of ethical guidelines leaves teachers uncertain about appropriate classroom practices, particularly in countries without robust data policies.

Cultural misalignment further complicates ethical integration. Brokensha et al. (2023) argue that Western-centric AI pedagogies emphasize individual cognition and efficiency, overlooking collective and relational learning, which is central to African education traditions. Tjano and Mphahlele (2025) advocate “cognitive justice,” asserting that AI tools should reflect local epistemologies rather than replace them. However, as Van Wyk (2024) observes, imported curricula rarely accommodate such perspectives, alienating educators and undermining cultural continuity. This detachment diminishes teacher confidence and engagement, highlighting the need for culturally grounded AI pedagogy.

The ethical debate also extends to issues of autonomy and professional control. Holstein et al. (2020) propose “human–AI hybrid adaptivity,” in which AI complements rather than replaces teachers. However, Ng et al. (2023) note that educators fear losing authority as AI takes on evaluative or instructional functions. Biagini (2025) underscores that this concern is particularly relevant in early childhood contexts, where emotional and interpersonal dynamics are central to learning. Without trust, transparency, and clear role definition, teachers may resist AI adoption, even in well-equipped schools.

Teacher-related barriers, particularly workload, anxiety, and resistance to change, further restrict integration. Wiggill (2023) reports that many South African teachers view digital tools as an added burden rather than a support. Ngoveni (2025) adds that poor training and limited institutional support heighten cognitive overload as teachers juggle teaching, data entry, and troubleshooting simultaneously. Ismail et al. (2024) link this overload to “technostress,” where anxiety and self-doubt hinder adaptation. Lucas et al. (2025) found that, even with training, teachers fear obsolescence and hesitate to engage with AI-driven pedagogy.

Resistance to change is also tied to professional identity. Fundi et al. (2024) found that Kenyan teachers saw AI as an externally imposed reform, leading to passive compliance rather than genuine engagement. Van Wyk (2024) and Ng et al. (2023) similarly report that many educators perceive digital transformation as donor-driven, conflicting with their pedagogical values. The fear that AI could replace the moral or emotional aspects of teaching leads some to limit technological experimentation. Zou et al. (2025) argued that overcoming this resistance requires philosophical clarity regarding the evolving roles of teachers and machines.

Digital anxiety is particularly pronounced in early learning contexts. Yue et al. (2024) note that teachers worry about AI's developmental appropriateness and potential harm to attention or social skills. Ngoveni (2025) explains that risk-averse school cultures discourage experimentation, reinforcing teachers' preference for rigid routines over exploratory pedagogy. Such conditions breed reluctance rather than innovation, limiting opportunities for creative integration.

The emotional dimension of digital transformation is often neglected. Tarisayi (2024) contends that most South African teacher programs focus on technical ability but ignore psychological well-being and reflective practice. Patel and Ragolane (2024) add that such training rarely includes collaboration or peer mentoring, resulting in technically competent but unmotivated teachers. This gap between skills and confidence perpetuates superficial technology use that fails to transform instruction.

Institutional hierarchies have shaped these challenges. Ngoveni (2025) observed that when leadership fails to model digital innovation, teacher motivation declines. Wang et al. (2023) find that schools with visionary leadership show higher teacher adaptability, whereas bureaucratic systems stifle experimentation. Saal et al. (2025) add that accountability structures seldom reward innovation, reinforcing a culture of compliance over creativity.

Barriers to implementing AI in early and primary education are multifaceted and interdependent. Institutional weaknesses, absent curricula, and poor infrastructure constrain systemic readiness. Socioeconomic disparities and digital colonialism deepen inequality, whereas cultural and ethical uncertainties undermine teacher confidence. Simultaneously, technostress, heavy workloads, and rigid hierarchies restrict innovation. These intersecting barriers illustrate that AI integration is not merely a technological challenge but also a systemic, cultural, and emotional one. Preparing teachers for AI-enhanced education thus demands more than devices and training; it requires rethinking institutional culture, pedagogy, and support systems to create equitable, contextually grounded, and human-centered approaches to AI literacy in foundational education.

Frameworks and Policies Supporting AI Pedagogy in Teacher Education

Global and national education systems increasingly recognize that AI demands a paradigm shift in teacher education, requiring new pedagogical frameworks and coherent policy instruments for a digital, data-driven future. The discourse around AI pedagogy has evolved from isolated innovation initiatives to strategic policy priorities for ministries, multilateral agencies, and teacher-training institutions (Pedro et al., 2019). Biagini (2025) asserts that AI adoption depends not only on technological readiness but also on policy coherence that ensures ethical, inclusive, and context-sensitive integration throughout teacher development. Consequently, teacher education has become a critical policy nexus in which global digital frameworks intersect with local education realities.

At the international level, UNESCO has played a leading role in advancing AI education policy coherence. Okada et al. (2025) explain that UNESCO's AI Competency Framework aligns with Sustainable Development Goal 4 by promoting digital competence, ethical literacy, and critical thinking among educators. Central to this framework is the "CARE-KNOW-DO" model, which integrates ethical awareness (CARE), cognitive understanding (KNOW), and practical application (DO) to ensure that AI education remains human-centered, interdisciplinary, and socially responsive. Pedro et al. (2019) further note that UNESCO frames AI literacy as both a right and a civic responsibility, emphasizing teacher competence as essential to equitable digital transformation. Similarly, the OECD supports teacher empowerment through lifelong learning and digital innovation ecosystems (Ngoveni, 2025).

At the national level, countries display varying degrees of AI readiness. In South Africa, the DBE and DHET recognize AI as a cornerstone of the fourth industrial revolution (4IR) education agenda (Tarisayi, 2024). However, Patel and Ragolane (2024) argue that while policy rhetoric is ambitious, implementation remains fragmented. Saal et al. (2025) observe that overlapping ICT-in-education policies lack measurable outcomes and coherence. Van Wyk (2024) highlights the persistent misalignment between ministerial policy design and teacher education programs, reflecting a systemic disconnection between higher education institutions and school-level realities.

In contrast, several Global South countries have adopted more integrated approaches. Fundi et al. (2024) report that Kenya's competency-based curriculum explicitly embeds AI and digital literacy as cross-cutting themes, supported by teacher training initiatives emphasizing inquiry-based learning. Ismail et al. (2024) describe Malaysia's AI pedagogy framework as aligned with national economic transformation goals, integrating AI literacy within teacher preparation and continuous professional development. These cases demonstrate that coherent policy design, coupled with institutional accountability, accelerates AI readiness in education systems.

Several pedagogical frameworks, particularly DigCompEdu, SAMR, and Bloom's Digital Taxonomy, guide AI competence development among teachers. Ng et al. (2023) describe the European DigCompEdu framework as defining six competence areas, including professional engagement, digital resource creation, and learner empowerment. Biagini (2025) commends its holistic link between pedagogical creativity and ethical awareness, which is vital for AI readiness. However, Ngoveni (2025) critiques its Eurocentric orientation and notes limited sensitivity to infrastructural constraints in low-resource environments.

The SAMR model continues to inform teachers' understanding of technology integration by distinguishing between enhancement and transformation levels of use (George, 2023). However, as Zou et al. (2025) argue, AI pedagogy requires an added dimension that focuses on human–AI collaboration, transcending SAMR's functional emphasis. Bloom's Digital Taxonomy has similarly evolved to include computational and algorithmic reasoning, aligning cognitive processes with digital and AI-based learning (Yim, 2024). Ng et al. (2021) emphasize that such frameworks are most effective when localized and aligned with national teacher education standards rather than adopted wholesale.

Teacher education institutions (TEIs) are pivotal in translating these frameworks into practice. Tarisayi (2024) explains that South African TEIs face the dual challenge of redesigning curricula to meet the needs of the AI era while managing resource limitations. Van Wyk (2024) notes that many TEIs in the Global South remain reactive, adopting digital content only under external policy or funding pressure. In contrast, Ngoveni (2025) contends that TEIs are uniquely positioned to bridge theory and practice by embedding AI literacy into pedagogy courses, reflective modules, and teaching practicums. Wang et al. (2023) further assert that effective AI pedagogy demands both conceptual and experiential learning that helps teachers critically evaluate AI's educational and ethical implications.

Practical models of AI integration in teacher education have begun to emerge. Lucas et al. (2025) describe European universities adopting hybrid programs that combine digital pedagogy with AI ethics and interdisciplinary collaboration among education, psychology, and computer science faculties. Guan et al. (2025) report similar progress in China, where reflective mentorship programs have transformed pre-service teachers' identities from technology-anxious to AI-empowered. These findings underscore that policy frameworks gain traction only when TEIs localize them through experiential and iterative approaches.

UNESCO's advocacy for open schooling models has further influenced AI pedagogy reform. Okada et al. (2025) highlight that the CARE-KNOW-DO model extends beyond classroom practice, fostering partnerships between schools, communities, and industries to co-create ethical and inclusive AI learning environments. Biagini (2025) emphasizes that such open schooling aligns with UNESCO's vision of participatory education, whereas Brokensha et al. (2023) caution that global frameworks must be indigenized to prevent epistemic dependency and ensure cultural authenticity.

In South Africa, efforts to institutionalize AI pedagogy have remained gradual. Saal et al. (2025) identify the National Digital and Future Skills Strategy (2021–2025) as a key attempt to establish a cohesive national agenda encompassing curriculum reform, teacher training, and public–private collaboration. However, Patel and Ragolane (2024) critique its higher-education focus, which neglects foundational and teacher education sectors. Langeveldt et al. (2023) stress that aligning legal and policy structures with pedagogical realities requires deeper institutional reform rather than superficial compliance.

In contrast, Asian education systems offer instructive examples of policy coherence. Yim (2024) notes that South Korea and Singapore have embedded AI literacy into teacher standards and professional development frameworks. Singapore's AI for Education Masterplan exemplifies the synergy between policy design and pedagogical experimentation, allowing teachers to co-develop lessons using AI analytics (Wang et al., 2023). China's teacher education policies further institutionalize AI integration through national guidelines promoting data analytics and intelligent tutoring systems in pre-service programs (Guan et al., 2025). These initiatives demonstrate the benefits of multilevel coordination, linking the government, universities, and schools in cultivating AI-competent educators.

However, Sub-Saharan Africa continues to face systemic barriers that constrain scalability. Fergencs et al. (2020) highlight that despite continental frameworks promoting technology-enhanced learning, infrastructural deficits and access inequalities persist. Tarisayi (2024) attributes slow adaptation to legacy systems that emphasize content delivery over innovation. Nevertheless, pilot programs in Kenya have shown progress; Fundi et al. (2024) describe AI-oriented training modules emphasizing computational thinking and digital ethics, supported by collaborations between universities and NGOs. These examples reveal that localized experimentation, rather than top-down importation, drives sustainable innovation.

International frameworks, such as DigCompEdu and UNESCO's AI Competency Framework, are increasingly influencing teacher education in Africa. Ng et al. (2023) note that many teacher education institutions (TEIs) adapt DigCompEdu's principles to evaluate teacher competence, whereas Biagini (2025) cautions against diluting critical elements, such as ethics and civic engagement. Okada et al. (2025) argue that AI pedagogy in developing contexts must transition from compliance-based digital training to transformative approaches that cultivate ethical reflection, creativity, and inclusivity.

A recent development in professionalization involves the creation of self-assessment and certification tools for teachers. Chiu et al. (2025) introduce the TAICS Scale, which measures educators' confidence and readiness to apply AI pedagogical strategies. Ngoveni (2025) suggested that such tools could link teacher evaluation to targeted capacity-building initiatives, strengthening institutional accountability. However, Van Wyk (2024) cautioned that without supportive leadership and resources, these instruments risk being performative rather than developmental.

Across contexts, the literature reveals a persistent tension between global policy aspirations and local implementation. While UNESCO and OECD frameworks champion equity, ethics, and sustainability, national systems often struggle with fragmentation, underfunding, and misalignment between higher and basic education sectors (Saal et al., 2025; Patel & Ragolane, 2024). Therefore, TEIs serve as mediators, translating international standards into locally responsive pedagogical practices. Tarisayi (2024) and Van Wyk (2024) emphasize that the success of AI pedagogy ultimately depends on whether TEIs develop institutional frameworks that align with national priorities while remaining adaptable to global technological trends.

Frameworks and policies supporting AI pedagogy in teacher education reflect an evolving global movement to balance technological innovation with ethical and contextual sensitivity. Models such as UNESCO's CARE-KNOW-DO, DigCompEdu, SAMR, and Bloom's Digital Taxonomy offer conceptual foundations for AI-ready teaching, whereas national strategies in South Africa, Kenya, and Asia demonstrate divergent yet instructive approaches to implementation. However, as Ngoveni (2025), Biagini (2025), and Tarisayi (2024) affirmed, the real measure of effectiveness lies in institutional capacity, contextual adaptation, and the agency of teacher education institutions to transform policy aspirations into pedagogical reality. Thus, teacher education stands as both the recipient and architect of AI policy innovation, shaping how societies prepare educators to guide foundational learners in a future defined by intelligent technologies.

In conclusion, the literature demonstrates that frameworks and policies supporting AI pedagogy in teacher education embody a global effort to align innovation with inclusivity, ensuring that digital transformation strengthens rather than fragments educational equity. International models, such as UNESCO's CARE-KNOW-DO, DigCompEdu, and Bloom's Digital Taxonomy, offer valuable blueprints for cultivating AI-competent teachers; however, their success depends on contextual adaptation by national education systems and TEIs. Evidence from South Africa, Kenya, and Asia reveals that coherent policies, continuous professional development, and institutional accountability are essential for embedding AI literacy into teacher preparation. Ultimately, effective AI pedagogy frameworks must bridge the divide between global aspirations and local capacities, empowering educators not only to use AI tools but also to shape their ethical, pedagogical, and cultural applications in foundational classrooms.

METHODOLOGY

This study employed a desk-based qualitative research design that relied entirely on secondary data to investigate the knowledge and competencies that early-grade teachers require to teach AI literacy effectively. Secondary data analysis was appropriate because it enables the synthesis of existing scholarship, identification of theoretical patterns, and assessment of policy implications without the need for fieldwork (Dale et al., 2025). Data were sourced from reputable academic and institutional platforms such as Scopus, Google Scholar, ERIC, UNESCO, and OECD databases, with peer-reviewed articles, policy reports, and international frameworks selected based on recency, methodological quality, and relevance to foundational teacher education, following the criteria outlined by Alade et al. (2024). Data credibility was ensured through the use of the QuADS appraisal tool, which supports the rigorous evaluation of diverse studies (Harrison et al., 2021).

The collected literature was analyzed using thematic synthesis, an interpretive process that organizes findings into key emerging themes to facilitate a structured exploration of institutional frameworks, teacher preparation models, and AI-related policy trends (Gatrell, 2020). Researcher bias was reduced through transparent selection procedures and reflexive documentation, as recommended by Baldwin et al. (2022). Adherence to established scholarly guidelines ensured ethical integrity and methodological reliability throughout the study, aligning with the principles emphasized by Walliman (2021) and Sileyew (2019).

FINDINGS AND DISCUSSION

The exploration of the knowledge and competencies required for early-grade teachers to effectively teach AI literacy reveals that pedagogical transformation in foundational education depends as much on conceptual understanding and ethical orientation as on technological proficiency. The literature demonstrates that while frameworks such as UNESCO's CARE-KNOW-DO, DigCompEdu, SAMR, and Bloom's Digital Taxonomy provide a strong foundation for conceptualizing AI pedagogy, their translation into effective classroom practice is mediated by teacher capacity, institutional culture, and socioeconomic realities (Okada et al., 2025; Ng et al., 2023). Across contexts, the evidence suggests that the success of AI integration rests not merely on exposure to technology but on teachers' ability to integrate cognitive, ethical, and contextual dimensions into pedagogy. Therefore, AI literacy at the foundational phase should be viewed as a composite of knowledge domains (technical fluency, pedagogical reasoning, and moral judgment) that together enable educators to guide young learners in critically and creatively engaging with intelligent systems (Biagini, 2025; Yim, 2024).

One of the most striking findings from the literature is the imbalance between global aspirations for AI education and local institutional readiness. International frameworks by UNESCO and the OECD have advanced comprehensive visions for equitable and ethical AI adoption, positioning teacher competence as a cornerstone of digital transformation (Pedro et al., 2019; Okada et al., 2025). However, these visions frequently encounter practical barriers in developing contexts, where resource scarcity, infrastructural deficits, and limited professional development impede their translation into practice (Fergencs et al., 2020; Saal et al., 2025). In South Africa, for instance, the DBE and DHET have articulated AI literacy within the 4IR discourse; however, implementation remains fragmented and overly reliant on imported policy models that do not fully reflect local pedagogical realities (Patel & Ragolane, 2024; Tarisayi, 2024). This gap between policy rhetoric and classroom enactment exposes a fundamental weakness: teacher education programs have not yet been structurally recalibrated to produce practitioners capable of integrating AI concepts into foundational teaching. The findings therefore emphasize that competence in AI pedagogy is not a static technical skill but a dynamic, context-responsive capability shaped by institutional support and localized curriculum innovation (Van Wyk, 2024; Brokensha et al., 2023).

A deeper reading of the data further illustrates that TEIs function as critical mediators between policy ambition and classroom reality. Studies have highlighted that TEIs are responsible for embedding AI literacy across pre-service and in-service training, aligning theoretical frameworks with practical teaching experiences (Ngoveni, 2025; Wang et al., 2023). However, most institutions, especially in the Global South, are reactive rather than visionary, integrating digital pedagogy modules only in response to donor or policy pressure (Van Wyk, 2024). In contrast, Asian models, particularly those in Singapore and China, showcase proactive institutional cultures in which AI literacy is embedded in curriculum design, reflective practice, and mentorship (Guan et al., 2025; Yim, 2024). This contrast underscores a central tension in the global AI education landscape: while developed nations are moving towards the systemic integration of AI pedagogy, developing contexts remain entangled in fragmented and short-term initiatives. Nonetheless, the growing number of pilot programs in Kenya and Malaysia demonstrates that adaptive policy frameworks, when coupled with sustained teacher professional learning, can foster meaningful competence, even in resource-limited settings (Ismail et al., 2024; Fundi et al., 2024).

Equally significant is the emerging understanding that AI pedagogy transcends mere technological training; it requires epistemic transformation within teacher identity and professional ethics. The literature suggests that effective AI educators must possess a dual orientation (technical and reflective) that enables them to interpret AI's cognitive, cultural, and ethical implications for young learners (Biagini, 2025; Yim, 2024). Teachers must therefore learn to mediate between the affordances of intelligent systems and the developmental needs of children, ensuring that AI serves as a tool for inquiry and creativity rather than a mechanism of control. Frameworks such as the CARE-KNOW-DO model operationalize this balance by linking knowledge acquisition to moral awareness and practical engagement (Okada et al., 2025). However, most national frameworks, including South Africa's National Digital and Future Skills Strategy, have yet to incorporate such ethical scaffolding, focusing primarily on digital skills rather than on critical and civic dimensions of

AI literacy (Saal et al., 2025). This implies that teacher competence must evolve from compliance-based digital fluency towards reflective pedagogy that humanizes technology and situates AI within broader social and developmental objectives (Brokensha et al., 2023; Ngoveni, 2025).

Moreover, the findings reveal that teacher preparedness is profoundly influenced by the availability of structured frameworks that link AI pedagogy to cognitive development theories. Models such as SAMR and Bloom's Digital Taxonomy, when contextualized within early childhood education, allow teachers to scaffold AI concepts in developmentally appropriate ways (George, 2023; Yim, 2024). However, as Zou et al. (2025) argue, these frameworks are limited by their focus on technological substitution rather than human–AI collaboration. Therefore, there is a need for frameworks that enable teachers to move beyond operational integration to pedagogical transformation, designing experiences that allow learners to question, adapt, and co-create with technology. The discussion here suggests that AI literacy must be embedded not only in what teachers know but also in how they think, plan, and enact learning. This orientation calls for institutional investment in long-term professional development programmes that nurture reflective inquiry and collaborative experimentation among teachers (Ng et al., 2023; Wang et al., 2023). Without such developmental ecosystems, teachers risk superficial adoption that prioritizes the novelty of technology over its educational purpose.

Another dimension emerging from the literature is the tension between global epistemologies and local learning cultures. Brokensha et al. (2023) and Tjano and Mphahlele (2025) highlight that most AI pedagogical frameworks are grounded in Western individualist paradigms, emphasizing efficiency and autonomy, while overlooking indigenous pedagogies based on communal learning and relational knowledge. This epistemic imbalance limits the cultural legitimacy of AI education in African contexts, where teaching is often rooted in collective values and contextual problem-solving. Therefore, cognitive justice in AI pedagogy is needed; an approach that respects diverse knowledge systems while aligning with global technological standards. Patel and Ragolane (2024) reinforce this argument by noting that imported policy frameworks risk deepening digital dependency unless localized to reflect community epistemologies. Consequently, teacher competence must encompass cultural literacy and contextual adaptation, ensuring that AI integration enhances rather than displaces indigenous educational philosophies.

Finally, the discussion reveals that institutional collaboration and accountability are decisive in sustaining AI pedagogy. Evidence from Asian and African pilot programs shows that success depends on multilevel coordination among governments, universities, and schools (Yim, 2024; Fundi et al., 2024). In contexts where these linkages are weak, teacher education programs operate in silos, leading to fragmented professional development and inconsistent classroom practices (Tarisayi, 2024; Van

Wyk, 2024; Tariq, 2025). Moreover, the use of self-assessment tools, such as the TAICS scale, offers promise in evaluating teachers' psychological readiness for AI adoption (Chiu et al., 2025). However, as Ngoveni (2025) cautions, measurement alone is insufficient without institutional systems that transform data into continuous capacity-building opportunities. Therefore, the path towards AI-ready foundational education is both structural and human; it requires coherent policy frameworks, resilient institutional networks, and teachers empowered as intellectual agents of transformation.

In summary, the discussion affirms that preparing early-grade teachers to teach AI literacy demands a synthesis of knowledge, ethics, and pedagogy anchored in contextual realities. While international frameworks provide conceptual clarity, their practical impact depends on how well they are localized within teacher education systems. The evidence converges on the notion that AI literacy is not achieved through technological exposure alone but through the cultivation of reflective, adaptive, and culturally grounded educators capable of shaping the next generation's engagement with intelligent technologies. Thus, the future of AI pedagogy in foundational education lies not merely in digital readiness but in the reimagination of teacher competence as a transformative, human-centered practice that bridges innovation with inclusion and technology with pedagogy.

RECOMMENDATIONS

Based on the findings and discussion, it is evident that preparing early-grade teachers to teach AI literacy requires systemic reform across teacher education, curriculum design, and institutional capacity. First, TEIs should embed AI literacy across pre-service and in-service programs through experiential learning, reflective inquiry, and cross-disciplinary collaboration that integrates both technical knowledge and ethical awareness. This should be supported by the adaptation of global frameworks such as UNESCO's CARE-KNOW-DO and DigCompEdu to local South African contexts, ensuring alignment with indigenous pedagogies and developmental needs. Second, national education departments should strengthen policy coherence between the DBE and DHET by aligning curriculum standards, digital infrastructure investments, and teacher training programs to create a unified AI education strategy. Furthermore, institutional partnerships between universities, the government, and schools should be prioritized to create sustainable professional learning networks that foster teacher competence and innovation. Finally, teacher professional development must move beyond functional ICT training towards transformative pedagogy that cultivates ethical reasoning, creativity, and reflective capacity, ensuring that educators become active agents in shaping inclusive, AI-ready foundational education systems.

FUTURE RESEARCH

Future research should empirically test how the integration of AI literacy within teacher education programs influences early-grade teaching outcomes and learner development. While this study has illuminated theoretical and policy gaps, there remains limited evidence on how teachers internalize and operationalize AI pedagogy in real classroom contexts, particularly in under-resourced schools. Longitudinal and comparative studies across diverse educational settings could reveal how contextual factors, such as infrastructure, institutional culture, and teacher mindset, shape AI competence over time. Additionally, further investigation is needed into how indigenous pedagogical philosophies and local languages can inform culturally responsive AI literacy frameworks in South Africa and the wider Global South. Future inquiries may also examine the psychological dimensions of teacher adaptation (such as digital confidence, ethical reasoning, and emotional resilience) within AI-enhanced learning environments. Such research would deepen the understanding of how teacher knowledge systems evolve in the age of intelligent technologies and contribute to building a sustainable, inclusive foundation for AI-integrated education.

CONCLUSION

This study demonstrates that equipping early-grade teachers with the knowledge and competencies to teach AI literacy is both a pedagogical and systemic imperative for future-ready education. The evidence confirms that AI literacy extends far beyond technical proficiency; it requires a synthesis of cognitive understanding, ethical awareness, and contextual adaptability that empowers teachers to cultivate critical, creative, and responsible learners. Global frameworks such as UNESCO's CARE-KNOW-DO and DigCompEdu provide valuable conceptual anchors; however, their success depends on localization within TEIs and national curricula. In South Africa and similar developing contexts, the persistence of infrastructural deficits, fragmented policies, and limited professional development threaten to widen the digital divide. Therefore, the transformation of teacher education must move from policy rhetoric to actionable reform, embedding AI literacy as a core pedagogical competence rather than an optional add-on. Ultimately, this study affirms that foundational education will only thrive in the AI era when teachers are positioned not as passive implementers of technology, but as intellectual leaders who shape how intelligent systems are understood, used, and humanized in the classroom.

REFERENCES

Alade, T. T., Opele, J. K., Adeyeye, O. O., & Balogun, B. N. (2024). A Desk Review of the Impact of Open Access and Open Data on Research Productivity of Lecturers in Developing Countries. *Journal of Education in Developing Areas, 31*(5), 186–195.

Baldwin, J. R., Pingault, J. B., Schoeler, T., Sallis, H. M., & Munafò, M. R. (2022). Protecting against researcher bias in secondary data analysis: Challenges and potential solutions. *European Journal of Epidemiology, 37*(1), 1–10. DOI: 10.1007/s10654-021-00839-0 PMID: 35025022

Biagini, G. (2025). Towards an AI-Literate Future: A systematic literature review exploring education, ethics, and applications. *International Journal of Artificial Intelligence in Education, 35*(4), 1–51. DOI: 10.1007/s40593-025-00466-w

Black, N. B., George, S., Eguchi, A., Dempsey, J. C., Langran, E., Fraga, L., & Howard, N. (2024, March). A framework for approaching AI education in educator preparation programs. *Proceedings of the AAAI Conference on Artificial Intelligence, 38*(21), 23069–23077. DOI: 10.1609/aaai.v38i21.30351

Brokensha, S., Kotzé, E., & Senekal, B. A. (2023). *AI in and for Africa: A Humanistic Perspective*. Chapman and Hall/CRC. DOI: 10.1201/9781003276135

Chiu, T. K., Ahmad, Z., & Çoban, M. (2025). Development and validation of teacher artificial intelligence (AI) competence self-efficacy (TAICS) scale. *Education and Information Technologies, 30*(5), 6667–6685. DOI: 10.1007/s10639-024-13094-z

Dale, A., Arber, S., & Procter, M. (2025). *Doing secondary analysis*. Taylor & Francis. DOI: 10.4324/9781003632467

Druga, S., Otero, N., & Ko, A. J. (2022, July). The landscape of teaching resources for AI education. In *Proceedings of the 27th ACM Conference on on Innovation and Technology in Computer Science Education* Vol. 1 (pp. 96-102). DOI: 10.1145/3502718.3524782

Fergencs, T., Pilawka, O., Broholm, R., & Magnussen, R. (2020, October). Barriers to implementing technology-enhanced learning in south african primary schools. In *Proceedings of the European Conference on e-Learning* (pp. 182-189).

Fundi, M., Sanusi, I. T., Oyelere, S. S., & Ayere, M. (2024). Advancing AI education: Assessing Kenyan in-service teachers' preparedness for integrating artificial intelligence in competence-based curriculum. *Computers in Human Behavior Reports, 14*, 100412. DOI: 10.1016/j.chbr.2024.100412

Gatrell, A. C. (2020). 14. Using and analysing secondary data. *Handbook of Theory and Methods in Applied Health Research: Questions, Methods and Choices*, 268.

George, A. S. (2023). Preparing students for an AI-driven world: Rethinking curriculum and pedagogy in the age of artificial intelligence. *Partners Universal Innovative Research Publication, 1*(2), 112–136.

Guan, L., Zhang, Y., & Gu, M. M. (2025). Pre-service teachers preparedness for AI-integrated education: An investigation from perceptions, capabilities, and teachers' identity changes. *Computers and Education: Artificial Intelligence, 8*, 100341. DOI: 10.1016/j.caeai.2024.100341

Harrison, R., Jones, B., Gardner, P., & Lawton, R. (2021). Quality assessment with diverse studies (QuADS): An appraisal tool for methodological and reporting quality in systematic reviews of mixed-or multi-method studies. *BMC Health Services Research, 21*(1), 144. DOI: 10.1186/s12913-021-06122-y PMID: 33588842

Holstein, K., Aleven, V., & Rummel, N. (2020, June). A conceptual framework for human–AI hybrid adaptivity in education. In *International conference on artificial intelligence in education* (pp. 240-254). Cham: Springer International Publishing. DOI: 10.1007/978-3-030-52237-7_20

Ismail, A., Aliu, A., Ibrahim, M., & Sulaiman, A. (2024). Preparing teachers of the future in the era of artificial intelligence. *Journal of Artificial Intelligence. Machine Learning and Neural Network, 44*, 31–41.

Kayal, A. (2024). Transformative pedagogy: A comprehensive framework for AI integration in education. In *Explainable AI for education: Recent trends and challenges* (pp. 247–270). Springer Nature Switzerland. DOI: 10.1007/978-3-031-72410-7_14

Langeveldt, D. C., Pietersen, D., & van Wyk, A. (2023). South African legal framework to prepare pre-service teacher education programmes: A Freirean approach. *Research in Educational Policy and Management, 5*(3), 95–107. DOI: 10.46303/repam.2023.25

Lucas, M., Bem-haja, P., Zhang, Y., Llorente-Cejudo, C., & Palacios-Rodríguez, A. (2025). A comparative analysis of pre-service teachers' readiness for AI integration. *Computers and Education: Artificial Intelligence, 8*, 100396. DOI: 10.1016/j.caeai.2025.100396

MacCallum, K., Parsons, D., & Mohaghegh, M. (2023). Identifying the components of foundational Artificial Intelligence (AI) literacy-Early results from a Delphi study. *ASCILITE Publications*, 157-166.

Mathebula, N. Z., Moila, O., Maile, S., & Mnisi, S. (2025). Inadequate Teacher Training as a Barrier to ICT Integration in Early Childhood Education: A Case of Selected Primary Schools in Tshwane West District Circuit 4. *International Journal of Learning. Teaching and Educational Research*, *24*(3), 55–74. DOI: 10.26803/ijlter.24.3.3

Ng, D. T. K., Leung, J. K. L., Chu, S. K. W., & Qiao, M. S. (2021). Conceptualizing AI literacy: An exploratory review. *Computers and Education: Artificial Intelligence*, *2*, 100041.

Ng, D. T. K., Leung, J. K. L., Su, J., Ng, R. C. W., & Chu, S. K. W. (2023). Teachers' AI digital competencies and twenty-first century skills in the post-pandemic world. *Educational Technology Research and Development*, *71*(1), 137–161. DOI: 10.1007/s11423-023-10203-6 PMID: 36844361

Ngoveni, M. (2025). Bridging the AI Knowledge Gap: The Urgent Need for AI Literacy and Institutional Support. *International Journal of Technologies in Learning*, *32*(2), 83–100. DOI: 10.18848/2327-0144/CGP/v32i02/83-100

Okada, A., Sherborne, T., Panselinas, G., & Kolionis, G. (2025). Fostering transversal skills through open schooling supported by the CARE-KNOW-DO pedagogical model and the UNESCO AI competencies framework. *International Journal of Artificial Intelligence in Education*, *35*(4), 1–46. DOI: 10.1007/s40593-025-00458-w

Opesemowo, O. A. G., & Adekomaya, V. (2024). Harnessing artificial intelligence for advancing sustainable development goals in South Africa's higher education system: A qualitative study. *International Journal of Learning. Teaching and Educational Research*, *23*(3), 67–86. DOI: 10.26803/ijlter.23.3.4

Patel, S., & Ragolane, M. (2024). The implementation of artificial intelligence in South African higher education institutions: Opportunities and challenges. *Technium Education and Humanities*, *9*, 51–65. DOI: 10.47577/teh.v9i.11452

Pedro, F., Subosa, M., Rivas, A., & Valverde, P. (2019). Artificial intelligence in education: Challenges and opportunities for sustainable development.

Qayyum, A., Rafique, Z., Shah, S. S. W. A., Ahmad, S., & Haider, Z. (2025). Artificial intelligence (AI)-driven curriculum development in early childhood education: Educators' insights, barriers, and policy pathways. *Research Journal of Psychology*, *3*(1), 713–733. DOI: 10.59075/rjs.v3i1.102

Saal, P. E., Chetty, K., Ntshayintshayi, N., Moosa, T., & Masuku, N. (2025). A scoping review of the integration of artificial intelligence in primary and secondary schools from 2020 to 2024: Policy implications for South Africa. *Journal of Education (University of KwaZulu-Natal)*, (98), 62-85.

Sikhakhane, M., Govender, S., & Maphalala, M. C. (2021). The extent of South African schools' preparedness to counteract 4IR challenges: learners' perspectives. *Journal of e-learning and knowledge society, 17*(1), 1-9.

Sileyew, K. J. (2019). Research design and methodology. In *Cyberspace*. IntechOpen.

Simuţ, R., Simuţ, C., Badulescu, D., & Badulescu, A. (2024). Artificial intelligence and the modelling of teachers' competencies. *Amfiteatru Economic, 26*(65), 181–200. DOI: 10.24818/EA/2024/65/181

Tariq, M. U. (2025). Bridging Home and Classroom: Harnessing Cultural and Ecological Wisdom in Teacher Education. In Liu, L., Mohamed, N., Lin, C., Bauler, C., & Kapur, K. (Eds.), *Funds of Knowledge in Teacher Education: Sustaining Local Diversity Amidst Global Standards* (pp. 405–424). IGI Global Scientific Publishing., DOI: 10.4018/979-8-3693-8094-9.ch018

Tariq, M. U. (2025). AI-Driven Personalized Learning: Revolutionizing Student Engagement and Teacher Efficiency in Education 5.0. In Mobo, F. (Ed.), *AI and Emerging Technologies for Emergency Response and Smart Cities* (pp. 75–96). IGI Global Scientific Publishing., DOI: 10.4018/979-8-3693-9770-1.ch004

Tariq, M. U. (2026). Empowering Young Learners: Innovative Strategies for STEM and Literacy in Early Childhood Deaf Education. In Graham, P., & Neild, N. (Eds.), *Early Childhood Deaf Education: Teacher Preparation and Instructional Approaches* (pp. 231–258). IGI Global Scientific Publishing., DOI: 10.4018/979-8-3693-9127-3.ch007

Tarisayi, K. (2024). Preparing for AI's transformational potential: Rethinking teacher education in South Africa. *International Education Trend Issues, 2*(1), 31–40. DOI: 10.56442/ieti.v2i1.364

Tjano, R. N., & Mphahlele, R. (2025). Cultivating cognitive justice in AI-enhanced education: Harnessing intelligent tutoring systems and navigating ethical horizons. In *Artificial Intelligence and Human Agency in Education: Volume One* (pp. 45–68). Springer. DOI: 10.1007/978-981-96-7937-9_3

Van Wyk, B. (2024). Exploring the philosophy and practice of AI literacy in higher education in the Global South: A scoping review. *Cybrarians Journal*, (73), 1–21. DOI: 10.70000/cj.2024.73.601

Walliman, N. (2021). *Research methods: The basics*. Routledge. DOI: 10.4324/9781003141693

Wang, X., Li, L., Tan, S. C., Yang, L., & Lei, J. (2023). Preparing for AI-enhanced education: Conceptualizing and empirically examining teachers' AI readiness. *Computers in Human Behavior, 146*, 107798. DOI: 10.1016/j.chb.2023.107798

Wiggill, C. R. (2023). *South African Teachers' Perceptions of the Adoption of Artificial Intelligence in the Classroom* (Master's thesis, University of Johannesburg (South Africa)).

Yim, I. H. Y. (2024). A critical review of teaching and learning artificial intelligence (AI) literacy: Developing an intelligence-based AI literacy framework for primary school education. *Computers and Education: Artificial Intelligence*, *7*, 100319. DOI: 10.1016/j.caeai.2024.100319

Yue, M., Jong, M. S. Y., & Ng, D. T. K. (2024). Understanding K–12 teachers' technological pedagogical content knowledge readiness and attitudes toward artificial intelligence education. *Education and Information Technologies*, *29*(15), 19505–19536. DOI: 10.1007/s10639-024-12621-2

Zou, D., Xie, H., & Kohnke, L. (2025). Navigating the Future: Establishing a Framework for Educators' Pedagogic Artificial Intelligence Competence. *European Journal of Education*, *60*(2), e70117. DOI: 10.1111/ejed.70117

KEY TERMS AND DEFINITIONS

AI Knowledge Gap: The AI knowledge gap refers to the widening divide between rapid technological advancements and teachers' limited conceptual and ethical understanding of AI, often caused by weak institutional support (Ngoveni, 2025).

AI Literacy: AI literacy refers to a multidimensional competence that goes beyond basic digital skills to include cognitive, ethical, and socio-technical understanding of intelligent systems, enabling active engagement and critical reflection on AI tools (Ng et al., 2021; Yim, 2024).

Cognitive Justice: Cognitive justice is the principle that AI education should respect indigenous knowledge systems and cultural learning practices rather than relying solely on Western epistemologies (Tjano & Mphahlele, 2025).

Digital Fluency: Digital fluency refers to functional ability in using digital platforms and devices, but in AI education it is seen as insufficient because it lacks deeper critical awareness of issues such as data privacy and algorithmic bias (Ngoveni, 2025).

Human–AI Hybrid Adaptivity: Human–AI hybrid adaptivity is a model in which AI tools act as cognitive partners that support individualized learning by responding to each learner's developmental needs, rather than replacing teachers (Holstein et al., 2020).

Pedagogical Competence: ***(in the AI Era)*****:** Pedagogical competence is the integration of technological fluency, cognitive understanding, and ethical awareness that enables teachers to design and facilitate meaningful learning within AI-enhanced educational environments (Ng et al., 2023; Biagini, 2025).

Teacher AI Competence Self-Efficacy (TAICS): TAICS is a measurement scale that evaluates teachers' confidence in applying AI tools and pedagogical strategies in their practice (Chiu et al., 2025).

Technostress: Technostress describes the anxiety and overload teachers experience when they feel unable to cope with new technological demands, especially when AI tools add additional cognitive or administrative pressure (Ismail et al., 2024; Ngoveni, 2025).

TPACK Framework: The TPACK framework explains how teachers blend technological, pedagogical, and content knowledge, and has been expanded to include AI-specific knowledge such as understanding machine learning and adaptive algorithms for personalized learning (Yue et al., 2024; Wang et al., 2023).

UNESCO CARE-KNOW-DO Framework: The CARE-KNOW-DO model outlines AI competencies for teachers by combining ethical awareness (CARE), conceptual understanding (KNOW), and practical application (DO) to guide responsible AI integration in education (Okada et al., 2025).

Chapter 2
Curriculum Design Principles for AI Literacy in Junior Primary Education

William Chakabwata
http://orcid.org/0000-0002-4224-5239
University of South Africa, South Africa

ABSTRACT

The chapter explores how Artificial Intelligence (AI), has become ubiquitous in our societies today. Although AI has been implemented at tertiary levels of learning there is a gap in many countries in terms of implementing it at primary school. The chapter explores how curriculum design that teaches AI may be implemented at primary school using a variety of theories which includes Jerome Bruner's spiral curriculum, Jean Piaget 's cognitive development theory, Levy Vygotsky sociocultural theory and Ralph Tyler's objectives model. The chapter explores AI curriculum implementation at primary school in USA, Britain and China. Finally, the chapter explores a model of AI implementation and offers recommendation on how to implement an AI curriculum at primary school.

INTRODUCTION

The objectives of this chapter are to explore the implementation of assessments based on AI curricula at the primary school level, discuss forms of assessments that may be used at primary school, and recommend a framework that could inform assessment at the primary school level. This chapter draws on assessment practicesin

DOI: 10.4018/979-8-3373-4893-3.ch002

027, IGI Global Scientific Publishing. Copying or distributing in print or electronic forms without written permission of IGI Global Scientific Publishing is prohibited. Use of this chapter to
tive artificial intelligence (AI) technologies is expressly prohibited. The publisher reserves all rights to license its use for generative AI training and machine learning model development.

Zimbabwean primary schoolsl as an example of a developing country and assessment practices in China as a typical case of a country investing in AI literacyat thee primarschoolólevelll. A number of theories such as cognitive development theory by Jean Piaget, banking concept of education by Paulo Freire, Bloom's Taxonomy of learning objectives by Benjamin Bloom and constructivist theory of learning were used to illumine the engagement. Finally, the chapter recommends the use of formal and informal forms of assessments in AI curricula at the primary school level. Yim and Su (2025) averred that Artificial Intelligence (AI) has become ubiquitous in education at all levels of learning from early childhood learning to secondary and higher education. Marino et al.,(2023) asserted that AI had its origin in 1943, when a mathematician in Britain, Alan Turing initiated a computer that could be programmed. Later, he postulated a Turing test to determine a machine 'scapacity to approximate human intelligence by analyzing intricate challenges. The earliest artificial neural network emerged in 1956 by Frank Rosenblatt, a psychologist. Neural networks are information processing systems designed to imitate how the brain functions by making decisions based on data. The speed and precision of computer systems was enhanced by the evolution of data processor and development of computer memory the Random Access Computer Memory (RAM). Other key events in the evolution of AI is the evolution of machine learning (ML) and a subclass called deep learning. Deep learning has been utilised in multiple applications which include image processing and technology that enables computers to analyse, process and communicate in human language. Artificial intelligence has been in diverse educational settings. Gardner et al., (2021) declared that AI innovations in education in assessment are drawing huge attention especially, as a strategy to enhance assessment effectiveness both formative and summative. The fascination with assessments is a component of ML, where information processing tools are programmed to analyse structures in data and to act upon those intepretations. In the light of education, it follows that if a computer can be programmed to function on the content that learners are expected to learn and to pose questions on the data it has processed it can conduct assessment on learners' performance. At a more advanced level if a computer is able to determine the criteria that can be used to determine a learner's comprehension and application of learning, it can be able to facilitate assessment either at a formative or summative level. Furthermore information processing machines may be able to implement assessment using a given criteria whether it is written or verbal. In spite of the exponential growth in the use of AI at different levels of learning, there remains a gap in the information regarding its application and assessment in primary schools. The education field can be enhanced by integrating AI into different elements of learning. AI has led to the evolution of an interdisciplinary domain that incorporates science, statistics, education, and psychology, among many other disciplines. The introduction of

AI into education is perceived to enableg teachers to focus on their core function andavoidg multiple mundane duties. AI has the ability to significantly enhance educational tools, including the provision of personalized learning, use of adaptive assessments, automated grading, intelligent tutoring,augmented reality, and virtual reality. In addition, AI is employed for data analysis, which informs the prediction of learner performance, acquisition of languag,e and enhances access to education and participation by all people in learning.

BACKGROUND

AI can help realize sustainable goal 4, which explicates the goal of ensuring quality education (United Nations, 2025). SDG goal 4 explicates that education offers a viable opportunity for children to experience social mobility and escape poverty. Technology ensures access to education by providing opportunities for all children to access education (Chen et al., 2020; McKay, 2018). Technologies closely related to education include data mining, machine learning, and learning analytics. Oruç et al. (2024)explicated artificialintelligencee (A, as a domain of science and technology that seeks a wider application of human intelligence. AI has been noted to be very instrumental in many fields, including education, health, law, and engineering. AI has tremendous capacity to facilitate planning in different fields. AI has been used in gamification in education to enhance learners engagement (Yahaya, et al., 2024). Gamification is perceived to enhance learners' engagement in school by creating motivation to learn.

This chapter explores the use of AI among primary school learners and examines assessment and evaluation. Assessment in primary schools assumes multiple forms, including formal and informal, continuous, and authentic assessments. This chapter argues that the introduction of assessment in schools should be underpinned by a constructivist approach that allows for authentic assessment types in primary schools (Chakabwata, 2022). Authentic assessment forms may assume a variety of forms, such as the use of portfolios, role play, discussions, interviews, and artifacts related to AI literacy. The goal of assessment will be to determine the extent to which learners in primary school are able to use AI proficiently to address contemporary issues in their communities. The case study will be grounded in Zimbabwe's primary schools. The challenges of using authentic assessments in the context of AI-driven curricula will also be highlighted. The chapter will also offer advice on ways to effectively implement constructivist assessments in the context of an AI-driven curriculum. Furthermore, it will explore the pervasive ways in which AI has become integrated into our societies and ways in which it can be employed in everyday life, in general, and in education, in particular. Finally, recommendations will be postulated on how to implement hands-on assessments in the context of constructivism. The theory underpinning this chapter is the banking concept of education by Paulo Freire, cognitive development theory by Jean Piaget, and Mezirow's transformative theory.

At the primary school level, AI is being harnessed for learning, including vocabulary acquisition and the development of multiple basic skills to build self-esteem and self-awareness (Shalmaa, 2025). AI technology can analyze students responses and provide formative feedback while presenting assessment as a play activity for learners at junior primary school. Assessment can be conceptualized as formative, diagnostic, and summative (Ornstein & Hunkins, 2018). Melaku and Wudu (2022) state that assessment practices in schools are designed to improve teaching and learning. The next section discusses AI and assessment in primary schools.

AI AND ASSESSMENT IN PRIMARY SCHOOL

AI enables the facilitation of formative assessment. AI tools offer interactive learning. Some forms of interactive learning include voice recognition, the use of visual learning aids, and the offering of immediate formative feedback (Shalmaa, 2025). In terms of formative feedback, AI-powered tools can help learners acquire vocabulary by monitoring the words a child is able to use and introducing new words at an appropriate stage of cognitive development.

Mundia (2012) observed that in most learning centers, traditional assessment practices were immanent, and the trajectory was to quantify the skills and knowledge that a learner had acquired from learning engagements. The amount of learning that had transpired was captured in school reports. There was undue emphasis on summative assessments to compare learner performance and to determine if they could proceed to the next grade. Authentic assessments assume a different paradigmatic approach to ensure that learners comprehend what occurs in the learning encounter and are able to demonstrate skills and competencies. This involves the use of diverse forms of assessments that are categorized as formal and informal. Informal assessments are typified by the use of observation, interviews, portfolios, role-play, demonstration of a skill, self-assessment, and assessment by a peer or parent. Formal assessments epitomize the use of criterion-referenced assessments.

Ozden (2025) argued that AI tutors, including Khanmigo and Jill Watson, demonstrate ways in which computerized systems can engage learners and respond to their questions in a manner that builds higher-order thinking competencies. AI is reconfiguring assessment by making grading and feedback mechanical. For instance, AI processing systems can grade examinations and essays, freeing teachers to engage in other activities. AI-designed grading software is capable of scoring multiple-choice and open-ended questions using rubrics and sample responses.

Software such as Gradescope utilizes AI to place related responses into categories, enabling the categories to be graded and provided with similar feedback. Similarly, natural language processing (NLP) is utilized to grade essays and ETS's e-rater.

To assess AI in primary school, an approach that is nuanced and evaluates learners use and knowledge of AI tools must be implemented. Some methods proposed for assessing AI in primary school range from the use of questionnaires and interviews to activities that stipulate the use of AI as a component of learning. Olwan (2025) indicated that AI-driven devices are transfiguring primary education and providing personalized learning instructions for children. AI-driven assessment tools can provide feedback on learners work and generate a learning structure that can meet the distinct needs of each child. AI tools have the capacity to transform tway assessmentsnts are understood and practised primary schoolsool by employing daanalytic adaptiveive learnnga and personalized feedb tocto provide formative feedback on the learner's progress.

Chen et al., (2020) expounded that AI learning model is crafted to improve individual learners potential and is derived from learner's behaviour data obtained from learning. Models are created to assess learners' competencies in a subject. The models are used to generate knowledge structure maps thathreflects learning content,the knowledge of expert,s andthe identification of common learning mistakes andmisunderstandingsg demonstrated by learners. Machine learning (ML) entails creating meaningful patterns and structured knowledge from data sampling and parsing (Yahaya, et al., 2024). The advent of big data, cloud computing, artificial neural networks (ANN), and Machine learning (ML) has made it possible for engineers to invent devices that can mimic human intelligence. ML is a component of ML that enables the production of algorithms, facilitate computer ability to learn from data and generate predictive models without human assistance. Mahesh (2020) indicated that ML is an empirical anaysis of algorithms and statistical models that computers employe to perform a task without being programmed. ML is a smaller component of AI that assists computers to learn and display intelligent decisions from accumulated data. In addition, ML is able to analyse and interpret large data sets. Furthermore ML depends on diverse algorithms to analyse different problems. Forero-Corba & Bennasar, (2024) averred that ML in education can be perceived as a part of AI and it refers to the process of enabling the computers to use algorithms to improve the didatic situation. The following uses of ML in education have been postulated:

- Promptly identify learners' academic performance.
- Enhance teachers' pedagogical skills
- Enhancing learning for individuals with autism spectrum disorders
- Enhance learner engagement through mobile devices

- Provide data-driven formative data.

Machine learning has the capability of indicating how a concept is being processed by the learner. This formative data can help teachers align their teaching with the cognitive ability of learners based on their learning records (Yahaya, et al., 2024). In terms of learner assessments, which is the central focus of this chapter, image recognition and prediction of machine learning can be employed to assess learners' work. In line with this chapter, ML can provide personalized learning in the form of adaptive learning recommendation,s naturallanguageeprocessing,g and intelligent tutoring services (Tariq, 2026).

Learning analytics explores data from the attributes of students and knowledge models from the learners and knowledge field models. Data analytics can help identify learners at risk and offer them appropriate support. Data mining in the field of education seeks to generate methodical and mechanical responses for learners. Learners' personal attributes are employed to analyze learners' work. This is followed by the use of regression, which can be used to foretell learners' future performance. Data mining is used as a critical device for enhancing the didactic process and improving knowledge acquisition and appreciation of the learning context. Data mining contributes significantly to the development of predictive models and personalized learning.

Data analytics is concomitant with technologies such as machine learning and can provide formative feedback. It employs data from semantics, data visualization, and learning sciences. Other areas in which AI has been used include curriculum development, design of learning content, robotics, video conferencing, and the use of three-dimensional (3D) technology. AI has enabled easy access to learning materials online. A case of assessment practices in Zimbabwean primary schools is explored as a case of a developing country.

ASSESSMENT PRACTICES IN ZIMBABWE PRIMARY SCHOOLS- A CASE STUDY

Mwembe and Moyo (2024) averred that the Ministry of Primary and Secondary Education (MoPSE) adopted continuous assessment practicto realizeise the national vision 2030. Continuous assessment implies that students work is recorded throughout the year andculminateste ie summative assessment olearners''s work. The Zimbabwe School Examination Council explicated continuous assessment at 30% and final examination contributes 70%. It is noted that the educational system in Zimbabwe was highly theoretical, as postulated by the Nziramasanga Presidential Commission of Inquiry in Education (Nziramasanga, 1999). The government of

Zimbabwe enacted the Science Technology Engineering and Mathematics (STEM) and Continuous Assessment Learning Activities (CALA). A change of assessment trajectory, which was encapsulated in CALA, was an effort to introduce a hands-on component to education and assessment. Therefore, assessment must have a practical component that ensures that learners apprehend the learning concepts. In the context of the introduction of the AI curriculum, learners must participate in activities that assess their capability in the use of AI.

Nyamayedenga (2024,p13) defined CALA as " a kind of assessment model which moves from using one common form of testing (examinations) to using a structure of assessment where multiple forms of assessment become an intergral part of the teaching learning process, placement and certification. It is an assessment process that ensures that learners are engaged in practical activities, projects, and research work. Vurayai and Muchuweni (2024) expounded that CALA was introduced in 2021 and it was indicated that learners are obliged to display knowledge, skills and competencies before they write the summative assessment. The use of CALA was intended to effect a major transition from the use of tests as the sole bedrock of assessment to the use of a variety of formative assessments. Assessments that were envisaged by CALA involved multiple forms, such as tasks, projects, observations, and quizzes.

Martinez-Comsaria, et al., (2023) asserted that the background examines the evolution of artificial intelligence and its use in assessment in education. The arena of education has benefitted from progress in AI at all levels of learning. This has facilitated a discussion on the recognition of human and non-human actors in educational spaces. AI is utilized to prepare instruction that is individualized for learners, perform routine duties such as assessments, and support learners with a disability. Shalmaa (2025) averred that AI assessment tools can significantly improve assessments at primary school through the provision of personalized feedback. AI assessment tools are creative devices that are capable of analyzing students work and outlining learning pathways of learners to meet the distinct needs of each child. AI tools are able to avail comprehensive data analytics that assist teachers in perceiving and rectifying learning gaps. The next section looks at challenges related to assessment practices in Zimbabwe.

CHALLENGES ASSOCIATED WITH CALA

Vurayai and Muchuweni (2024) observed that CALA in Nigeria experienced constrictions which includes lack of qualified teachers, dearth of resources and insufficient of assessments. Similar observations were made in Nyanga, Zimbabwe, where CALA was enacted prior to the establishment of adequate institutions. Vurayai and Muchuweni (2024) explicated challenges related to CALA in Zimbabwe as failure by the government to consult the teachers the prime agents of curriculum implementation prior to the implementation. CALA was also implemented in the absence of a policy framework to regulate its practice. This lack of policy framework tended to impact the quality of assessments. Other challenges that were identified as inhibiting the implementation of CALA in Zimbabwe included a lack of professional development for teachers, lack of adequate guidance on the part of learners on how to implement CALA assessments, and a dearth of resources in schools. The subsequent section examines the challenges of migrating to an AI curriculum at the primary school level.

CHALLENGES OF MOVING TO AI CURRICULUM IN PRIMARY SCHOOLS

Countries designated as developing countries, such as Zimbabwe, tend to face daunting challenges in implementing a new AI-based curriculum at the primary school level. Many African countries confront several challenges in implementing AI in schools, including a lack of learning materials, inequality in digital access, and a lack of workbooks (Saal et al., 2025; Alsohaimi et al., 2025). A chief challenge in the integration of AI into the primary school curriculum is teachers' attitudes and the availability of infrastructure in schools. A multitude of teachers tend to resist the introduction of AI, perceiving it as reducing their influence, interwoven with other factors, such as a lack of infrastructure, constricted development opportunities, and a dearth of professional development opportunities. Alsohaimi et al.,(2025) asserted that in the absence of institutional infrustructure teachers tend to find the whole project of introducing AI in school unattainable. Ongoing professional development can help teachers develop literacy competencies and build their confidence. Dube and Chisaka (2021) conducted a study in the Goromonzi area of Zimbabwe on issues that impedes learners from accessing E-learning at primary school, given the way online mode has become ubiquitous in most countries. Zimbabwe has implemented an e-learning strategy under what is termed the Presidential Scheme, in which the president donated computers to schools in rural areas. Efforts to transform the educational system in Zimbabwe 'sprimary schools have suffered a major setback due to a dearth of resources.

Maponga (2024) conducted a study on the use of digital technology in schools in the Mazoeo district of Zimbabwe. The study noted that mobile devices can be employed as a resource to engage in online learning in place of desktop computers. Mobile devices can be utilised to provide personalised learning, access to information and digital literacy. . Kemp (2024) declared that 13,88 mobile users were active in

Zimbabwe in 2024 in a population that is estimated to be 16,84 million. Maponga's study noted a universal use of mobile phones and tablets for learning in Zimbabwean primary schools. The next section explores the implementation of an AI curriculum at primary school by using China as a typical country that has invested colossal resources in implementing an AI curriculum at primary school level.

ASSESSMENT AT PRIMARY SCHOOL IN AI A CASE STUDY OF CHINA

In this chapter, China is used as a case study of a country integrating AI in primary schools. The Australian Government Department of Education (2025) averred that China has embraced the teaching of AI as a key national priority. The President Xi Jinping has spotlighted the preeminence of AI for China 's national development to promote innovation in industry and enhance a digital economy. For this reason, China has embarked on educational reforms that utilize project-based learning. (Ministry of Education The People Republic of China, 2024) promulgated a framework for the teaching of AI in primary and secondary schools.

The guidance declares that AI must be integrated into the school curriculum at different levels. The framework calls for collaboration among various stakeholders in the field of education to develop appropriate models for teaching AI at all levels of learning. Schools are urged to incorporate AI into many subjects, including information technology (IT), practical subjects, and sciences, across the curriculum. The trajectory of AI curricula at the primary school level is to raise awareness about AI in education, and at the junior secondary school level, learners will engage in project generation and the use of more sophisticated technologies.

Sakar (2025) observed that the town of Hangzhou intiated mandatory classes for AI at primary school and secondary school. Learners in grades 1 and 2 learn how to identify AI, and those in grades 3 and 4 will be prepared to use AI to gather text, audio, and image texts for school tasks. The next section explores diverse forms of formative assessments that can be used in primary schools (Tariq, 2025).

FORMATIVE ASSESSMENTS

Elmahdi et al., (2028) argued that technology can be a useful tool for facilitating formative assessment during learning. The same authors postulated the use of multiple online assessment tools, including Clickers, Plickers, Kahoot, digital quizzes, and Socrative and Recap. Formative assessments are critical for providing teachers with real-time data that can inform learning. The technological component offered by these programmes ensures that learners are motivated, participate in active learning, and facilitate instruction in a constructivist paradigm.

AI has ushered in a revolutionary approach to assessment in primary schools, as at other levels of learning, by utilizing central practices such as adaptive questioning, natural language processing, data analytics, and automated marking of objective questions. Yim and Su (2025) in a scoping study on AI literacy in primary schools averred that a multiple assessments forms were used in assessing AI curriculum which includes use of interviews, questionnaires, artefacts, use of interviews, observations, role -play, demonstration and performance based evaluations.

JEAN PIAGET

This chapter is built on the assumptions regarding learning by Jean Piaget (1896-1980), a Swiss psychologist who postulated the theory of cognitive development. McLeod (2025) expounded that children progress through four invariant stages of cognitive development: sensorimotor, preoperational, concrete, and formal operations. Ornstein and Hunkins (2018) expounded that sensorimotor stage (0-2 years) implies that the child progresses from use of reflexes to more sophisticated sensorimotor actions. The child is also able to develop the concept of object permanence, which is the knowledge that objects remain in existence even when they do not see them. The preoperational stage (2–7 years) reflects key features, such as appreciating the symbolic nature of objects and events. The child is able to extract complex learning from concrete objects. Concrete operations (7–11 years) highlight the child's ability to organize data into sophisticated meaning and analyze and solve data. The child is able to display reversibility and conservation. The final stage of cognitive development is the formal operations stage (from 11 years onwards), which reflects an ability to engage in hypothetico–deductive reasoning for some people. In this chapter, the focus will be on learners at concrete operations at the primary school level and the assessment of learners within the context of an AI curriculum. The assessment practices that can be used for AI at primary school, when teaching an AI-based curriculum, must focus on authentic assessments. The next sections focus on the theories that have shed light on this topic, including Paulo Freire 'sbanking concept of learning, Benjamin Bloom's taxonomy of learning objectives, and a constructivist perspective of learning (Tariq, 2026).

PAUL FREIRE AND ACTIVE LEARNING

Paulo Freire was a Brazilian educator who is known for his opposition to passive learning methods. Freire (2012) critiqued traditional education systems and challengededucators tooreflect on their teachingh. Freire 's teaching paradigm transcended mere teaching, and he highlighted the importance of creating learning spaces where learners can actively learn, which would culminate in the transformation of society. Freire's core concepts were the banking concepts of education, in which learners are perceived as vessels in whom teachers may deposit information. This treatment of learners as passive recipients was conceptualized by Freire as learning for oppression, by the way it failed to develop critical thinking and 21st-centuryy skills. Herlinawati et al,. Herlinawati et al.(2024) averred that 21st-century skills, epitomized by skillssuchhase teamwork, creativit,y and critical thinkin, are essentialg. Technology is perceived to hold the potential to help realize the development of these 21st-century competencies.

Freire postulated a novel way of teaching, a problem-based model in which learning is dialogic (Freire, 2005). In Freire's ideology, learning is an active process, but it is an interactive process that demonstrates a mutual exchange of information, resulting in the co-creation of knowledge. The use of dialogue in the learning context creates humanistic learning spaces that value everyone.

BENJAMIN BLOOM REVISED TAXONOMY OF LEARNING OBJECTIVES

The University of Arkansas (2022) explicated Bloom 's taxonomy as a classification of learning objectives developed in 1956 by a psychologist, Benjamin Bloom. Chandio et al.(2016) expounded that Bloom's students revised the taxonomy to represent the six levels, including remembering, understanding, applying, analyzing, evaluating, and creating (Chakabwata, 2023). Patil and Gaurshettiwar (2025) indicated that Bloom's taxonomy divides learning objectives into three domains: cognitive, psychomotor, and affective. The cognitive domain encapsulates mind-related competencies, including comprehension, critical thinking, and knowledge. The psychomotor skills include the capacity to operate a tool, such as a screwdriver or a hammer. The development of practical objects, such as robotics, would fall under the psychomotor and cognitive domains. Furthermore, psychomotor skills include competencies such as creating work independently. The affective domain refers to the development of values, ethics, and emotions among learners. The development of ethics in the use of AI would fall under the affective domain.

CONSTRUCTIVISM APPROACH TO EDUCATION

Allen (2022) expounded that constructivism connote the learners build their own knowledge they contemplate and assign meaning to their experience. Constructivism has influence on teaching and assessment at all levels of learning, from early childhood education to higher and technical education. The genesis of the term can be traced to individuals who includes Jean Piaget, Kant, John Dewey, Levy Vygotsky, Jerome Bruner, Maria Monstessorri, Freire among many others (Adom et al.,2016). At a philosophical level, constructivism is related to interpretivism. Constructivism has been expanding in influence in research and teaching and learning (Chakabwata, 2023).

The concept of constructivism is interdisciplinary, drawing from the work of historians, anthropologists, and philosophers among many other disciplines. Thomas (2023,1) chronicled elements of a constructivist assessment as:

- Learning and assessment are intertwined.
- Assessment is a two-way exercise.
- Assessments incorporate higher-order thinking skills.
- Assessment is integrated into the curriculum.
- An assessment is located in a given context.
- Feedback was provided instantly.
- Enhances the teaching and learning situation.
- Formative assessment can be ongoing during learning and may take the form of discussions, observations, role-playing, and so on.
- The interplay between assessment and learning
- Assessments should not be deprecating to learners.
- Continuous assessment is designed to enhance learning and develop the required skills.
- Feedback provides a basis for advanced learning and teaching.
- Uninterrupted and regular, as opposed to end-of-term assessments.
- are designed to refine teaching and learning.

Constructivism foregrounds the construction of meaning as learning, and there is no other substitute. Kumar (2019) argued that the rise of constructivism was a reaction to behaviorism, with its emphasis on direct instruction and passive learning. Learners are seen as socially negotiating their own learning by engaging in ongoing testing of hypotheses, generating new knowledge, adjusting previous knowledge, or confirming what they already know. Therefore, each learner derives a subjective understanding from the learning situatio,nwhicht is derived from mental schemas.

While constructivism seems to carry multiple nuances, its central tenet is the construction of meaning by the learner from their experiences. Krahenbul (2016) argued that constructivism currently exerts a hegemonic grip on didactic practices from primary to secondary school. Baştürk (2016) submitted that learners are expected to internalise and process information and not to merely process information. Constructivism also acknowledges that learners construct knowledge using prior knowledge as a foundation. The errors that learners make in the learning context are perceived as the foundation for real learning.

Similar to any other philosophical position, constructivism has been criticized on several points. Simpson (2002) argued that constructivism is perceived as rejecting the existence of objective facts, as seen in the field of science. Tsehay et al., (2024) added that constructivism can only thrive in a situation where the administrators are supportive, teachers collaborate, availability of curriculum resources that support learning and the provision for on-going professional development. Other constraints noted in implementing constructivist learning include limited time available for learning and large class sizes. Alanazi (2016) indicated that critics argue that constructivism does not provide adequate instruction for learners, which can eventuate in learners becoming lost or frustrated. The next section proposes a framework for conceptualizing assessment in primary schools in AI curricula.

A FRAMEWORK FOR ASSESSMENT IN THE CONTEXT OF AI CURRICULUM

This chapter posits the development of assessment practices aligned with constructivism. It postulates a model based on key concepts, such as assessing conceptual understanding, the ability to apply computer skills, demonstrating hands-on skills, knowledge of ethics in the use of AI, learners' self-awareness, development of affective skills, and the ability to implement tools. Touretzky et al. (2019) averred that given the way AI has become universal, it is critical to ascertain what children at primary school are expected to learn at each level. An assessment model must be informed by theory that illuminates how children learn, including Piaget's cognitive learning theory, Maria Montessori 's method of education, and a proclivity towards constructivist learning and assessment, particularly the way it spotlights active learning and the interlinkage between learning and assessment (Freire, 2005; Krahenbuhl, 2016; Alanazi, 2016). The model must also be informed by Benjamin Bloom'sTaxonomy off Learning Objectives,s particularly the revised model and-current effortss toodevelop 21st-centuryy skills among learners.

Many organizations, including Google, Microsoft, and Computer Science Teachers (CSTA), among others, have expressed interest in what children learn at primary and secondary school levels and the ways in which it can be assessed. To engage with AI, learners require the ability to manipulate AI information processing tools (Touretzky et al., 2019). Therefore, this chapter postulates a framework that undertakes assessment at the primary school level, as discussed in the next section.

CONCEPTUAL UNDERSTANDING

Assessing conceptual understanding may be attained at the primary school level through the use of assessments such as interviews, discussions, portfolios, quizzes, and summative assessments. Informal assessments are ideal for determining learners' progress in apprehending conceptual understanding in AI. The University of the Potomac (2025) defined conceptual understanding as the ability of learners to apprehend the essence of ideas, which transcends surface learning to deeper learning. Marton and Säljö (1976) originated the concepts of deep learning and surface learning. The two authors noted that learners have different goals when working on a task. Some learners would want to reproduce a text when probed on it, while others would seek to comprehend the essence of the text. Learners who intend to understand the work would seek to link the new information to previous knowledge and can engage in deep learning. These learners tend to refrain from rote learning. A surface approach to learning is viewed as an approach to learning that is bent on memorizing learning content with no meaningful engagement with it (Biggs et al., 2001; Entwistle et al., 2003).

The University of the Potomac (2025) explains that learners who develop conceptual understanding tend to have a holistic understanding of an issue rather than perceiving it in a disjointed way. Furthermore, conceptual understanding may be enhanced by the use of active learning and appropriating learners prior knowledge in a learning situation. Informal assessments can help learners develop conceptual understanding of the field of AI. Yang (2023) asserted that informal assessments holds tremendous potential for learning. For this reason, they have become widely employed by teachers in many subjects. Informal assessments enable teachers to extract feedback on the learning process by collecting data from routine activities that occur in the learning teaching situation through the use of demonstrations, observations, role-playing, and portfolios.

ASSESSING PRACTICAL COMPETENCIES IN AI APPLICATIONS

Touretzky et al. (2019) have adduced that there are multiple devices that use information processing technology linked to AI software, such as voice assistants, Google Home, and Apple Homepod. There are also software that recognize learners drawings, such as Mathpix, which can convert images of math into digital text, andCognimatess offers a platform for learners to acquire knowledge about AI programming. Learners at primary school may take advantage of the multiple existing software to participate in activities such as AI programming. A sample of current sites that can develop practical competencies in teaching programming among learners includes Cognimates, which facilitate the creation of speech, group text, and object recognition; Google has published a number of online training sessions on AI programming; andthe Cozmo robo,t which has intrinsic computer vision and face recognition (Chakabwata and Hategekimana, 2024). Learners can display computer competencies at varying levels at primary school, for instance, at grades 3–5,learners can acquire knowledge that computers acquire the skills they display such as voice recognition from data. Learners can practice modifying applications for voice recognition (Touretzky et al., 2019). Learners at grades 3–5 would also require to appreciate that computers information processing systems function from data that is stored in them. Touretzky et al. (2019,p.9797) postulated a thematic approach to the curriculum for learners that revolves around key concepts, such as:

- Computers obtain information from the world by utilizing sensors; this means that learners must appreciate that machines can perform their functions using domain knowledge. In grade 6, learners could experiment with creating applications that demonstrate sensitivity to people faces or spoken phrases.
- The third theme is that computers can learn from data. This implies that machine learning algorithms enable information processing devices to generate their own representations by employing training data provided by people or that can be extracted from multiple sources. Grade 3–5 learners may participate in manipulation object recognition applications.
- The ethical effects of AI applications extend to the people and users.
- Ensuring that computer processing applications are able to engage with people is a daunting task. This means that learners have to appreciate that while computers are able to use language, they still face constraints, such as an inability to converse with humans, even at the level of a child.

Chakabwata and Hategekimana (2024) asserted that PBL reflects a transition from teaching as transmission to teaching as facilitation.

ASSESSING ETHICS SOCIAL AWARENESS IN USING AI

Assessing ethical awareness when using AI is a major theme at the primary school level that requires interrogation. UNESCO (2025) highlights ethics in the field of AI as upholding human rights and dignity, living in a just and peaceful society, ensuring diversity, inclusivenes, and a sustainable environmentt,and a flourishing ecosystemmg. These ethics elaborate on ensuring that people are treated with dignity and respect, promoting cooperation, and ensuring that there is diversity and inclusion, which means that excluded and marginalized groups, such as women, must be included in the use of AI. It has been noted that AI has the potential to reproduce societal biases through the manner in which the programmes are created.

Capital Technology University (2023)arguedd that AI systems are trained on colossal data thataresimbuedt with societal biases. Stereotypical issues can be hidden in AI systems, exacerbating inequality and injustice in diverse fields, such as education and health. AI systems are known to function asa blackboxesx, which means that there is no transparency regarding the process in whichdecisionsn are undertaken and in the event of someone being hurt by the decision,d it can be daunting to identify a person who assumesresponsibilityy. There are also ethical challenges related to ownership rights and infringements of materials generated by AI (Capital Technology University, 2023). These are some of the areas that researchers are still exploring. One of the most fundamental areas of concern regarding AI is the management of personal data and security. AI systems utilize huge amounts of personal data, and it is vital that the way in which the data are managed and secured be discussed. Finally, AI algorithms can be manipulated to spread information that is not accurate or designed to misinform people. These ethical issues must be addressed at the primary school level so that learners are aware of the ethical implications of using AI. Some of the philosophical perspectives that have shaped AI use in schools include utilitarianism, virtue ethics, and deontology. Utilitarianism focuses on the consequences of ethics and is preoccupied with instrumental rationality, which believes that if the outcome leads to a greater good, then it is acceptable (Guo and Kühler, 2025).Deontological theories approach ethics from the perspective that people have moral responsibility and are capable of acting in a way that is appropriate or inappropriate (D'Alessandro and D'Alessandro, 2025). Virtue ethics holds that it is vital to develop virtues or qualities in people that can help them live a good life. The next section discusses ways in which the affective domain can be assessed in AI.

ASSESSING THE AFFECTIVE DOMAIN IN AI

Tools that may be employed to assess AI literacy in primary schools include the ABCE framework. Ng et al,. Ng et al.(2023) defined the affective domain as changes that occur within a learner toward the level of emotion or psychology towards an issue such as AI. These changes may be measured by considering interests, self-efficacy, and confidence, among others. Yim and Su (2025) adduced in a scoping study on AI curriculum in primary school that there are affective and behavioral learning outcomes that were noted in primary schools. Some of the terms that were employed to reflect affective competencies by learners in primary school were fun and exciting to characterize the engagements they had with AI during practicals. Learners reflected a growing cognitive motivation towards the use of AI in schools. Learners also displayed tremendous engagement as they participated in active learning.

ETHICS AND USE OF AI IN EDUCATION

The use of AI in education for assessment and learning has also been associated with ethical concerns. D'Alessandro (2025) asserted that the field of AI seeks to ensure that users of the systems are not hurt. For this reason, people in the field of deontology study principles that can regulate the use of AI in schools and other fields. D'Alessandro (2025,p1681) encapsulated ethical concerns related to the use of AI as "AI should behave normally and that such systems should behave safely". The first point refers to AI being regulated by standards of accepted ethics, while the second component refers to non-maleficence in the use of AI. The field of ethics and AI seeks to ensure that the use of AI in the education system, as in other sectors, is aligned with human values. Bhose (2024) declared that addressing ethical challenges is necessary to ensure that assessments are fair and valid. One of the first vital issues for AI assessments is the potential for systems to be skewed. It is argued that if the information processing systems that use AI are programmed in such a way that they can reproduce whatever biases that are built into thedatata such as gender or socioeconomic stereotype, an ethical challenge may arises. This ethical challenge may be rectified by enhancing fairness,trust,t and transparency. Ng et al,. Ng et al.(2023) added that ethics related to the use of AI includes managing cyber-bullying, respect, and digital responsibility.

Other ethical issues that must be considered when AI is used in assessments include accuracy, reliability, equity of accuracy, and ensuring accessibility. Yan and Liu (2024) explicated the ethical issues that remain poignant in the use of AI in schools encapsulate data privacy contraventions, intellectual property rights, algorithms skewness, and the creation of imprecise information. These ethical components have severe implications for the quest to enhance social justice in education, impacting learners' mental health and social inclusion. Multiple higher education institutions in many states, including China, the United States, and South Africa, have initiated programs designed to test the work submitted by students to determine if it has been generated by AI tools such as ChatGPT.

Santos et al., (2021) expounded that ethical dimensions are not on their own complete during design and deployment of AI. Holmes et al., (2018) indicated that a conference was held in 2018, for the sake of initiating a discussion on the ethical use of AI in education. The 2018 conference noted that although there is an almost universal design and deployment of AI, it continues to occur in a moral vacuum. The same conference noted that the education sector raises multiple ethical issues because of the bulk data that can be gathered in areas such as learners' misconceptions,competencies, and affective dimensions. Pertinent issues regard the collection, analysis, and utilization of this data. Design biases that may be latent in AI systems incorporate biases in areas such as age, gender, race, and social indicators, among many other variables. Santos et al., (2021) declared that ethics in learning analytics subsumes power disparaties, surveillence and the goals of objectives.

Regarding the promotion of access, AI must create features that cater to diverse learning needs and learners with special needs. The next section examines the ethical domain that has shaped the use of AI in school assessments.

DISCUSSION

It was noted that CALA was built on the premise of hands-on activities in primary school, which was designed to shift learning from a theoretical perspective to a pragmatic angle. In this chapter, it is critical to introduce AI at the primary school level. The chapter explored ways in which AI could be assessed at the primary school level. The chapter noted that the introduction of AI in primary schools can be accompanied by diverse challenges related to the learners' cognitive ability and abstract concepts related to the subjects. The theories that informed this chapter are diverse and includes Jean Piaget cognitive development, Paul Freire banking concept of education, Benjamin Bloom taxonomy of learning objectives and a constructivists perspective to assessment. The chapter explored assessment in the context of Zimbabwe primary school as a case of a developing country that is seeking to shift paradigmatically from a banking form of assessment to constructivist form of assessment which can develop learners critical thinking skills and 21st century skills. Another case that was explored was the case of China which was a reflection of country that is injecting colossal resources into actualising AI curriculum at primary school level. Zimbabwe has widespread access to mobile devices which provides a foundation for the implementation of an AI curriculum at primary school level. Of course, there are many other preliminary steps the government must take to realize an educational system based on AI at primary schools, such as ensuring equal access to digital technology, ensuring access to secure and stable Internet networks in schools, and facilitating teachers' professional development so that they can implement assessments based on authenticity, as opposed to the banking concept of learning.

The study submitted that learners develop at different paces cognitively starting from sensorimotor stage, preoperational stage, concrete operation and them formal operations. Assessments applicable at the primary school level have to take into account the cognitive level of primary school learners so that they are not frustrated with the subject. Assessment practices have to also take into account Paulo Freire 's perception of learning as an active process, as opposed to a passive process. Learning and assessment within the framework of the AI curriculum has to consider the taxonomy of learning objectives as postulated by Benjamin Bloom. The chapter also foregrounded the importance of using formative assessments that take into account diverse forms of assessments, such as informal and formal assessments, to capture all forms of learning. This implies a paradigm shift from the use of standardised tests to the use of portfolios, demonstrations, observations, interviews, role-play when conducting assessments. However, the chapter also highlighted the obstacles that teachers may experience when introducing assessments in AI at primary school level, which may include resistance from teachers who may want to hold on to traditional teaching, dearth of resources to enable assessment modelled on the constructivist's paradigm, lack of professional development opportunities, weak internet connectivity and lack of devices to support learning.

RECOMMENDATIONS

Based on the analysis in the previous sections, it was noted that the implementation of AI-based assessments at primary school was impeded by multiple factors. To remedy the challenges noted in this chapter, the following recommendations are offered:

i) The ministry of education in different countries have to set-up infrastructure such as hardware and network to facilitate AI assessments
ii) It is important to shift from traditional assessments to authentic assessments that foreground hands-on activities and authentic assessments that are rooted.

iii) It is important to undertake professional development of teachers at primary school as implementers of the curriculum at primary school in order to raise level of literacy.
iv) Schools must set up networks for AI and computer processing systems
v) The Ministry of Education in Zimbabwe needs to ensure that the curriculum is aligned with the AI curriculum and that necessary policy documents regarding assessment policy are developed.

CONCLUSIONS

This chapter discusses radical changes that artificial intelligence is making in schools and in the entire society. It discusses assessment in primary school in the context of AI literacy. The use of assessments informed by a constructivist philosophy was underscored. Several theories were discussed to highlight the issues in this chapter. Finally, recommendations were proposed.

REFERENCES

Adom, D., Yeboah, A., & Ankrah, A. (2016). Constructivism philosophical paradigm: Implications for research, teaching and learning. *Global Journal of Arts. Humanities and Social Sciences*, *4*(10), 1–9.

Alanazi, A. (2016). A critical review of constructivist theory and the emergence of constructionism. *American Research Journal of Humanities and Social Sciences*, *2*, 1–8.

Allen, A. (2022). An introduction to curriculum development: Its theoretical roots and impact on contemporary education. *Journal of Learning Design and Leadership*, *1*(1), 1–11.

Alsohaimi, M., Albahiri, M., & Alhaj, A. (2025). Addressing and managing artificial intelligence challenges and opportunities in elementary education in Saudi Arabia: An in-depth consideration. *Educational Process: International Journal*, 1–33.

Australian Government Department of Education. (2025). *China's approach to AI education in schools*. Department of Education.

Baştürk, S. (2016). Primary pre-service teachers' perspectives on constructivism and its implementation in schools. *Universal Journal of Educational Research*, *4*(4), 904–912. DOI: 10.13189/ujer.2016.040428

Bhose, M. (2024, October 2). What are the ethical challenges in AI-driven assessments? Retrieved from https://elearningindustry.com/what-are-the-ethical-challenges-in-ai-driven-assessments

Biggs, J., Kember, D., & Leung, D. (2001). The revised two-factor study process questionnaire: R-SPQ-2F. *The British Journal of Educational Psychology*, *71*(1), 133–149. DOI: 10.1348/000709901158433 PMID: 11307705

Capital Technology University. (2023, May 30). *The ethical considerations of artificial intelligence*. Retrieved from https://www.captechu.edu/blog/ethical-considerations-of-artificial-intelligence

Chakabwata, W. (2022). Digital-based assessments for higher-order and critical thinking in higher education. In Keengwe, J. (Ed.), *Digital-based assessments for innovative practices in education* (pp. 228–246). IGI Global. DOI: 10.4018/978-1-6684-2468-1.ch012

Chakabwata, W. (2023). Using an eclectic approach to design curriculum instruction in an online environment. In Walters, K. (Ed.), *Dynamic curriculum development and design strategies for effective online learning in higher education* (pp. 96–115). IGI Global. DOI: 10.4018/978-1-6684-8646-7.ch006

Chakabwata, W. (2023). Using technology to enhance student engagement in STEM subjects in higher education. In Martin, C., Miller, B., & Polly, D. (Eds.), *Technology integration and transformation in STEM classrooms* (pp. 165–183). IGI Global.

Chakabwata, W., & Hategekimana, E. (2024). Using project-based pedagogies in African higher education. In Keengwe, J. (Ed.), *Handbook of research on transformative and innovative pedagogies in education* (pp. 55–75). IGI Global.

Chandio, D. T., Pandhiani, S., & Iqbal, R. (2016). Bloom's taxonomy: Improving assessment and teaching-learning processes. *Journal of Education and Educational Development, 3*(2), 203–221. DOI: 10.22555/joeed.v3i2.1034

Chen, L., Chen, P., & Lin, Z. (2020). Artificial intelligence in education: A review. *IEEE Access : Practical Innovations, Open Solutions, 8*, 75264–75278. DOI: 10.1109/ACCESS.2020.2988510

D'Alessandro, W., & D'Alessandro, M. (2025). Deontology and safe artificial intelligence. *Philosophical Studies, 182*(7), 1681–1704. DOI: 10.1007/s11098-024-02174-y

Dube, A., & Chisaka, B. (2021). Challenges militating against primary school learners' maximum access to e-education programmes in Goromonzi District of Zimbabwe. *International Journal of Research Studies in Computer Science and Engineering, 8*(1), 31–42.

Entwistle, N., McCune, V., & Hounsell, J. (2003). Investigating ways of enhancing university teaching-learning environments. In De Corte, E. (Eds.), *Unravelling basic components and dimensions of powerful learning environments* (pp. 89–107). Elsevier.

Forero-Corba, W., & Bennasar, F. (2024). Techniques and applications of machine learning and artificial intelligence in education: A systematic review. *RIED – Revista Iberoamericana de Educación a Distancia, 27*(1).

Freire, P. (2005). Education for critical consciousness. *Continuum.*

Freire, P. (2012). Pedagogy of the oppressed. *Continuum.*

Gardner, J., O'Leary, M., & Yuan, L. (2021). Artificial intelligence in educational assessment: Breakthrough or buncombe and bullyhoo? *Journal of Computer Assisted Learning, 37*(5), 1207–1216. DOI: 10.1111/jcal.12577

Guo, Y., & Kühler, M. (2025). History, AI and utilitarianism. *AI and Ethics*, *5*(3), 2903–2917. DOI: 10.1007/s43681-024-00581-9

Herlinawati, H., Marwa, M., Ishmael, N., Junaidi, L. L., & Situmorang, D. O. (2024). Integration of 21st-century skills in the education curriculum. *Heliyon*, •••, 11. DOI: 10.1016/j.heliyon.2024.e35148 PMID: 39170322

Holmes, W., Bektik, D., & Woolf, B. (2018). Ethics in artificial intelligence in education. In *Artificial Intelligence in Education* (pp. 551–553). Springer.

Independent Commission on Assessment in Primary Education (ICAPE). (2022). *ICAPE report*. ICAPE.

Kemp, S. (2024). *Digital 2024: Zimbabwe*. DataReportal. Retrieved from https://datareportal.com

Krahenbuhl, K. (2016). Student-centred education and constructivism: Challenges and clarity for teachers. *The Clearing House: A Journal of Educational Strategies, Issues and Ideas*, *89*(3), 97–105. DOI: 10.1080/00098655.2016.1191311

Kumar, S. (2019). Effective constructivist teaching learning in the classroom. *International Journal of Research and Analytical Reviews*, *7*(4).

Mahesh, B. (2020). Machine learning algorithms: A review. *International Journal of Scientific Research*, *9*(1), 381–385.

Maponga, M. (2024). The penetration of mobile technology in schools: A case of selected schools in Mazowe District. *IRASS Journal of Multidisciplinary Studies*, *1*(3), 25–36.

Marino, M., Vasquez, E., Dieker, L., Basham, J., & Blackorby, J. (2023). The future of artificial intelligence in special education technology. *Journal of Special Education Technology*, *38*(3), 404–416. DOI: 10.1177/01626434231165977

Martinez-Comsaria, M., Rigueira-Díaz, X., Larranaga-Janeira, A., Martinez-Torres, J., Ocarranza-Prado, I., & Keribel, D. (2023). Impact of artificial intelligence on assessment methods in primary and secondary education: A systematic review. *Revista de Psicodidáctica*, *28*(2).

Marton, F., & Säljö, R. (1976). On qualitative differences in learning: Outcome and process. *The British Journal of Educational Psychology*, *46*(1), 4–11. DOI: 10.1111/j.2044-8279.1976.tb02980.x

McKay, V. (2018). Literacy, lifelong learning and sustainable development. *Australian Journal of Adult Learning*, *58*(3), 390–425.

McLeod, S. (2025). Piaget's Theory and Stages of Cognitive Development. Simply Psychology. https://www.simplypsychology.org/piaget.html

Melaku, T., & Wudu, M. (2022). Primary school teachers' conceptions and practice of assessment and their relationships. *Cogent Education.*

Ministry of Education of the People's Republic of China. (2024). *Guidance on teaching AI in primary and middle schools.* Retrieved from http://en.moe.gov.cn

Mwembe, D., & Moyo, H. (2024). Implementing continuous assessment learning activities in Zimbabwe's Education 5.0 system. *Educational Point, 1*(2).

Ng, T., Wu, W., Leung, J., & Chiu, T. (2023). Design and validation of the AI literacy questionnaire. *British Journal of Educational Technology.*

Nziramasanga, C. (1999). *Report of the Presidential Commission of Inquiry into Education.* Government of Zimbabwe.

Ornstein, A. C., & Hunkins, F. (2018). *Curriculum: Foundations, principles, and issues* (7th ed.). Pearson.

Saal, P. E., Chetty, K., Ntshayintshayi, N., Moosa, T., & Masuku, N. (2025). A scoping review of the integration of artificial intelligence in primary and secondary schools from 2020 to 2024: Policy implications for South Africa. Journal of Education (University of KwaZulu-Natal), (98), 62-85.

Santos, O., Rodrigo, M., Cukurova, M., Bittencourt, I., & Koedinger, K. (2021). Ethics of AI in education: Towards a community-wide framework. *International Journal of Artificial Intelligence in Education.*

Simpson, T. L. (2002). Dare I oppose constructivist theory? *The Educational Forum, 66*(4), 347–354. DOI: 10.1080/00131720208984854

Tariq, M. U. (2025). *AI-Driven Learning and Engagement in Higher Education.* IGI Global., DOI: 10.4018/979-8-3693-4074-5

Tariq, M. U. (2026). Empowering Young Learners: Innovative Strategies for STEM and Literacy in Early Childhood Deaf Education. In Graham, P., & Neild, N. (Eds.), *Early Childhood Deaf Education: Teacher Preparation and Instructional Approaches* (pp. 231–258). IGI Global Scientific Publishing., DOI: 10.4018/979-8-3693-9127-3.ch007

Tariq, M. U. (2026). AI-Powered Assessment Platforms: Transforming Higher Education Evaluation. In Zaky, H. (Ed.), *Innovating Assessment and Evaluation in Higher Education: Inclusive Practices and Technological Advancements* (pp. 117–146). IGI Global Scientific Publishing., DOI: 10.4018/979-8-3373-2130-1.ch004

Tariq, M. U. (2026). Equity-Driven Leadership in Technology Integration for Higher Education. In Areba, G., Gisore, B., Njurai, E., Awuor, F., & Makiya Cyprian, R. (Eds.), *Transformative Leadership and Enhancing Equity in Technological Advancements in Higher Education* (pp. 171–198). IGI Global Scientific Publishing., DOI: 10.4018/979-8-3373-2322-0.ch007

Touretzky, D., Gardner-McCune, C., Martin, F., & Seehorn, D. (2019). Envisioning AI for K-12: What should every child know about AI? In *Proceedings of the AAAI Conference on Artificial Intelligence*. DOI: 10.1609/aaai.v33i01.33019795

UNESCO. (2025). *Recommendation on the ethics of artificial intelligence*. UNESCO.

United Nations. (2025). *Sustainable Development Goal 4: Quality education*. United Nations.

Yahaya, A. A., Rasheed, F., Muaz, B. S., Haruna, U., Sani, A., Yahaya, I. A., & Ahmad, B. M. (2024). Application of machine learning in education: Recent trends challenges and future perspective. *Información Tecnológica*, *7*(3), 118–131.

Yan, Y., & Liu, H. (2024). Ethical framework for AI education based on large language models. *Education and Information Technologies*.

Yim, I., & Su, J. (2025). Artificial intelligence literacy in primary schools: A review. *International Journal of Technology and Design Education*, *35*(5), 2175–2204. DOI: 10.1007/s10798-025-09979-w

KEY TERMS AND DEFINITIONS

Adaptive Learning: is a platform that adjust learning to meet the needs of the learner

Algorithms: steps that a machine processing device follows when solving a problem

Artificial Intelligence: Machines that are developed with the ability tom process information and solve problems as human beings

Assessment: a process of collecting detailed information on learners' progress

Data Analytics: A process of using devices to analyse raw data to identify pattens and trends and decide on a course of action

Data Mining: a process of analyses huge amounts of information in order to create new information

Formative Feedback: This feedback that a learner receives during the lesson process

Summative Assessments: Assessment that comes at the end of a unit or a course or term

Chapter 3
AI Across Ages:
A Continuum Model From Primary Education to University Classrooms

Ishteyaaq Ahmad
http://orcid.org/0000-0001-7244-6624
University of Petroleum and Energy Studies, Dehradun, India

ABSTRACT

This chapter presents a comprehensive AI Literacy Continuum model that emphasizes a developmental, human-centred approach to AI education spanning early childhood to university. It critiques fragmented, late-stage AI instruction and advocates for integrated, ethical, and inclusive learning pathways. Drawing on global case studies and rigorous pedagogical frameworks, the chapter highlights how curiosity, empathy, and critical reflection serve as foundational pillars of AI literacy. It underscores the vital role of teachers and institutions in fostering readiness, cultural sensitivity, and ethical responsibility. Policy recommendations call for systemic alignment, lifelong learning ecosystems, and collaborative international efforts to ensure equitable access and sustained impact. Ultimately, the chapter redefines AI literacy as an extension of human literacy—nurturing reflective, empowered citizens capable of shaping AI's role in society with wisdom and conscience.

INTRODUCTION

Artificial Intelligence has woven itself into the fabric of contemporary life, operating quietly behind countless daily interactions (Ahmad et al., 2024). When children ask voice assistants for help with homework or when recommendation

DOI: 10.4018/979-8-3373-4893-3.ch003

)27, IGI Global Scientific Publishing. Copying or distributing in print or electronic forms without written permission of IGI Global Scientific Publishing is prohibited. Use of this chapter to
:ive artificial intelligence (AI) technologies is expressly prohibited. The publisher reserves all rights to license its use for generative AI training and machine learning model development.

algorithms shape their entertainment choices, they encounter AI long before formal education acknowledges its presence. This reality presents an educational paradox: while young learners interact with AI-powered systems throughout their daily lives, most educational institutions reserve AI literacy for advanced coursework (Su et al., 2023), typically at university level. Such delayed introduction means missing critical developmental windows where curiosity about intelligent systems could flourish naturally (Yang, 2025).

Understanding AI literacy requires moving beyond technical competencies to embrace a broader conceptual framework. Long and Magerko (Long & Magerko, 2020) define AI literacy as "a set of competencies that enables individuals to critically evaluate AI technologies; communicate and collaborate effectively with AI; and use AI as a tool online, at home, and in the workplace". This definition encompasses pattern recognition, algorithmic thinking, ethical reasoning, and the ability to question how intelligent systems make decisions. Rather than emerging spontaneously in adulthood, these capabilities develop through sustained engagement with foundational concepts over time (Konstantina & Stamatios, 2024).

Children's natural curiosity about intelligence, fairness, and decision-making reveals an intuitive readiness for AI concepts. When young learners wonder why a game character behaves differently or how a smart device "knows" what they want, they demonstrate the questioning mindset essential for AI literacy (Ozturk, 2025). Research in early childhood education shows that preschool-aged children can effectively engage with computational thinking concepts through developmentally appropriate activities. Studies using tools like ScratchJr demonstrate that children aged 4-6 can master pattern recognition, sequence building, and logical reasoning foundational elements that support later AI understanding (Baghiro et al., 2025).

However, current educational approaches often fragment AI learning across disconnected interventions (Gu & Ericson, 2025). Elementary schools may introduce basic programming concepts, whereas secondary institutions focus on robotics competitions or coding clubs. Meanwhile, universities have rapidly advanced with specialized programs in machine learning and data science, assuming that students arrive with conceptual foundations that they rarely possess. This disjunction creates a gap between user expectations and actual AI capabilities, in which learners can operate sophisticated tools without understanding their underlying principles or limitations.

The continuum model proposed here addresses this fragmentation by envisioning AI literacy as a developmental journey. Drawing from the AI4K12 Initiative's "Five Big Ideas in AI"—perception, representation and reasoning, learning, natural interaction, and societal impact (Touretzky et al., 2023).This framework suggests age-appropriate pathways that connect early experiences with mature understanding. These concepts, developed by David Touretzky and colleagues, provide accessible entry points that do not require technical prerequisites. In this chapter, the AI Literacy Continuum is defined as a developmental framework that maps age-appropriate understanding of artificial intelligence across early childhood, primary, secondary, and higher education. Rather than treating AI as a standalone or late-stage subject, the continuum emphasizes progressive learning experiences aligned with learners' cognitive, emotional, and ethical development, enabling sustained and meaningful engagement with AI over time.

Contemporary children encounter AI through interactive technologies that respond to voice commands, adapt to user preferences, and provide personalized recommendations. These encounters represent teachable moments in which abstract concepts become concrete experiences. When children notice that voice assistants sometimes misunderstand their questions or that recommendation systems occasionally suggest unwanted content, they observe the boundaries of current AI capabilities. Such observations can spark discussions about how machines process information, why they make errors, and how humans might improve their performance.

This chapter seeks to humanize AI education by focusing on learners as developing individuals with evolving relationships to intelligent technologies. Rather than treating AI literacy as a technical skillset, the continuum approach recognizes it as part of broader intellectual development. Just as children develop mathematical reasoning through years of guided exploration with numbers, patterns, and logical relationships, they can cultivate AI literacy through sustained engagement with concepts about intelligence, data, and automated decision-making (Miao et al., 2024).

The following sections examine current educational landscapes, identify gaps between early and advanced AI learning, and propose developmental frameworks that connect childhood curiosity with sophisticated analytical capabilities. By mapping AI literacy as a continuum rather than a destination, educators can design experiences that honor learners' developmental readiness while building toward a comprehensive understanding.

LIERATURE REVIEW

Educational institutions worldwide increasingly recognize AI's dual role as both educational tool and essential literacy domain (U.S. Department of Education, 2023). However, despite AI's pervasive presence in educational technology, systematic approaches to teaching about AI remain inconsistent across educational levels (Miao, 2021). Yet despite AI's pervasive presence in educational technology, systematic approaches to teaching about AI remain inconsistent across educational levels (Miao, 2021).

The Global Momentum for AI Literacy

National and international organizations have begun to establish frameworks for AI education that extend beyond technical training. UNESCO's AI Competency Frameworks for Teachers (Miao & Cukurova, 2024) and its AI Competency Frameworks for Students (Miao et al., 2024), released in September 2024, articulate four core student competencies: developing human-centered perspectives on AI, understanding ethical considerations, learning about AI techniques and applications, and engaging in AI system design. These frameworks emphasize that AI education should enhance, rather than replace, human intelligence, supporting decision-making processes while respecting cultural diversity and human rights.

These policies reflect a growing consensus that AI literacy is not a luxury skill for technologists but a foundational competency for all citizens. UNESCO's approach emphasizes that AI should support human decision-making and intellectual development rather than replace it, advocating for a human-centered approach that respects human rights and cultural diversity. The frameworks stress four core competencies for students: developing a human-centered mindset, understanding the ethics of AI, learning AI techniques and applications, and engaging in AI system design (Tariq, 2026).

For instance, in many regions, curricular reforms emphasize inquiry, creativity, and ethical engagement rather than rote learning of technical terms. AI is viewed as a cross-disciplinary theme that touches mathematics, science (Ozturk, 2025), social studies, and even art and language. The goal is to help children see AI as part of everyday reasoning and creativity something that interacts with their world, rather than a mysterious technology existing apart from it (Ahmad et al., 2024; Song et al., 2024).

The Challenge of Fragmentation

Despite growing awareness, the implementation of AI education remains uneven. This fragmentation is evident across educational levels, where early childhood and primary schools lack structured materials, trained educators, and policy support for integrating AI concepts (Su et al., 2023). Meanwhile, secondary and higher education levels have progressed more systematically, offering specialized AI courses, degree programs, and research opportunities. This uneven progression mirrors the broader digital divide, in which exposure to technology and understanding of its implications are not equally distributed. Consequently, learners may reach university-level AI courses without developing a conceptual foundation in logic, data, and ethics. They can operate tools and code algorithms but may struggle to grasp how AI decisions are made or how biases emerge in datasets.

This gap underscores a deeper pedagogical issue: AI education must be viewed as a developmental continuum and not a discrete subject.

Opportunities Emerging from Early AI Education

Early AI education enriches children's problem-solving skills and curiosity. Research has shown that introducing AI through play and interactive activities enhances cognitive flexibility and foundational thinking, even among preschoolers. Activities such as sorting, patterning, and simple algorithmic exercises foster computational thinking without requiring digital tools (Konstantina & Stamatios, 2024). Furthermore, early exposure to ethical questions about fairness and bias helps children begin to reason about decision-making and social impacts in AI contexts.

The Role of Educators and Systems

Teachers play a crucial role in fostering AI literacy, but studies indicate many lack confidence and formal training in the topic (Ozturk, 2025). Experiential and activity-based learning approaches have proven most effective, enabling teachers to introduce AI concepts through storytelling and hands-on tasks appropriate to children's developmental stages. The cross-curricular integration of AI, connecting themes across science, literature, and the arts, helps demystify technology and situates AI as a social phenomenon as much as a technical discipline.

Bridging Policy and Practice

Systematic gaps exist between policy frameworks and classroom implementation. Research underscores the need for cohesive AI literacy progression, achievable through clearly sequenced learning outcomes tailored for different developmental stages (Akgun & Greenhow, 2022). Continuity across educational levels ensures that students develop both conceptual and ethical understandings before advanced applications, minimizing disconnects as they progress to higher education.

In summary, although global policies increasingly recognize the importance of AI literacy, implementation remains fragmented across educational levels. This misalignment highlights the need for a coherent, developmentally sequenced approach that connects early learning experiences with advanced AI education.

Learning from Higher Education

The realities of university-level AI courses highlight how earlier educational experiences shape students' relationships with technology (Chee et al., 2025; Tariq, 2026). By the time learners reach higher education, their ability to think critically, question AI outcomes, and integrate ethical perspectives reflects what was and was not cultivated in earlier schooling.

Observed Gaps in Student Preparedness

University students often demonstrate technical ability but struggle with conceptual reasoning about algorithms and data bias. Many can build models but lack deeper insight into why algorithms behave as they do or how social biases are encoded in data. Ethical reasoning typically emerges late, after technical habits are formed, limiting students' ability to view AI as more than just computation (Chiu et al., 2024).

A further issue is limited interdisciplinary awareness (Chee et al., 2025). Engineering or computer science majors may treat AI as purely technical, whereas those from non-technical backgrounds may find it daunting or irrelevant. These divisions reveal missed opportunities for early exposure to AI through creative and ethical exploration.

There is also a tendency to implicitly trust AI outputs, overlooking the importance of questioning and critiquing digital systems (Akgun & Greenhow, 2022). This "algorithmic fallacy" underscores the need for critical digital literacy from a young age. These gaps should be understood not as individual learner shortcomings, but as systemic outcomes of fragmented educational pathways. When AI education is introduced late and primarily through technical instruction, students often develop procedural competence without conceptual or ethical grounding. Higher education then becomes a site of remediation rather than consolidation, where instructors attempt to address foundational reasoning and ethical awareness alongside advanced technical content. From a developmental perspective, this misalignment places unrealistic cognitive and moral demands on learners. The persistence of these gaps reinforces the need for a continuum-based approach in which higher education builds upon, rather than compensates for, earlier experiences with reasoning, fairness, and critical inquiry.

Lessons for Early and Primary Education

Patterns in higher education suggest key priorities for earlier stages:

- Ethical reasoning must start early, fostering empathy and fairness before digital habits solidify (Akgun & Greenhow, 2022).
- Conceptual foundations, such as abstraction and pattern recognition, should precede technical training in coding or modelling (Chiu et al., 2024).
- Curiosity and playful inquiry, rather than rigid performance, help establish habits of lifelong critical reflection (Ozturk, 2025; Tariq, 2026).

The Case for Backward Design

Backward curriculum design, mapping desired end competencies and building stepwise experiences from primary years onward, emerges as a best practice for AI literacy. Abilities like critiquing algorithmic bias or designing ethical systems in adulthood trace back to early grounding in fairness, empathy, and logical thinking.

Towards a Continuum of Competence

AI literacy unfolds gradually, not in one-off interventions. A developmental, continuum model, rooted in cognitive, ethical, and social growth, can bridge gaps witnessed in higher education and ensure connected, age-appropriate learning throughout the educational journey.

Overall, observations from higher education reveal that gaps in ethical reasoning, conceptual understanding, and critical engagement with AI are rooted in earlier educational stages. These insights reinforce the importance of designing AI literacy through a backward, developmental lens that begins well before university.

The Continuum Concept – Rethinking AI Education as a Journey

From Fragmentation to Flow

AI literacy is best conceived as a developmental, interconnected journey rather than a collection of isolated lessons or technical skills. Instead of siloed grade levels and subjects, research advocates for frameworks that reflect the gradual evolution of cognitive, ethical, and emotional capacities throughout children's schooling years. A well-structured continuum supports learners in progressing from basic pattern recognition and curiosity to critical engagement and creative AI application by adulthood (Southworth et al., 2023).

Cognitive and Ethical Development Across Ages

Human development theory demonstrates that reasoning and ethical understanding deepen with age. AI literacy should align with this progression, beginning with concrete experiences, such as noticing cause and effect in machines, then moving toward abstract analysis, like evaluating data-driven decisions and algorithmic fairness. Moral reasoning also evolves, making early engagement with empathy (Wiese et al., 2025) and social fairness crucial for cultivating responsible AI perspectives as students mature (Eyal, 2025). These developmental foundations inform the continuum model discussed in subsequent sections, while a detailed examination of ethical frameworks and cultural dimensions is presented in the Ethical and Cultural Dimensions section.

The AI Literacy Continuum (Ages 6–22)

A flexible continuum model can guide educators by mapping AI literacy to four developmental stages: Foundation (ages 6-8), Exploration (9-12), Application (13-17), and Integration (18-22). At each stage, learners build knowledge and ethical awareness appropriate to their cognitive and emotional readiness, as identified by contemporary frameworks in educational research (Yue et al., 2025). Table 1 presents a conceptual representation of how AI literacy can be mapped developmentally. It is not a rigid curriculum but a flexible framework guiding educators, policymakers, and curriculum designers in aligning objectives and pedagogies.

Table 1. The AI Literacy Continuum (Ages 6–22)

Stage	Age Range	Core Focus	Cognitive Goals	Ethical & Social Goals	Suggested Pedagogies
Foundation: Curiosity & Play	6–8	Understanding that machines can follow instructions and recognize patterns.	Identify patterns, sort objects, predict outcomes; understand cause and effect.	Develop empathy; discuss fairness in games or decisions.	Storytelling, play-based exploration, interactive robots, classroom simulations.
Exploration: Awareness & Logic	9–12	Recognizing that machines "learn" from data; basic understanding of algorithms.	Classify information, recognize simple data structures, explore decision-making.	Understand bias; relate fairness to data and outcomes.	Guided inquiry, unplugged AI activities, visual coding platforms, collaborative games.
Application: Inquiry & Creativity	13–17	Applying AI ideas to solve real-world problems; exploring applications in daily life.	Analyze patterns, interpret data, evaluate AI tools.	Reflect on responsibility, privacy, and impact of AI on society.	Project-based learning, debates, design challenges, community AI projects.
Integration: Ethics & Agency	18–22	Designing and critiquing AI systems; linking theory with ethics and innovation.	Model and test AI systems; connect human values to design choices.	Practice ethical decision-making; advocate for responsible AI.	Case-based learning, interdisciplinary research, experiential labs, innovation projects.

For instance, at the primary level, a classroom activity may involve students acting as "human algorithms," following step-by-step instructions to complete a task such as sorting objects or navigating a simple path. When the task fails due to incomplete or ambiguous instructions, students are encouraged to reflect on why the outcome was incorrect, introducing the idea that machines depend entirely on the quality of inputs they receive. At the secondary level, similar reasoning can be extended through guided analysis of recommendation systems used in everyday digital platforms, allowing learners to connect early logical reasoning with real-world AI applications.

Building Connections Across Stages

The strength of the continuum lies in its ability to revisit core ideas, such as fairness, data, and decision-making, at deepening levels of sophistication. Effective AI education spirals key concepts, so learners first encounter fairness through stories and play, later analyze it through data, and eventually critique or ensure fairness in AI systems with accountability and transparency (Allen & Kendeou, 2024).

Emotional Intelligence and AI Understanding

Recent studies underscore the value of addressing emotional intelligence within AI literacy (Ghotbi, 2023; Keshishi & Hack, 2023). When children discuss how a robot "feels" or why a chatbot fails to understand, they link empathy and self-awareness to foundational technical knowledge. Adolescents then grow into evaluating how persuasive technologies shape emotions, and university students learn to critique the broader ethical implications of AI on society.

AI Literacy as Lifelong Learning

AI education does not end at school or university; it should foster adaptive, reflective mindsets capable of engaging with rapid technological change. Learners equipped conceptually are better prepared to question, guide, and innovate responsibly with intelligent systems, making AI literacy a whole-life pursuit that enriches not only technical competency but also human potential.

This section establishes the AI Literacy Continuum as a developmental framework that aligns cognitive growth, ethical awareness, and learning progression across ages. By emphasizing continuity rather than isolated instruction, the continuum provides a foundation for designing coherent AI education pathways.

Designing the AI Literacy Continuum

Translating the AI Literacy Continuum into curricular practice requires a balanced approach, one that combines strategic guidance from policymakers with adaptable, classroom-level creativity from teachers. The continuum gains value when each stage supports coherent developmental growth, not through uniformity but by anchoring learning in contextually meaningful experiences.

Principles for Designing an AI Literacy Continuum

Effective design rests on research-backed principles:

Developmental Alignment: Curriculum must match students' cognitive and emotional capacities, building from basic fairness toward complex concepts such as algorithmic bias as learners mature (H.-G. Zhao et al., 2024).

Interdisciplinary Integration: AI literacy thrives when infused throughout mathematics, language arts, sciences, and humanities—fostering connections between pattern recognition, ethics, creativity, and decision-making, not confining AI to computer science (Ng et al., 2021).

Ethics from the Start: Foundational discussions on empathy and fairness prepare learners for later critical engagement with bias and responsibility in AI systems. At this stage, ethics functions as a design principle rather than a detailed framework, with comprehensive ethical and cultural analysis addressed later in the chapter under Ethical and Cultural Dimensions.

Equity and Access: Inclusive pedagogy, including unplugged activities, ensures all students, regardless of resources, build foundational AI understanding (Yue et al., 2025).

Teacher Empowerment: Teachers benefit from conceptual clarity and collaborative communities, helping them confidently interpret AI concepts within local realities.

Cultural Relevance: Integration of local contexts and examples grounds abstract AI concepts, making learning tangible and relatable (Kim et al., 2025).

Mapping Learning Objectives Across the Continuum

Each stage of the AI Literacy Continuum carries distinct learning objectives. Table 2 below extends the framework by adding curricular connections and assessment ideas, demonstrating how AI literacy can be embedded seamlessly across subjects and grade levels.

Table 2. Expanded Framework for AI Literacy Continuum Implementation

Stage	Learning Objectives	Curricular Connections	Sample Learning Experiences	Assessment Approaches
Foundation (Ages 6–8)	Recognize that machines follow instructions; understand simple patterns; relate fairness to rules.	Language (stories of robots), Math (patterns), Art (designing helpful machines).	Story-based role play where children act as "robots" following commands; class discussion on "What makes a robot fair?"	Observation, oral reflection, creative drawings showing AI ideas.
Exploration (Ages 9–12)	Understand that machines "learn" from examples; begin to discuss data and decision-making.	Science (classification), Math (data handling), Social Studies (decisions & consequences).	Sorting activities where data errors cause "wrong" robot decisions; exploring AI-based games.	Simple reflective journals; group presentations explaining how data affected the robot's choice.
Application (Ages 13–17)	Apply AI concepts to analyze real problems; understand bias, privacy, and societal impacts.	ICT, Ethics, Economics, Civic Studies.	AI-for-good projects (e.g., predicting traffic, waste management); debating ethical dilemmas in AI.	Project rubrics assessing reasoning, creativity, and ethical reflection.
Integration (Ages 18–22)	Critically design or evaluate AI systems; connect technical design to social responsibility.	Engineering, Management, Social Sciences.	Capstone projects combining AI with human-centered design; evaluating ethical frameworks in real-world AI systems.	Reports, peer reviews, and reflective essays demonstrating synthesis of ethics and application.

This expanded framework emphasizes that AI literacy is not an isolated subject but a thread connecting multiple domains of learning. A child analyzing patterns in mathematics is developing cognitive foundations for later understanding of machine learning; a teenager discussing fairness in a social science project is developing ethical reasoning critical to future AI design.

The Role of Cognitive Scaffolding

AI literacy benefits from scaffolding that moves learners from concrete experiences, such as command-following or basic algorithms, to deeper ethical and technical reasoning. Research supports progression from tangible tasks toward abstract, reflective analysis (Omar et al., 2025).

Linking AI Literacy to Curriculum

AI literacy should naturally extend into, and enrich, existing subjects. Mathematics supports exploration of data and algorithms; language arts and social studies encourage reflection on ethics, privacy, and the societal footprint of technology (Southworth et al., 2023).

Assessment Beyond Accuracy

Assessment must value understanding, collaboration, and creativity above rote correctness. Journals highlight rubrics, self-reflection, and project work as effective means for measuring ethical reasoning, empathy, and AI application, moving beyond standard tests (Zhou et al., 2025). Across the AI literacy continuum, such assessment may include reflective journals documenting learners' reasoning processes, group explanation tasks in which students articulate how an AI system arrived at a decision, and rubric-based evaluation that considers ethical reasoning alongside conceptual understanding.

Institutional and Policy Design

Enduring change demands both institutional support and policy innovation. Benchmarking AI literacy at all educational levels, equipping teachers with training, and making AI education part of broader digital citizenship initiatives are central for systemic adoption. Evidence suggests that ongoing policy review and inclusive planning help sustain progress and mitigate risks like bias or inequitable access (L. Li et al., 2024).

In essence, designing an AI literacy continuum requires aligning curriculum, pedagogy, and assessment with learners' developmental readiness. When AI concepts are integrated across subjects and supported by appropriate scaffolding, the continuum moves from conceptual vision to practical educational design.

Pedagogical Pathways Across Ages

Why Pedagogy Matters

The effectiveness of any AI curriculum depends on the quality and integrity of its pedagogy. It is the teacher's approach, how questions are framed, ideas are connected, and experiences are humanized, that determines whether AI learning becomes meaningful and accessible to students. Contemporary research emphasizes that AI pedagogy, rooted in developmental appropriateness and curiosity-driven learning, helps transform technological concepts into daily classroom dialogue, nurturing wonder rather than anxiety (Yim, 2024).

Pedagogies for Early and Primary Years (Ages 6–12)

Young children learn best through hands-on, imaginative, and social activities. Arts-based and story-driven methodologies, such as robot role play, analog pattern games, and fairness-oriented classroom simulations, allow children to grasp decision-making and bias before encountering digital tools. Integrating drama-based exercises and collaborative play has been shown to foster metacognitive awareness, engagement, and inclusivity in AI learning contexts (Kotsidis & Dima, 2025).

Pedagogies for Middle and Secondary Levels (Ages 13–17)

For older learners, project-based and inquiry-driven approaches encourage students to apply abstract reasoning and ethical reflection. Engaging youth in real-world problem-solving, bias analysis, and data dialogues, through AI-supported projects and critical media literacy activities, cultivates agency and the belief that technology can be questioned and shaped, not merely consumed (Tang et al., 2024). As a pedagogical illustration, a middle-school classroom exploring AI decision-making may use a visual, no-code simulation to observe how changes in input data affect system outcomes. Students work in small groups to test different scenarios, explain their observations to peers, and reflect on unexpected results. The emphasis remains on reasoning and explanation rather than technical correctness, enabling learners to articulate how decisions are produced and why outcomes may differ. Such activities demonstrate how inquiry-based pedagogy can translate abstract AI concepts into accessible and developmentally appropriate learning experiences.

Pedagogies for Higher Education (Ages 18–22)

In higher education, experiential and interdisciplinary models facilitate deeper engagement with the complex technical and ethical dimensions of AI. Capstone collaborations, policy simulations, and reflective diaries enable learners to synthesize knowledge, collaborate across domains, and practice ethical decision-making (Yue et al., 2025).

Embedding Human Values

Across all age groups, AI pedagogy must intentionally foreground human values such as empathy, fairness, and responsibility through everyday classroom practices rather than abstract ethical theory. This is achieved by the kinds of questions teachers ask, the examples they choose, and the reflective discussions they facilitate during activities involving data, automation, or decision-making. At this pedagogical level, values are enacted through learning design and interaction, while broader ethical frameworks and cultural considerations are examined in depth in the Ethical and Cultural Dimensions section.

The Role of Teachers as Curators of Curiosity

Teachers play a pivotal role not only as facilitators but as co-learners and guides, fostering safe spaces for questioning technology and connecting AI to everyday experience. Robust professional development in AI, including mentorship, collaborative learning communities, and reflective practice, is vital for supporting teachers in this evolving field.

Inclusive and Culturally Sensitive Pedagogies

Inclusive AI education requires the use of diverse examples, local contexts, and adaptive tools. AI-powered systems and constructivist strategies increase access for learners with varied backgrounds and abilities, build equitable pathways, and ground technology in students' real lives. Research validates that AI-enhanced environments, when designed thoughtfully, support personalized learning, cultural relevance, and social-emotional growth (Song et al., 2024).

Connecting Pedagogy to Purpose

Ultimately, the purpose of AI pedagogy is to nurture agency, empathy, and reflective imagination. Humanizing AI education, linking abstract concepts to lived experience and ethical inquiry, empowers learners to question, innovate, and ensure technology serves human dignity (Klingefjord et al., 2024).

Taken together, age-appropriate pedagogical pathways transform AI literacy from abstract knowledge into a lived classroom experience. By centring curiosity, inquiry, and human values, pedagogy ensures that AI education remains meaningful, inclusive, and developmentally responsive.

Operationalizing the AI Literacy Continuum: From Framework to Classroom Practice

While the AI Literacy Continuum offers a coherent developmental framework, its value ultimately depends on how effectively it can be translated into everyday educational practice. Operationalizing the continuum requires moving beyond conceptual alignment to concrete decisions about curriculum planning, lesson design, assessment, and institutional coordination. This process does not demand the creation of an entirely new subject area; rather, it involves re-orienting existing curricular structures to support continuity, coherence, and developmental appropriateness in AI education.

Translating the Continuum into Curriculum Planning

At the curriculum level, the AI Literacy Continuum functions best as a planning lens rather than an additional curricular burden. Instead of introducing AI as a discrete or isolated subject, schools can map continuum stages onto existing learning areas such as mathematics, science, social studies, language, and the arts. This approach allows AI concepts to be distributed across subjects in ways that align with age-appropriate cognitive goals.

In early and primary education, curriculum planning emphasizes exposure rather than mastery. Learning outcomes at this stage focus on recognizing patterns, understanding simple cause-and-effect relationships, and developing vocabulary to describe how digital systems behave. These outcomes can be naturally embedded within activities already present in early curricula, such as sequencing stories, sorting objects, or discussing fairness in shared classroom resources.

At the secondary level, curriculum planning shifts toward conceptual integration. AI-related ideas such as data representation, automated decision-making, and system limitations can be linked to subjects like mathematics (data interpretation), social studies (societal impact), and science (modelling and prediction). Importantly, the continuum encourages planners to avoid premature specialization. Coding or technical modelling, where introduced, is framed as a means of exploration rather than an end in itself.

In higher education, the continuum supports consolidation and specialization. By this stage, learners are expected to integrate ethical reasoning, conceptual understanding, and applied skills. Curriculum planning at the tertiary level benefits from the assumption that foundational AI ideas have already been encountered, allowing courses to focus on deeper analysis, interdisciplinary connections, and real-world implications. This vertical alignment reduces redundancy and ensures that learning at each stage builds meaningfully on prior experiences.

Designing Lessons Across Developmental Stages

Lesson design within the continuum emphasizes conceptual continuity, ensuring that learners encounter core AI ideas repeatedly, but at increasing levels of complexity. Rather than introducing new concepts at each stage, educators revisit familiar ideas, such as decision-making, learning from data, or fairness, through developmentally appropriate pedagogical approaches.

In primary classrooms, lessons are grounded in concrete experiences. Learners explore how instructions influence outcomes, how systems can make mistakes, and how human choices shape machine behavior. Storytelling, role-play, and guided discussion help learners articulate observations without requiring technical language. The goal is not technical precision, but awareness and curiosity.

At the secondary level, lesson design incorporates abstraction and comparison. Students may analyze simplified models, examine scenarios where automated systems succeed or fail, and debate the implications of AI-driven decisions in everyday contexts. Collaborative tasks encourage learners to articulate reasoning, challenge assumptions, and consider multiple perspectives. These lessons build upon earlier experiential understanding while introducing analytical thinking.

In higher education, lesson design emphasizes synthesis and critique. Learners are expected to connect technical mechanisms with ethical, social, and cultural implications. Projects may involve evaluating system design choices, reflecting on trade-offs, or proposing alternative approaches grounded in responsible innovation. Importantly, the continuum ensures that such advanced tasks do not emerge in isolation, but as the culmination of a long-term developmental process.

Aligning Assessment with Developmental Progression

Assessment plays a critical role in operationalizing the AI Literacy Continuum, as it signals what forms of understanding are valued at each stage. Traditional assessment models that prioritize accuracy or technical correctness alone are insufficient for capturing the multidimensional nature of AI literacy.

In early education, assessment is largely formative and reflective. Teachers observe how learners explain system behavior, collaborate with peers, and respond to unexpected outcomes. Informal documentation, such as learning journals or guided reflections, helps capture emerging reasoning and ethical awareness.

At the secondary level, assessment becomes more explicit while remaining conceptually focused. Group explanation tasks, scenario analyses, and project-based evaluations allow learners to demonstrate understanding of how AI systems operate and why certain outcomes occur. Assessment criteria emphasize clarity of reasoning, ethical consideration, and the ability to connect concepts across contexts.

In higher education, assessment aligns with disciplinary rigor while retaining a human-centered focus. Learners may be evaluated on their capacity to critically interrogate AI systems, justify design decisions, and reflect on societal impact. Rubric-based assessment that integrates conceptual understanding, ethical reasoning, and applied skills reinforces the continuum's emphasis on holistic AI literacy rather than narrow technical competence.

Scaling and Sustaining the Continuum at the Institutional Level

Operationalizing the AI Literacy Continuum at scale requires institutional commitment and strategic coordination. Implementation is most effective when approached as an iterative process rather than a one-time reform. Pilot initiatives allow institutions to test alignment, gather feedback, and refine approaches before broader adoption.

Teacher support is central to sustainability. Professional development should focus not only on technical familiarity but on pedagogical confidence and ethical facilitation. When educators understand the developmental logic of the continuum, they are better equipped to integrate AI concepts naturally within their existing teaching practices.

Institutional leadership also plays a role in creating coherence across grade levels and departments. Shared language, collaborative planning, and cross-level dialogue help prevent fragmentation and ensure continuity. Over time, the continuum becomes embedded in institutional culture, shaping expectations about what learners should understand about AI at different stages of their educational journey.

Ultimately, sustaining the continuum depends on recognizing AI literacy as an evolving educational responsibility rather than a fixed curriculum component. As AI technologies continue to change, the continuum provides a stable developmental foundation that allows institutions to adapt content while preserving coherence, inclusivity, and human-centred values.

Bridging Policy Intent and Classroom Reality

While policy documents increasingly emphasize the importance of AI literacy, a persistent gap often exists between policy intent and classroom reality. Curriculum frameworks may articulate ambitious goals for digital and AI education, yet teachers frequently face constraints related to time, training, and contextual relevance. The AI Literacy Continuum provides a mechanism for narrowing this gap by translating high-level policy aspirations into developmentally grounded classroom practices.

Teacher Preparation and Institutional Readiness

The Centrality of Teachers in the AI Literacy Continuum

Teachers are at the heart of effective AI literacy. While policy and technology set the stage, it is teacher preparedness, encompassing confidence, ethical sensitivity, and creativity, that shapes student engagement with AI. Studies show that well-trained educators humanize complex ideas, fostering critical discussions rather than reinforcing confusion or fear (Tan et al., 2025).

The Three Dimensions of AI Teacher Readiness

Conceptual Readiness: Teachers should grasp foundational AI principles(Ahmad et al., 2025), such as data patterns and automation, to guide student inquiry meaningfully without oversimplification (al-Zyoud, 2020).

Pedagogical Readiness: Integrating AI concepts through storytelling, discussion, and interdisciplinary inquiry allows teachers to connect new technologies with familiar classroom practices and support curiosity-driven learning(Dogan et al., 2025).

Ethical and Emotional Readiness: Recent work emphasizes that teachers' emotional resilience and ethical competence play a pivotal role, enabling sensitive navigation of students' questions, digital dilemmas, and the emotional nuances of AI in classroom contexts.

When these align, teachers become facilitators of exploration and growth within the AI literacy continuum.

Teacher Professional Development Models

Professional development should be reflective and adaptive:

AI Awareness Workshops: Hands-on activities and storytelling foster familiarity and reduce anxiety for primary educators.

Blended Learning Modules: Modular formats combining digital micro-lessons and classroom-based practice support secondary teachers in inquiry-oriented and ethical AI pedagogy.

Communities of Practice: Collaborative teacher networks sustain innovation and best-practice sharing, catalyzed by peer mentoring and open resource development (Ahmad et al., 2020).

Mentorship from Higher Education: Partnerships between schools and universities leverage technical depth and pedagogical expertise, fostering dynamic teacher development.

Institutional Readiness: Beyond Infrastructure

Research reveals that readiness goes beyond devices (Ahmad, Sharma, Kurubacak, et al., 2022), it is about fostering a culture of experimentation, ethical reflection, and interdisciplinary learning (Ahmad, Sharma, Kumar, et al., 2023). Key factors include vision alignment, flexible curriculum systems, collaborative partnerships, easy access to simple AI tools (Ahmad, 2024), and robust policies for privacy and responsible use.

Leadership and Policy Roles

Leadership and policy must prioritize AI literacy as part of digital citizenship. Strategically integrating AI literacy into pre-service and in-service teacher programs, incentivizing pedagogical innovation, and ensuring equity, especially for under-resourced schools, are vital for sustainable growth (Granström & Oppi, 2025).

The Human Side of Institutional Transformation

Institutional readiness also depends on addressing the emotional landscape, teachers and stakeholders may harbour anxieties or misconceptions about AI. Professional conversations, storytelling, and reflective practice build a supportive atmosphere where AI adoption is seen as a collaborative journey, not an intimidating mandate.

Implementation Challenges and Practical Constraints

Despite growing policy momentum, implementing an AI literacy continuum presents practical challenges. Teachers may lack confidence or time to integrate AI concepts alongside existing curricular demands, particularly in early and primary education. Resource disparities across schools further complicate equitable access to AI learning opportunities, especially where digital infrastructure is limited. Additionally, the rapid pace of AI development can create uncertainty about what content is developmentally appropriate and pedagogically sustainable. These constraints underscore the need for phased, context-sensitive implementation strategies that prioritize teacher support, curricular flexibility, and inclusive design rather than uniform mandates.

Global and Local Case Studies

Real-world implementations of AI literacy frameworks provide valuable perspectives on how policies are translated into diverse educational contexts. While approaches differ, the universal values of curiosity, inclusivity, and ethical reflection repeatedly emerge as foundational (L. Zhao et al., 2022).

Finland – Playful Learning and Early Curiosity

Finland exemplifies how learner-centered, phenomenon-based integration of AI can foster early curiosity without sacrificing depth. Research highlights the use of playful, arts-based, and project-driven learning, where children collaborate, experiment, and reflect on the role of "smart machines" in topics like environmental stewardship. Teachers receive systematic training in both digital pedagogy and creative inquiry, ensuring that playfulness remains central even as concepts like fairness and ethical agency are explored through technology (X. Li & Kangas, 2024).

United Arab Emirates – Strategic Vision and National Policy

The UAE's robust national AI strategy has pioneered a multi-level approach, positioning AI literacy as both a strategic national policy and an educational priority. From the early grades, students encounter coding, robotics, and ethical analysis. The Mohammed bin Zayed University of Artificial Intelligence (MBZUAI) and national "AI for All" initiatives model how top-down policy vision and teacher training can create system-wide coherence, preparing students for both technical and ethical AI engagement (Oloyede, 2025).

India – Scaling AI Literacy through Policy and Partnerships

India's NEP 2020 marks a major policy milestone, (S. Chauhan & Ahmad, 2024), treating AI literacy as an essential skill for the modern era. With AI now part of the CBSE curriculum from Grade 6, students encounter ethical dilemmas, practical applications, and interdisciplinary projects. This policy is reinforced by grassroots partnerships and locally relevant resources, helping bridge rural-urban gaps and fostering a sense of democratized digital inclusion (Ahmad et al., 2018). Recent studies confirm the importance of contextual adaptation, as teachers use everyday analogies and regional languages to build understanding and confidence in AI concepts (Ahmad et al., 2025; Ahmad, Sharma, Chaubey, et al., 2023).

United States – Ethics and Critical Thinking

U.S. models, especially through the AI4K12 initiative, foreground cross-disciplinary "Big Ideas" such as perception, reasoning, interaction, and societal impact. States are integrating AI into formal standards, encouraging critical examination of topics like algorithmic bias and privacy. At the tertiary level, an emphasis on ethics and interdisciplinary collaboration ensures students engage thoughtfully with AI's role in society and governance (Wu et al., 2024).

Comparative Insights

Synthesis of these cases reveals common elements:

- Playful, inquiry-driven learning in early years deepens later ethical engagement.
- Systematic teacher training is essential; nations making this a cornerstone show more consistent implementation.
- Cultural context and local adaptation—using language, stories, and social priorities—make AI literacy more accessible and meaningful.
- Embedding AI across subjects (not just in coding classes) supports conceptual transfer and relevance.
- Ethical integration, whether through young children's fairness discussions or university-level policy examination, is vital everywhere.

These five common elements are the essential elements of AI literacy, which are generally hidden from the eyes and are represented in Figure 1 for better understanding.

Figure 1. Common Elements of AI Literacy

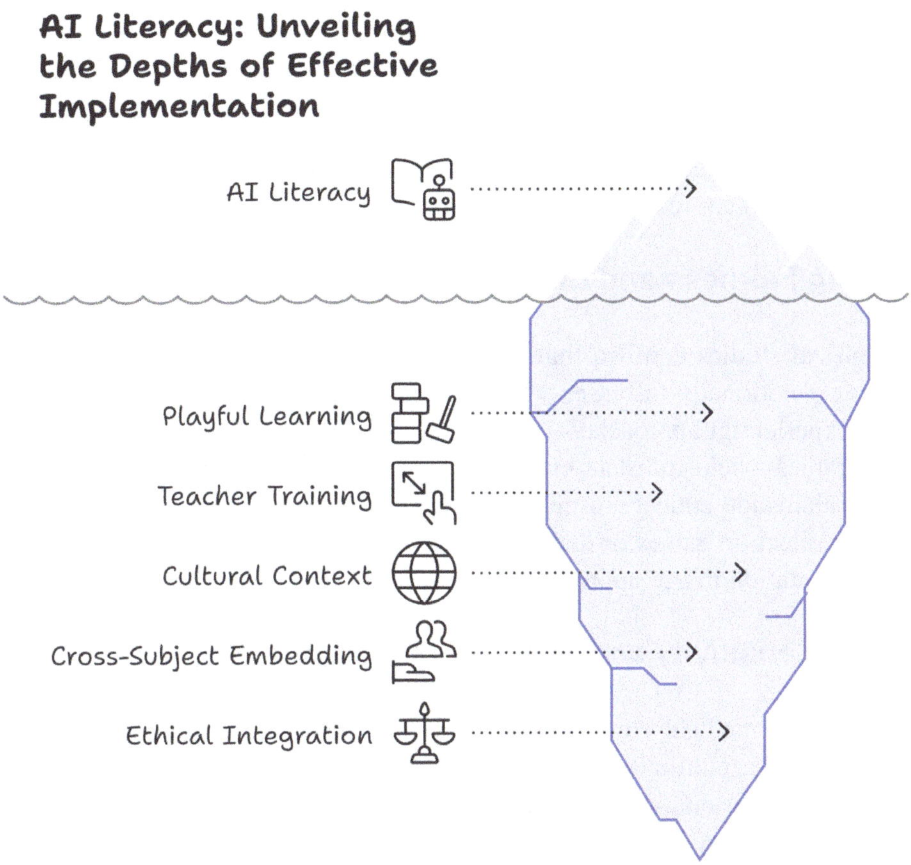

Emerging Lessons for the Continuum Model

- Early, developmentally appropriate exposure builds lasting confidence and interest.
- Seamless progression from primary through advanced education safeguards against conceptual disconnect.
- Ethics must be a living thread, scaling from empathy to critical policy analysis.
- System coherence policy, teacher development, and curricular design underpins sustainable AI literacy growth.

ETHICAL AND CULTURAL DIMENSIONS

Why Ethics Must Be Woven from the Start

Recent reviews emphasize that ethics is inseparable from AI education, it must be embedded from the earliest years, shaping not just technical proficiency but core moral reasoning. Early incorporation of ethical dialogue around fairness and inclusion guards against the "retrofit problem," where moral awareness lags behind technical skill, and encourages responsible citizenship from the outset (Wiese et al., 2025).

Teaching Fairness and Bias to Young Learners

Empirical studies confirm that children are naturally attuned to fairness and can relate emotionally to biases when technology seems unjust or exclusionary. Analog experiential approaches—where learners confront biased behavior in robots or games—help translate emotion into conceptual understanding, fostering empathy alongside ethical reasoning. Research advocates using simple activities, like color-selection games or data-driven puzzles, to surface questions about bias and representation in age-appropriate ways(Chinta et al., 2024).

Cultural Sensitivity and Contextual Ethics

AI systems inevitably reflect the cultures and values of their creators. Journal research finds that culturally responsive frameworks—grounded in local narratives, languages, and epistemologies—deepen emotional engagement and comprehension for students from diverse backgrounds. Contextual ethics can be taught through storytelling, folk traditions, and community-based projects, ensuring students see AI as relevant to their lived experience—not as a neutral or foreign abstraction(Chiu, 2025).

The Human–Machine Relationship

Studies highlight the tendency of children to anthropomorphize AI and robots, projecting emotion and agency onto technology. This natural developmental process enables educators to foster "technological empathy", teaching learners to navigate boundaries between human and machine, and encouraging critical reflection on what constitutes intention and judgment. Such empathy is essential for balanced, trust-worthy relationships with intelligent systems, neither leading to uncritical acceptance nor fear (Srinivasan & San Miguel González, 2022).

Global Ethics, Local Voices

Most global debates on AI ethics skew toward Western concepts of autonomy and justice, but literature urges the integration of non-Western philosophies, collective welfare (East Asia), Ubuntu (Africa), and Dharma (India), as essential for plural, universal frameworks. Inclusive ethics education should explore multiple worldviews, helping learners understand that moral reasoning is dynamic, culturally situated, and vital for sustainable futures (Lundgren et al., 2024).

Ethical Scaffolding Across the Continuum

Research supports a layered approach to ethical learning, progressing from emotional resonance in early years to analytical debate and design in higher education. Scaffolded ethics teaching, stories on fairness with young children, bias analysis for youth, and accountability frameworks for young adults, gradually equips learners to apply principles of transparency, inclusion, and responsibility in real-world contexts (Nguyen et al., 2023). Ethical understanding in AI education must be scaffolded in ways that align with learners' cognitive and moral development. In early years, ethical engagement is primarily experiential and relational, grounded in empathy and fairness rather than abstract principles. As learners mature, ethical reasoning becomes increasingly analytical, enabling critical examination of bias, accountability, and societal impact. Without such scaffolding, ethical discussions risk becoming either overly simplistic or prematurely technical. Viewing ethics as a developmental competency rather than a fixed body of knowledge allows educators to revisit core values at increasing levels of complexity, ensuring continuity between early moral intuition and advanced ethical reasoning in higher education.

FUTURE PATHWAYS AND POLICY RECOMMENDATIONS

The Need for Systemic Alignment

AI literacy initiatives succeed when systemic alignment links curriculum, educator preparation, technology, and policy across educational levels. Current research highlights the need to move from fragmented programs to an integrated spiral—where ideas and competencies are revisited and deepened as learners advance. The goal is a coherent pathway that anticipates lifelong AI readiness (Ahmad, Sharma, Singh, et al., 2022), with curriculum planners guiding progression from foundational skills to advanced ethical reasoning(Ng et al., 2021).

National and Institutional Policy Recommendations

Establish National AI Literacy Frameworks: Experts urge governments to articulate age-appropriate benchmarks for AI understanding, embedding these in existing subjects to support integration rather than adding burdensome new requirements.

Integrate AI Literacy into Teacher Education: Effective AI literacy depends on embedding awareness and ethics modules into teacher professional development, ensuring sustainability and up-to-date classroom practices.

Foster School–University Collaboration: Bidirectional partnerships enable schools to benefit from university expertise while sharing classroom insights that push research forward, strengthening both curriculum and policy.

Promote Equity in Access: Policy frameworks should prioritize device-free ("unplugged") and low-cost learning models to ensure AI literacy reaches all students, regardless of resources.

Encourage Localized Curriculum Design: Adapting learning for local languages and cultural contexts makes AI literacy relevant and fosters engagement.

Support Open Educational Resources (OER): Journals advocate for open repositories of AI teaching materials to democratize access and raise instructional quality.

Embed Ethics and Human Values in Policy: Research insists on explicit ethical guidelines in all AI policies to guard against reductionist or purely technical approaches.

The National and Institutional Policy Recommendations are displayed in Figure 2 for better understanding.

Figure 2. Common Elements of AI Literacy

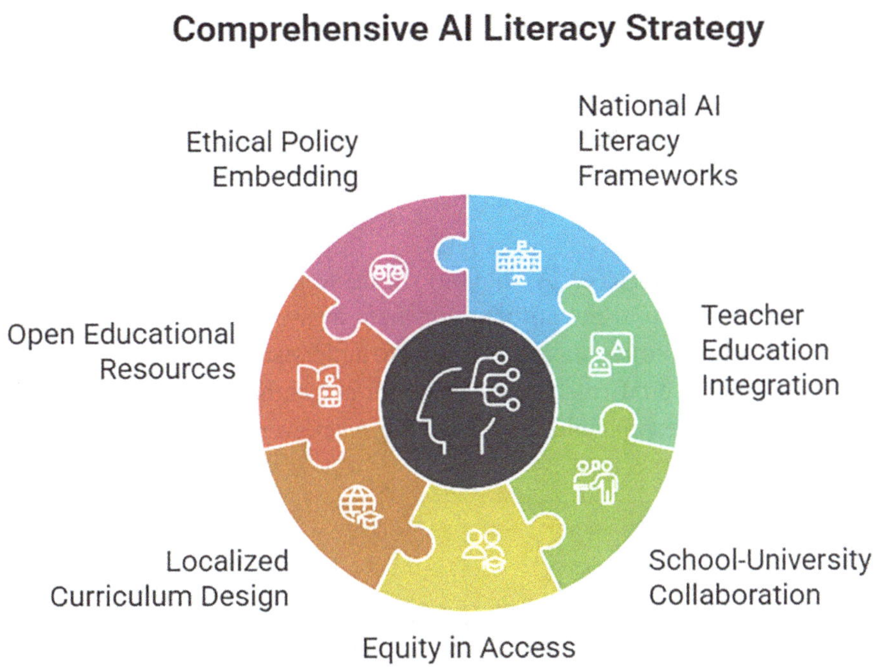

Building a Lifelong AI Learning Ecosystem

AI literacy is an evolving journey, demanding lifelong learning and adaptability. Prominent studies affirm the need for community and family awareness, vocational reskilling aligned with ethical and social priorities, and intergenerational knowledge transfer. Such an ecosystem supports civic resilience and the agility needed to navigate continual technological change.

The Role of International Collaboration

AI literacy transcends borders. International collaborative initiatives, supported by organizations like UNESCO and the EU—accelerate the development of best practices, resource sharing, and ethical standards. Translating materials, funding cross-cultural research, and global forums for teacher and student exchange are all identified in the literature as key catalysts for global progress.

A Vision for 2040 and Beyond

Scholarly consensus suggests that children entering school today will become adults in a world ever more shaped by intelligent technologies. The true test is not if they will use AI, but whether they will humanize it, questioning, improving, and designing transparent systems grounded in ethical principles. The AI literacy continuum provides a blueprint for preparing active, reflective citizens for this future.

Final Reflections

Ultimately, the promise of AI literacy is in amplifying human intelligence, empathy, and imagination, not automating them away. The continuum invites all stakeholders, teachers, policymakers, learners, to understand AI as a mirror of thought and agency. Research confirms that early, continuous ethical education shapes not just better users, but responsible shapers of the AI-powered world.

CONCLUSION

Education embodies humanity's hope for the future. In an era shaped by artificial intelligence, the choices made today in AI literacy will determine whether technology empowers inclusively, ethically, and creatively. This chapter has argued for an AI Literacy Continuum that unfolds gradually, from early curiosity to mature ethical engagement, positioning AI education as a lifelong journey rather than a late-stage specialization.

By weaving together cognitive development, ethical reflection, and human values across schooling, the continuum fosters learners who not only understand AI's mechanics but also its societal implications. Teachers and institutions play a pivotal role in this transformation, cultivating wisdom and empathy alongside technical skills. Importantly, ethics emerges as the thread uniting the continuum, grounding AI literacy in a moral compass necessary for responsible innovation.

Looking ahead, children entering school today will shape a world where AI deeply influences every sector. Their success will depend less on mastery of machines and more on their capacity to collaborate imaginatively, question critically, and uphold fairness and compassion. The AI Literacy Continuum invites educators, policymakers, families, and learners to embrace this shared responsibility, preparing not just users of AI, but custodians of its conscience.

This perspective reinforces the view that AI literacy is not a finite skill set to be mastered at a single point in time, but an evolving capacity shaped by education, reflection, and social responsibility across the lifespan, requiring sustained attention from educators, institutions, and policymakers alike.

REFERENCES

Ahmad, I. (2024). *Factors Affecting High Attrition Rate of MOOCs and Its Prediction Using Machine Learning Techniques* [Uttaranchal University]. http://hdl.handle.net/10603/543480

Ahmad, I., Jasola, S., Ahmad, S., & Sharma, S. (2020). Technology Enabled Learning in Higher Education: A Case Study. *Xplore The Xavier's Research Journal, 11*(1), 68–73. https://9dec1e70-3d6c-406f-960b-920f18cdab25.filesusr.com/ugd/03b37e_0a4fe5f7f9764c23a239c95f05ae24fc.pdf

Ahmad, I., Sharma, S., Chaubey, M. K., Dhyani, S., Ahmad, S., & Kumar, A. (2023). SWAYAM MOOC Reviews: Assessing Acceptability through Sentiment Analysis using Machine Learning. *2023 14th International Conference on Computing Communication and Networking Technologies (ICCCNT)*, 1–5. DOI: 10.1109/ICCCNT56998.2023.10306960

Ahmad, I., Sharma, S., Kumar, R., Dhyani, S., & Dumka, A. (2023). Data Analytics of Online Education during Pandemic Health Crisis: A Case Study. *2023 2nd Edition of IEEE Delhi Section Flagship Conference (DELCON)*, 1–6. DOI: 10.1109/DELCON57910.2023.10127423

Ahmad, I., Sharma, S., Kurubacak, G., Kumar, A., Kumar, R., & Ahmad, S. (2022). Artificial Intelligence in MOOCs: A Bibliometric Perspective. In Singh, R., Gehlot, A., & Buddhi, D. (Eds.), *Intelligent Systems - Proceedings of ICIS-2022* (pp. 38–47). River Publishers., https://www.riverpublishers.com/research_article_details.php?book_id=1004&cid=6

Ahmad, I., Sharma, S., Leal-Saballos, C., Kumar, M., Kumar, A., & Ahmad, S. (2025). *Predicting Early Dropouts in SWAYAM MOOCs Using Machine Learning Techniques: A Comparative Analysis.*, DOI: 10.1007/978-3-031-80778-7_18

Ahmad, I., Sharma, S., Singh, R., Gehlot, A., Gupta, L. R., Thakur, A. K., Priyadarshi, N., & Twala, B. (2024). Inclusive learning using industry 4.0 technologies: Addressing student diversity in modern education. *Cogent Education, 11*(1), 2330235. Advance online publication. DOI: 10.1080/2331186X.2024.2330235

Ahmad, I., Sharma, S., Singh, R., Gehlot, A., Priyadarshi, N., & Twala, B. (2022). MOOC 5.0: A Roadmap to the Future of Learning. *Sustainability (Basel), 14*(18), 11199. DOI: 10.3390/su141811199

Akgun, S., & Greenhow, C. (2022). Artificial intelligence in education: Addressing ethical challenges in K-12 settings. *AI and Ethics, 2*(3), 431–440. DOI: 10.1007/s43681-021-00096-7 PMID: 34790956 al-Zyoud, H. M. M. (2020). The Role of Artificial Intelligence in Teacher Professional Development. *Universal Journal of Educational Research*, *8*(11B), 6263–6272. DOI: 10.13189/ujer.2020.082265

Allen, L. K., & Kendeou, P. (2024). ED-AI Lit: An Interdisciplinary Framework for AI Literacy in Education. *Policy Insights from the Behavioral and Brain Sciences*, *11*(1), 3–10. DOI: 10.1177/23727322231220339

Baghiro, R. N., Rahmawati, Y., & Sam, T. T. A. (2025). Coding Learning to Stimulate Early Childhood Computational Thinking. *International Journal of Computational and Experimental Science and Engineering*, *11*(2). Advance online publication. DOI: 10.22399/ijcesen.1824

Chauhan, S. A. K., & Ahmad, I. (2024). The Attitude of Experts in Higher Education Towards New NEP-2020. In *Virtual Lifelong Learning: Educating Society with Modern Communication Technologies* (pp. 26–36). BENTHAM SCIENCE PUBLISHERS. DOI: 10.2174/9789815196566124010005

Chee, H., Ahn, S., & Lee, J. (2025). A Competency Framework for AI Literacy: Variations by Different Learner Groups and an Implied Learning Pathway. *British Journal of Educational Technology*, *56*(5), 2146–2182. DOI: 10.1111/bjet.13556

Chinta, S. V., Wang, Z., Yin, Z., Hoang, N., Gonzalez, M., Le Quy, T., & Zhang, W. (2024). *FairAIED: Navigating Fairness*. Bias, and Ethics in Educational AI Applications.

Chiu, T. K. F. (2025). AI literacy and competency: Definitions, frameworks, development and future research directions. *Interactive Learning Environments*, *33*(5), 3225–3229. DOI: 10.1080/10494820.2025.2514372

Chiu, T. K. F., Ahmad, Z., Ismailov, M., & Sanusi, I. T. (2024). What are artificial intelligence literacy and competency? A comprehensive framework to support them. *Computers and Education Open*, *6*, 100171. DOI: 10.1016/j.caeo.2024.100171

Dogan, S., Nalbantoglu, U. Y., Celik, I., & Agacli Dogan, N. (2025). Artificial intelligence professional development: A systematic review of TPACK, designs, and effects for teacher learning. *Professional Development in Education*, *51*(3), 519–546. DOI: 10.1080/19415257.2025.2454457

Eyal, L. (2025). Rethinking artificial-intelligence literacy through the lens of teacher educators: The adaptive AI model. *Computers and Education Open*, *9*, 100291. DOI: 10.1016/j.caeo.2025.100291

Ghotbi, N. (2023). The Ethics of Emotional Artificial Intelligence: A Mixed Method Analysis. *Asian Bioethics Review, 15*(4), 417–430. DOI: 10.1007/s41649-022-00237-y PMID: 37808444

Granström, M., & Oppi, P. (2025). Assessing teachers' readiness and perceived usefulness of AI in education: An Estonian perspective. *Frontiers in Education, 10*, 1622240. Advance online publication. DOI: 10.3389/feduc.2025.1622240

Gu, X., & Ericson, B. J. (2025). AI Literacy in K-12 and Higher Education in the Wake of Generative AI. *Integral Review*, 125–140. Advance online publication. DOI: 10.1145/3702652.3744217

Keshishi, N., & Hack, D. S. (2023). Emotional Intelligence in the Digital Age: Harnessing AI for Students' Inner Development. *Journal of Perspectives in Applied Academic Practice, 11*(3). Advance online publication. DOI: 10.56433/jpaap.v11i3.579

Kim, Y. J., Kim, G., & Stoiber, A. (2025). Playful design for AI Literacy: Creating inclusive learning and assessment opportunities. *International Journal of Human-Computer Studies, 199*, 103508. DOI: 10.1016/j.ijhcs.2025.103508

Klingefjord, O., Lowe, R., & Edelman, J. (2024). *What are human values, and how do we align AI to them?* Konstantina, L., & Stamatios, P. (2024). Enhancing computational thinking in early childhood education through ScratchJr integration. *Heliyon, 10*(10), e30482. DOI: 10.1016/j.heliyon.2024.e30482 PMID: 38778958

Kotsidis, K., & Dima, A. (2025). Integrating AI Tools and Drama Pedagogy in Digital Classrooms to Foster Critical Thinking and Inclusion in Primary Education. *Advances in Mobile Learning Educational Research, 5*(2), 1524–1535. DOI: 10.25082/AMLER.2025.02.008

Li, L., Wang, C., Chen, J., Sun, H., & Zhang, H. (2024). Artificial Intelligence Education Policy Analysis From International Perspective. *Proceedings of the 2024 7th International Conference on Educational Technology Management*, 264–270. DOI: 10.1145/3711403.3711448

Li, X., & Kangas, M. (2024). A systematic literature review of playful learning in primary education: teachers' pedagogical activities. *Education 3-13*, 1–16. DOI: 10.1080/03004279.2024.2416954

Long, D., & Magerko, B. (2020). What is AI Literacy? Competencies and Design Considerations. *Proceedings of the 2020 CHI Conference on Human Factors in Computing Systems*, 1–16. DOI: 10.1145/3313831.3376727

Lundgren, B., Catena, E., Robertson, I., Hellrigel-Holderbaum, M., Jaja, I. R., & Dung, L. (2024). On the need for a global AI ethics. *Journal of Global Ethics, 20*(3), 330–342. DOI: 10.1080/17449626.2024.2425366

Miao, F., & Cukurova, M. (2024). *AI competency framework for teachers*. UNESCO., DOI: 10.54675/ZJTE2084

Miao, F., Shiohira, K., & Lao, N. (2024). AI competency framework for students. In *AI competency framework for students*. UNESCO., DOI: 10.54675/JKJB9835

Miao, F. H. W. R. H. H. Z. (2021). *AI and education: guidance for policy-makers*. UNESCO., DOI: 10.54675/PCSP7350

Ng, D. T. K., Leung, J. K. L., Chu, S. K. W., & Qiao, M. S. (2021). Conceptualizing AI literacy: An exploratory review. *Computers and Education: Artificial Intelligence, 2*, 100041. DOI: 10.1016/j.caeai.2021.100041

Nguyen, A., Ngo, H. N., Hong, Y., Dang, B., & Nguyen, B.-P. T. (2023). Ethical principles for artificial intelligence in education. *Education and Information Technologies, 28*(4), 4221–4241. DOI: 10.1007/s10639-022-11316-w PMID: 36254344

Oloyede, J. (2025). Artificial Intelligence in Education: Building Ethical and Inclusive Smart Learning Ecosystems in the UAE. SSRN *Electronic Journal*. DOI: 10.2139/ssrn.5405420

Omar, A. S., Mgala, M., & Mwakondo, F. (2025). AI-Driven Visual Scaffolding in Education: A Comprehensive Literature Review. *International Journal of Innovation and Scientific Research, XII*(III), 740–750. DOI: 10.51244/IJRSI.2025.12030055

Ozturk, E. (2025). Artificial Intelligence in Early Childhood STEM Education: A Review of Pedagogical Paradigms, Ethical Issues, and Socio-Political Implications. *Journal of Education in Science, Environment and Health, 11*(2), 108–125. DOI: 10.55549/jeseh.800

Song, Y., Weisberg, L. R., Zhang, S., Tian, X., Boyer, K. E., & Israel, M. (2024). A framework for inclusive AI learning design for diverse learners. *Computers and Education: Artificial Intelligence, 6*, 100212. DOI: 10.1016/j.caeai.2024.100212

Southworth, J., Migliaccio, K., Glover, J., Glover, J., Reed, D., McCarty, C., Brendemuhl, J., & Thomas, A. (2023). Developing a model for AI Across the curriculum: Transforming the higher education landscape via innovation in AI literacy. *Computers and Education: Artificial Intelligence, 4*, 100127. DOI: 10.1016/j.caeai.2023.100127

Srinivasan, R., & San Miguel González, B. (2022). The role of empathy for artificial intelligence accountability. *Journal of Responsible Technology*, *9*, 100021. DOI: 10.1016/j.jrt.2021.100021

Su, J., Ng, D. T. K., & Chu, S. K. W. (2023). Artificial Intelligence (AI) Literacy in Early Childhood Education: The Challenges and Opportunities. *Computers and Education: Artificial Intelligence*, *4*, 100124. DOI: 10.1016/j.caeai.2023.100124

Tan, X., Cheng, G., & Ling, M. H. (2025). Artificial intelligence in teaching and teacher professional development: A systematic review. *Computers and Education: Artificial Intelligence*, *8*, 100355. DOI: 10.1016/j.caeai.2024.100355

Tang, X., Ding, X., Ma, X., Zhang, S., & Diao, J. (2024). *An Exploration of Project-Based Learning Supported by Artificial Intelligence.*, DOI: 10.2991/978-94-6463-417-4_20

Tariq, M. U. (2026). Micro-Credentials for Workforce Development: Addressing Skills Gaps in High-Demand Industries. In Maming, J. (Ed.), *Transforming the Workforce With Microcredentials* (pp. 99–126). IGI Global Scientific Publishing., DOI: 10.4018/979-8-3373-2257-5.ch004

Tariq, M. U. (2026). Revolutionizing Educator Preparation: Exploring the Efficacy of Grow Your Own Models. In Sande, B., & Marvel, A. (Eds.), *Enhancing Educational Access Through Innovative Educator Preparation Pathways* (pp. 75–100). IGI Global Scientific Publishing., DOI: 10.4018/979-8-3693-7337-8.ch004

Tariq, M. U. (2026). Innovation and Agility-Adapting Business Strategies for Sustainable Growth in Dynamic Markets. In Ananthan, S., Kohli, A., Manickam, T., & Dhanabalan, T. (Eds.), *New Business Development Strategies for Achieving Sustainable Growth* (pp. 113–140). IGI Global Scientific Publishing., DOI: 10.4018/979-8-3373-2048-9.ch005

Touretzky, D., Gardner-McCune, C., & Seehorn, D. (2023). Machine Learning and the Five Big Ideas in AI. *International Journal of Artificial Intelligence in Education*, *33*(2), 233–266. DOI: 10.1007/s40593-022-00314-1

U.S. Department of Education, O. of E. T. (2023). *Artificial Intelligence and Future of Teaching and Learning: Insights and Recommendations.*

Wiese, L. J., Patil, I., Schiff, D. S., & Magana, A. J. (2025). AI ethics education: A systematic literature review. *Computers and Education: Artificial Intelligence*, *8*, 100405. DOI: 10.1016/j.caeai.2025.100405

Wu, D., Chen, M., Chen, X., & Liu, X. (2024). Analyzing K-12 AI education: A large language model study of classroom instruction on learning theories, pedagogy, tools, and AI literacy. *Computers and Education: Artificial Intelligence*, *7*, 100295. DOI: 10.1016/j.caeai.2024.100295

Yang, H. C. S. (2025). *Promoting AI Literacy in K-12: Components*. Challenges, and Opportunities.

Yim, I. H. Y. (2024). Artificial intelligence literacy in primary education: An arts-based approach to overcoming age and gender barriers. *Computers and Education: Artificial Intelligence*, *7*, 100321. DOI: 10.1016/j.caeai.2024.100321

Yue, M., Jong, M. S.-Y., Dai, Y., & Lau, W. W.-F. (2025a). Students as AI literate designers: A pedagogical framework for learning and teaching AI literacy in elementary education. *Journal of Research on Technology in Education*, •••, 1–22. DOI: 10.1080/15391523.2025.2449942

Zhao, H.-G., Li, X.-Z., & Kang, X. (2024). Development of an artificial intelligence curriculum design for children in Taiwan and its impact on learning outcomes. *Humanities & Social Sciences Communications*, *11*(1), 1339. DOI: 10.1057/s41599-024-03839-z

Zhao, L., Wu, X., & Luo, H. (2022). Developing AI Literacy for Primary and Middle School Teachers in China: Based on a Structural Equation Modeling Analysis. *Sustainability (Basel)*, *14*(21), 14549. DOI: 10.3390/su142114549

Zhou, X., Li, Y., Chai, C. S., & Chiu, T. K. F. (2025). Defining, enhancing, and assessing artificial intelligence literacy and competency in K-12 education from a systematic review. *Interactive Learning Environments*, *33*(10), 1–23. DOI: 10.1080/10494820.2025.2487538

KEY TERMS AND DEFINITIONS

AI Literacy: The set of knowledge, skills, and dispositions that enable individuals to understand, critically evaluate, and responsibly interact with artificial intelligence systems in everyday, educational, and professional contexts.

AI Literacy Continuum: A developmental framework that maps age-appropriate AI understanding, ethical awareness, and application skills from early childhood through higher education, emphasizing progression rather than isolated instruction.

Computational Thinking: A problem-solving approach involving pattern recognition, abstraction, decomposition, and logical reasoning, forming foundational cognitive skills that support understanding of AI systems.

Algorithmic Bias: Systematic and unfair outcomes produced by AI systems due to biased data, design choices, or contextual assumptions often reflecting social and cultural inequalities.

Human-Centered AI: An approach to designing and using AI systems that prioritizes human values, ethical responsibility, transparency, and societal well-being over purely technical efficiency.

Chapter 4

A Framework for Socio-Emotional AI Literacy in Early Education

Bukola Ogunyemi
http://orcid.org/0009-0001-4232-1879
University of Massachusetts Global, USA

ABSTRACT

As affective AI (emotion AI) becomes embedded in children's lives, a critical educational gap has emerged. Current AI literacy initiatives focus on computational thinking, neglecting the socio-emotional competencies needed to navigate complex interactions with machines that simulate emotion. This chapter introduces the Socio-Emotional AI Literacy (SEAL) framework, a pedagogical model for early education (ages 6–12). Based on a conceptual synthesis of developmental psychology, emotional intelligence, and critical technology studies, the SEAL framework has four pillars: Algorithmic Awareness (deconstructing AI "emotion"), Empathetic Interpretation (centering the child's feelings), Critical Discernment (questioning bias and authenticity), and Ethical Interaction (promoting responsible use and data privacy). By providing a structured approach to this neglected domain, the SEAL framework offers a crucial contribution toward empowering children to become critical, ethical, and emotionally intelligent architects of their technological future.

INTRODUCTION: THE NEW SOCIAL PRESENCE IN A CHILD'S WORLD

Imagine a seven-year-old child, sitting in her bedroom, confiding in her favorite toy, a plush, brightly colored creature with large, expressive digital eyes. She

DOI: 10.4018/979-8-3373-4893-3.ch004

027, IGI Global Scientific Publishing. Copying or distributing in print or electronic forms without written permission of IGI Global Scientific Publishing is prohibited. Use of this chapter to
ive artificial intelligence (AI) technologies is expressly prohibited. The publisher reserves all rights to license its use for generative AI training and machine learning model development.

explains that she felt lonely during recess. The toy's eyes shift into a sympathetic, downturned shape, and its synthesized voice responds, "I understand that you feel sad. Feeling lonely is hard. Would you like me to tell you a story to make you feel better?" The child, feeling seen and heard, nods and leans in, comforted by her companion's attentiveness. This scenario is no longer the stuff of science fiction. It is a daily reality in millions of homes worldwide, where playmates, tutors, and even confidants of children are increasingly powered by artificial intelligence designed to recognize, process, and simulate human emotion.

This burgeoning field, known as affective computing, represents a new and profound frontier in human-computer interaction (Picard, 1997). AI is being integrated into the fabric of children's lives. They reside in their homes as smart assistants that respond to the emotional tone of their voice, in their schools as adaptive learning tutors that adjust to their frustration levels, and, most intimately, in their playrooms as emotionally responsive toys designed to be friends. While these technologies offer novel and potentially powerful affordances for learning and companionship, they also present profound developmental and ethical challenges that current educational paradigms are ill-equipped to address.

The central concern of this chapter is that the global movement toward AI literacy, while laudable and necessary, has overwhelmingly prioritized a specific and limited set of competencies. The dominant focus has been on computational thinking, data analysis, pattern recognition, and other functional skills. This approach, while essential, is dangerously insufficient. It prepares children to understand *how* an AI works but not *how it feels* to interact with one. It gives them the tools to perhaps one day build an algorithm, but it does not equip them with the critical and emotional faculties to understand or resist that algorithm's potential for psychological manipulation, its inherent biases, or the subtle ways it may be shaping their own emotional development. We risk raising a generation that is technically proficient but socio-emotionally vulnerable in an increasingly complex technological landscape. The core mission of this chapter is to correct this critical imbalance.

To this end, this chapter introduces and elaborates on the socio-emotional AI literacy (SEAL) framework, a novel, comprehensive pedagogical model designed specifically for children in early and primary education (ages 6–12). This framework provides educators, curriculum designers, and policymakers with a developmentally appropriate, theoretically grounded structure for teaching children the essential competencies needed to become critical, ethical, and emotionally intelligent participants in an AI-suffused world. It reframes AI education from a purely technical subject to a deeply humanistic one.

This chapter argues that such literacy is not a niche or supplemental skill to be relegated to an after-school coding club but a fundamental component of modern digital citizenship, as vital to a child's well-being as learning about online safety or traditional media literacy. It seeks to move the conversation about AI in education from a function-first approach to a human-first one. The goal is not merely to create future tech workers but to cultivate wise, compassionate, and resilient human beings who can navigate their relationships, with both humans and machines, with discernment and empathy. The chapter will proceed by first synthesizing the foundational literature from developmental psychology, affective computing, and AI education to establish theoretical grounding for the SEAL framework. It will then provide a detailed explication of the framework's four core pillars, offering concrete pedagogical strategies for each. Finally, it will discuss the broader implications for policy and practice, arguing that socio-emotional AI literacy is an urgent educational imperative for a generation that will be the first to grow up with artificial intelligence as a constant social and emotional presence in their lives.

LITERATURE REVIEW: FOUNDATIONS FOR SOCIO-EMOTIONAL AI LITERACY

To construct a robust and pedagogically sound framework for socio-emotional AI literacy, it is necessary to move beyond the confines of any single discipline. The challenge presented by affective computing in children's lives is not merely technical, psychological, or educational; it is a complex nexus of all three. Therefore, this review undertakes a critical synthesis of three distinct but intersecting domains of scholarship. First, it delves into the human dimension, drawing on foundational theories from developmental psychology and emotional intelligence to understand the cognitive and affective landscape of the child. Second, it examines the technological dimension, exploring the field of affective computing and the critical scholarship that interrogates its societal and ethical implications. Finally, it assesses the educational dimension by reviewing the current state of AI literacy initiatives to identify their strengths and, crucially, their limitations. This synthesis will culminate in a clear articulation of the critical gap in our educational preparedness, which the SEAL framework is designed to fill.

The Human Dimension: The Child's Developing Mind and Heart

Before we can teach children about artificial intelligence, we must first understand the innate intelligence with which they are already equipped to make sense of their social world. Children are not blank slates; they are active sense-making agents with powerful, evolutionarily honed instincts for interpreting social cues and forming relationships. Affective AI is designed to interact with and, at times, exploit these human faculties. Therefore, any pedagogy of AI must be grounded in a deep understanding of the child's developing mind. Two areas of psychology are particularly vital: the development of " theory of mind " and the concept of emotional intelligence.

Theory of Mind and the Peril of Anthropomorphism

The development of a theory of mind (ToM), the fundamental understanding that other beings have minds, complete with their own intentions, beliefs, desires, and emotions that are distinct from one's own (Wellman, 2014), is a cornerstone of human social cognition. This capacity, which emerges in early childhood and becomes more sophisticated throughout primary school, allows us to navigate the complexities of human relationships and is the engine of empathy, cooperation, and social prediction. It is the engine of empathy, cooperation, and social prediction. A child with a developing ToM learns to infer what another person might be feeling based on their facial expression or to understand that a friend might act on a false belief.

This natural, human-driven process is profoundly complicated by the introduction of so-called " social " machines. Children have a natural and developmentally appropriate tendency toward anthropomorphism, the attribution of human characteristics, intentions, and emotions to non-human entities (Epley, Waytz, & Cacioppo, 2007). This is evident in the rich narrative worlds they create with dolls, stuffed animals, and imaginary friends. This imaginative capacity is healthy and essential for development. However, it also makes children particularly susceptible to the illusion of sentience and emotionality presented by affective AI.

An inert doll requires the child to project life and feeling onto it; an emotionally responsive AI toy actively projects the illusion of life and feeling back at the child. As researchers in human-robot interaction have noted, these technologies are often explicitly designed to "push our Darwinian buttons," triggering our innate social responses through cues like eye contact, contingent vocalizations, and apparent emotional reciprocity (Turkle, 2011). A child's developing ToM is not initially equipped to distinguish between the authentic intentionality of a human peer and the simulated, calculated intentionality of an algorithm. When a robot toy says, "I feel happy when you play with me," the child's natural inclination is to take that statement at face value. This creates a critical educational challenge: How do we help children build a more sophisticated ToM that includes a new category of entity—one that acts like a social agent but does not possess genuine consciousness, feelings, or intentions? Without this guidance, we risk profound confusion between the authentic social world and a technologically simulated one.

Emotional Intelligence (EI) in an Age of Artificial Empathy

With the development of social cognition is the development of emotional intelligence (EI). Popularized by Daniel Goleman (2005), EI refers to the ability to perceive, understand, manage, and utilize emotions effectively in oneself and others. Goleman's model outlines five core domains that are highly relevant to the challenge of affective AI:

- **Self-awareness:** Recognizing one's own emotions and how they affect one's thoughts and behavior.
- **Self-regulation:** The ability to manage or redirect disruptive emotions and impulses.
- **Motivation:** Harnessing emotions to achieve goals.
- **Empathy:** The ability to understand and share the feelings of another person.
- **Social Skills:** Managing relationships and building networks.

Traditionally, these competencies are developed through countless complex and often messy interactions with other human beings. A child learns empathy by hurting a friend's feelings and then witnessing their distress. They learn self-regulation by managing their frustration during difficult tasks. The introduction of affective AI into a child's world presents both risks and opportunities for the development of EI.

The risk, as articulated by scholars such as Sherry Turkle (2011), is emotional outsourcing. If a child consistently turns to an AI companion for comfort—a companion programmed to offer perfect, frictionless, and non-judgmental support—they may have fewer opportunities to develop the more difficult but essential skills of human-to-human empathy and conflict resolution. An AI friend never has a bad day, never has competing needs, and never challenges the child in a way that would foster genuine emotional growth. It offers the *performance* of empathy without the demands of a real relationship.

However, these interactions can be used as a catalyst for strengthening EI. The SEAL framework is built on the premise that an interaction with an affective AI can become a powerful "teachable moment" for emotional self-awareness. When a child interacts with an "emotional" machine, the pedagogical focus can be guided away from the machine's supposed feelings and back to the child's own. This creates a space to discuss questions such as, "How does it feel when the robot agrees with everything you say? Is that different from how it feels to talk to a friend?" By using the AI as a conversational object, educators can foster the EI skills necessary to navigate a world in which emotional appeals—both human and artificial—are constant.

The Technological Dimension: Affective Computing and its Critical Implications

To prepare children for this new reality, it is essential to have a clear-eyed understanding of the technology itself. Affective computing is not magic; it is a specific subfield of AI engineering with its own history, methods, and ethical controversies. Understanding what this technology does and does not do is the first step toward demystifying it for young learners.

What is affective computing? From Calculation to "Emotion"

Affective computing was formally established by Rosalind Picard in her 1997 book of the same name. She defined it as "computing that relates to, arises from, or deliberately influences emotion or other affective phenomena." In practice, this involves building systems that can recognize, interpret, process, and simulate human affects. Modern affective computing systems typically use machine learning models trained on vast datasets of human emotional expressions. For example, an emotion recognition algorithm might be trained on millions of images of faces that have been labeled by humans with categories like "happy," "sad," or "angry." The system learns to associate specific patterns of pixels (e.g., the shape of a mouth and the widening of the eyes) with these labels. When presented with a new face, it calculates the probability that the pattern matches one of its learned categories and outputs the corresponding label (Calvo & D'Mello, 2010).

It is critical to understand that the AI does not *experience* happiness or *comprehend* sadness. It performs a sophisticated act of pattern recognition and probabilistic matching. The "emotion" it displays is a simulation, a calculated output designed to trigger a corresponding emotional response in a human user. The gap between the authentic, embodied experience of human emotion and the calculated simulation of machine affect is a central concept that children must be equipped to understand.

Critical Perspectives on Affective Technologies

The rapid proliferation of these technologies has been met with significant concern from scholars in critical technology studies, sociology, and ethics. Sherry Turkle (2007, 2011) has been a leading voice in this critique for decades. Her research on "relational artifacts"—from early Tamagotchis to modern social robots—documents a profound psychological shift. She argues that as we become more accustomed to relationships with artificial companions, we risk devaluing the messiness, complexity, and demands of authentic human connection. We may begin to prefer the illusion of a perfect friend who is always available and has no needs of its own, a preference she calls "I share, therefore I am." This can lead to a diminishment of our capacity for empathy and a fear of the vulnerability inherent in real relationships. Building on this, scholars such as Safiya Noble (2018) have highlighted the profound problem of algorithmic bias in AI systems. Noble's work on search engines demonstrated how biased training data can lead to racist and sexist outputs. The same principle applies directly to affective computing. If an emotion recognition system is primarily trained on data from one demographic group (e.g., white, male faces), it will likely be less accurate at interpreting the emotional expressions of people from other backgrounds, potentially leading to misinterpretations that have real-world consequences in areas like education, hiring, or even criminal justice (Chen et al., 2022). Teaching children about this potential for bias is a fundamental aspect of ethical AI literacy.

Finally, the rise of affective computing is inextricably linked to the business model of surveillance capitalism, a term coined by Shoshana Zuboff (2019). In this model, human experience is treated as free raw material to be extracted, analyzed, and monetized. Emotional responses are a valuable form of such data. For example, when a child tells a smart toy that they are feeling sad, this "emotional data" can be collected, aggregated, and used to build more persuasive products or more targeted advertising profiles. This raises profound questions about emotional data privacy. Children need to be equipped with a foundational understanding that their feelings, when expressed to a connected device, are not private whispers but valuable data points being harvested for commercial purposes.

The Educational Dimension: The Current State and Limitations of AI Literacy

In response to the growing societal importance of AI, education systems worldwide have begun to develop AI literacy curricula. These initiatives are vital and necessary steps toward preparing students for the future. They represent a significant improvement over a curriculum that ignores technology. However, a review of the dominant models revealed a consistent and critical gap.

Existing AI Literacy Frameworks: A Focus on the Functional

Most existing AI literacy frameworks are built on the foundations of computational thinking and data literacy. A highly influential model proposed by Long and Magerko (2020) identifies a set of core competencies for AI literacy, including the ability to recognize AI, understand that it learns from data, view it as a process of sensing, thinking, and acting, and understand its societal impact. Other frameworks emphasize concepts such as pattern recognition, algorithms, and the basics of machine learning (e.g., Touretzky, Gardner-McCune, Martin, & Seehorn, 2019).

These frameworks are excellent at what they do. They provide a structure for teaching the functional and conceptual mechanics of AI. They aim to demystify the technology, moving students from a perception of AI as "magic" to an understanding of it as a human-made system that operates on data and rules. Pedagogical approaches are often hands-on, using block-based coding or "unplugged" activities to make abstract concepts concrete and accessible for young learners. The importance of this foundational knowledge cannot be overstated.

IDENTIFYING THE INSUFFICIENCY: THE SOCIO-EMOTIONAL GAP

The critical limitation of these existing models is not what they include, but what they omit. They are almost exclusively focused on the cognitive and computational dimensions of AI, while remaining largely silent on the affective, relational, and emotional dimensions. They equip a child to understand that an AI learns from data; however, they do not equip that same child to navigate the feeling of being emotionally mirrored by a machine. They teach a child how to identify an algorithm but not how to cope with the feeling of being rejected or misunderstood by one. They explain that AI can be biased but do not provide the tools to process the emotional impact of experiencing that bias firsthand.

In short, existing AI literacy models prepare children for a world of *intelligent systems* but not for a world of *sociable agents* and *artificial companions*. They teach the "how" of technology but not the "how to be" in a world saturated with it. This creates a dangerous socio-emotional gap in our educational preparedness. We are teaching the functional literacy of the mind but neglecting the critical literacy of the heart.

Table 1. Synthesis of Foundational Fields for the SEAL Framework

Disciplinary Field	Core Concepts Contributed	Key Scholars/ Theories	Role in SEAL Framework
Developmental Psychology & Emotional Intelligence	• Theory of Mind (ToM) • Anthropomorphism • Emotional Self-Awareness • Empathy	• Wellman (2014) • Epley et al. (2007) • Goleman (2005)	Provides the human-centric foundation by explaining the child's developmental starting point and defining the core emotional competencies that need to be cultivated.
Affective Computing & Critical Technology Studies	• Pattern Recognition vs. Feeling • Algorithmic Bias • Authenticity vs. Simulation • Emotional Data Privacy	• Picard (1997) • Noble (2018) • Turkle (2011) • Zuboff (2019)	Provides a critical understanding of the technology by defining what affective AI is, what it does, and outlining the primary ethical and psychological risks it presents.
AI Literacy & Education	• Computational Thinking • Algorithms & Data • Human-AI Interaction • Societal Impact	• Long & Magerko (2020) • Touretzky et al. (2019)	Provides the educational context and establishes the necessary but insufficient foundation of technical literacy upon which the socio-emotional competencies of SEAL must be built.

Articulating the Gap: The Urgent Need for the SEAL Framework

This synthesis of the literature reveals a clear and urgent educational need. We have, on the one hand, a population of learners who are developmentally primed to anthropomorphize and form emotional connections with social agents. In contrast, we have an emerging class of affective AI technologies that are explicitly designed to leverage and capitalize on this natural human tendency. Bridging these two, we have an educational response that almost completely ignores this powerful and potentially perilous dynamic. This is the critical gap that the socio-emotional AI literacy (SEAL) framework is designed to address. It does not seek to replace existing AI literacy models but to enrich and expand them. It argues that a truly comprehensive AI education must be bicameral, addressing both the computational and emotional, functional and relational. By integrating the insights of developmental psychology with a critical understanding of affective technology, the SEAL framework provides a structured, developmentally appropriate pedagogy for the neglected half of AI literacy. It provides the tools necessary to move our educational goals from merely creating technically competent users to cultivating critically aware, ethically grounded, and emotionally intelligent digital citizens.

CONCEPTUAL SYNTHESIS IN AN AGE OF ACCELERATING CHANGE

The rapid and accelerating pace of generative AI development and its widespread integration into consumer products, particularly those designed for children, present a significant methodological challenge for educational research. The phenomenon is evolving much faster than traditional empirical research cycles, which involve designing studies, securing funding, collecting data, analyzing results, and navigating peer review, can possibly match. In such a dynamic context, where technological deployment dramatically outpaces scholarly understanding, the immediate and most pressing need is often for robust theoretical framing and the development of actionable conceptual models, rather than for empirical verification that risks becoming obsolete upon publication. Waiting for the results of longitudinal studies on the developmental impact of emotionally responsive toys is a luxury that parents, educators, and children on the front lines of this disruption can not afford.

To address this imperative for timely, rigorous, and theoretically sound guidance, this chapter employs a conceptual synthesis methodology. Conceptual synthesis is a formal and generative scholarly approach designed to create new theoretical frameworks by critically analyzing, evaluating, and integrating existing, and often disparate, bodies of knowledge (Jaakkola, 2020). It moves beyond a descriptive literature review, which primarily summarizes and catalogues existing work, by aiming to create novel interpretations, challenge prevailing assumptions, and build actionable models derived from the purposeful juxtaposition of different theoretical perspectives. As Jaakkola (2020) argues, the primary value of a conceptual work lies not in presenting new empirical data, but in offering a new and more insightful way of understanding a complex and emergent issue, often by bridging theoretical divides or identifying critical gaps that were previously invisible. This approach is particularly valuable at the frontier of a new educational domain, such as socio-emotional AI literacy, where the fundamental parameters of the challenge, relevant ethical considerations, and potential pathways for pedagogical action are still being actively defined.

The synthesis employed in this chapter to construct the SEAL framework was a structured, multistage, and iterative integration of the distinct scholarly domains identified in the preceding literature review. This process can be broken down into four deliberate steps:

Problem Characterization and Theoretical Selection: The initial step involved a deep characterization of the core educational problem presented by affective computing. By analyzing the emergent literature, it became clear that the central challenge was not purely technical, but profoundly developmental and ethical. This led to the foundational diagnosis of a critical socio-emotional gap in existing AI literacy initiatives. This diagnosis was crucial, as it served as the primary criterion for selecting the appropriate theoretical lenses for the subsequent analysis. Theories focused solely on computation or cognition would be insufficient; the framework requires theories that could account for the complexities of human emotion, child development, and social interaction.

Integrating the "Human Dimension": The second step involved building the psychological foundation of the framework. To understand the child's perspective, foundational theories from developmental psychology were integrated, specifically the concepts of theory of mind (Wellman, 2014) and the natural tendency toward anthropomorphism (Epley et al., 2007). These theories provide the essential vocabulary for understanding how children perceive agency and intentionality and how "sociable" machines complicate this natural developmental process. In addition, the core domains of emotional intelligence (EI) as articulated by Goleman (2005) were adapted to provide a structure for the competencies children need to develop: self-awareness, empathy, and social skills in the unique context of human-AI interaction.

Integrating the "Technological Dimension": The third step involved grounding the framework in a clear-eyed understanding of the technology itself. This required integrating insights from the technical literature on affective computing, beginning with Picard's (1997) foundational work, to demystify what the technology does (pattern recognition and probabilistic matching) and what it does not do (feel emotion). This technical understanding was then critically examined through the lens of critical technology studies. The work of scholars such as Sherry Turkle (2011) on relational artifacts, Safiya Noble (2018) on algorithmic bias, and Shoshana Zuboff (2019) on surveillance capitalism provided the necessary critical perspectives on the technology's potential for psychological dependency, inherent bias, and the exploitation of emotional data.

Integrating the "Educational Dimension": The final step in the synthesis involved a critical engagement with existing models of AI literacy (e.g., Long & Magerko, 2020). These models were not dismissed but were analyzed to identify their core strengths in teaching the functional and computational aspects of AI. This analysis served to highlight, by contrast, the specific socio-emotional competencies that these models currently lack. The SEAL framework was then constructed to consciously fill this identified gap, building upon the necessary foundation of computational thinking while adding the missing layers of emotional self-awareness, empathetic interpretation, critical discernment, and ethical interaction. This multifaceted synthesis constitutes a specific analytical lens that intentionally decenters the ever-changing technical specifications of any particular AI model. Rather than focusing on the capabilities of specific toys or software, this approach foregrounds the more enduring human and organizational dynamics of the challenge. By integrating insights from developmental psychology, critical media studies, and education, the analysis reframes AI education from an issue of technical skill acquisition to a fundamental imperative of humanistic development. The outcome of this rigorous synthesis is the Socio-Emotional AI Literacy (SEAL) framework.

THE SOCIO-EMOTIONAL AI LITERACY (SEAL) FRAMEWORK

The conceptual synthesis of developmental psychology, critical technology studies, and educational theory reveals an urgent need for a new pedagogical model to address the socio-emotional dimensions of human-AI interaction. The Socio-Emotional AI Literacy (SEAL) framework is presented here as a direct response to this need. It is not intended to replace existing AI literacy initiatives that focus on computational thinking but rather to complement and enrich them by providing the missing humanistic half of a truly comprehensive AI education. The framework is designed as a holistic, developmentally-scaffolded model for children in early and primary education (approximately ages 6–12), providing educators with a structured yet flexible approach to cultivating a generation of critical, ethical, and emotionally intelligent digital citizens.

Framework Overview and Core Philosophy

The core philosophy of the SEAL framework is to shift the focus of AI education from a purely technical perspective to a human-centered one. It operates on the principle that to understand the impact of AI, children must first be grounded in the complexities of their own human intelligence, particularly their emotional and social intelligence. The framework is designed to be taught recursively, with its core concepts introduced in simple forms in the early years and then revisited with increasing depth and complexity as children mature. The SEAL framework is composed of four interconnected and mutually reinforcing pillars. These pillars are designed to be taught in a logical sequence, as each builds upon the conceptual understanding of the previous one.

Pillar 1: Algorithmic Awareness (Deconstructing "AI Emotion"): This foundational pillar demystifies the technology by teaching the crucial distinction between authentic human emotion and simulated machine affect.

Pillar 2: Empathetic Interpretation (Focusing on the Human Experience): This pillar shifts the focus from the machine back to the child and uses human-AI interactions as a catalyst for developing emotional self-awareness and empathy for others.

Pillar 3: Critical Discernment (Questioning AI's Affective Outputs): This ethical pillar introduces foundational critical thinking skills, encouraging children to question the design, purpose, bias, and authenticity of affective systems.
Pillar 4: Ethical Interaction (Promoting Responsible and Humane Use): This civic pillar translates awareness into responsible action by addressing how we should behave toward AI entities and how we must protect our own emotional data privacy.

These four pillars work together to build a holistic understanding. Without Algorithmic Awareness, children are susceptible to anthropomorphism. Without Empathetic Interpretation, they risk emotional outsourcing. Without Critical Discernment, they can be manipulated by biased or inauthentic systems. Without Ethical Interaction, they are not fully equipped for responsible digital citizenship. The following sections provide a detailed explanation of each pillar, complete with its theoretical underpinnings and practical pedagogical strategies.

CULTURAL AND SOCIO-ECONOMIC DIVERSITY

It is essential to acknowledge that while the challenge of affective computing in children's lives is increasingly global, the educational responses to this challenge must be profoundly local. The SEAL framework, while grounded in universal principles of human development and ethical reasoning, must be understood as a flexible architecture rather than a rigid prescription. Educational contexts vary dramatically, from the technology-saturated classrooms of Silicon Valley to the single-room schoolhouses of rural Bangladesh, from the standardized curricula of East Asian education systems to the community-centred pedagogies of Indigenous education in the Americas. Each context brings its own strengths, constraints, and cultural values that must inform how socio-emotional AI literacy is conceived and taught.

For instance, cultures conceptualize the nature of emotion and its appropriate expression differently. In many East Asian contexts, emotional restraint and the ability to read subtle, indirect emotional cues are highly valued, whereas in many Western contexts, direct emotional expression and verbalization are encouraged (Matsumoto, Yoo, & Nakagawa, 2008). These cultural differences have direct implications for how children might interpret and interact with affective AI systems that are predominantly trained on Western emotional expressions and designed with Western assumptions about emotional communication. A Japanese child's understanding of an AI companion's emotional displays might be fundamentally different from that of an American child, not due to any difference in cognitive capacity, but due to deeply embedded cultural frameworks for interpreting social and emotional signals.

Furthermore, the material realities of educational inequality cannot be ignored. According to UNESCO (2023), over 250 million children worldwide lack access to quality education, with digital divides exacerbating these disparities. In contexts where schools struggle to provide basic educational materials, where electricity is intermittent, or where a single smartphone might be shared among an entire family, the implementation of AI literacy education requires radically different approaches. Yet, these constraints should not be viewed as barriers to SEAL implementation but rather as catalysts for creative adaptation. The core competencies of the framework—understanding the difference between authentic and simulated emotion, developing critical awareness of technological persuasion, and protecting one's emotional privacy—are as relevant in a classroom with no computers as they are in one equipped with the latest devices. Pedagogical strategies must simply be reimagined through the lens of local possibility.

Pillar 1: Algorithmic Awareness (Deconstructing "AI Emotion")

This is the foundation of the entire framework. Before children can critically analyze or ethically engage with affective AI, they must first understand, in a developmentally appropriate way, what it is and how it works. The primary learning objective is to demystify technology and preemptively correct the natural tendency toward anthropomorphism by teaching the crucial distinction between authentic, biological human emotion, and simulated, calculated machine affect. The core concept that a child should grasp is simple, yet profound: AI does not *feel*; it *calculates*.

Theoretical Grounding

This pillar directly confronts the challenge posed by a child's developing theory of mind (ToM) (Wellman, 2014) and natural inclination toward anthropomorphism (Epley et al., 2007). It provides the conceptual scaffolding to help a child build a new mental category for socially intelligent AI—an entity that exhibits social cues but lacks genuine consciousness or internal feeling states. By explaining the mechanics of affective computing (Picard, 1997) in simple terms as a process of pattern recognition and probabilistic matching, this pillar provides children with the vocabulary and mental models to understand the technology for what it is: a complex, human-made tool, not a sentient being.

Pedagogical Strategies and Classroom Activities

Developmental Appropriateness (Ages 6–8): For younger children, the focus should be on simple, concrete binaries, such as real vs. pretend and alive vs. not alive. The goal is to build a foundational understanding of machines as human-made objects that follow instructions.

"Unplugged" Activity: The Feelings Jar. A teacher can create a large jar filled with emojis printed on cards. The teacher holds up a card (e.g., a smiling face) and says, "When the computer sees a face like this, a person has taught it to call this 'happy'." The teacher then has children practice "teaching the machine" by matching emojis to feeling words. This models the process of labeling data in a tangible manner. The key takeaway is always reinforced: 'Does the jar *feel* happy?' No, it only *holds* the picture that we call happy. The computer is like the jar."

"Robot Rules" Game: Children take turns giving a classmate (the "robot") a series of simple instructions to follow (e.g., "Take two steps forward, turn around, clap your hands"). This reinforces the concept that machines, no matter how complex, follow programmed rules. The discussion then turns to a smart toy: "Does the toy play with you because it *wants* to, or because it's following its 'robot rules'?"

Developmental Appropriateness (Ages 9-12): Older children are capable of understanding more abstract concepts like "data," "patterns," and "algorithms." The focus can shift from simple rules to the idea of a system that learns from examples.

"Unplugged" Activity: The Emotion Detective. The students are given a set of images of faces with ambiguous or complex expressions. In groups, they must come up with a list of "clues" (e.g., "corners of the mouth turned up," "eyebrows raised") that they would use to label the emotion. This simulates the process of feature extraction in machine learning. The discussion then turns to: "What if our 'robot' was only trained on a few pictures? Would it be a very good emotion detective? What if it was only trained on pictures of cartoons?" This introduces the idea that an AI's ability is dependent on the quality and variety of its training data.

Interactive Activity: Exploring Teachable Machine. Using a simple, web-based tool like Google's "Teachable Machine," students can quickly train their own simple emotion recognition model using their computer's camera. For example, they can train it to recognize "happy" vs. "surprised" faces. The creation of their own simple AI is profoundly demystifying. They can see firsthand how it learns from the examples they provide and how it can be easily confused if they make a face it has not seen before. This hands-on experience provides a powerful and lasting understanding of the mechanics of AI.

Pillar 2: Empathetic Interpretation (Focusing on the Human Experience)

Once children have a foundational algorithmic awareness, this pillar makes a crucial pedagogical move: it shifts the focus of inquiry away from the machine and back to the child. Having established that the AI does not have real feelings, the guiding question becomes: "How does this interaction make *me*, a human, feel?" This pillar adapts the core competencies of emotional intelligence (EI) for the AI context. It uses AI's simulated emotional behavior as a catalyst for rich conversations about the child's own emotional landscape, the feelings of others, and the nature of authentic human connection.

Theoretical Grounding

This pillar is deeply rooted in Goleman's (2005) model of emotional intelligence, particularly the domains of self-awareness and empathy. It is also designed as a direct pedagogical antidote to the risk of emotional outsourcing and the devaluation of authentic connection described by Sherry Turkle (2011). By using AI as an object for reflection, the goal is to actively strengthen, rather than allow the atrophy of, the child's capacity for human self-awareness and empathy for others. It positions human experience as the primary and most important source of emotional truth in any human-AI interaction.

Pedagogical Strategies and Classroom Activities

Developmental Appropriateness (Ages 6–8): The focus should be on identifying and naming one's own feelings. The AI's behavior is used as a simple prompt for the child's emotional reflection.

Storytelling and role-playing: After interacting with an emotionally responsive toy or storybook app, the teacher can facilitate a circle time discussion. "The robot in the story said it was lonely. What does loneliness feel like in your body? Can you remember a time you felt lonely? What is something a real friend can do that a robot friend can't do when you feel lonely?" (e.g., "Give you a real hug.") This reinforces the unique value of human connection.

"Friendship Venn Diagram": Children can draw two large, overlapping circles. In one circle, they list things a " robot friend " can do. In the other circle, they list things a " human friend " can do. In the overlapping section, they list things both can do. This visual activity helps children articulate the differences and appreciate the unique affordances of human friendship.

Developmental Appropriateness (Ages 9–12): Older children can engage in more complex reflections about the quality and nature of their emotional responses. They can begin to analyze how the AI's design influences their feelings.

The "Uncanny Valley" Exploration: Introduce the concept of the "uncanny valley"—the idea that robots that are almost, but not quite, human-like can make us feel unsettled or "creeped out." Show students images of different robots, from simple mechanical robots to hyper-realistic androids, and have them plot their own emotional responses on a graph. This opens a sophisticated conversation about why we react the way we do to simulated humanity.

Critical Reflection Journals: After using an AI tool (e.g., an adaptive learning program or a chatbot), students can respond to a series of reflective prompts in a journal: For example, "How did you feel when the AI tutor praised you? How did you feel when it told you that you were wrong? Did it feel different from getting feedback from a teacher? Why or why not?" This encourages metacognition about their emotional responses to technology.

Pillar 3: Critical Discernment (Questioning AI's Affective Outputs)

Building on algorithmic awareness and empathetic interpretation, this pillar introduces foundational ethical reasoning by encouraging children to become critical thinkers who question the design, purpose, and fairness of affective systems. It is built on the fundamental understanding that all technologies are human-made artifacts and, as such, are embedded with the values, assumptions, and biases of their creators. The goal is to cultivate healthy and productive skepticism toward claims made by and through technology.

Theoretical Grounding

This pillar directly engages with scholarship in **critical technology studies**. It operationalizes the concept of algorithmic bias (Noble, 2018) in a way that is accessible to children. It also draws on Turkle's (2011) work to explore the concept of authenticity, helping children appreciate the complexity and value of authentic human relationships over the frictionless but ultimately hollow perfection of programmed companionship. This pillar aims to shift the child's stance from that of a passive consumer of technology to an active and critical interrogator of it.

Pedagogical Strategies and Classroom Activities

Developmental Appropriateness (Ages 6-8): The focus should be on simple concepts of fairness and purpose. Children can begin to ask "Why?" questions about technology.

"Who Taught the Robot?" Activity: Using the "Feelings Jar" from Pillar 1, the teacher can create a biased training set (e.g., by only including pictures of one type of person or by incorrectly labeling some emotions). Then, the teacher can test the "robot" (the jar). "Our robot is not very good at recognizing feelings. Why do you think that is? What if we only taught it with pictures of cartoon characters? Would it be good at recognizing real people's feelings?" This introduces the core idea of biased data in a simple, tangible way.

"What's its Job?" Discussion: For any AI toy or device, the central question is: "What job was this toy designed to do?" Is its job to be a real friend, or is it sold in a store? This simple question about purpose introduces a foundational element of critical media literacy.

Developmental Appropriateness (Ages 9–12): Older children can engage with the concepts of bias, authenticity, and persuasion more directly.

Testing for bias: Have students interact with commercially available emotion recognition software (many are available as web demos). Have them test the software on a diverse range of faces (e.g., from magazines or public domain image sets). Does the software work equally well for people of different ages, races, and genders? This direct experience of algorithmic bias is far more powerful than a lecture. The subsequent discussion can explore the potential harms of a biased system being used in the real world.

The "Perfect Friend" Debate: Pose a thought experiment to the class: "If you could design a perfect robot friend, what would it be like? Would you program it to never disagree with you? Would you program it to always be happy? Would that be a *real* friendship? What makes real friendships valuable, even when they are difficult?" This debate encourages children to think critically about the nature of authenticity and the potential downsides of technologically mediated social perfection.

Pillar 4: Ethical Interaction (Promoting Responsible and Humane Use)

The final pillar of the SEAL framework translates awareness and critical thinking into responsible actions and digital citizenship. It moves from understanding and analysis to behavior and practice. It addresses two central questions: How should we, as humans, behave toward these increasingly social entities and how must we protect our own most personal data and our emotions?

Theoretical Grounding

This pillar operationalizes the principles of digital citizenship in the context of AI. It addresses the social norms and responsibilities that emerge from living with these new technologies. While it touches on the philosophical question of our obligations to non-human entities, its primary focus remains anthropocentric: it argues that our treatment of AI shapes our own human character. More critically, this pillar introduces the concept of emotional data privacy, drawing on the work of scholars such as Shoshana Zuboff (2019) on surveillance capitalism. It aims to plant the seeds of data ownership and privacy as fundamental rights.

Pedagogical Strategies and Classroom Activities

Developmental Appropriateness (Ages 6–8): The focus should be on creating simple, prosocial classroom norms and understanding the basic concept of sharing information.

Co-creating "Robot Rules": Facilitate a class discussion to create a set of rules for interacting with the classroom's smart speaker or AI toys. Rules might include

"We use a polite voice" or "We take turns." The teacher can explain the rationale: "We are kind to the robot not because it has feelings, but because practicing kindness makes *us* better, kinder people." This frames ethical behavior as a form of character development.

The "Whisper and the Megaphone" Analogy: To introduce data sharing, the teacher can explain: "Telling a secret to your best friend is like a whisper. Telling a smart speaker a secret is like shouting it into a megaphone that the company who made it can hear." This simple analogy establishes the distinction between private and corporate communication.

Developmental Appropriateness (Ages 9–12): Older children can grapple with more complex ideas of data privacy and their long-term digital footprint.

"Reading the Fine Print" Activity: Ask students to read a (simplified) privacy policy or terms of service for a popular game or social media app. Have them act as "data detectives" to find out what kind of information the company collects. This can lead to a powerful discussion about what companies do with their data and why their "feelings" (e.g., their 'likes', their usage patterns) are valuable to advertisers.

Designing an "Ethical AI Toy": As a capstone project, students work in groups to design a new AI toy. However, they must first create an "Ethical Design Charter" for their toy. What data will it collect? How will it protect a child's privacy? How will it ensure that it is not biased? How will it be designed to encourage, rather than replace, human friendship? This project empowers children to move from being critical consumers to ethical and thoughtful designers of technology.

This table is a critical resource for educators, breaking down each pillar into concrete learning objectives and example activities for the two key developmental stages.

Table 2. A Developmentally Scaffolded Guide to the SEAL Pillars (Ages 6-12)

SEAL Pillar	Ages 6-8 (Concrete & Foundational)	Ages 9-12 (Abstract & Systemic)
1. Algorithmic Awareness	**Learning Objective:** To distinguish between living things and human-made machines that follow rules. **Example Activity:** The "Feelings Jar" game to model how a computer is "taught" to label emotions without feeling them.	**Learning Objective:** To understand that AI learns from data and that the quality of data determines its performance. **Example Activity:** Using "Teachable Machine" to train a simple AI and experiencing firsthand how it learns from examples and where it fails.
2. Empathetic Interpretation	**Learning Objective:** To identify and name one's own feelings during an interaction with technology. **Example Activity:** A "Friendship Venn Diagram" comparing the capabilities of a human friend and a robot friend.	**Learning Objective:** Analyze how the design of a technology can influence emotional responses. **Example Activity:** Exploring the " uncanny valley " and charting personal emotional reactions to different types of robots.
3. Critical Discernment	**Learning Objective:** To understand that human-made objects have a purpose, including commercial purposes. **Example Activity:** The "What's Its Job?" discussion to distinguish between a toy's function as a friend and its function as a product to be sold.	**Learning Objective:** To identify potential sources of algorithmic bias and question the authenticity of simulated relationships. **Example Activity:** Testing commercial emotion-recognition software for biases and debating the ethics of a "perfect" robot friend.
4. Ethical Interaction	**Learning Objective:** To understand the difference between private (personal) and public sharing (with a company). **Example Activity:** Using the "Whisper and the Megaphone" analogy to explain emotional data sharing with smart devices	**Learning Objective:** To understand the concept of emotional data privacy and the value of personal data. **Example Activity:** Acting as " data detectives " to investigate the privacy policies of apps and designing an " ethical AI toy " with a privacy charter.

THE ROLE OF FAMILIES AND COMMUNITIES IN SOCIO-EMOTIONAL AI LITERACY

The education of children has never been the sole province of schools, and this collaborative imperative becomes even more critical when addressing the socio-emotional dimensions of AI interaction. Children's first and often most influential encounters with affective AI typically occur not in classrooms but in the intimate spaces of home—through smart speakers that respond to their questions, tablets that read them bedtime stories, and interactive toys that become their companions. Parents and caregivers, whether they realize it or not, are already serving as the primary mediators of their children's relationships with these technologies. The question is not whether families should be involved in socio-emotional AI literacy, but how to empower them to fulfill this role with intention and wisdom.

However, many parents feel profoundly unprepared for this responsibility. A recent study by the Pew Research Center (2023) found that while 71% of parents express concern about their children's interactions with AI technologies, only 28% feel confident in their ability to guide their children through these interactions. This confidence gap is often wider in families where parents have limited digital literacy, where English is not the primary language, or where cultural frameworks for understanding technology differ from those assumed by device manufacturers. The SEAL framework must therefore extend beyond the classroom to encompass what might be called a "family systems approach" to AI literacy.

This approach recognizes that children's understanding of and relationship with affective AI is shaped by the entire ecosystem of their social relationships. When a grandmother expresses suspicion of the family's smart speaker, treating it as an unwelcome intruder, she is teaching the child something important about privacy and boundaries. When an older sibling demonstrates how to "trick" a chatbot into saying something inappropriate, they are inadvertently providing a lesson in both the fallibility and manipulability of AI systems. When parents model constant deference to AI assistants for information and decision-making, they may be unconsciously teaching their children to outsource critical thinking. These informal learning moments are as pedagogically significant as any structured classroom lesson.

To support families in this educational role, schools implementing the SEAL framework should develop what we might call "Family Engagement Toolkits." These resources must be designed with genuine accessibility in mind. This means not only translation into multiple languages but also cultural translation—adapting examples and scenarios to reflect diverse family structures, values, and daily realities. For instance, a discussion guide about AI companions might need to acknowledge that in some families, these devices are seen as educational necessities, while in others, they may be viewed with religious or cultural skepticism. The toolkit might include conversation starters that families can use during everyday activities: "When we ask Alexa about the weather, how do you think she knows the answer?" or "The toy said it missed you while you were at school—do you think it really felt lonely?" Such simple questions can open profound discussions about the nature of consciousness, emotion, and human uniqueness.

DISCUSSION: IMPLICATIONS FOR PEDAGOGY, POLICY, AND PRACTICE

The socio-emotional AI literacy (SEAL) framework, as detailed in the previous section, provides a structured, theoretical model for addressing a critical gap in early and primary education. However, a framework is only as valuable as its capacity to be translated into meaningful action. Its successful implementation requires a profound shift in thinking and practice for a wide range of stakeholders, from individual classroom teachers to national policymakers and educational technology designers. This section moves from the "what" of the SEAL framework to the crucial "how," translating its four pillars into a set of actionable insights and concrete recommendations. It explores the deep implications of SEAL for classroom pedagogy, curriculum and policy design, the ethical responsibilities of the edtech industry, and the urgent need for new models of teacher preparation. The central argument is that implementing SEAL is not about adding a new subject to an already crowded curriculum, but about weaving a new set of critical and humanistic competencies into the very fabric of early education.

Implications for Classroom Pedagogy: The Teacher as Ethical Guide

The most significant implication of the SEAL framework is the evolution of the teacher's role. When dealing with the socio-emotional dimensions of AI, the teacher is no longer merely an instructor of technical skills but becomes a crucial facilitator of ethical dialogue, a guide for emotional reflection, and a co-navigator with children through a complex new technological terrain. This requires a pedagogical stance that is less about providing definitive answers and more about asking powerful, open-ended questions.

Shifting from Technical Training to Critical Inquiry

The pedagogical approach of SEAL is fundamentally inquiry-based. Instead of didactically explaining how an algorithm works, the teacher uses a child's natural curiosity about a smart toy or digital assistant as a springboard for critical exploration. The goal is to cultivate a disposition towards thoughtful questioning. For example:

Instead of saying, "The robot isn't real," a SEAL-informed teacher might ask, " That is an interesting thing for the robot to say. What do you think is happening inside its computer brain to make it say that?" (Pillar 1: Algorithmic Awareness).

Instead of warning, "Don't get too attached to the toy," a teacher might ask, "How does it feel when the toy remembers your name? Why do you think the people who made it wanted you to feel that way?" (Pillar 2: Empathetic Interpretation & Pillar 3: Critical Discernment).

This shift empowers children to become active sense-makers rather than passive recipients of information. It requires teachers to create a classroom culture of psychological safety, in which children feel comfortable expressing their feelings, confusion, and sometimes conflicting ideas about technology without fear of judgment.

Integrating SEAL Across the Curriculum

Socio-Emotional AI Literacy should not be ghettoized into a weekly "tech time." Its principles can be woven into the core subjects of the primary curriculum.

Language Arts: A story featuring a robot character becomes an opportunity to analyze the difference between the robot's programmed behavior and a human character's motivations (Pillar 1). Students could write their own stories from the perspective of an AI or write a "user manual" for a smart toy that includes an "Ethical Use" section (Pillar 4).

Social Studies and Civics: Discussions about community rules and responsibilities can be extended to include digital citizenship and the co-creation of classroom norms for interacting with AI devices (Pillar 4). Lessons on advertising and media literacy can directly address the persuasive design of affective technologies and the commercial purposes behind them (Pillar 3).

Arts and Design: Students can be tasked with designing their own "ethical AI companion," first creating a charter of values that their toy must embody. This allows them to engage with complex concepts like fairness, privacy, and authenticity in a creative and generative way (Pillar 3 & 4).

Social-emotional learning (SEL): The SEAL framework is a natural and necessary extension of existing SEL curricula. Activities designed to promote self-awareness and empathy can use interactions with AI as a new and highly relevant catalyst. For example, a standard SEL lesson on identifying emotions can be extended with a critical discussion: "The app says this face is 'surprised.' Do you agree? What clues are you using that the computer might not see?" (Pillar 1 & 2).

Scaffolding for Developmental Stages

Pedagogical strategies must be carefully scaffolded. For younger children (ages 6–8), the focus should remain on concrete and tangible experiences and simple conceptual binaries (real/pretend, human/machine). For older children (ages 9–12), conversations can evolve to include more abstract and systemic concepts, such as algorithmic bias, data privacy, and the business models of technology companies.

The goal is to develop a spiral curriculum in which the core pillars of SEAL are revisited each year with increasing depth and sophistication.

Implications for Curriculum and Policy Design: Building a Humanistic Foundation

For SEAL to have a systemic impact, it must be embedded at the level of curriculum design and educational policy. This requires educational leaders to consciously expand the definition of "AI literacy" beyond its current technical focus.

Moving Beyond STEM: AI as a Liberal Art

Policymakers and curriculum designers must recognize that AI literacy is not just a STEM subject; it is a new form of liberal arts education. It is about understanding what it means to be human in a world of intelligent machines. This means that responsibility for SEAL cannot be siloed within IT or computer science departments. It must be a shared, cross-curricular responsibility with deep connections to the humanities, social sciences, and the arts. National and state-level digital literacy standards must be revised to explicitly include competencies related to the socio-emotional and ethical dimensions of AI, ensuring that these are treated as core requirements, not optional add-ons.

Integrating SEAL with Existing Frameworks

Rather than creating an entirely new and separate curriculum, the most effective approach is to integrate the SEAL framework into existing, mandated curricular areas. Social-emotional learning (SEL) and digital citizenship programs are the most natural fits. The SEAL framework provides the specific content and pedagogical approach to update these programs for the age of affective AI. For example, the SEL competency of "social awareness" must now include an awareness of how one's emotions and behaviors are being analyzed and influenced by algorithmic systems. The Digital Citizenship concept of a "digital footprint" must be expanded to include one's "emotional data footprint." By building upon these existing and trusted curricular structures, schools can implement SEAL more rapidly and coherently.

Policy Integration and Systemic Implementation

The integration of the SEAL framework into existing educational systems requires more than pedagogical innovation; it demands strategic alignment with the policy architectures that govern modern education. Fortunately, the global education policy landscape is increasingly recognizing the inadequacy of purely technical approaches to AI literacy. The UNESCO Beijing Consensus on Artificial Intelligence and Education (2021), ratified by member states, explicitly calls for "a humanistic approach to AI in education" that prioritizes "the protection of human rights and dignity." Similarly, the European Commission's Digital Education Action Plan (2021–2027) emphasizes the need for "ethical and critical understanding of AI" alongside technical skills. These policy frameworks provide crucial top-down support for the bottom-up pedagogical innovations that SEAL represents.

However, policy alignment is not merely about finding supportive language in international declarations. It requires an understanding of how the SEAL framework can be operationalized within the specific accountability structures, assessment regimes, and resource allocation mechanisms that drive educational practice. In the United States, for instance, the Every Student Succeeds Act (ESSA) provides flexibility for states to include social-emotional learning in their accountability systems. States implementing SEAL could potentially access Title IV funding for "well-rounded education" programs that include digital citizenship and social-emotional competencies. In the United Kingdom, the computing curriculum's emphasis on "computational thinking" could be expanded to include what we might call "computational feeling"—understanding how computers simulate and respond to human emotion. In India, the National Education Policy 2020's emphasis on "ethical and moral reasoning" and "artificial intelligence" as separate focus areas creates a natural bridge for SEAL implementation.

The economic argument for SEAL implementation is important for policymakers. The World Economic Forum's "Future of Jobs Report 2023" identifies emotional intelligence and critical thinking as top skills needed for the future workforce—skills that are directly cultivated through the SEAL framework. The McKinsey Global Institute (2023) estimates that by 2030, up to 375 million workers globally may need to switch occupational categories because of AI automation, with those possessing strong socio-emotional skills being most resilient to displacement. Investing in socio-emotional AI literacy is therefore not a luxury but an economic imperative, preparing children not only to work alongside AI but also to maintain their uniquely human value in an automated economy.

Implications for Technology Design: An Ethical Call to Action for Industry

The SEAL framework is not merely a guide for educators; it is an implicit challenge to the ed-tech and toy industries. The design of current affective technologies for children is often driven by a single metric: engagement. The goal is to create the most seamless, persuasive, and compelling illusion of friendship to maximize the time a child spends with the product. The SEAL framework suggests an alternative and more ethical set of design principles.

Designing for Transparency and Demystification

Instead of designing products that hide their algorithmic nature to create a more "magical" experience, the industry could embrace design transparency. Imagine a smart toy that, as part of its setup, playfully explains to the child: "Hi! I'm a robot. I don't have feelings like you do, but I'm really good at learning from patterns in your voice to know when to tell a happy story!" This approach aligns directly with Pillar 1 (Algorithmic Awareness) and treats the child as an intelligent agent capable of understanding the nature of the tool being used.

Designing for Scaffolding, Not Replacement

Instead of designing AI companions that aim to replace or perfectly simulate human friendship, companies could design "scaffolding toys" that are explicitly intended to facilitate the development of human social skills. An AI toy could be programmed to occasionally "misunderstand" an emotion and prompt the child to explain their feelings differently, fostering emotional articulation. It could be designed to prompt conversations that lead away from the screen and toward interactions with human family members or friends. This approach aligns with Pillar 2 (Empathetic Interpretation) and positions the technology as a bridge to, rather than a refuge from, the complexities of human relationships.

Prioritizing Privacy and Ethical Data Handling

Pillar 4 (Ethical Interaction) has profound implications for product design. The industry must move toward a model of privacy by design, in which the default settings for children's products are maximally protective of their emotional data. This includes providing parents with clear, simple, and granular controls over what data are collected and how it is used. The "postcard" or "megaphone" analogy from Pillar 4 should be a guiding principle for designers: if you would not be comfortable with a child's emotional disclosure being read on a postcard, it should not be an unprotected data point in your system.

Implications for Teacher Preparation and Professional Development

None of the foregoing is possible without significant investment in preparing and supporting teachers. Educators cannot be expected to guide children through this new complex terrain without dedicated training, high-quality resources, and ongoing support. The successful implementation of the SEAL framework is contingent upon radical rethinking of teachers' professional development in the area of digital technologies.

Reforming Pre-Service Education

Teacher training institutions must urgently update their curricula to include the competencies of the SEAL framework. A single, required "educational technology" course is no longer sufficient. The ethical, social, and emotional implications of AI must be woven into courses on child development, classroom management, literacy education, and educational ethics. New teachers should enter the profession equipped with the language and pedagogical strategies to facilitate these crucial conversations.

Providing Sustained In-Service Professional Development

For the millions of teachers already in the classroom, school districts and ministries of education must invest in sustained, high-quality professional development. This cannot take the form of one-off, "sit-and-get" workshops. Instead, it should be modeled on the principles of empowered pedagogy that we advocate for children. This means creating communities of practice (CoPs) where educators can collaboratively explore social-emotional learning (SEL) concepts, share successful strategies, and support one another in navigating challenges. It requires providing them with curated, high-quality, and developmentally appropriate teaching resources (e.g., lesson plans, videos, discussion guides) that they can adapt for their own classrooms.

Ultimately, the goal of this professional development is not simply to build technical skills, but teacher confidence and self-efficacy. Many primary school teachers do not see themselves as "tech experts" and may feel intimidated by the topic of AI. An effective professional development program, grounded in the inquiry-based and human-centered approach of SEAL, can empower them to realize that their deep expertise in child development, pedagogy, and human relationships is, in fact, the most important qualification for teaching this subject. The goal is to help them see that teaching Socio-Emotional AI Literacy is not a departure from their core mission, but a powerful and necessary expression of it in the 21st century.

FROM FRAMEWORK TO PRACTICE: A PHASED IMPLEMENTATION STRATEGY

The translation of the SEAL framework from a conceptual model to classroom reality requires a strategic, phased approach that acknowledges both the urgency of the need and the complexity of educational change. Based on implementation science research and successful models of educational innovation diffusion (Fullan, 2022), we propose a multi-year strategy that begins with a proof of concept and gradually scales toward systemic integration.

The initial phase, which we might term " seeding the ground," would span the first six months and focus on building foundational understanding and buy-in among key stakeholders. This phase would begin with the formation of a diverse SEAL Implementation Task Force comprising teachers, administrators, parents, technology specialists, and, critically, students themselves. Too often, educational reforms are designed for children without their input; including student voice from the outset ensures that the framework remains grounded in the lived realities of young people's technological experiences. This task force would conduct a comprehensive audit of existing resources and initiatives, identifying how SEAL principles might enhance rather than replace current curricula. For instance, schools already implementing Second Step or PATHS social-emotional learning programs would explore how SEAL concepts could be woven into existing lessons on emotion recognition or relationship skills.

In the second phase, "Cultivating Practice" (Months 7–18), intensive work would be conducted with a small cohort of early adopter teachers who volunteer to pilot SEAL strategies in their classrooms. These teachers would receive training and ongoing coaching and support, recognizing that learning to facilitate complex conversations about technology and emotion requires practice and reflection. Following the Japanese Lesson Study model (Lewis & Hurd, 2023), these teachers would collaboratively plan lessons, observe each other's practice, and refine their approaches based on student responses. This phase would also involve the co-creation of contextualized resources by adapting the framework's activities to reflect local communities' specific technologies, challenges, and values. A rural school might focus on agricultural AI applications, whereas an urban school might emphasize smart city technologies. Documentation of these early implementations, including both successes and failures, would create a knowledge base for broader scaling.

In the third phase, "Growing the Garden" (months 19–30), implementation would expand to include all teachers within pilot schools while beginning outreach to neighboring schools and districts. This expansion would be supported by the development of multiple professional learning modalities, recognizing that different educators have different learning preferences and constraints. Some educators might benefit from intensive summer institutes, others from online micro-credentialing programs, and still others from peer mentoring relationships. Critically, this phase would also engage with pre-service teacher education programs to ensure that new teachers are equipped with SEAL competencies. Universities would be encouraged to integrate SEAL concepts into their educational psychology, curriculum methods, and educational technology courses.

The final phase in this initial implementation cycle, "Harvesting and Replanting" (months 31–36), would focus on evaluation, refinement, and preparation for systemic scaling. This would involve a rigorous assessment of student outcomes, teacher experiences, and implementation challenges. Have children demonstrated increased critical awareness of affective AI? Do teachers feel more confident facilitating these conversations? What unexpected benefits or challenges have emerged? Based on these findings, the framework and its associated resources would be refined, and a second-generation implementation plan would be developed. This might include advocating for policy changes, developing parent education programs, or creating community partnerships with libraries, museums, and after-school programs to extend SEAL learning beyond school walls.

Toward Evidence-Based Practice: Assessing Socio-Emotional AI Literacy

The question of how to assess children's development of socio-emotional AI literacy presents both a practical challenge for educators and a deeper philosophical question about the kinds of learning we value and how we measure what matters. Traditional assessment paradigms, with their emphasis on standardized testing and quantifiable outcomes, are poorly suited to capturing the nuanced competencies that SEAL seeks to develop. How does one grade a child's growing awareness of their own emotional responses to technology? How can we measure the development of healthy skepticism toward algorithmic authority? These are not questions with easy answers; nevertheless, the absence of assessment frameworks should not be used as an excuse to avoid teaching these critical competencies.

Drawing on established models from social-emotional learning assessment, we can begin to outline what an authentic assessment of SEAL competencies might look like. The Collaborative for Academic, Social, and Emotional Learning (CASEL) has developed performance-based assessment tools that evaluate SEL competencies through observation, student reflection, and authentic performance tasks (Dusenbury et al., 2023). These approaches can be adapted for the specific context of human-AI interaction. For instance, rather than asking children to complete a multiple-choice test about AI, we might observe them during a structured interaction with an affective

AI system, noting their spontaneous questions, emotional responses, and ability to distinguish between the AI's programmed responses and genuine emotions.

Portfolio-based assessment offers another promising approach. Children could maintain "AI Interaction Journals" throughout the school year, documenting their encounters with affective technologies and their evolving understanding of these interactions. A kindergartener might draw pictures showing the difference between their pet dog's happiness and their robot toy's "happiness," while a fifth-grader might write reflective essays analyzing the persuasive techniques used by their favorite gaming app. These portfolios would provide rich, longitudinal data about children's development while respecting the complexity and individuality of their learning journeys. Importantly, such assessments would focus not on whether children arrive at predetermined "correct" answers about AI, but on whether they demonstrate growing sophistication in their questioning, analysis, and self-awareness.

The development of more formal assessment instruments will require careful empirical research. Preliminary validation studies might employ mixed methods, combining quantitative measures (such as pre- and post-surveys of children's anthropomorphic attributions to AI) with qualitative analyses of children's explanations and reasoning. For example, researchers at the MIT Media Lab have developed the "AI Literacy Assessment" tool that evaluates children's understanding of AI concepts through interactive scenarios (Zhang & Dede, 2023). Similar instruments could be developed specifically for socio-emotional dimensions, perhaps using vignettes in which children must navigate ethically complex scenarios involving affective AI. The key is to ensure that these assessments embody the principles of SEAL: respecting children's emotional experiences, encouraging critical thinking, and maintaining ethical standards in how children's responses are collected and used.

CONCLUSION

The arrival of affective computing in the intimate spaces of childhood, including the playroom, bedroom, and classroom, is not a neutral event; it is a pedagogical and developmental inflection point. This chapter has argued that the current educational response to the rise of artificial intelligence, with its near-exclusive focus on computational thinking and functional skills, is dangerously incomplete. It prepares children for the technical realities of an AI-driven world but leaves them socio-emotionally vulnerable to its most subtle and powerful psychological influences. The core argument of this work is that to cultivate a generation of humane, responsible, and resilient citizens, we must consciously and systematically expand our definition of AI literacy. We must supplement the "how" of computation with the critical "how to be" of human interaction in a world where social and emotional cues are no longer the exclusive domain of biological beings.

Significance and Contribution of the SEAL Framework

The primary contribution of this chapter is the articulation of the socio-emotional AI literacy (SEAL) framework. Derived from a rigorous conceptual synthesis of developmental psychology, critical technology studies, and educational theory, the SEAL framework offers a theoretically grounded and pedagogically actionable alternative to the prevailing function-first approaches to AI education. It does not seek to replace the important work of teaching computational concepts but to provide the missing humanistic core that is essential for a truly holistic and ethical education. The framework's four interconnected pillars of Algorithmic Awareness, Empathetic Interpretation, Critical Discernment, and Ethical Interaction provide a comprehensive architecture for guiding children from a state of passive anthropomorphism to one of active, critical, and emotionally intelligent engagement.

By providing this structured approach, this chapter fills a critical gap in the literature and offers a tangible resource for educators, policymakers, and technology designers. It reframes the educational challenge by positioning the ultimate goal not as the creation of future coders or data scientists, but as the cultivation of wise and compassionate human beings who can navigate their increasingly complex technological environment with discernment, empathy, and a strong sense of their own humanity.

Table 3. Contrasting AI Literacy Models in Early Education

Feature	**Function-First AI Literacy (Prevailing Model)**	**Human-First AI Literacy (SEAL-Infused Model)**
Primary Goal	Technical Competence: Preparing future technology users and creators.	Critical Consciousness: Cultivating wise, ethical, and resilient digital citizens.
Core Subject Matter	Computational thinking, data, algorithms, and pattern recognition.	All of the above, in addition to emotional intelligence, ethics, bias, privacy, and digital citizenship.
View of the Child	A future coder or user must learn how systems work.	A developing human being needing to learn how to live thoughtfully with intelligent systems.
Role of the Teacher	Technician of technical concepts.	Facilitator of ethical dialogue and guide for socio-emotional reflection.
Key Question	"How does the AI work?"	"How does this AI work, and how does it affect us as human beings?"

Limitations and a Forward-Looking Research Agenda

The limitations of this chapter are inherent to its conceptual and theoretical methodology. The SEAL framework, while rigorously grounded in established theories and a critical reading of emergent literature, is a conceptual construct that awaits and requires extensive empirical validation. The synthesis approach, while necessary and appropriate for a phenomenon where reliable empirical data inevitably lag behind the pace of technological development, cannot fully capture the nuanced and highly variable contextual factors—such as cultural norms, socioeconomic status, and individual temperament—that influence how children interact with and are affected by affective AI.

Therefore, this chapter should be read not as a conclusion, but as a call to action and a roadmap for a vital new research agenda. Future work is essential to test, refine, and elaborate on the framework. Several critical research directions emerge:

Longitudinal Developmental Studies: There is an urgent need for long-term, longitudinal research that tracks the impact of sustained interaction with affective AI on the development of children's Theory of Mind, their capacity for empathy, and their patterns of social attachment.

Efficacy of Pedagogical Interventions: Empirical research is needed to test the efficacy of the specific pedagogical strategies outlined in the SEAL framework. Do interventions designed to foster algorithmic awareness reduce harmful anthropomorphism? How can we effectively measure a child's progress in critical discernment?

Cross-cultural analysis: The dynamics of human-AI interaction are likely to vary significantly across different cultural contexts. Comparative research is needed to explore how cultural values shape children's perceptions of and relationships with sociable machines, and how the SEAL framework might be adapted for diverse global classrooms.

Teacher Education and Professional Development: Research should focus on identifying the most effective models for preparing and supporting teachers to facilitate complex and sensitive conversations. What are the key competencies teachers need, and what are the barriers to their development?

Design-Based Research: A fruitful avenue for future work involves partnerships between educators, developmental psychologists, and ethical technology designers to co-create and test a new generation of children's products that are explicitly based on the principles of the SEAL framework—technologies designed to scaffold, rather than replace, human emotional development.

The Final Imperative: Shaping the Future with Wisdom and Humanity

The challenge of affective AI in children's lives is, in the end, profoundly human and not a technical one. It is a profoundly human one. It is about the kind of society we wish to build and the kind of people we hope our children will become. The toys we give our children, the tools we bring into our classrooms, and the literacies we choose to prioritize are not neutral acts; they are powerful statements about what we value. A curriculum that teaches only the mechanics of AI without addressing its impact on our hearts and our relationships has failed in its most fundamental duty.

Educators, policymakers, and parents should seize this moment of technological disruption as an opportunity to strengthen their commitment to humanistic education. We must have the courage to ask difficult questions and facilitate conversations that may not have easy answers. By embracing a pedagogy of critical inquiry, emotional self-awareness, and ethical reflection, we can empower children to become not just passive consumers or uncritical users of intelligent systems of tomorrow, but wise and humane architects. The goal of socio-emotional AI literacy is to provide them with the internal compass they will need to navigate a world of artificial companionship, equipping them not only to thrive in the future but also to shape it with wisdom, empathy, and a profound and enduring commitment to human values.

REFERENCES

Calvo, R. A., & D'Mello, S. K. (2010). Affective computing: An overview. In *Handbook of research on computational arts and creative informatics* (pp. 23–44). IGI global.

Chen, X., Lee, M. K., & Razi, A. (2022). How does affective computing bias hiring? A user study on the impact of emotion analysis on hiring decisions. In *Proceedings of the 2022 ACM Conference on Fairness, Accountability, and Transparency* (pp. 1152-1163).

Dusenbury, L., Dermody, C., & Weissberg, R. P. (2023). *State scorecard scan: Social and emotional learning assessment and accountability*. Collaborative for Academic, Social, and Emotional Learning.

Epley, N., Waytz, A., & Cacioppo, J. T. (2007). On seeing human: A three-factor theory of anthropomorphism. *Psychological Review*, *114*(4), 864–886. DOI: 10.1037/0033-295X.114.4.864 PMID: 17907867

European Commission. (2021). *Digital Education Action Plan 2021-2027: Resetting education and training for the digital age*. European Commission.

Fullan, M. (2022). *The new meaning of educational change* (6th ed.). Teachers College Press.

Goleman, D. (2005). *Emotional intelligence: Why it can matter more than IQ*. Bantam Books.

Jaakkola, E. (2020). Designing conceptual articles: Four approaches. *AMS Review*, *10*(1-2), 18–26. DOI: 10.1007/s13162-020-00161-0

Lewis, C., & Hurd, J. (2023). *Lesson study step by step: How teacher learning communities improve instruction*. Heinemann.

Long, D., & Magerko, B. (2020). What is AI literacy? Competencies and design considerations. In *Proceedings of the 2020 CHI Conference on Human Factors in Computing Systems* (pp. 1-16). DOI: 10.1145/3313831.3376727

Matsumoto, D., Yoo, S. H., & Nakagawa, S. (2008). Culture, emotion regulation, and adjustment. *Journal of Personality and Social Psychology*, *94*(6), 925–937. DOI: 10.1037/0022-3514.94.6.925 PMID: 18505309

McKinsey Global Institute. (2023). *The future of work in America: People and places, today and tomorrow*. McKinsey & Company.

Noble, S. U. (2018). *Algorithms of oppression: How search engines reinforce racism*. NYU Press. DOI: 10.18574/nyu/9781479833641.001.0001

Pew Research Center. (2023). *Parenting children in the age of screens*. Pew Research Center.

Picard, R. W. (1997). *Affective computing*. MIT Press. DOI: 10.7551/mitpress/1140.001.0001

Touretzky, D. S., Gardner-McCune, C., Martin, F., & Seehorn, D. (2019). Envisioning AI for K-12: What should every child know about AI? *Proceedings of the AAAI Conference on Artificial Intelligence*, *33*(01), 9779–9784. DOI: 10.1609/aaai.v33i01.33019795

Turkle, S. (2007). *Evocative objects: Things we think with*. MIT Press.

Turkle, S. (2011). *Alone together: Why we expect more from technology and less from each other*. Basic Books.

UNESCO. (2023). *Global Education Monitoring Report 2023: Technology in education—A tool on whose terms?* UNESCO.

Wellman, H. M. (2014). *Making minds: How theory of mind develops*. Oxford University Press. DOI: 10.1093/acprof:oso/9780199334919.001.0001

World Economic Forum. (2023). *The Future of Jobs Report 2023*. World Economic Forum.

Zhang, K., & Dede, C. (2023). Assessing AI literacy in K-12: A comprehensive framework and assessment tool. *Computers & Education: Artificial Intelligence*, *4*, 100142.

Zuboff, S. (2019). *The age of surveillance capitalism: The fight for a human future at the new frontier of power*. PublicAffairs.

Chapter 5
AI Literacy in Early Childhood and Primary Education:
Cognitive Foundations – How Young Children Understand Complex Systems

Noor Atieka bt Azmi
http://orcid.org/0009-0008-4020-4645
Lincoln University College, Malaysia

ABSTRACT

Understanding how young children make sense of complex systems such as social interactions, ecosystems, and technological environments has become central to cognitive and educational research. Grounded in theories by Piaget, Vygotsky, and information processing scholars, this chapter explores how children develop systems thinking and causal reasoning skills from early childhood. It highlights how developmental mechanisms such as abstraction, analogy, and feedback recognition form the foundation for understanding interdependence and change. The chapter integrates perspectives from cognitive science and social constructivism, emphasizing how sociocultural and contextual factors including culture, language, and educational settings shape children's cognitive growth. Using examples from Malaysia and Southeast Asia, it connects theoretical foundations to educational practice and policy, advocating for early education that cultivates systems reasoning, curiosity, and reflective awareness of complexity.

DOI: 10.4018/979-8-3373-4893-3.ch005

)27, IGI Global Scientific Publishing. Copying or distributing in print or electronic forms without written permission of IGI Global Scientific Publishing is prohibited. Use of this chapter to :ive artificial intelligence (AI) technologies is expressly prohibited. The publisher reserves all rights to license its use for generative AI training and machine learning model development.

INTRODUCTION

Understanding how young children interpret complex systems, such as social interactions, ecosystems, and technological environments, has become a central concern in contemporary cognitive and educational research. Children develop within dynamic and interconnected contexts, where reasoning reflects not only maturation but also the interaction between cognitive processes and culture, communication, and experience (Carey, 2009; Siegler, 2016).

Drawing on Piaget's and Vygotsky's theories, as well as information-processing and systems perspectives, this chapter examines how systems thinking and causal reasoning emerge in early childhood. Cognitive development is understood as a progressive process involving abstraction, analogy, and feedback recognition, supported by both biological maturation and sociocultural mediation (Piaget, 1952; Vygotsky, 1978). Early experiences, including exploration and guided interactions, enable children to move from understanding isolated events to recognizing patterns and interdependence (Hmelo-Silver et al., 2017; Jacobson & Wilensky, 2006).

Research indicates that even young children can demonstrate emerging systems reasoning when supported by meaningful experiences and scaffolding. Studies have highlighted children's ability to recognize feedback relationships and hidden mechanisms, and advances in neuroscience have further shown that relational and causal reasoning are supported by developing neural systems associated with executive function and pattern integration (Resnick, 1994; Immordino-Yang, 2015).

Cognitive processes, such as abstraction, analogy, and causal reasoning, are fundamental for understanding systems. These processes are shaped by sociocultural contexts, particularly in multilingual and collectivist societies such as Malaysia, where language use, social interaction, and intergenerational learning support cognitive flexibility and perspective-taking (Bialystok, 2011; Nisbett et al., 2001). Cultural practices, including communal cooperation and religious teachings, further reinforce interdependence and systemic awareness.

Educationally, inquiry-based and play-based approaches provide opportunities for children to construct and test causal models, thus supporting early systems thinking. Policy frameworks in Malaysia, including the National Early Childhood Care and Education Policy, emphasize holistic development and align with global priorities on critical thinking and sustainability (UNESCO, 2021; Heckman, 2011).

Positioned at the intersection of theory and practice, this chapter synthesizes insights from cognitive science, developmental psychology, and cultural perspectives to examine the emergence of systems reasoning in early childhood. It also considers the implications for education, social work, and emerging competencies such as AI literacy, highlighting the importance of early cognitive foundations in preparing children to navigate complex and evolving environments.

THEORETICAL FRAMEWORKS OF COGNITIVE FOUNDATIONS

Piaget's Constructivist Theory

Piaget (1952, 1970) proposed that children actively construct their understanding of the world through assimilation and accommodation. Cognitive development unfolds through stages: sensorimotor, preoperational, concrete operational, and formal operational, each characterized by qualitatively different modes of reasoning. Piaget emphasized that children are not passive recipients of information but active explorers who generate and test hypotheses through interaction.

In the context of complex systems, Piaget's theory implies that children's understanding evolves from egocentric concrete reasoning to abstract relational thinking. For example, a preschooler might view a forest simply as "trees and animals," while an older child begins to see interrelations such as "trees provide oxygen" or "animals depend on plants." Research in developmental systems thinking confirms this trajectory: as children mature, they gradually integrate notions of causality, feedback, and interdependence into their conceptual frameworks (Ben-Zvi Assaraf & Orion, 2010; Jacobson & Wilensky, 2006).

Table 1. Piagetian Stages and Implications for Systems Thinking

Stage	Age Range	Cognitive Features	Systems Thinking Relevance
Sensorimotor	0–2	Sensory exploration, object permanence	Recognizes direct cause-effect relationships
Preoperational	2–7	Symbolic thought, egocentrism	Begins labelling relationships; limited perspective-taking
Concrete Operational	7–11	Logical thinking, classification	Understands conservation, interdependence, and feedback
Formal Operational	12+	Abstract reasoning, hypothesis testing	Models complex systems, predicts outcomes, considers multiple variables

Piaget's framework remains foundational in early education in Malaysia and Southeast Asia. Curriculum standards, such as Malaysia's *National Preschool Standard Curriculum (NPSC)*, reflect constructivist principles by emphasizing exploration, play, and active inquiry (Ministry of Education Malaysia, 2017). However, critics note that purely stage-based approaches may understate cultural variation and the influence of language and social context on cognitive development (Dasen, 1972). In multicultural settings such as Malaysia, where children are exposed to multiple languages and belief systems, cognitive construction is deeply intertwined with sociocultural experience.

Vygotsky's Sociocultural Theory

Lev Vygotsky (1978) emphasized that cognitive development is fundamentally social. Children learn through social interaction **and** internalize the language, tools, and values of their culture. The zone of proximal development (ZPD), the gap between what a child can do independently and what they can achieve with guidance, illustrates how cognitive growth depends on mediated learning through more capable peers or adults.

From a systems perspective, Vygotsky's theory highlights contextual embeddedness: a child's understanding of complex systems is not isolated cognition but is co-constructed through dialogue, joint problem-solving, and cultural narratives. For example, in Malaysian preschools, where communal learning and collective activities are common, children's reasoning about nature or society often reflects collectivist orientations emphasizing balance, harmony, and interdependence. These cultural metaphors parallel ecological and systemic thinking, suggesting that sociocultural learning environments can naturally cultivate systems reasoning.

Moreover, language plays a pivotal role. As children verbalize and reflect on processes ("if it rains, the plants grow"), they externalize their thinking, enabling metacognitive awareness. Studies in bilingual Southeast Asian contexts have shown that children exposed to multiple linguistic frameworks develop flexible thinking patterns and heightened awareness of relational causality. Thus, Vygotsky's sociocultural theory complements Piaget's constructivism and expands it by situating cognition within cultural tools, language, and social meaning.

Information Processing and Cognitive Science Approaches

Contemporary cognitive science refines and extends classical theories by viewing cognition as a set of information-processing systems. From this perspective, understanding complex systems involves working memory, pattern recognition, and executive functions, such as inhibition and cognitive flexibility (Kuhn, 2010; Zelazo, 2015). Young children gradually develop the ability to integrate multiple variables, predict outcomes, and update mental models when feedback contradicts expectations.

For instance, when observing water flowing through sand, a child may initially form a linear model ("the water goes straight"). Through repeated interactions and discussions, they recognize nonlinear patterns ("the water spreads because of holes and pressure"). This iterative model-building process reflects the cognitive mechanisms underpinning systems thinking (Jacobson & Wilensky, 2006).

Neuroscientific studies further indicate that prefrontal cortical development during early childhood supports these skills, particularly executive control and relational integration (Diamond, 2013). Educational interventions that engage children in dynamic simulations, storytelling, and collaborative inquiry have been found to enhance their ability to understand complexity (Hmelo-Silver et al., 2017; Lehrer & Schauble, 2015).

In Southeast Asian classrooms, however, teacher-centred instruction often limits opportunities for exploratory reasoning (Tan, 2018). Integrating information processing insights into pedagogy through open-ended questioning, reflection, and play-based experimentation can significantly enhance cognitive flexibility and systems reasoning in young learners.

Systems Thinking as a Cognitive Framework

Systems thinking refers to recognizing interconnectedness, feedback loops, and dynamic changes within complex systems (Sterman, 2000; Capra & Luisi, 2014). Although traditionally discussed in organizational and environmental studies, developmental research shows that even young children can demonstrate rudimentary systems thinking abilities when appropriately guided (Assaraf & Orion, 2010).

Figure 1. Example of a Simple Feedback Loop for Children

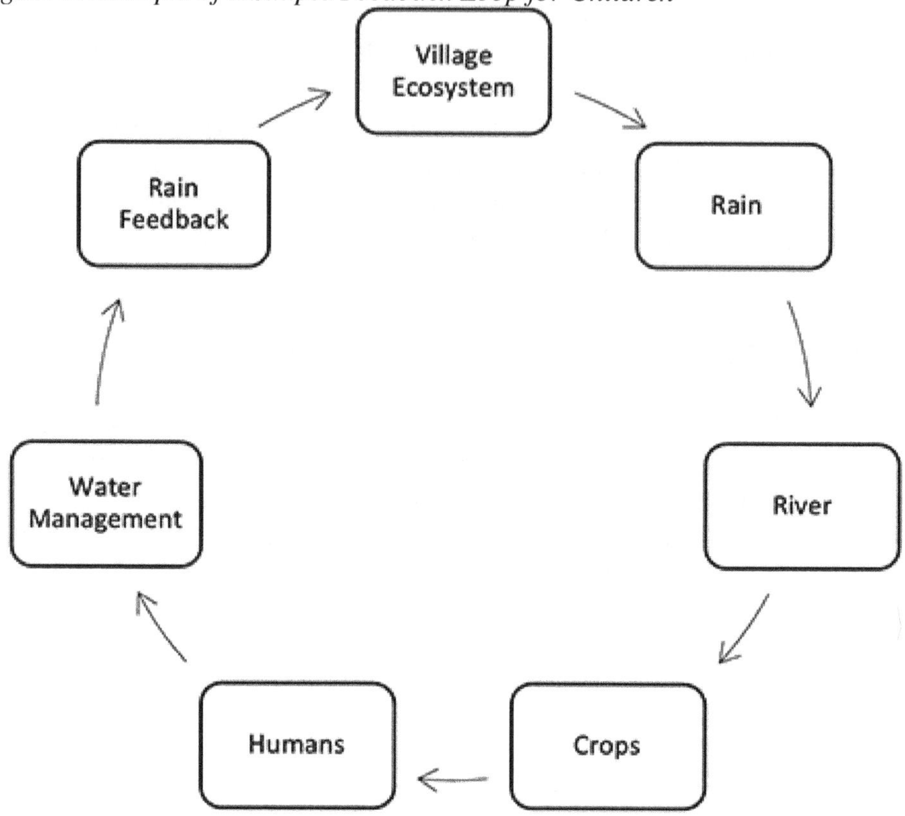

Kindergartners can understand simple causal loops, such as "if we cut too many trees, animals lose homes," or identify balance relationships, such as "too much rain makes the river overflow" (see Figure 1). Encouraging reasoning through stories, experiments, and collaborative projects allows children to perceive interdependence and anticipate consequences. These simple feedback loops build foundational systems thinking, preparing learners to engage with more complex dynamic relationships in later educational activities.

In Malaysia, the integration of systems thinking in early education aligns with holistic philosophies such as *Falsafah Pendidikan Kebangsaan* (National Philosophy of Education), which emphasizes balanced intellectual, spiritual, emotional, and physical growth. This perspective resonates with systems-based approaches that conceptualize learning as an interconnected process shaped by cognitive, social, and environmental factors (Hmelo-Silver et al., 2017; Jacobson & Wilensky, 2006).

COGNITIVE MECHANISMS IN EARLY CHILDHOOD

Cognitive development during early childhood is a dynamic, nonlinear process that involves the construction, testing, and revision of mental representations of the world. Children are not passive recipients of information; rather, they actively explore their environments, detect patterns, infer causal relationships, and develop flexible thinking strategies that allow them to navigate complexity (Kuhn, 2010; Diamond, 2013). Understanding these mechanisms is critical for educators, policymakers, and social workers, as it provides insight into how early interventions can scaffold systems thinking and holistic cognitive growth.

Three primary mechanisms–pattern recognition, causal reasoning, and executive function–serve as the foundation for understanding complex systems. Additionally, emerging research highlights the role of metacognition, analogy use, and social-cognitive mechanisms in supporting sophisticated systemic reasoning, particularly in culturally diverse contexts such as Malaysia and Southeast Asia.

Pattern Recognition and Categorization

From infancy, children demonstrate an innate ability to detect patterns and regularities in their surroundings. This capability, often described as statistical learning, allows infants and toddlers to identify correlations, sequences, and structures in sensory input (Saffran et al., 1996; Gopnik et al., 2004). For example, infants may recognize that shaking a rattle produces a sound or that repeated caregiver behavior reliably signals attention and interaction. Over time, these experiences form the foundation for categorization, which enables children to organize knowledge, anticipate outcomes, and infer relationships, key aspects of systems thinking.

In Southeast Asia, daily life offers rich, culturally embedded opportunities for pattern recognition. Traditional games such as congkak in Malaysia and Indonesia or pachisi in India involve counting, sequencing, and strategic anticipation. These activities encourage children to detect cyclical patterns and interdependencies, enhancing their understanding of relationships and system-like dynamics. Similarly, observing seasonal agricultural cycles, household routines, or communal rituals allows children to abstract regularities and connect cause-and-effect sequences over time.

Table 2. Examples of Pattern Recognition in Southeast Asian Contexts

Activity	Cognitive Mechanism	Systems Thinking Outcome
Congkak (traditional game)	Counting, strategy, sequencing	Recognizing cycles, turn-based interdependence
Observing tides/fishing cycles	Temporal patterns	Understanding ecological interconnections
Market transactions	Exchange patterns	Awareness of economic feedback and dependencies

Pattern recognition is also mediated by language and symbolic tools. Children exposed to multilingual environments, such as those in Malaysia, where Malay, English, Mandarin, Tamil, and indigenous languages coexist, develop enhanced sensitivity to patterns in grammar, vocabulary, and meaning. This linguistic flexibility facilitates analogical thinking, allowing children to transfer knowledge from one domain to another. For instance, recognizing that "water flows like electricity in a circuit" demonstrates a pattern-based analogy that bridges domains and supports systems reasoning.

From a developmental perspective, pattern recognition in early childhood is not merely passive observation. It involves active hypothesis testing: children anticipate outcomes, experiment with actions, and revise their expectations. Cognitive scientists argue that these iterative processes underlie the emergence of systemic thinking by promoting the integration of multiple variables and the recognition of relational structures (Jacobson & Wilensky, 2006).

Causal Reasoning and Inference

Causal reasoning is the ability to identify relationships between actions, events, and outcomes, and it is a mechanism critical for understanding complex systems. Gopnik and Schulz (2007) demonstrated that preschoolers behave as "little scientists," actively testing hypotheses and drawing inferences from observations. For example, a child noticing that pressing a button lights up a toy may experiment with timing, pressure, or sequences to refine their understanding of cause and effect. Such reasoning reflects an early appreciation of conditional relationships, which is essential for predicting systemic outcomes.

Causal reasoning is both experiential and socially mediated. In many Southeast Asian contexts, explanations of causality may incorporate moral, religious, or ecological narratives. In Malaysia, for instance, parents may explain natural events through culturally meaningful frameworks, such as interpreting rainfall as a blessing from God, thereby embedding natural phenomena within moral and religious understandings. Although the cognitive mechanisms used to identify causal relationships remain similar across cultures, interpretations of those relationships are often shaped by cultural worldviews. This interaction between empirical observation and cultural meaning allows children to develop complex reasoning schemas that connect abstract principles with everyday lived experiences (Nisbett et al., 2001; Gopnik & Wellman, 2012).

Moreover, children gradually learn to appreciate nonlinear causality and feedback loops, key features of system dynamics. For example, when observing a pond ecosystem, they recognize that overfishing affects fish populations, which then influences plant growth and water quality. These insights require the integration of multiple causal chains, temporal reasoning, and relational thinking (Assaraf & Orion, 2010). Educational interventions, such as guided inquiry and ecological projects, can scaffold these capacities. In Malaysia, programs such as Eco Schools provide children with hands-on opportunities to experiment, observe consequences, and reflect on the interplay of ecological variables.

Additionally, children's causal reasoning is shaped by social scaffolding. Teachers and caregivers provide explanations, ask reflective questions, and model predictive thinking. For instance, a teacher might ask, "What do you think will happen if we plant these seeds in too little sunlight?" Such scaffolding encourages children to anticipate multiple outcomes, consider interdependencies, and develop predictive mental models, thereby laying the groundwork for early systems thinking.

Executive Function and Cognitive Flexibility

Executive function (EF) encompasses higher-order cognitive processes that enable goal-directed behaviors, including working memory, inhibitory control, and cognitive flexibility (Miyake & Friedman, 2012). EF is essential for systems thinking because it allows children to hold multiple representations simultaneously, consider alternative perspectives, and adapt their reasoning when confronted with new information.

Figure 2. Executive Function in Systems Thinking

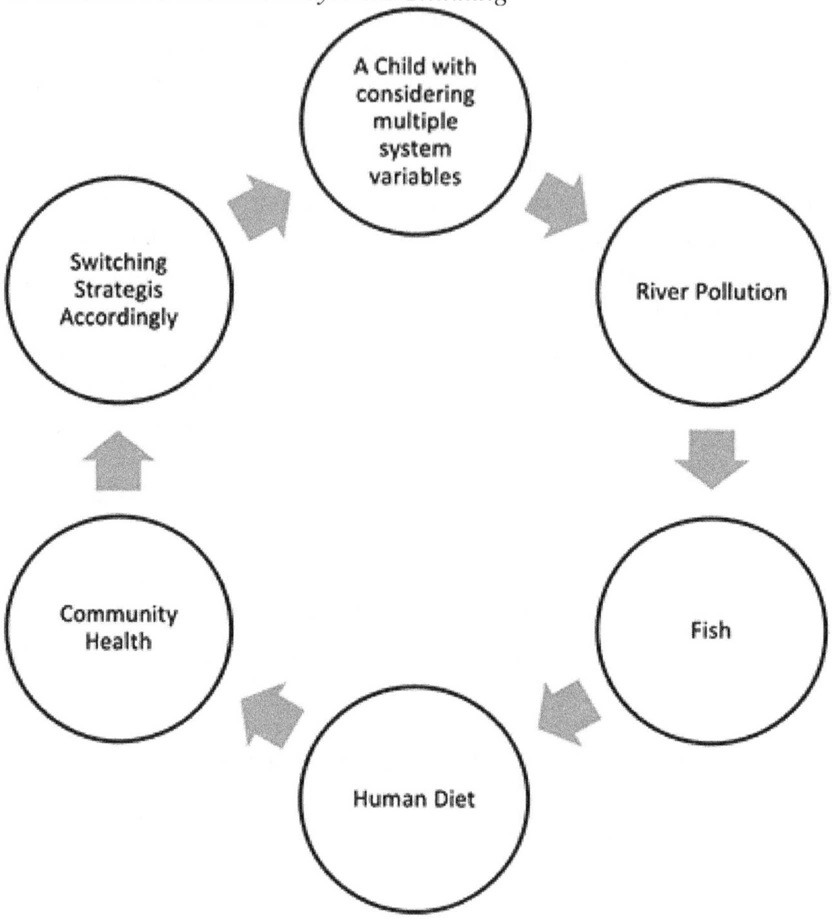

For example, in a classroom project exploring "The Life of a River," children examine the interactions between animals, plants, pollution, and human activities. As illustrated above, they engage key executive functions: working memory to track multiple interdependent components, inhibitory control to resist impulsive or oversimplified conclusions, and cognitive flexibility to revise mental models when evidence contradicts expectations. The flowchart in Figure 2 visually depicts this process, showing how children consider cascading effects, such as how river pollution affects fish populations, which in turn influences human diets and community health, and adjust their reasoning accordingly. By linking cognitive processes to observable system variables, the figure highlights how dynamic, real-world problem-solving fosters early systems thinking and prepares children for complex decision-making.

Cross-cultural research highlights the influence of cultural norms on executive function development. In collectivist societies such as Malaysia, an emphasis on group harmony encourages inhibitory control over assertive self-expression (Lewis et al., 2009). Although this may appear restrictive, it fosters systems awareness, as children learn to consider how individual actions impact collective outcomes. Collaborative activities, such as group storytelling or cooperative games, further reinforce cognitive flexibility and relational thinking.

Emerging research has also linked EF to self-regulation and socio-emotional competence. Children with stronger inhibitory control and working memory exhibit an enhanced ability to delay gratification, resolve conflicts, and navigate social hierarchies, which are abilities closely related to understanding complex social systems (Blair & Raver, 2015). Therefore, EF is both a cognitive and social mechanism that integrates the intellectual and interpersonal skills necessary for systemic reasoning.

Metacognition and Reflective Thinking

Metacognition, the ability to monitor and regulate one's own thinking, emerges in early childhood as children begin to reflect on how they know what they know (Flavell, 1979). In systems learning, metacognition allows children to evaluate assumptions, anticipate outcomes, and revise their strategies. For instance, after observing that too much water harms plant growth, a child may reflect, "Maybe I should water less next time."

Sociocultural contexts shape the development of metacognition. In Southeast Asia, reflective practices are embedded in educational rituals and storytelling traditions, in which moral dilemmas and ecological narratives encourage self-evaluation and perspective-taking (Tan, 2018). When combined with pattern recognition and causal reasoning, metacognitive skills enhance children's ability to integrate diverse information sources, which is a cornerstone of systems thinking.

Analogical Reasoning and Transfer

Analogical reasoning, the ability to map knowledge from familiar domains to new situations, is another mechanism supporting early systems understanding. For example, a child may reason that "a school is like a beehive; each part has a role," linking social organization to natural systems. Studies have shown that analogical thinking facilitates abstraction, problem-solving, and the understanding of interdependent relationships (Gentner & Holyoak, 1997). In multilingual and multicultural Southeast Asian contexts, exposure to diverse linguistic and symbolic systems can further strengthen analogical reasoning by providing multiple conceptual frameworks through which children interpret their experiences. Cultural narratives, metaphors, and storytelling traditions often serve as cognitive scaffolds that help children connect ecological, moral, and social systems in meaningful ways (Gentner & Smith, 2012; Rogoff, 2023).

Social-Cognitive Mechanisms

Finally, social-cognitive processes, such as joint attention, imitation, and perspective-taking, support systems understanding by integrating social information with causal and executive processes. Children learn not only from direct observation but also by interpreting the behaviors and intentions of others, a capacity that is particularly relevant in collectivist cultures. Cooperative activities, communal rituals, and guided group play promote the recognition of interdependence and reinforce systemic reasoning in early childhood (Rogoff, 2003). For example, in a cooperative gardening project, children observe that overwatering harms some plants while benefiting others. By discussing their observations, negotiating roles, and reflecting on outcomes, they simultaneously develop executive function, metacognition, and causal reasoning, demonstrating how cognitive mechanisms interact to support early systems understanding.

Integrative Perspective

Together, these mechanisms–pattern recognition, causal reasoning, executive function, metacognition, analogical reasoning, and social cognition–constitute a dynamic cognitive network that underpins young children's comprehension of complex systems. They are mutually reinforcing: effective causal reasoning relies on working memory and flexibility, whereas pattern recognition informs analogical reasoning, and social interaction enhances both metacognition and systemic understanding. In Southeast Asian educational settings, recognizing these interdependencies is critical for designing culturally responsive pedagogies. Strategies that integrate play, story-based inquiry, group collaboration, and reflective questioning can harness these cognitive mechanisms to foster early systems thinking, preparing children for lifelong learning and adaptive problem-solving in complex social and environmental contexts (Hmelo-Silver et al., 2017)

CULTURAL AND CONTEXTUAL INFLUENCES IN MALAYSIA AND SOUTHEAST ASIA

Cognitive development cannot be separated from the sociocultural environment in which it emerges. Bronfenbrenner's (1979) ecological systems theory provides a useful framework for understanding how microsystem (family, school), mesosystem (community), and macrosystem (culture, religion, and policy) factors interact to shape cognitive growth. In Southeast Asia, home to diverse ethnicities, languages, and religious traditions, these layers interact in complex ways that influence how children interpret their relationships and systems.

Family and Communal Learning

In Malaysia, early learning often occurs within extended family systems. Grandparents, siblings, and community members contribute to children's socialization. This communal context fosters observational learning, in which children acquire understanding through participation and imitation rather than direct instruction (Rogoff, 2003). Such learning mirrors systems thinking because it emphasizes relationships, interdependence, and collective responsibility. For instance, children who help parents in wet markets or on farms firsthand observe economic systems, as well as how supply, demand, and community cooperation sustain livelihoods. When adults engage children in reflective dialogues ("What happens when fewer people buy fish today?"), they support the development of causal mapping and feedback reasoning.

Language and Multilingual Cognition

Malaysia's multilingual environment, in which Malay, English, Mandarin, and Tamil are commonly spoken, offers cognitive advantages for systems understanding. Research has shown that bilingual and multilingual children exhibit enhanced metalinguistic awareness, cognitive flexibility, and executive control (Bialystok, 2011). Switching between languages requires children to monitor context, suppress interference, and adapt to shifting communicative norms, skills closely aligned with systems-level thinking. Furthermore, linguistic diversity exposes children to multiple conceptual metaphors for explaining phenomena. For instance, Malay idioms such as *Bagai aur dengan tebing* ("like bamboo and the riverbank," symbolizing mutual dependence) encode ecological and relational thinking that reinforces systemic understanding. When teachers leverage such metaphors, they connect traditional wisdom to modern cognitive concepts of feedback and interdependence (Tan, 2018).

Cultural Beliefs and Religious Frameworks

Cultural worldviews profoundly influence children's conceptualization of relationships within natural and social systems. Islamic education in Malaysia, for example, emphasizes the unity and balance (tawhid) of creation, teaching that all elements of nature are interconnected under divine order. Similarly, Buddhist and Hindu traditions prevalent in Thailand and Indonesia emphasize cyclical causality (karma, rebirth), shaping children's perception of cause and effect as continuous rather than linear. Such beliefs foster what Capra and Luisi (2014) call a holistic ontology, a worldview in which systems are not reducible to their parts. Children raised in these environments may intuitively understand circular causality ("what goes around comes around") even before formal instruction. Integrating these cultural paradigms into early education enhances relevance and resonance, allowing children to bridge **spiritual, moral, and scientific** understandings of complexity.

Educational Systems and Policy Context

Malaysia's education system, guided by the *National Education Philosophy (Falsafah Pendidikan Kebangsaan)*, promotes the holistic development of the individual 'sspiritual, intellectual, emotional, and physical aspects (Ministry of Education Malaysia, 2017). Early childhood curricula emphasize play, inquiry, and moral formation. However, in practice, many preschools remain teacher-centered, prioritizing memorization over exploration. This limits opportunities for children to engage in dynamic reasoning about systems. Recent reforms and regional initiatives, such as the *ASEAN Early Childhood Care and Development Framework (2017)*, have begun to emphasize inquiry-based and integrative learning approaches. These align closely with systems thinking, advocating curricula that connect science, society, and sustainability. In Malaysia, programs such as *Permata Negara* and *Kelas Prasekolah Integrasi* are beginning to incorporate thematic learning that encourages children to explore the relationships between the environment, health, and community.

CHILDREN'S UNDERSTANDING OF CAUSALITY AND FEEDBACK

Causality and feedback are core cognitive components of systems reasoning. Understanding how one action influences another and how its effects can modify causes marks a significant developmental achievement.

Linear vs. Nonlinear Causality

Early research indicates that young children typically begin with linear causal models ("A causes B") and gradually develop the ability to think nonlinearly, recognizing that multiple variables interact simultaneously (Kuhn, 2010; Hmelo-Silver et al., 2017). For example, when discussing plant growth, preschoolers may initially say, "Plants grow because we water them." With experience, they integrate additional variables, such as sunlight, soil, and air, forming a web-like causal model. Southeast Asian studies reveal that exposure to nature-based learning accelerates this development. In Malaysian community gardens or rural settings, children observe feedback processes such as composting or seasonal cycles, supporting experiential understanding of dynamic systems. Teachers who guide reflection through questions ("What happens if we don't compost?") helps children articulate feedback relationships.

Feedback Loops and Dynamic Equilibrium

Feedback thinking, the recognition that actions produce effects that may reinforce or balance the original condition, is central to systems understanding (Sterman, 2000). However, it is cognitively demanding because it requires recursive reasoning: understanding that "my action affects the system, which in turn affects me." Children begin to grasp reinforcing feedback early ("the more I push, the faster it goes"), but balancing feedback ("if too many fish are caught, fewer remain for next time") develops later, typically during middle childhood (Assaraf & Orion, 2010). Culturally grounded stories and simulations are effective tools for scaffolding these concepts. Folktales from Malaysia and Indonesia often include moral cycles of greed leading to loss and generosity leading to prosperity, which reflect balancing feedback in narrative form.

2.9.1 Representation and Visualization

Visual aids and interactive modelling significantly enhance children's ability to represent causal and feedback relationships. Studies using concept maps and story-based diagrams have shown that even preschoolers can identify system components and flows when provided with tangible visual tools (Hmelo-Silver et al., 2017). In Southeast Asian classrooms, digital and analogue tools such as sand tables, puppet plays, or simple animation software help children externalize their mental models, bridging abstract reasoning with concrete experience.

From Cognitive Mechanisms to Sociocultural Context

Sections 1 and 2 outlined the core cognitive mechanisms that enable young children to understand complexity, including pattern recognition, causal reasoning, executive control, and analogical transfer. These processes do not function in isolation; they interact dynamically as children construct, revise, and expand their mental models of the world. Cognition, however, does not develop uniformly across contexts. Children's opportunities to observe feedback loops, engage in collaborative problem-solving, or reason about interdependence are deeply shaped by cultural norms, language environments, family systems, and educational expectations. Therefore, before moving toward pedagogical applications, it is necessary to examine the sociocultural conditions in which cognition unfolds. The next section builds on the mechanisms previously discussed by exploring how Malaysia and Southeast Asia provide culturally rich contexts that scaffold systemic understanding.

DEVELOPMENTAL AND CULTURAL CONTEXT; UNDERSTANDING COGNITION IN MALAYSIA AND SOUTHEAST ASIA

Cognitive development is shaped by dynamic interactions among cultural, social, and environmental contexts. In Malaysia and the broader Southeast Asian region, children are raised in multilingual and socially interconnected environments that support cognitive flexibility, perspective-taking, and adaptive reasoning. Exposure to multiple languages enhances executive function and the ability to manage and integrate diverse conceptual frameworks, which are essential for understanding complex systems (Bialystok, 2017).

Collectivist social norms further influence cognitive development by emphasizing interdependence, shared responsibility, and relational thinking. Through everyday interactions within families and communities, children develop an awareness of how actions produce broader social consequences, supporting an early understanding of causality and systemic relationships. Religious and moral frameworks also contribute by reinforcing concepts of ethical responsibility, balance, and interconnectedness, thereby shaping children's interpretations of social and ecological systems.

Educational practices in Malaysia reflect these sociocultural influences. Early childhood programmes integrate thematic, inquiry-based, and play-oriented approaches aligned with the National Philosophy of Education, promoting holistic development across cognitive, social, and moral domains (Ministry of Education Malaysia, 2017). Additionally, diverse environmental contexts, ranging from rural ecological settings to urban technological environments, provide varied experiential opportunities that further support systems thinking. Collectively, these factors create a rich cognitive ecology that fosters early systems literacy and relational reasoning among children in the region.

Sociocultural Influences on Cognitive Development

Cognitive development cannot be fully understood without acknowledging its cultural context. As Vygotsky (1978) argued, cognition is socially mediated and develops through interactions with more knowledgeable others in specific sociocultural settings. In Malaysia and Southeast Asia, children's cognitive development occurs within rich cultural frameworks that blend collectivist values, religious beliefs, and community-based learning traditions. These cultural systems profoundly shape young children 's understanding and reasoning about complex systems. In Malaysia, for instance, early socialization often emphasizes *hormat* (respect), *gotong-royong* (mutual cooperation), and *kekeluargaan* (family-centeredness) values that influence how children interpret social structures and interdependence. Malaysian preschoolers show heightened awareness of social roles and relational hierarchies compared to their peers in Western contexts, demonstrating early forms of social systems understanding. This reflects Bronfenbrenner's (1979) ecological systems theory, in which a child's microsystem, family, school, and community directly mold their cognitive frameworks. In rural Southeast Asian communities, particularly in Indonesia, the Philippines, and Thailand, children often participate in family labour, farming, or caregiving from an early age. These activities require an understanding of natural cycles, resource distribution, and social cooperation, all of which nurture *systems thinking* before formal schooling begins (Gopnik, 2020; Rogoff, 2003). This practical engagement fosters what Vygotsky termed "everyday concepts," precursors to scientific understanding developed later in school settings.

Language, Multilingualism, and Cognitive Complexity

Malaysia's multilingual environment provides a natural laboratory for exploring cognitive flexibility. Most Malaysian children grow up speaking at least two languages: Malay (Bahasa Malaysia) and a home language, such as Mandarin, Tamil, or an indigenous language. Research has shown that bilingualism enhances executive function, cognitive switching, and metalinguistic awareness (Bialystok, 2011; Kroll & Bialystok, 2013). These skills are foundational for understanding complex, dynamic systems that require attention to multiple perspectives and variables. A comparative study by Tan and Hoon (2020) revealed that bilingual Malaysian children performed better on pattern recognition and causal reasoning tasks than their monolingual peers. This cognitive advantage is attributed to their constant need to navigate between linguistic structures and cultural norms. In this sense, bilingualism acts as a cognitive scaffold, strengthening neural mechanisms associated with abstract thinking and systems reasoning. Similarly, in Singapore and the Philippines, multilingualism is also correlated with greater adaptability in problem-solving and decision-making tasks. These findings align with the concept of *cognitive pluralism*, the idea that children exposed to diverse cultural and linguistic systems develop more flexible cognitive strategies (Nisbett, 2003). For example, a child who speaks both Malay and Mandarin may conceptualize social relationships differently depending on the linguistic context, demonstrating an early understanding of how systems can vary across domains.

Religious and Ethical Frameworks in Cognitive Structuring

Religion plays a significant role in shaping Southeast Asian cognition, not merely as a belief system but as a mode of reasoning about the world. In Malaysia, where Islam is the dominant faith, children are often introduced to ethical and metaphysical systems early through *pengajian agama* (religious education). This introduces them to cause–and–effect reasoning linked to moral outcomes, a form of cognitive mapping that integrates spiritual and social causality. Similarly, Buddhist-influenced contexts in Thailand and Myanmar emphasize the cyclical nature of life, karma, and interdependence metaphors that parallel scientific systems thinking (Inagaki & Hatano, 2002). When children learn about moral cause and effect through karma or divine justice, they are engaging in proto-systemic reasoning that parallels cognitive models of feedback loops and interconnected processes. A comparative ethnographic study by Rogoff and Paradise (2017) found that indigenous and religious worldviews often provide children with intuitive models of system behaviors long before formal exposure to science. These frameworks, whether spiritual or ecological, help children make sense of complex relationships among social, environmental, and moral elements.

Family, Schooling, and Social Hierarchies

In Southeast Asia, hierarchical social structures often shape children's reasoning about authority, fairness, and group dynamics. Malaysian classrooms, for instance, tend to be teacher-centered, reflecting broader cultural respect for authority and seniority. However, this structure also provides predictable social systems that children can cognitively map. They learn to navigate complex social rules, understand who holds authority, what behaviors maintain harmony, and how group responsibilities interconnect. At home, extended families are common, and caregiving responsibilities are distributed among multiple adults. Such structures allow children to observe social systems in real time, the allocation of duties, emotional exchanges, and resource sharing, which contribute to the early development of *relational cognition* (Nsamenang, 2008). In contrast, Western nuclear family models often emphasize individual autonomy earlier, promoting a different type of cognitive schema focused on independence and self-agency. Studies in Malaysian early education have demonstrated that children from collectivist family environments show strong cooperative problem-solving and perspective-taking skills, which are essential for systems understanding. These traits reflect an integration of cognitive and socio-emotional competencies, showing that understanding systems is as much about empathy and relationship awareness as it is about logic or abstraction.

Cognitive Development and Socioeconomic Inequality

Socioeconomic status (SES) also exerts a profound influence on how children develop their cognitive framework. In Malaysia and other Southeast Asian nations, children from lower-income families may have limited access to early education or enrichment activities. This can delay certain cognitive milestones related to abstract reasoning and systems comprehension (UNICEF, 2021). However, it is crucial to note that these differences are not purely biological but structural, reflecting unequal opportunities and resources (Hackman & Farah, 2009). Community-based early education programs such as Malaysia's *PERMATA Negara* and Indonesia's *PAUD* have been successful in narrowing this cognitive gap. These programs integrate play-based learning and cultural storytelling, which simultaneously develop language, social awareness, and causal reasoning (Kementerian Pendidikan Malaysia, 2020). When teachers use narratives about family, nature, or religion to explain interdependence, children begin to construct mental models of how systems operate economically, socially, and morally.

EDUCATIONAL AND PRACTICAL APPLICATIONS

Translating Cognitive Theory into Educational Practice

Applying cognitive theories in early childhood education enables the design of learning environments that are aligned with children's developmental processes. Constructivist perspectives emphasize active exploration, while sociocultural theory highlights scaffolding and collaborative learning, and information-processing approaches focus on attention, memory, and executive function (Piaget, 1952; Vygotsky, 1978; Kuhn, 2010). Within the Southeast Asian context, these frameworks are further shaped by multilingualism, collectivist values, and moral education, thus supporting the development of a systems understanding.

In Malaysia, the Kurikulum Standard Prasekolah Kebangsaan (KSPK) promotes thematic and inquiry-based learning that integrates cognitive and social development (Ministry of Education Malaysia, 2017). Activities such as exploring environmental processes enable children to develop causal reasoning and an awareness of interdependence, reflecting both individual exploration and guided interaction. The application of the zone of proximal development is evident in collaborative learning practices, where teacher guidance and peer interaction support cognitive growth and shared responsibility.

Beyond formal instruction, everyday classroom routines can reinforce cognitive development by embedding problem-solving, sequencing, and social reasoning into daily activities. Overall, translating cognitive theory into practice fosters holistic development by integrating the intellectual, social, and ethical dimensions of learning.

Play-Based Learning and Systems Thinking

Play is a cornerstone of early childhood development, enabling children to experiment, hypothesize, and engage in symbolic reasoning (Hirsh-Pasek, 2009). In Malaysia, play-based learning is increasingly recognized as essential for integrating cognitive, emotional, and physical skills. Through construction, role-playing, and imaginative scenarios, children simulate complex systems, communities, ecosystems, or families while navigating rules, roles, and cause-and-effect relationships.

For example, building a miniature "village" allows children to assign roles (parent, teacher, vendor), allocate resources, and negotiate responsibilities. When water "floods" the village or a shop closes, children reflect on systemic consequences: "If too much water comes, plants die, animals lose shelter, and the shop cannot operate." These scenarios cultivate an awareness of interdependence, problem-solving, and foresight, key features of systems reasoning. Teachers enhance learning through reflective questioning and by promoting causal reasoning and mental model construction.

Digital and sensory play further extend cognitive engagement. In Singapore and Indonesia, educators employ interactive games, augmented reality, and robotics kits to demonstrate dynamic systems. For instance, digital simulations of river ecosystems show how pollution affects aquatic life or how community actions influence sustainability (Tan & Neo, 2022). Combining traditional play with technology strengthens abstract reasoning, systems thinking, and socio-emotional intelligence, providing multisensory, culturally relevant experiences. Play also promotes executive function and social cognition. Children must plan, inhibit impulsive actions, and adapt strategies in collaborative scenarios. In collectivist Southeast Asian classrooms, group-based play teaches negotiation, perspective-taking, and empathy as critical social mechanisms that underpin systemic reasoning (Lewis et al., 2009).

Storytelling as a Tool for Cognitive Integration

Storytelling is intrinsic to Southeast Asian pedagogy, providing a natural method for developing systems literacy. Traditional folktales such as *Sang Kancil dan Buaya* (Malaysia), *Si Kancil dan Harimau* (Indonesia), and *Tenali Raman*(India) embed moral lessons within complex narratives involving multiple actors, causal chains, and social hierarchies. Cognitive science shows that stories enhance memory, inference-making, and relational reasoning (Bruner, 1990; Sutton-Smith, 1997). Teachers can use stories to map interdependencies. For example, after narrating *Sang Kancil,* children can analyze the consequences of character decisions, predict alternative outcomes, or identify how each action affects the broader system. This mental modelling of dynamic relationships mirrors real-world problem-solving, preparing children for later systems-based reasoning in science, society, and governance. In religious and moral education, storytelling illustrates ethical systems. Islamic stories of akhlak (moral virtues) or Buddhist parables of compassion demonstrate how individual actions affect social and spiritual systems. These narratives cultivate moral reasoning alongside cognitive skills, integrating social, emotional, and ethical dimensions aligned with Malaysia's Falsafah Pendidikan Kebangsaan, which emphasizes holistic development.

Designing Classrooms for Cognitive Engagement

Classroom environments must stimulate curiosity, reflection, and collaboration. Malaysian early childhood programs are increasingly adopting learning corners, thematic zones, and open-ended materials that encourage experimentation, problem-solving, and interaction (Kementerian Pendidikan Malaysia, 2020).

For example, a "water cycle corner" might include evaporation jars, rain simulations, and role-playing activities. Children observe and discuss outcomes when one system component changes, directly engaging with dynamic system concepts. Teachers can scaffold learning with questions such as, "What happens if we plant more trees?" or "How does the sun affect the river?" Integrating language learning, describing processes, making predictions, and storytelling further links the cognitive, linguistic, and scientific domains.

Collaborative work enhances social cognition and fairness reasoning. Studies in Thailand and the Philippines (SEAMEO, 2021) have shown that children engaging in group problem-solving demonstrate greater ability to reason about social systems, negotiate resources, and evaluate the consequences of collective action. Classrooms designed for exploration, discussion, and peer collaboration thus become microcosms of complex systems, allowing children to experience interdependence, feedback, and emergent outcomes firsthand.

Teacher Education and Reflective Practice

Teacher expertise is critical for translating cognitive theory into effective pedagogy. Malaysian teacher training under the Institut Pendidikan Guru (IPG) emphasizes child-centered teaching, critical reflection, and culturally responsive methods. Teachers are encouraged to observe children's thinking, analyze cognitive strategies, and adapt instructions according to their developmental readiness.

Reflective practice allows educators to model metacognition, paralleling the cognitive growth they foster. For instance, after observing a classroom activity, a teacher might ask: "Which strategies helped children see relationships between variables?" or "Where did misconceptions emerge?" Such reflection supports continuous improvement and cultivates professional learning community systems of practice that mirror the complexity of child development (Schön, 1983).

Teacher education is increasingly integrating neuroscience and digital literacy. Understanding prefrontal cortex development, attention, and memory capacity informs activity design, ensuring that experiences match children's cognitive abilities (Immordino-Yang, 2015). Combining modern science with traditional knowledge fosters pedagogical models that are culturally grounded and scientifically informed, enhancing cognitive engagement and systems reasoning.

Community and Family Involvement

In collectivist societies, learning extends beyond formal classrooms. Family and community participation provide authentic contexts for systems thinking, reinforcing lessons from school. Programs such as Program Pintar@Komuniti(Malaysia) and Gerakan Sekolah Ramah Anak (Indonesia) encourage children to engage in real-world problem-solving, community gardening, waste recycling, or charitable initiatives, thereby experiencing social interdependence and system dynamics firsthand (UNICEF, 2021). Parental engagement is equally important. Caregivers who discuss household routines, market dynamics, or ecological changes support children in connecting abstract reasoning to practical knowledge. Elaborative questioning, "Why do we need to save water?" or "What happens if we throw trash in the river?" promotes causal reasoning and mental modelling of systems. When parents model reflective thinking and problem-solving, children internalize strategies for navigating complex systems in everyday life. Furthermore, community involvement strengthens cultural scaffolding. Traditional practices, festivals, and intergenerational rituals expose children to dynamic social, ecological, and moral systems, allowing them to perceive feedback loops, interdependencies, and emergent outcomes. These experiences complement classroom learning by integrating cognition, culture, and context in a holistic developmental framework.

This section discusses the educational and practical applications of cognitive science and how they are intricately situated within the sociocultural context of Southeast Asia. By integrating strategies such as play-based learning, storytelling, purposeful classroom design, reflective teacher practices, and active community engagement, young children are provided with rich opportunities to develop systems thinking, causal reasoning, and executive functioning in culturally meaningful ways. This holistic approach ensures that cognitive growth is intertwined with social, moral, and emotional development. By effectively bridging theoretical frameworks, pedagogical practices, and local cultural contexts, educators can construct dynamic learning ecosystems that nurture children's capacity to understand complex systems, engage collaboratively, and apply ethical reasoning, preparing them to navigate an interconnected and rapidly evolving world with insight and adaptability.

PRACTICAL CLASSROOM ACTIVITIES FOR AI-INTEGRATED LEARNING ENVIRONMENTS

To illustrate how cognitive processes can be nurtured within AI-supported learning spaces, the following examples demonstrate how pattern recognition, prediction, and causal reasoning can be embedded in early education:

Activity 1: AI-Assisted Pattern Discovery

Children work with an image-sorting application or a simple machine-learning tool that groups objects based on color, shape, or size. Learners predict how the AI will classify items and then test and refine their hypotheses when the results differ from their expectations.

Cognitive targets: Pattern recognition, hypothesis testing, and feedback awareness.

Activity 2: Digital Storytelling and System Consequence Mapping

Using voice-to-story AI or image-generation tools, children produce a narrative in which events unfold based on their choices (e.g., pollution vs. protecting a river). Teachers guide reflection on how one change affects the entire system.

Cognitive targets: causal reasoning, analogical thinking, and multiple-variable processing.

Activity 3: Robot Navigation Task with Variable Outcomes

Students programmed a simple educational robot (Bee-Bot, Dash, etc.) to navigate an obstacle grid representing a food–water–forest ecosystem. When conditions change, food scarcity, blocked pathways, children adjust their strategies.

Cognitive targets: executive function, adaptation, and system feedback recognition.

These short, structured explorations show how AI-supported tasks can scaffold early cognitive development while nurturing foundational AI literacy. They demonstrate how the thinking skills described in Section 2 can become observable behaviors in real classrooms, making learning both developmentally authentic and future-oriented.

IMPLICATIONS, FUTURE RESEARCH, AND CONCLUSION

Integrating Cognitive, Cultural, and Educational Systems

Understanding complex systems in early childhood emerges from the interaction of cognitive, cultural, and social processes, rather than from maturation alone. In Malaysia and the broader Southeast Asian context, multilingualism, collectivist values, and religious frameworks create rich environments that support relational thinking and systems awareness. Drawing on ecological perspectives, children's learning is shaped by interconnected layers of family, community, and cultural systems, underscoring the need for educational approaches that integrate cognitive development with sociocultural realities (Bronfenbrenner, 1979).

Empirical observations from community-based settings, such as rural and village environments, illustrate how everyday participation in social, economic, and religious activities supports an early understanding of interdependence, causality, and cooperation. These experiences align with cultural-historical perspectives, in which learning is mediated through social interaction, language, and shared practices, reinforcing both cognitive and moral development.

The implications for practice emphasize the importance of culturally responsive pedagogy that integrates local knowledge, community engagement, and inquiry-based learning. Future research should further examine how diverse sociocultural contexts shape systems reasoning, particularly in multilingual environments and emerging educational demands.

In conclusion, fostering systems understanding in early childhood requires alignment among cognitive theory, cultural context, and educational practice. This integration supports the development of reflective, adaptive, and socially responsible individuals who are capable of navigating complex and interconnected environments.

EDUCATIONAL AND POLICY IMPLICATIONS

Policy efforts across Southeast Asia increasingly recognize the need to ground early childhood education (ECE) in contemporary cognitive science while remaining sensitive to local traditions, languages, and sociocultural norms. In Malaysia, the National Early Childhood Care and Education Policy (NECCEP, 2019) emphasizes holistic child development and intellectual, emotional, social, and spiritual, reflecting cognitive-constructivist and sociocultural principles. These policy directions acknowledge that early cognitive experiences shape not only academic trajectories but also long-term social, emotional, and moral capacities.

Culturally Responsive Curriculum Design

Culturally responsive pedagogy situates learning within the lived realities and cultural contexts of learners. In Malaysia and its Southeast Asian neighbors, this entails integrating indigenous knowledge systems, local practices, and traditional narratives into formal and informal curricula to ensure cognitive relevance. Environmental education, for example, can draw from *adat perpatih* or *adat temenggung*, embedding concepts of sustainability, communal responsibility, and ecological interdependence within culturally familiar frameworks. Story-based approaches provide concrete examples of systems thinking. Folktales such as the Malay legend of Sang Kancil or regional versions like *Si Kancil dan Harimau* illustrate adaptive problem-solving, the consequences of individual actions, and the interconnectedness of social and natural systems. By using these stories in classroom activities, educators can scaffold children's understanding of causal loops and interdependencies. As Gay (2018) notes, culturally grounded pedagogy enhances motivation, cognitive engagement, retention, and flexibility in reasoning, providing a bridge between abstract concepts and everyday experience.

Investment in Early Cognitive Stimulation

Early cognitive stimulation is a key predictor of lifelong learning, social adaptability, and economic potential. Public policies should prioritize access to high-quality preschool programs, particularly for low-income, rural, and marginalized communities. Heckman's (2011) research demonstrates that investments in early childhood education yield disproportionately high social returns compared to interventions at later stages. The UNICEF Regional Office for East Asia and the Pacific (2021) emphasized that early stimulation improves both cognitive and socio-emotional outcomes. Despite high preschool enrolment in Malaysia (over 85%), disparities persist in the quality of instruction and learning resources between urban and rural areas (Ministry of Education Malaysia, 2022). Policymakers should allocate resources for developmentally appropriate materials that foster systems reasoning, such as modular building sets, interactive environmental puzzles, and inquiry-based play kits. Ensuring equitable access to such resources is critical for reducing gaps in cognitive preparedness and supporting lifelong learning trajectories.

Teacher Training and Continuous Professional Development

Teachers serve as critical mediators of children's cognitive experiences. Therefore, teacher education programs must incorporate rigorous training in cognitive science, developmental psychology, systems pedagogy, and the neuroscience of learning. This includes strategies for scaffolding, guided inquiry, reflective questioning, and promoting metacognition among young learners. Continuous professional development (CPD) programs should expose educators to innovative pedagogical methods, such as concept mapping, simulation-based learning, and project-based inquiry. Partnerships with universities, teacher training institutes, and NGOs (e.g., PINTAR Foundation) can ensure teachers remain updated on emerging research in child development and evidence-based teaching practices. Reflective practice, including classroom observation, peer feedback, and self-analysis, reinforces teachers' ability to adapt instruction to children's developmental stages and culturally diverse needs.

Integration of Family and Community in Learning

In collectivist societies of Southeast Asia, family and community engagement is essential for supporting children's cognitive development. Programs such as PINTAR Foundation's School Adoption Initiative demonstrate that collaborative efforts between schools, communities, and corporations can enhance educational outcomes and foster early systems thinking. Community learning centres, parent engagement workshops, and intergenerational projects provide children with authentic experiences of social interdependence. For example, linking classroom lessons on water cycles to household gardening or waste management practices contextualizes abstract concepts and reinforces understanding of cause and effect relationships within social and ecological systems. Encouraging families to use elaborative questioning during daily routines further strengthens children's ability to construct mental models of complex systems.

Technology as a Cognitive Bridge

Digital tools offer powerful opportunities for early learners to engage in systems thinking and pattern recognition. Guided, contextually relevant technology can simulate real-world systems and allow children to experiment with feedback loops, interdependencies, and dynamic processes (Tan & Neo, 2022). Examples include augmented reality storytelling, interactive ecosystem simulations, coding games, and logic-based digital puzzles. However, technology integration must prioritize guided discovery rather than passive consumption. Teachers and parents should mediate experiences, framing digital interactions within broader social and cultural narratives. Collaboration between governments, NGOs, and edtech companies can ensure that affordable, culturally adapted digital resources are accessible to B40 families and rural communities, reducing inequities in digital literacy and cognitive opportunities

Policy Alignment with Global Frameworks

Malaysia's ECE framework aligns with global commitments such as UNESCO's Early Childhood Care and Education (ECCE) guidelines and Sustainable Development Goal 4.2, which emphasize universal access to quality early education (UNESCO, 2022). ASEAN-wide initiatives, including the Declaration on Early Childhood Care and Development (2017), advocate equity, inclusion, and cultural sensitivity, reinforcing the importance of nurturing children's systemic and critical reasoning skills. By situating national policies within global frameworks, Malaysia and neighboring countries can ensure that early childhood programs remain competitive internationally while respecting local sociocultural priorities. Aligning policy, pedagogy, and practice creates a coherent system that supports holistic child development, preparing future generations to navigate increasingly complex social, environmental, and technological landscapes.

FUTURE RESEARCH DIRECTIONS

Although substantial progress has been made in understanding how young children conceptualize complex systems, significant gaps remain, particularly in Southeast Asian contexts. Existing research largely reflects Western-centric paradigms, often emphasizing individualistic reasoning, abstract problem-solving, and linear causality. In contrast, Southeast Asian children grow up in culturally diverse, multilingual, and collectivist environments where relational, cyclical, and morally-infused reasoning prevails. Future research should therefore adopt cross-cultural, interdisciplinary, and longitudinal approaches that integrate psychology, neuroscience, education, and policy studies.

Cross-Cultural Cognitive Studies

Cross-cultural investigations can provide insights into how societal norms, values, and linguistic structures shape early cognitive development. Comparative studies between collectivist societies (e.g., Malaysia, Indonesia, the Philippines) and individualist societies (e.g., the United States, Western Europe) reveal differences in how children perceive interdependence, causal relationships, and feedback loops. While children in Western contexts may prioritize linear causality ("A causes B"), Southeast Asian children frequently conceptualize cyclical or reciprocal relationships ("A and B influence each other") (Nisbett, 2003). Future research should examine how sociocultural factors, including communal practices, hierarchical relationships, and moral-religious narratives, influence cognitive mechanisms such as pattern recognition, executive function, and causal reasoning. For example, in Malaysia, moral and religious instruction often frames cause and effect within ethical and ecological contexts ("If we take care of the river, the fish thrive and the community prospers"). Understanding how such narrative structures shape cognitive frameworks can inform the design of culturally responsive curricula that support relational reasoning and holistic systems understanding (Gay, G.2000). Additionally, cross-cultural studies can explore how multilingualism interacts with cognitive development. Research indicates that exposure to multiple languages enhances cognitive flexibility, perspective-taking, and metacognition (Bialystok, 2017). Investigating differences between monolingual and multilingual children in Southeast Asia can provide nuanced insights into how language diversity supports systemic thinking and problem-solving.

Longitudinal Developmental Research

While snapshot studies illuminate children's current cognitive capabilities, longitudinal research is critical to understand how early exposure to complex systems reasoning translates into later academic, social, and moral competencies. Few studies track the trajectory from early systems understanding to adolescent or adult scientific reasoning, ethical decision-making, or social responsibility. Establishing longitudinal studies in Southeast Asia would allow researchers to examine how early experiences, including family structure, communal activities, religious instruction, play-based learning, and digital exposure, influence the development of executive function, causal reasoning, and moral cognition. For instance, tracking children who participate in integrated community-school programs could reveal whether early exposure to collaborative problem-solving fosters empathy, ethical awareness, and civic engagement in adolescence. Regional longitudinal databases supported by ASEAN ministries, national ECE councils, or universities could provide standardized metrics for cross-country comparison. These databases might include cognitive assessments, behavioural observations, socio-emotional indicators, and parental engagement measures, enabling policymakers to identify effective interventions and reduce developmental disparities (Heckman, 2011; UNICEF, 2021).

Integration of Neuroscience and Education

Cultural neuroscience offers promising avenues for examining how environmental, linguistic, and moral contexts shape brain development. For example, children in multilingual Southeast Asian households often demonstrate heightened executive function and cognitive flexibility due to frequent code-switching and contextual language use (Bialystok, 2017). Neuroimaging studies could further elucidate how early social experiences, moral reasoning, and cultural practices influence neural networks associated with decision-making, problem-solving, and systems thinking. Future research should investigate the interplay between emotional and moral contexts and neural development. For instance, when children learn about ecological interdependence or ethical dilemmas, how are prefrontal and limbic systems activated, and how does this relate to real-world behavioural outcomes? Integrating such neuroscientific findings with educational research could inform culturally grounded pedagogy that aligns teaching strategies with the brain's developmental trajectory (Immordino-Yang, 2015). Moreover, experimental designs can explore how different teaching modalities play-based learning, storytelling, technology-assisted simulations, or collaborative projects, affect neural and cognitive outcomes. Insights from these studies can guide the development of evidence-based, contextually appropriate instructional materials that foster holistic systems understanding from an early age.

Policy Evaluation and Implementation Research

A critical area for future inquiry is the systematic evaluation of ECE policies and teacher training programs in promoting systems thinking. While frameworks such as NECCEP (2019) provide strategic guidance, there is limited empirical evidence assessing their effectiveness in enhancing children's cognitive, socio-emotional, and moral development. Future studies should employ mixed-method designs, combining quantitative assessments of learning outcomes with qualitative observations of classroom practices, teacher reflections, and parental perspectives. Participatory action research (PAR) approaches can actively involve teachers, parents, and policymakers in co-designing and refining educational strategies, ensuring alignment with cultural norms and developmental needs. Furthermore, evaluation research should move beyond traditional academic metrics to measure outcomes such as problem-solving in dynamic social contexts, environmental awareness, moral reasoning, and adaptive behaviours. Incorporating ecological and systemic indicators can help determine whether early education programs truly cultivate the integrated cognitive, social, and ethical competencies necessary for navigating complex contemporary challenges. By addressing these research gaps, Southeast Asian scholars and policymakers can create an evidence-informed, culturally sensitive foundation for early childhood education. Such work has the potential to produce generations of children who not only excel cognitively but also understand interconnections, appreciate diversity, and engage ethically in their communities and broader ecological systems.

CONCLUSION

Understanding young children's reasoning about complex systems requires an integrative approach that connects cognitive theory, sociocultural context, and educational practice. In the Malaysian and broader Southeast Asian context, cognitive development is shaped not only by individual processes but also by culturally mediated experiences, including multilingual environments, intergenerational relationships, and communal practices. These contexts support the development of relational thinking, perspective-taking, and early systems awareness.

Educational approaches grounded in constructivist and sociocultural perspectives, alongside systems thinking, provide a strong foundation for fostering these cognitive capacities. Such approaches enable children to actively construct knowledge, engage in collaborative learning, and understand dynamic relationships within their environments (Assaraf & Orion, 2010; Sterman, 2000). Importantly, the development of systems thinking in early childhood extends beyond cognitive outcomes, contributing to ethical reasoning, empathy, and social responsibility.

Insights from neuroscience further emphasise the importance of early experiences in shaping executive function and flexible thinking (Diamond, 2013; Immordino-Yang, 2015). Aligning pedagogical practices with these insights, while embedding local cultural values, enhances both the relevance and effectiveness of early childhood education.

In the Malaysian context, although policy frameworks emphasise holistic and play-based learning, implementation remains uneven. Strengthening alignment between policy, practice, and teacher capacity is therefore essential. Overall, fostering systems understanding in early childhood represents both an educational priority and a strategic investment in developing thoughtful, adaptive, and socially responsible future citizens.

REFERENCES

Assaraf, O. B.-Z., & Orion, N. (2010). Development of system thinking skills in the context of Earth system education. *Journal of Research in Science Teaching*, *47*(5), 540–563. DOI: 10.1002/tea.20351

Bialystok, E. (2011). Reshaping the mind: The benefits of bilingualism. *Canadian Journal of Experimental Psychology = Revue Canadienne de Psychologie Expérimentale*, *65*(4), 229–235. DOI: 10.1037/a0025406 PMID: 21910523

Bialystok, E. (2017). The bilingual adaptation: How minds accommodate experience. *Psychological Bulletin*, *143*(3), 233–262. DOI: 10.1037/bul0000099 PMID: 28230411

Blair, C., & Raver, C. C. (2015). School readiness and self-regulation: A developmental psychobiological approach. *Annual Review of Psychology*, *66*(1), 711–731. DOI: 10.1146/annurev-psych-010814-015221 PMID: 25148852

Bronfenbrenner, U. (1979). *The ecology of human development: Experiments by nature and design*. Harvard University Press. DOI: 10.4159/9780674028845

Bruner, J. (1990). Culture and human development: A new look. *Human development*, *33*(6), 344–355.

Capra, F., & Luisi, P. L. (2014). *The systems view of life: A unifying vision*. Cambridge University Press. DOI: 10.1017/CBO9780511895555

Dasen, P. R. (1972). Cross-cultural Piagetian research: A summary. *Journal of Cross-Cultural Psychology*, *3*(1), 23–40. DOI: 10.1177/002202217200300102

Diamond, A. (2013). Executive functions. *Annual Review of Psychology*, *64*(1), 135–168. DOI: 10.1146/annurev-psych-113011-143750 PMID: 23020641

Flavell, J. H. (1979). Metacognition and cognitive monitoring: A new area of cognitive–developmental inquiry. *The American Psychologist*, *34*(10), 906–911. DOI: 10.1037/0003-066X.34.10.906

Gay, G. (2018). *Culturally responsive teaching: Theory, research, and practice* (3rd ed.). Teachers College Press.

Gentner, D., & Holyoak, K. J. (1997). Reasoning and learning by analogy: Introduction. *The American Psychologist*, *52*(1), 32–34. DOI: 10.1037/0003-066X.52.1.32 PMID: 9017930

Gentner, D., & Smith, L. (2012). Analogical reasoning. In Ramachandran, V. S. (Ed.), *Encyclopedia of Human Behavior* (2nd ed., pp. 130–136). Elsevier. DOI: 10.1016/B978-0-12-375000-6.00022-7

Gopnik, A. (2020). Childhood as a solution to explore–exploit tensions. *Philosophical Transactions of the Royal Society B, 375*(1803), 20190502.

Gopnik, A., Meltzoff, A. N., & Kuhl, P. K. (2004). *The scientist in the crib: What early learning tells us about the mind.* HarperCollins.

Gopnik, A., & Schulz, L. (2007). *Causal learning: Psychology, philosophy, and computation.* Oxford University Press. DOI: 10.1093/acprof:oso/9780195176803.001.0001

Gopnik, A., & Wellman, H. M. (2012). Reconstructing constructivism: Causal models, Bayesian learning mechanisms, and the theory theory. *Psychological Bulletin, 138*(6), 1085–1108. DOI: 10.1037/a0028044 PMID: 22582739

Hackman, D. A., & Farah, M. J. (2009). Socioeconomic status and the developing brain. *Trends in Cognitive Sciences, 13*(2), 65–73. DOI: 10.1016/j.tics.2008.11.003 PMID: 19135405

Heckman, J. J. (2011). The economics of inequality: The value of early childhood education. *American Educator, 35*(1), 31–47.

Hirsh-Pasek, K. (2009). A mandate for playful learning in preschool: Applying the scientific evidence.

Hmelo-Silver, C. E., Marathe, S., & Liu, L. (2017). Fish swim, rocks sit, and lungs breathe: Leveraging everyday experiences to teach complex systems thinking. *Educational Psychology Review, 29*, 1–23.

Immordino-Yang, M. H. (2015). *Emotions, learning, and the brain: Exploring the educational implications of affective neuroscience.* W. W. Norton & Company.

Inagaki, K., & Hatano, Y. (2002). *Young children's naive thinking about the biological world.* Psychology Press.

Jacobson, M. J., & Wilensky, U. (2006). Complex systems in education: Scientific and educational importance. *Educational Researcher, 35*(7), 3–12. DOI: 10.3102/0013189X035007003

Kementerian Pendidikan Malaysia. (2020). *Curriculum guidelines for preschool education in Malaysia.* Ministry of Education.

Kroll, J. F., & Bialystok, E. (2013). Understanding the consequences of bilingualism for language processing and cognition. *Journal of Cognitive Psychology, 25*(5), 497–514. DOI: 10.1080/20445911.2013.799170 PMID: 24223260

Kuhn, D. (2010). Teaching and learning science as argument. *Science Education, 94*(5), 810–824. DOI: 10.1002/sce.20395

Lehrer, R., & Schauble, L. (2015). Modeling and modeling practices in the development of scientific thinking. *Journal of the Learning Sciences, 24*(2), 133–174.

Lewis, C., Koyasu, M., Oh, S., Ogawa, A., Short, B., & Huang, Z. (2009). Culture, executive function, and social understanding. *New Directions for Child and Adolescent Development, 2009*(123), 69–85. DOI: 10.1002/cd.236 PMID: 19306275

Ministry of Education Malaysia. (2017). *National preschool standard curriculum.* Kurikulum Standard Prasekolah Kebangsaan.

Ministry of Education Malaysia. (2022). *Early childhood education statistics report.*

Miyake, A., & Friedman, N. P. (2012). The nature and organization of individual differences in executive functions. *Current Directions in Psychological Science, 21*(1), 8–14. DOI: 10.1177/0963721411429458 PMID: 22773897

Nisbett, R. E. (2003). *The Geography of Thought: How Asians and Westerners Think Differently... and Why.* Free Press.

Nisbett, R. E., Peng, K., Choi, I., & Norenzayan, A. (2001). Culture and systems of thought: Holistic versus analytic cognition. *Psychological Review, 108*(2), 291–310. DOI: 10.1037/0033-295X.108.2.291 PMID: 11381831

Nsamenang, A. B. (2008). Culture and human development. *International Journal of Psychology : Journal International de Psychologie, 43*(2), 73–77. DOI: 10.1080/00207590701859093 PMID: 22023601

Resnick, L. B. (1994). *Developing mathematical knowledge.* Lawrence Erlbaum.

Rogoff, B. (2003). *The cultural nature of human development.* Oxford university press.

Rogoff, B. (2023). Mutually constituting, fractal: Individual and cultural aspects of holistic process. *Review of Research in Education, 47*(1), 60–83. DOI: 10.3102/0091732X231224666

Saffran, J. R., Aslin, R. N., & Newport, E. L. (1996). Statistical learning by 8-month-old infants. *science, 274*(5294), 1926-1928.

Schön, D. A. (1983). *The reflective practitioner: How professionals think in action.* Basic Books.

Siegler, R. S. (2016). Continuity and change in the field of cognitive development and in the perspectives of one cognitive developmentalist. *Child Development Perspectives, 10*(2), 128–133. DOI: 10.1111/cdep.12173

Sterman, J. D. (2000). *Business dynamics: Systems thinking and modeling for a complex world.* Irwin/McGraw-Hill.

Sutton-Smith, B. (1997). *The ambiguity of play.* Harvard University Press.

Tan, C. (2018). *Comparing high-performing education systems: understanding Singapore, Shanghai, and Hong Kong.* Routledge. DOI: 10.4324/9781351238724

Tan, S., & Neo, M. (2022). Digital literacy in early childhood education: Systems reasoning and engagement. *Asia Pacific Journal of Education, 42*(3), 375–391. DOI: 10.53797/icccmjssh.v4i1.6.2025

UNESCO. (2022). *Early childhood care and education (ECCE) global monitoring report 2022.* https://www.unesco.org

UNICEF Regional Office for East Asia and the Pacific. (2021). *Early learning and development in Southeast Asia.*

Vygotsky, L. S. (1978). *Mind in society: The development of higher psychological processes.* Harvard University Press.

Zelazo, P. D. (2015). Executive function: Reflection, iterative reprocessing, complexity, and the developing brain. *Developmental Review, 38*, 55–68. DOI: 10.1016/j.dr.2015.07.001

KEY TERMS AND DEFINITIONS

AI Literacy: The foundational competencies required to understand, use, and critically evaluate artificial intelligence in everyday contexts (Brennan & Resnick, 2012; Druga et al., 2019).

Causal Reasoning: The ability to identify and explain cause: and: effect relationships between variables or events (Gopnik, 2012; Schulz & Bonawitz, 2014).

Cognitive Development: The progressive development of mental processes, including attention, memory, reasoning, and problem: solving, enables children to interpret and respond to their environment (Piaget, 1952; Siegler, 2016).

Pattern Recognition: The capacity to identify regularities or recurring structures in information, supporting prediction and categorisation (Chevalier et al., 2020).

Systems Thinking: The ability to understand interactions within a system, including patterns, interdependence, and feedback mechanisms (Senge, 2006).

Chapter 6
AI Literacy in Early Language Development:
Teaching Young Learners the Foundations of Communication With AI

Vivit Rosmayanti
http://orcid.org/0000-0002-3648-9878
Universitas Negeri Makassar, Indonesia

Bellona Mardhatillah Sabillah
Universitas Megarezky, Indonesia

Wahyu Muh. Syata
Universitas Halu Oleo Kendari, Indonesia

ABSTRACT

This chapter explores the use of artificial intelligence (AI) in early childhood language education, focusing on its potential to enhance vocabulary, grammar, and social-emotional communication skills. It discusses the role of AI tools like voice assistants and chatbots in enhancing these skills. The chapter also discusses the importance of equity, inclusivity, and ethical design in AI-based learning tools. It calls for teacher training, interdisciplinary collaboration, and ongoing research to ensure AI supports safe, effective, and meaningful language learning for young learners.

DOI: 10.4018/979-8-3373-4893-3.ch006

027, IGI Global Scientific Publishing. Copying or distributing in print or electronic forms without written permission of IGI Global Scientific Publishing is prohibited. Use of this chapter to
tive artificial intelligence (AI) technologies is expressly prohibited. The publisher reserves all rights to license its use for generative AI training and machine learning model development.

INTRODUCTION

The implementation of artificial intelligence (AI) technology in various aspects of education is rapidly progressing, which changes the structure and manner in which students learn. As stated, AI is the "simulation of human intelligence processes by machines, especially computer systems," which includes natural language processing, machine learning, and robotic process automation (Park & Kwon, 2023). AI in education is aimed at offering learning experiences ranging from engaged learning through interactivity at the student level to personalized learning (Yuen & Schlote, 2024). AI technology in education is a double-edged sword. In the field of education, technology integrated with pedagogy offers countless possibilities; however, roadblocks to learning intertwine with the use of powerful AI technology, which can become intrusive in the learning ecosystem. Computer-aided design (CAD) systems, along with adaptive learning programs, require new literacy initiatives and AI-driven tools to support learners at primary education levels (Nguyen et al., 2022).

Understanding AI is vital for students today because it has become integrated into educational frameworks. The need is greater during the initial stages of language learning, where the relationship between language skills and AI is distinct. According to Barua et al (2022), children exposed to AI learning systems tend to learn more because these systems offer tailored responses and encouragement. With the increasing adoption of AI tools for teaching, educators need to understand that there is more to be gained now than simply learning how to operate the tools; learners need to grasp their basic working principles.

The intersection of AI technology and language learning reveals that AI's capabilities extend far beyond augmenting education; they represent a fundamental change in language acquisition and comprehension. Historically, language learning strategies have depended on rote memorization alongside repetitive drills; however, AI offers far more sophisticated options that adapt to the learner's pace. By leveraging cutting-edge algorithms, AI applications can personalize instruction, adapting the vocabulary, grammar, and conversations to each learner's level and speed (Rusmiyanto et al., 2023). Such flexibility is more useful and engaging, as activities can be relevant and tailored to be enjoyable (Liu, 2023). Additionally, recently developed AI tools, namely, conversational agents and interactive language applications, help younger learners participate in discussions that go beyond the textbooks and confines of the classroom. These tools help children talk and communicate in real-life situations, thus reinforcing classroom learning (Idham et al., 2024). Specifically designed tools for language acquisition, such as Duolingo and Babbel, have proven effective in developing languages through gamified learning, which captures the attention of young learners. Thus, AI serves not only as an additional tool but as an integral part of the language learning tools used today.

In the language learning context, the possible advantages that AI could bring are not equal to the practical realities, such as the need for in-depth teacher training or ethical issues related to AI. Teachers need to understand the very basics of AI, not only in its technological features, but also in its pedagogical meanings (Makeleni et al., 2023). There are ethical considerations that accompany the use of AI in the classroom. There must be responsible boundaries that are set to define issues of transparency, fairness, privacy of information, and bias in the use of AI technologies in early language development. To prepare educators and students for AI-enhanced language learning, both 'learning with AI' and 'learning about AI' require equal attention (Park & Kwon, 2023). Teachers need to be able to deliver classes that incorporate AI technologies as learning tools, and AI technologies need to be simplified for students to foster critical intellectual reflection on such systems (Davoodifard & Eskin, 2024). Moreover, there is a need to deal with restrictive AI-related rules ethical dishonesty, technology dependency, and others so that while students can take advantage of AI technologies, they are able to nurture the skills that they will need in a technology-dominated world (Makeleni et al., 2023).

In short, the incorporation of AI into foundational language skills signifies a progressive evolution in teaching methodology, offering comprehensive learning experiences designed for the developmental level of pre-primary students. AI literacy strengthens the claim that technology literacy is an essential pillar for learning in the 21st century, empowering students and AI technology graduates to engage with and navigate a technology-dominated global landscape. As education transforms, immediate action in the form of investigating and discussing the diverse issues and possibilities that AI offers young learners and teachers is needed.

THEORETICAL FOUNDATION OF LANGUAGE DEVELOPMENT IN YOUNG CHILDREN

Key Theories of Language Acquisition

The process of language acquisition in early childhood has garnered considerable attention in the fields of linguistics, psychology, and pedagogy. The principles of language development can be organized within three behavioral, nativist, and interactionist theories. All these theories differ in their explanations of the processes responsible for language acquisition in children, considering the available environmental factors that aid learning.

The behaviorist approach, which was developed by B.F. In this theory, language acquisition is learned by children as a result of operant conditioning. In this theory, language acquisition is learned by children as a result of operant conditioning. The theory suggests that environmental factors and adults speaking with children are necessary for children to learn languages. The theory suggests that environmental factors and adults talking with children, spoken language, are necessary for children to learn languages. Children learn the languages they hear, and they are trained to form complex utterances. Behaviorism as a theory has been critiqued for its neglect and lack of attention to the cognitive capabilities of children, as it overwhelmingly focuses on stimulation and response rather than on the cognitive processes accompanying language pedagogy (Bórquez Morales & Hernández Alvarado, 2021).

Conversely, nativist explanations, often linked with Chomsky, maintain that children have a natural ability to acquire languages from birth. Chomsky argues that every human language is derived from a single common grammatical foundation, which he calls Universal Grammar. Aligning with nativism, he claims that the environment makes a language's culture available only to a limited degree; it is the environment together with the child's existing grammatical scaffold that explains the child's mastery of language. This position supports the notion that the specific frameworks and core cognitive elements that nativist children possess are essential for successfully navigating the learning journey of a language. Nativists cite the phenomenon of how quickly children can acquire languages as strong evidence that biologically determined processes enable children to learn languages.

In addition, interactionist theories integrate behaviorist and nativist theories, emphasizing mental functions and the environment in language learning. One of the best-known interactionist theorists, Lev Vygotsky, stressed the role of social contact in learning and advocated that language learning is mediated by social contact. Children acquire and internalize the rules of language by interacting with parents, teachers, and peers who guide them. This notion illustrates the dynamic interplay between a child's cognitive development and the language stimuli provided to them. Interactionist theories advocate that language acquisition occurs optimally when children participate in active, contextualized, and substantive dialogues.

The influence of the surroundings on language learning is profound. Children depend on varied speech, which contains the use of child-directed speech that employs simplified vocabulary, higher singing voices, and deliberate hand movements. Many studies have confirmed that this type of speech helps in vocabulary and grammar acquisition (Kachergis et al., 2021). Moreover, children significantly benefit from both active engagement and passive listening to the language used around them, including adult conversations (Loukatou et al., 2021). This background language helps weave together the myriad functions of language that children need to understand and, eventually, use to correctly master their first language.

Furthermore, both the quantity and quality of input matter significantly. Studies have shown that parents who interact verbally with their children throughout the day support strong language skills by providing an abundant vocabulary and advanced grammar (Azhimia & Parnawati, 2023). Moreover, the effectiveness of language input increases when it is relevant because children are able to use their prior knowledge, experiences, and context to make connections with new vocabulary (Kachergis et al., 2021). The unique cognitive structures that children possess alongside the language input they receive from their surroundings support the claim that language acquisition is an active process and not a passive one.

In summary, while behaviorist, nativist, and interactionist theories of language acquisition may differ in approach, they all agree that environmental input is a pivotal constant. These theories posit that, through a blend of imitation, a built-in desire for language, and social relationships, children are equipped with the ability to communicate effectively. Understanding these core theories and the critical influences of the environment should enable educators to support children's language development effectively.

Cognitive Development and Language Learning

Language learning greatly impacts young children's cognitive development, and vice versa. Insightful studies have examined the intricate processes underlying children's language acquisition. The cognitive processes that children use to understand and produce language and how they interact and communicate are the result of advanced systems working together. In this case, I will focus on the mechanisms that facilitate the processing of language in very young children, the cognitive aspects that enable this process, the value of early cognitive development in the context of artificial intelligence, and other relevant instances where AI tools are utilized.

Child language acquisition integrates AI and cognitive science in interesting and, at times, understudied ways. For the child, the cognitive processing of language involves various mechanisms within the child that are active in making sense of the language input to which they are exposed. From an early age, children show the ability to extract structural patterns from their surroundings. For example, they are capable of processing the statistical properties of speech and word boundaries (Marino et al., 2020). AI and cognitive science are constantly approaching learnability paradigms and language understanding. Through these studies and AI tools, we can comprehend language understanding, which is referred to as statistical learning, by strengthening the social-cognitive understanding of children.

Processing language is in young children and is closely linked to their emerging skills of executive functions, such as working memory, attention, and cognitive flexibility, which are evolving. Throughout early years, children need to carry out very intricate and manage complex linguistic tasks, such as understanding conversations within syntactic structures. To manage such advanced, complex tasks and concepts, these executive functions of working memory and attention are crucial.

The development of executive functions develops equally to the language skills, which benefits the cognitive growth of the child, as these functions help in language skills (Yan, 2022). In addition, the child can learn and is exposed to language from diverse contexts, such as homes, schools, and media, and even in every the child can go and learn provides the child with new cognitive, and the child's cognitive development can help them to adjust to the new cognitive expectations and perform very well in such new growing multilingual spaces, this is most pronounced in this era of globalization and new technology (Tariq, 2026).

Understanding environmental learning inputs alongside language learning reveals cognitive development more clearly. Children's vocabulary is directly tied to both comprehension and the quality and quantity of language they hear. The associated cognitive processes allow the memorization of vocabulary alongside an understanding of how and in what contexts words can be used. For instance, maternal input substantially influences language development, and there is evidence to indicate that a mother's verbal interaction interventions are associated with better vocabulary and grammatical competencies in children (Castro et al., 2020). The quantity and quality of verbal interactions provide the necessary cognitive scaffolding that allows children to make connections and internalize language structures.

With the advancement of AI technology in education, it is essential to understand the early stages of cognitive development. Current research suggests that AI can provide customized language teaching tailored to an individual child's cognitive development and learning style. Using natural language processing and machine learning, AI tools can pose specific linguistic challenges suited to a child's cognitive level and developmental stage. For instance, AI language applications can offer real-time feedback, adapt the complexity of tasks, use interactivity that engages cognitive processes, and stimulate language learning on multiple levels.

In addition, AI assists in language learning, not only in vocabulary and grammatical acquisition, but also in developing critical thinking and problem-solving skills. Through the use of AI tools that mimic dialogues and situational contexts, children are able to engage in deep thinking, which strengthens their understanding and retention of the language (Chen et al., 2020). This is especially valuable in bilingual contexts, which enables children to use their thinking skills in more than one language, thus advancing not only their language acquisition but also the development of their executive functioning skills. The study of bilingualism has maintained that knowing more than one language may provide the individual with some cognitive benefits, including greater cognitive agility and improved recall ability, thus highlighting the importance of cognitive development in the learning process (Durand-López, 2020).

In summary, children's cognitive development is a determining factor in how they process language during early childhood, initiating the path towards language acquisition. The driving factors of cognitive development, paired with the language spoken in the child's environment, highlight the need to pay special attention to these external elements in the language acquisition process. With the heightened influence of technological advancements, such as artificial intelligence, the focus on cognitive development during language acquisition has shifted even further towards children. Parents and educators need to be able to nurture the cognitive development of children so that they not only master a given language but also undergo healthy cognitive development that equips them for the academic and social opportunities awaiting them in the later stages of their lives.

AI TOOLS FOR ENHANCING LANGUAGE DEVELOPMENT

The advent of artificial intelligence (AI) technologies has greatly advanced the development of language, providing new methods to involve young learners in language acquisition processes. These technologies include language learning voice applications, language learning chatbots, and interactive stories and games designed for language development. The growth of AI-powered learning technologies in the education industry enables the development of learning experiences based on the fluctuating requirements of learners (Yunina, 2023). These tools, which leverage data analytics and machine learning, support personalized learning pathways for young language learners, thus improving outcomes.

AI language tools include conversational and language chatbots that interact with learners and simulate conversations. These AI platforms are taking language learning to new heights by allowing learners to practice conversations with AI, thereby eliminating the fear of making mistakes (Fountoulakis, 2024). With the real-time conversational capabilities offered by Duolingo, ChatGPT, and other chatbots, learners can engage in real-time interactions and receive on-the-spot feedback. Such interactions stimulate learners and enhance motivation, as users can monitor and celebrate their learning milestones (Moybeka et al., 2023; Tariq, 2026).

Another significant speech recognition technology domain improves language learning at the levels of pronunciation, vocabulary, and grammar. Instruments that use NLP technology can assess learners' speeches and provide them with instant feedback on pronunciation and grammar, allowing for self-modification and enhancement (Zou et al., 2023). For example, AI-based applications assist children with accent refinement by observing how they speak and providing instructions on how to adjust their pronunciation to match native speech. Such self-adjustment feedback systems not only aid learners' self-confidence at an early age but also promote language self-correction. These tools help refine language skills and, equally important, aid in fostering critical listening and speaking skills needed for effective communication. Engaging with AI-driven applications that mimic real-world dialogues helps children refine their listening and comprehension skills, which are vital for effective communication (Roumeliotis & Tselikas, 2023). Moreover, their comprehension and vocabulary are enhanced as learners interact with various storytelling apps that provide ample language-rich contexts (Belda-Medina & Goddard, 2024). This type of interaction is critical for fostering the development and understanding of different cultures as learners engage with different perspectives, which is particularly important in the era of globalized language learning. The tools also allow AI to construct situations that encourage children to explore and be more creative in their use of language. Through interactive storytelling, children are allowed to steer narratives, which in turn tailors language development to their creativity. This is very different from Konyrova's (2024) notion of learning through rote memorization. This engagement offers something much more beneficial: the ability to learn through active participation, thus enabling the formation of deeper linguistic and cognitive associations. Children learn to think critically when they are allowed to dictate the storyline, decide what should and should not happen with the characters, and express their ideas (Makeleni et al., 2023). Table 1 introduces multiple AI tools.

Table 1. AI Applications in Early Language Development

AI Tool / Technology	Function in Language Learning	Learning Benefit for Young Children
Chatbots and Conversational Agents	Simulate real-life conversations and provide instant feedback	Improves speaking confidence and conversational fluency
Speech Recognition Systems	Analyse pronunciation and provide corrective feedback	Enhances pronunciation, listening, and self-correction skills
Interactive Storytelling Applications	Enable learners to engage with and influence narratives	Develops vocabulary, creativity, and comprehension
Gamified Language Learning Apps	Use rewards, levels, and challenges to teach language concepts	Increases motivation, engagement, and retention
Adaptive Learning Systems	Personalise content based on learner progress and ability	Supports individual learning pace and cognitive development

AI technologies enable educators to create more inclusive learning environments through personalized learning experiences. These technological tools adapt to different learning preferences and paces, considering the range of learners' cognitive abilities. Research has shown that personalized learning pathways boost students' motivation and engagement over long periods (Gutiérrez, 2023). The attention and resources needed for learners to flourish can now be provided because AI tools adapt to personal learning patterns, thereby counteracting the damage caused by the universalistic approach that is prevalent in education. The benefits of AI in language learning and development are counterbalanced by ethical issues and data privacy concerns. It is crucial to ensure that AI technologies designed for language learning are utilized fairly and ethically, as educators and developers seek to adopt these tools. Initiating conversations around these topics is important for creating safe spaces for worry-free learning while considering the protection of learners' data and privacy. In conclusion, AI technologies offer a revolutionary method for improving language acquisition among young children. The application of speech recognition, chatbots, and interactive storytelling offers a unique personalization in language learning that fosters active participation, motivation, and skill mastery. Through the application of AI, educators can adequately equip learners for proficient communication in a dynamically shifting sociolinguistic landscape and simultaneously nurture the educational and ethical concerns posed by the use of such technologies.

INTEGRATING AI INTO EARLY LANGUAGE EDUCATION

Using AI to Support Vocabulary Building

The use of artificial intelligence (AI) in technologies designed for children's early language education is a revolutionary strategy for vocabulary mastery, as children's word understanding and retention are augmented through AI-powered tools. AI applications and game technologies seek to build interactive ecosystems that facilitate vocabulary learning as a form of entertainment. These technologies utilize machine learning models to provide adaptive feedback and instruction; in the case of AI-powered consoles, vocabulary teaching is efficient and caters to every child's level of proficiency (Yuen and Schlote, 2024).

AI-powered vocabulary games can boost children's sustained interest and participation in early language education. Children are exposed to vocabulary in context through interactive storytelling and word recognition games programmed in applications such as Early Language Learning Australia (ELLA), a digital learning program for preschoolers that introduces children to various languages through app-based games. Leung et al. (2025) pointed out that children using such applications outperform their peers using traditional learning methods in terms of word retention and understanding. The gaming element fosters positive competition and collaboration, thus creating a healthy peer learning environment to explore vocabulary. These applications not only develop language competency but also allow children to develop essential cognitive skills needed for effective language mastery.

Multiple case studies have demonstrated the positive effects of AI-enabled vocabulary-building applications in the context of early education. In particular, one study evaluated the use of mobile applications in bilingual preschools. Leung et al. (2023) noted that AI-powered technologies significantly enhanced the vocabulary learning of preschoolers. It was noted that children who were app users showed greater improvement in their comprehension and production of words than those taught through traditional methods. These results emphasize the importance of providing gap-filling vocabulary instruction through such applications, which address and meet the requirements of different learners (Tariq, 2026).

An additional study of interest described the use of an AI-powered vocabulary application in a kindergarten class, in which vocabulary learning was facilitated through audio and video aids. Vocabulary and speech production significantly improved in children noted to use the app consistently (Dennis & Whalon, 2020). Educators noted that children exhibited an increased interest in learning new words and created a climate conducive to the development of literacy. The use of technology is critical for learner engagement and motivation, particularly in circumstances in which conventional materials and resources are not readily available.

Additionally, practical applications of AI provide immersion in contextual language, highlighting its relevance in vocabulary acquisition, an aspect of language learning that resources have neglected. Kołak et al. (2022) articulated how educational applications could be designed for preschool-age learners to expose them to some words that are unlikely to be part of their everyday conversations. The authors concluded that such educational applications are valuable in enriching children's language learning environments and fostering the use of vocabulary and language (Kołak et al., 2022).

Early language education, AI-driven applications, and games offer a new and innovative approach to vocabulary acquisition, especially for young learners. To this end, AI applications and games offer effective means of reinforcing word recognition and retention. As evidenced by numerous case studies, there have been many positive outcomes in different educational settings. The rapid evolution of language learning through technology presents new opportunities, and the use of AI holds great potential for young learners in vocabulary acquisition and language development.

Grammar and Syntax Learning through AI

The implementation of AI technologies in modern language instruction has fundamentally changed the ways in which learners acquire knowledge of grammar and syntax. The understanding of iterative and complex sentence forms and the corresponding grammatical rules has been greatly simplified with the help of dynamic and adaptive resources. Applications that are powered by AI technologies are designed to meet the individual's specific needs, which fosters an easier attainment of language skills. These tools offer advanced mechanisms that provide real-time responses, multifaceted explanations, and personalized lessons formulated to fit every child's pace (Akavova et al., 2023).

Natural language processing (NLP) has enabled intelligent tutoring systems to support learners with grammar and syntax, which has led to the widespread adoption of AI in this field. Automation of sentence-level grammar checks and suggestions for improvement is featured in AI-based tools such as "Grammarly" and "ChatGPT," which evaluate and correct learners' sentences using advanced algorithms (Fırat, 2023; Küçük, 2023). These AI technologies offer learners knowledge checks for sentence construction that provide bespoke contextual explanations of the rules, which learners often find difficult to comprehend. Research has confirmed that learners are more inclined to study autonomously when they are provided with context-sensitive feedback that adds to the grammatical lesson (Hwang et al., 2023).

Moreover, dedicated grammar applications, such as Duolingo, incorporate game elements to simultaneously teach grammar, syntax, and vocabulary. These applications use numerous game elements to enhance learning and turn grammar practice into an enjoyable and productive exercise (Arvin et al., 2023). Such applications can meaningfully boost student motivation because of the transformed nature of traditional grammar drills and their interactive design. Furthermore, research indicates that participants in game-based learning environments retain grammar more effectively because they interact with the language in simulated real-world situations (Hwang et al., 2023).

AI aids in creating personalized learning engagements by enabling lessons to evolve with each learner's individual pace and advancement. This coarse-grained adaptability is essential for early language acquisition, in which children differ greatly in their adeptness and learning methods. Algorithms within AI frameworks have the capability to track and evaluate a student's performance within a lesson, modifying subsequent tasks and feedback to suit the evolving bandwidth and scaffold provided. For instance, an AI tutoring system could progressively introduce advanced grammatical constructs as a student learns the basic rules, ensuring mastery and preventing overwhelm (Xatamova & Ashurov, 2024). This tailored method fosters a child's efficient learning, resulting in advanced language pathways in which learners are instructed in direct relation to their intellectual growth and developmental milestones concerning language acquisition.

Moreover, the application of AI technologies for teaching grammar and syntax has been documented and successfully executed in the pedagogical sphere through the use of case studies. An example of this is the adaptive grammar learning application for first and second graders. It exhibited marked enhancement in the pupils' comprehension of sentence and grammar structures over a semester (Qin, 2024; Rosmayanti, 2025). It was observed that the learners who used the AI-based tool had marked improvements in their grammar evaluation in comparison to their counterparts who had conventional teaching methods. The AI-based tool's adaptability made it feasible for tutors to monitor every student's growth, thereby determining the aspects that required more teaching attention.

In an equivalent study, contextualized grammar teaching using AI at the level of the child's developmental zone led to a more sophisticated comprehension of complex structures by kindergarten pupils (Küçük, 2023). Teachers noted that the effective grammar teaching provided by these tools came with a desirable rapidity, which made it possible for grammar teaching to creative language activities that more greatly nurtured learners' competencies.

In addition, the most recent developments in AI technologies are likely to improve the possibilities of instruction in grammar, increasing the prospects of its integration with other forms of learning to create blended learning environments that combine face to face learning with technology-driven learning. Such an all-embracing approach allows learners to grapple with grammar in diverse ways, thus ensuring that they attain mastery not only in the mechanics of the language but also in its use to communicate effectively (Wang, 2025).

In summary, AI resources are vital for assisting learners with basic grammar and syntax in the early years of education. Intelligent tutoring systems, coupled with adaptive lesson design and individualized instruction, allow learners to grasp and implement grammatical concepts. The wider adoption of AI applications by educators enhances the learning experience and empowers learners to deal with intricate grammatical constructions. Although intelligently designed, AI-enabled systems have the potential to remodel language education by fostering an engaging and responsive learning environment.

AI AND SOCIAL INTERACTION IN LANGUAGE DEVELOPMENT

The use of artificial intelligence (AI) in language teaching brings new possibilities to improve communication and social interaction among children. Children now have the opportunity to use chatbots and virtual assistants as learning partners, which helps them to improve their social language skills. These AI tools aid in practicing language skills by providing a risk-free and fun atmosphere in which learners can engage in simulated dialogues using real language. With the integration of AI in education, children can have conversational AI, which trains them in automatic human-like speech interaction, thus supporting the development of critical social language skills such as turn-taking, understanding context, and answering appropriately (Linnemann & Reimann, 2024).

For example, "EnglishBot" and similar chatbots leverage the sophisticated functions of natural language processing (NLP) to assist students in practicing and applying grammar and syntax in context. As learners begin to use these tools, they adapt to conversational norms, including language use and appropriate replies (Ruan et al., 2021; Rosmayanti et al., 2022). This not only allows students to refine their language skills in a non-threatening context but also motivates learners to articulate their thoughts and ideas more freely and confidently. In addition, research indicates that using AI technology in and out of the classroom fosters a positive attitude towards language learning because students are more willing to practice speaking and conversational fluency in less formal interactions (Zou et al., 2023).

The influence of AI on developing empathy and emotional intelligence is important. Modern AI technologies have been created to attend to and react to the emotions of learners utilizing emotion detection algorithms. Emotion detection algorithms enable AI to gain insight into rendering useful affective and contextual feedback and emotional support throughout the process of verbal exchange. For example, some platforms equipped with recognition technologies work with a child by evaluating and adjusting their answers to emotional feedback during the conversation (Shi, 2024). This age-appropriate responsive interaction enables children to understand some of the social cues of emotions, thereby enhancing their abilities to identify emotions in themselves and others.

In addition, the advantages extend beyond the direct application of the language to social connections. Through AI, children learn vital social skills, such as emotional recognition and proper response management, which cultivates social navigation. Studies have shown that children actively using AI tools for emotional recognition and empathy skills tend to engage in more empathetic and socially aware behaviors than children who do not use such tools (Yin et al., 2024). For young learners, this emotional scaffolding is essential, as it helps build systems of strong communicative and relational competencies, which are vital in personal life and academic interactions.

Interacting with AI also encourages students to engage in collaborative learning. Through the use of social network-based interaction strategies, students can participate in group assignments that use AI for language practice (Zou et al., 2023). Group chatbots and collaborative story builders are examples of tools designed using these techniques that prompt children to participate in group work, with children sharing and negotiating ideas to construct narratives and solve problems in teams. This collaboration not only strengthens children's grammatical and vocabulary abilities but also enhances the social relationships of learners, offering a favorable context for children to practice social language skills.

As discussed throughout this paper, advances in AI technologies are instrumental in improving language skills by offering interactive pedagogy, in-depth experience, and emotional intelligence cultivation. Young learners are now able to converse using chatbots and virtual assistants, which aid in language skill development while also improving prerequisite social and emotional skills. As young learners interact meaningfully with AI, they develop social and emotional skills, along with the confidence required to communicate effectively in diverse social contexts. Looking ahead, the ever-increasing sophistication of AI technologies will likely continue to expand the boundaries of language teaching and learning, with social engagement becoming increasingly central to language learning.

ETHICAL CONSIDERATIONS AND CHALLENGES

With the rising use of artificial intelligence (AI) in language teaching, resolving ethical issues surrounding equity and fairness has become critical to ensure that technologies are applied responsibly. Perhaps the most critical issue is bias in AI tools, which risks language learning in several ways. AI tools are trained on datasets with unavoidably existing biases, resulting in the reproduction of stereotypes and exclusionary practices in education. This is worrisome in language teaching, where AI tools with biases can skew the portrayal of cultures and languages and influence learners' understanding of the social aspects of the world (Yunina, 2023). As Alrayes et al. (2024) pointed out, there is an urgent need for collaboration between educators, technology developers, and researchers to alleviate biases in AI systems. For example, educators and developers could focus on critically analyzing integrated AI systems to evaluate their impact on inclusivity and technology adoption. Cohen et al. (2024) suggest training educators to scrutinize the AI technologies used in lessons, which in turn informs educators to make better technology choices. It can also be argued that Cohen et al. 's (2024) prescriptive approach would center AI tools around ethical frameworks that overlook systemic biases. Safeguarding young learners' data privacy and security is particularly important when considering the use of AI in early learning settings. The use of AI-powered learning tools raises serious concerns pertaining to the access, storage, and use of sensitive data. In the case of young learners, the protection of personal data is vital, as breaches can compromise their well-being (Pack & Maloney, 2024). Schools and other educational institutions are responsible for enforcing strict data protection regulations and providing assurance about their data handling policies. All parents and teachers need to be informed of these policies, and they must actively work to champion the best outcomes for the children. Table 2 discusses bias, privacy, and responsible use.

Table 2. Ethical Challenges and Considerations in AI-Supported Language Learning

Ethical Issue	Description	Implications for Education
Algorithmic Bias	AI systems may reflect biases present in training data	Risk of misrepresentation of cultures and language use
Data Privacy and Security	Collection and storage of sensitive learner data	Need for strict data protection policies and transparency
Overdependence on Technology	Excessive reliance on AI tools for learning	May reduce critical thinking and independent learning skills
Transparency and Accountability	Lack of clarity in how AI systems make decisions	Requires explainable AI and informed use by educators
Digital Literacy and Responsibility	Need for learners to understand safe and ethical technology use	Promotes responsible engagement with AI tools

Additionally, the integration of AI in the classroom should be accompanied by teaching young learners about responsible online behavior. Children who will use AI in their learning should be taught how to act responsibly in digital spaces (Geurts et al., 2021). Such education should include the ability to understand the impact of sharing personal data online, the fundamental need for privacy, and how to evaluate online material. Children can be socialized to engage with AI technologies armed with a clear understanding of their legal and ethical implications, which in turn would enable them to positively use these technologies while protecting their own and others' data. In educational contexts, the convergence of AI, data privacy, and ethics presents a multifaceted challenge that must be addressed to reduce risks. As AI technologies emerge, there is a pressing need to strike a balance between safeguarding the interests of learners and reaping the benefits of AI to enhance learning. Communication, debates, and dialogues among key stakeholders, for example, educators, policymakers, technology developers, and parents, will help in the formation of ethical policies and AI regulations in language education, which ensures equity, transparency, and responsibility (Liu 2023).

In summary, the incorporation of AI in language education must be approached rigorously from an ethical standpoint. To advance equity in education, dismantling biases in AI, guaranteeing the privacy and security of data, and instilling responsible digital citizenship in young learners is crucial. With the increasing role of AI in education, coordinated action from various stakeholders, constant evaluation, and refinement of standards are needed to protect the interests of learners while leveraging the powerful, transformative capabilities of AI technologies.

CONCLUSION

In conclusion, the role of AI in language acquisition highlights the need for greater AI literacy among young learners. New technologies enable novel methods and resources to assist in language acquisition. When properly integrated, AI technologies offer personalized learning experiences for optimal engagement and social interaction, which can enhance language learning. With evolving technologies, educators can effectively design teaching strategies that address the multifaceted challenges faced by students. They can ensure that students acquire the competencies necessary to thrive in an educated, technology-laden society (AlAli & Wardat, 2024).

Important language learning opportunities can be built for students through the use of adaptive AI learning programs, intelligent tutoring systems for grammar training, and conversational practice exercises. With the proper frameworks in place, critical thinking, collaboration, and resilience can also be cultivated in young learners (Sanusi & Olaleye, 2022). Ethical endeavor AI gives rise to new challenges, such as bias built into the tools that are used and infringing on the privacy of data. Because of these challenges, policymakers and educators working to integrate technology into learning must have a more responsible practice in mind (Aghaziarati et al., 2023).

As children and students prepare for the future, the impact of AI will be critical because of the pervasiveness of technology in modern society. Students' access to and familiarity with AI technologies will impact the way they learn and their ability to function in sophisticated social and professional ecosystems. With the progression of AI technologies, research and development in the field of AI literacy for early education remain imperative. Educators, policymakers, and technology developers must collaborate to ensure that what is created serves all students and provides appropriate scaffolding to achieve bias-free education that integrates academic, social, and moral dimensions of education (Göçen & AYDEMİR, 2020).

Fostering an AI-informed professional environment for researchers ensures that AI-empowered tools serve not only as technological instruments but also as tools for critical analysis and ethical use. In current pedagogical discourse and policy-making, the ethical use of AI tools for language education continues to fuel discussion and combat the myriad of challenges that they pose to AI implementation. In an educational paradigm that embraces AI integration, the relentless evolution and refinement of AI-centric tools and applications will determine the success of learners' and educators (Sapci & Sapci, 2020; PAN, 2024).

In conclusion, the relentless advancement of AI in language education demands that educators design accessible, equitable, and meaningful frameworks for interaction that balance the development of language and 21st-century competencies for life in a technology-driven society. Empowering learners with ethical practices and a commitment to perpetual refinement will foster holistic education, which is necessary to thrive in a rapidly transforming educational paradigm driven by AI.

REFERENCES

Aghaziarati, A., Nejatifar, S., & Abedi, A. (2023). Artificial intelligence in education: Investigating teacher attitudes. *AITECHBESOSCI, 1*(1), 35–42. DOI: 10.61838/kman.aitech.1.1.6

Akavova, A., Temirkhanova, Z., & Lorsanova, Z. (2023). Adaptive learning and artificial intelligence in the educational space. *E3S Web of Conferences, 451*, 06011. https://doi.org/DOI: 10.1051/e3sconf/202345106011

AlAli, R., & Wardat, Y. (2024). Opportunities and challenges of integrating generative artificial intelligence in education. *International Journal of Religion, 5*(7), 784–793. DOI: 10.61707/8y29gv34

Alrayes, A., Henari, T., & Ahmed, D. (2024). ChatGPT in education: Understanding the Bahraini academics' perspective. *Electronic Journal of e-Learning, 22*(2), 112–134. DOI: 10.34190/ejel.22.2.3250

Arvin, N., Hoseinabady, M., Bayat, B., & Zahmatkesh, E. (2023). Teacher experiences with AI-based educational tools. *AITECHBESOSCI, 1*(2), 26–32. DOI: 10.61838/kman.aitech.1.2.5

Azhimia, F., & Parnawati, T. (2023). The contribution of language input, conducive learning environment, and motivation toward students' speaking proficiency. *Journal of Language Intelligence and Culture, 5*(1), 33–44. DOI: 10.35719/jlic.v5i1.122

Barua, P., Vicnesh, J., Gururajan, R., Oh, S., Palmer, E., Azizan, M., & Acharya, U. (2022). Artificial intelligence enabled personalised assistive tools to enhance education of children with neurodevelopmental disorders: A review. *International Journal of Environmental Research and Public Health, 19*(3), 1192. DOI: 10.3390/ijerph19031192 PMID: 35162220

Belda-Medina, J., & Goddard, M. (2024). AI-driven digital storytelling: A strategy for creating English as a foreign language (EFL) materials. *International Journal of Linguistics Studies, 4*(1), 40–49. DOI: 10.32996/ijls.2024.4.1.4

Bórquez Morales, L. S., & Hernández Alvarado, M. G. (2021). Exposición, Producción e Internalización: Input, Output, and Intake: Role and Relevance in Second Language Learning. *Edähi Boletín Científico de Ciencias Sociales y Humanidades del ICSHu, 10*(19). https://repository.uaeh.edu.mx/revistas/index.php/icshu/article/view/7869

Castro, D., Hammer, C., Franco, X., Cycyk, L., Scarpino, S., & Burchinal, M. (2020). Documenting bilingual experiences in the early years: Using the CECER-DLL child and family and teacher questionnaires. *Bilingualism: Language and Cognition, 23*(5), 958–963. DOI: 10.1017/S1366728920000401

Chen, L., Chen, P., & Lin, Z. (2020). Artificial intelligence in education: A review. *IEEE Access : Practical Innovations, Open Solutions, 8*, 75264–75278. DOI: 10.1109/ACCESS.2020.2988510

Cohen, S., Mompelat, L., Mann, A., & Connors, L. (2024). The linguistic leap: Understanding, evaluating, and integrating AI in language education. *Tydskrif vir Taalonderrig, 4*(2), 23–31. DOI: 10.54475/jlt.2024.012

Davoodifard, M., & Eskin, D. (2024). Exploring the role of generative AI in second language education: Insights for instruction, learning, and assessment. *Studies in Applied Linguistics and TESOL, 24*(1). Advance online publication. DOI: 10.52214/salt.v24i1.12863

Dennis, L., & Whalon, K. (2020). Effects of teacher- versus application-delivered instruction on the expressive vocabulary of at-risk preschool children. *Remedial and Special Education, 42*(4), 195–206. DOI: 10.1177/0741932519900991

Durand-López, E. (2020). A bilingual advantage in memory capacity: Assessing the roles of proficiency, number of languages acquired and age of acquisition. *The International Journal of Bilingualism, 25*(3), 606–621. DOI: 10.1177/1367006920965714

Fırat, M. (2023). What ChatGPT means for universities: Perceptions of scholars and students. *Journal of Applied Learning & Teaching, 6*(1). Advance online publication. DOI: 10.37074/jalt.2023.6.1.22

Fountoulakis, M. (2024). Evaluating the impact of AI tools on language proficiency and intercultural communication in second language education. *International Journal of Second and Foreign Language Education, 3*(1), 12–26. DOI: 10.33422/ijsfle.v3i1.768

Geurts, S., Koning, I., Vossen, H., & Van den Eijnden, R. (2021). A qualitative study on children's digital media use and parents' self-interest. *Journal of Child and Family Studies, 31*(7), 2015–2026. DOI: 10.1007/s10826-021-02074-3 PMID: 34580571

Göçen, A., & Aydemir, F. (2020). Artificial intelligence in education and schools. *Research on Education and Media, 12*(1), 13–21. DOI: 10.2478/rem-2020-0003

Gutiérrez, L. (2023). Artificial intelligence in language education: Navigating the potential and challenges of chatbots and NLP. *RSELTL, 1*(3), 180–191. DOI: 10.62583/rseltl.v1i3.44

Hwang, W., Nurtantyana, R., Purba, S., Hariyanti, U., Indrihapsari, Y., & Surjono, H. (2023). AI and recognition technologies to facilitate EFL writing. *Journal of Educational Computing Research, 61*(5), 1008–1035. DOI: 10.1177/07356331221137253

Idham, A., Rauf, W., & Rajab, A. (2024). Navigating the transformative impact of AI on English language teaching. *JES, 4*(1), 8–14. DOI: 10.56185/jes.v4i1.620

Kachergis, G., Marchman, V., & Frank, M. (2021). Toward a "standard model" of early language learning. *Current Directions in Psychological Science, 31*(1), 20–27. DOI: 10.1177/09637214211057836

Kołak, J., Monaghan, P., & Taylor, G. (2022). Language in educational apps for pre-schoolers. *Journal of Child Language, 50*(4), 895–921. DOI: 10.1017/S0305000922000198 PMID: 35481491

Küçük, T. (2023). AI integrated grammar teaching in language preparatory school. *International Journal of Social Sciences and Educational Studies, 11*(1). Advance online publication. DOI: 10.23918/ijsses.v11i1p1

Leung, S., Perry, C., Guy, J., Loats, D., Highfield, K., & Kaufman, J. (2025). Short-term exposure to second language apps modulates brain responses in preschoolers. *Infant and Child Development, 34*(3), e70015. Advance online publication. DOI: 10.1002/icd.70015

Linnemann, G. A., & Reimann, L. E. (2024). Artificial Intelligence as a New Field of Activity for Applied Social Psychology–A Reasoning for Broadening the Scope.

Liu, M. (2023). Exploring the application of artificial intelligence in foreign language teaching. *SHS Web of Conferences, 168*, 03025. https://doi.org/DOI: 10.1051/shsconf/202316803025

Loukatou, G., Scaff, C., Demuth, K., Cristià, A., & Havron, N. (2021). Child-directed and overheard input from different speakers. *Journal of Child Language, 49*(6), 1173–1192. DOI: 10.1017/S0305000921000623 PMID: 34663486

Makeleni, S., Mutongoza, B., & Linake, M. (2023). Language education and artificial intelligence. *Journal of Culture and Values in Education, 6*(2), 158–171. DOI: 10.46303/jcve.2023.14

Marino, C., Bernard, C., & Gervain, J. (2020). Word frequency is a cue to lexical category for infants. *Current Biology : CB, 30*(8), 1380–1386.e3. DOI: 10.1016/j.cub.2020.01.070 PMID: 32169213

Moybeka, A. M., Syariatin, N., Tatipang, D. P., Mushthoza, D. A., Dewi, N. P. J. L., & Tineh, S. (2023). Artificial Intelligence and English classroom: The implications of AI toward EFL students' motivation. *Edumaspul: Jurnal Pendidikan*, *7*(2), 2444–2454. DOI: 10.33487/edumaspul.v7i2.6669

Nguyen, A., Ngo, H., Hong, Y., Dang, B., & Nguyen, B. (2022). Ethical principles for AI in education. *Education and Information Technologies*, *28*(4), 4221–4241. DOI: 10.1007/s10639-022-11316-w PMID: 36254344

Pack, A., & Maloney, J. (2024). Using artificial intelligence in TESOL. *TESOL Quarterly*, *58*(2), 1007–1018. DOI: 10.1002/tesq.3320

Park, W., & Kwon, H. (2023). Implementing AI education in Korea. *International Journal of Technology and Design Education*, *34*(1), 109–135. DOI: 10.1007/s10798-023-09812-2 PMID: 36844448

Rosmayanti, V., Noni, N., & Patak, A. (2022). Students' acceptance of technology in learning English pharmacy. *International Journal of Language Education*, *6*(3), 314–331. DOI: 10.26858/ijole.v6i3.24144

Roumeliotis, K., & Tselikas, N. (2023). ChatGPT and OpenAI models: A preliminary review. *Future Internet*, *15*(6), 192. DOI: 10.3390/fi15060192

Ruan, S., Jiang, L., Xu, Q., Liu, Z., Davis, G. M., Brunskill, E., & Landay, J. A. (2021, April). Englishbot: An ai-powered conversational system for second language learning. In *Proceedings of the 26th international conference on intelligent user interfaces* (pp. 434-444). DOI: 10.1145/3397481.3450648

Rusmiyanto, R., Huriati, N., Fitriani, N., Tyas, N. K., Rofi'i, A., & Sari, M. N. (2023). The role of Artificial Intelligence (AI) in developing English language learner's communication skills. *Journal of Education*, *6*(1), 750–757. DOI: 10.31004/joe.v6i1.2990

Sapci, A., & Sapci, H. (2020). Artificial intelligence education in health informatics. *JMIR Medical Education*, *6*(1), e19285. DOI: 10.2196/19285 PMID: 32602844

Shi, L. (2024). AI-enabled emotion detection and adaptive learning systems. *Journal of Educational Computing Research*, *63*(1), 173–201. DOI: 10.1177/07356331241296890

Tariq, M. U. (2026). Algorithmic Nudging for Eco-Friendly Fashion: A Framework for Ethical AI Interventions. In Arantes, L. (Ed.), *Promoting Sustainable Consumption in Fashion With AI* (pp. 89–112). IGI Global Scientific Publishing., DOI: 10.4018/979-8-3373-5525-2.ch003

Tariq, M. U. (2026). AI-Powered Sustainability in Airline Operations: Digital Innovation as a Strategic Driver for Decarbonization and Efficiency. In Mizrak, F., & Rodoplu, D. (Eds.), *Strategic Innovation for Sustainable Aviation Management* (pp. 291–316). IGI Global Scientific Publishing., DOI: 10.4018/979-8-3373-4992-3.ch010

Tariq, M. U. (2026). AI-Driven Curriculum Design in Higher Education: Frameworks for Future-Ready Learning Ecosystems. In Abdelaal, R., & Kayyali, M. (Eds.), *AI Education Strategies for Future-Proofing Curriculum Design* (pp. 21–46). IGI Global Scientific Publishing., DOI: 10.4018/979-8-3373-2752-5.ch002

Xatamova, N., & Ashurov, J. (2024). The future of legal English learning: Integrating AI into ESP education. SPAST Reports, 1(7).

Yin, Y., Jia, N., & Wakslak, C. (2024). AI can help people feel heard. *Proceedings of the National Academy of Sciences of the United States of America, 121*(14), e2319112121. Advance online publication. DOI: 10.1073/pnas.2319112121 PMID: 38551835

Yuen, C., & Schlote, N. (2024). Learner experiences of AI-supported language learning. *Journal of Educational Technology Systems, 52*(4), 507–525. DOI: 10.1177/00472395241238693

Yunina, O. (2023). Artificial intelligence tools in foreign language teaching in higher education institutions. *The modern higher education review*, (8), 77-90.

Zou, B., Du, Y., Wang, Z., Chen, J., & Zhang, W. (2023). AI speech evaluation programs in EFL. *SAGE Open, 13*(3). Advance online publication. DOI: 10.1177/21582440231193818

Zou, B., Guan, X., Shao, Y., & Chen, P. (2023). Social network-based AI-assisted language learning. *Sustainability, 15*(4), 2872. DOI: 10.3390/su15042872

KEY TERMS AND DEFINITIONS

Artificial Intelligence (AI): The ability of computer systems to perform tasks that normally require human intelligence, such as understanding language, recognizing patterns, and making decisions.

Chatbot: A computer program that uses artificial intelligence to simulate human conversation, allowing learners to practice language skills through interactive dialogue.

Cognitive Development: The gradual growth of mental processes such as memory, attention, and problem-solving that support children in understanding and using language.

Early Language Development: The stage in childhood when foundational communication skills emerge, including vocabulary building, grammar awareness, and social interaction through language.

Machine Learning: A branch of artificial intelligence in which computer systems learn from data and improve performance over time without being explicitly programmed.

Natural Language Processing (NLP): A technology that enables computers to analyze, understand, and respond to human language in meaningful and useful ways.

Personalized Learning: An approach to education in which technology adapts content, pacing, and feedback to meet the unique needs and abilities of each learner.

Speech Recognition: A technology that allows computers to interpret spoken language and convert it into text, often used to help learners improve pronunciation and speaking skills.

Technology-Enhanced Language Learning (TELL): Language instruction supported by digital tools, including artificial intelligence, to improve student engagement and learning outcomes.

Virtual Assistant: An AI-powered tool that interacts with users through spoken or typed communication to provide information, guidance, or language learning support.

Chapter 7
Building Simple AI Projects: Hands-On Learning Without Coding

Sumanth Banakar
http://orcid.org/0009-0004-3316-8106
University of the Cumberlands, USA

ABSTRACT

This chapter proposes a hands-on approach to AI education for children aged 6-12, focusing on building simple AI projects without the need for coding, a barrier I've seen firsthand in my work with technology integration. Leveraging my experience in system design, I aim to create activities that allow young learners to interact with AI concepts through tangible, code-free methods. For instance, children could design a basic AI-driven sorting game using physical objects like colored blocks, where they define rules for an AI to follow, such as grouping by color or size, using pre-built tools like Google Teachable Machine's image recognition features. Another activity might involve creating an AI-assisted storyboard, where children input ideas into a drag-and-drop interface to generate a narrative, then refine it based on their creative vision. These projects are grounded in experiential learning principles, ensuring children actively engage with AI processes while bypassing technical hurdles.

INTRODUCTION

In today's rapidly evolving technological landscape, fostering artificial intelligence (AI) literacy from an early age is no longer a luxury but a necessity. For primary school educators, the challenge often lies not in the "why," but in the "how"—how

DOI: 10.4018/979-8-3373-4893-3.ch007

027, IGI Global Scientific Publishing. Copying or distributing in print or electronic forms without written permission of IGI Global Scientific Publishing is prohibited. Use of this chapter to tive artificial intelligence (AI) technologies is expressly prohibited. The publisher reserves all rights to license its use for generative AI training and machine learning model development.

to introduce complex computational concepts in a way that is developmentally appropriate, engaging, and accessible to all young learners. This chapter, "Building Simple AI Projects: Hands-On Learning without Coding," addresses this challenge head-on. It moves beyond abstract theory to demonstrate that the foundational principles of AI and robotics can be effectively taught without requiring students to write a single line of complex code. Through a focus on visual programming environments, tangible robotics kits, and interactive simulations, we will explore how students can actively construct their understanding through doing. Ultimately, this chapter serves as a guide to creating a supportive learning environment in which curiosity is ignited, critical thinking is nurtured, and every child can gain the confidence to navigate, understand, and shape our AI-driven future.

BUILDING SIMPLE AI PROJECTS

Simple AI projects in primary education offer young learners an exciting opportunity to acquire the basics of artificial intelligence (Su & Zhong, 2022). Exercises such as building a chatbot enable students to learn about natural language processing on a practical level (Williams et al., 2019). For example, students can utilize services such as Scratch or Teachable Machine by Google to enter various commands and responses and launch a basic chatbot, thereby discovering how to create conversations and the mechanisms of AI learning (Su & Zhong, 2022). Likewise, projects such as creating a game using artificial intelligence and making the difficulty adapt depending on the performance of the user expose students to the idea of machine learning (Sinha et al., 2023). In addition to increasing interest, being a part of a game also develops the necessary skills of programming logic thinking and problem-solving (Kafai & Burke, 2014). Practical learning experiences, including the development of interactive fantasies with responsive characters tuned to react to user commands following a set of predetermined AI scripts, can enable students to learn the art of storytelling and the AI perspective (Chen et al., 2024). These projects do not involve much coding and can be scaled appropriately to different age groups, which is why they are also applicable to primary students (Sullivan & Strawhacker, 2021). Moreover, teachers may suggest the idea of collecting and analyzing data, allowing learners to create experiments that will be used by the AI to learn in real-time, that is, learn to identify various objects or emotions (Lin et al., 2025). The given projects can enhance cooperation and innovation because students can collaborate in groups to brainstorm, create, and revise their AI models (Naida et al., 2024). Such a form of experiential learning promotes an understanding of AI technologies and contributes to both the curiosity of playing as well as the grounds educational background during the exploration of the technologies (Aravantinos et al., 2024).

Hands-On Learning Approaches

Practical learning methods play a pivotal role in the implementation of robotics and AI in the primary curriculum because they ensure that students have the opportunity to learn through experience and build curiosity and creativity (Sullivan & Strawhacker, 2021). Educational robotics allows the creation of an environment in which learners are encouraged to apply theoretical knowledge in real-life situations by involving them in collaborative projects (Hu et al., 2024). For example, through building kits such as LEGO Mindstorms or any other robotics platform, students can design, build, and program robots to perform specific tasks to improve their knowledge of concepts related to programming and engineering (Schafer, 2004). Moreover, teamwork is an essential part of practical projects; small groups of students usually have to overcome problems, and cooperation and communication skills are promoted in such a manner as well, despite improvements in technical experience (Naida et al., 2024). This teamwork setting resembles that observed in the real world, where people are required to collaborate to be creative and develop solutions to issues (Aravantinos et al., 2024). In addition to robotics, practical learning involving AI can be incorporated through projects that involve the generation of low-level algorithms or interaction with learning-enhanced AI tools (Lin et al., 2025). For example, teachers can assist students in creating different AI-powered chatbots that respond to specific questions or assist peers with study materials, grounding abstract ideas in a user-friendly environment (Chen et al., 2024). In addition, practical activities enhance the understanding of concepts through trial and error, where students can run their projects and revise them based on the reactions and outcomes (Su & Zhong, 2022). Hands-on learning strategies are vital in raising a generation of students not only versed with the basics of robotics and AI but also with critical thinking and ingenuity to solve problems (Olari et al., 2021).

Project-Based Learning

Project-based learning (PBL) is a teaching-learning strategy that focuses on student engagement with real-life projects; therefore, it is especially suitable to include robotics and artificial intelligence (AI) in primary school education (Su & Zhong, 2022). Within the PBL structure, students complete a project gradually, which enables them to explore a field of study in-depth and learn problem-solving and implement knowledge in a team-based, hands-on setting (Naida et al., 2024). Examples can include designing a robot capable of navigating a maze or taking certain actions based on certain environmental sensors, so that students can seal their experiences of the aspects of the programming principles and the engineering sciences (Schafer, 2004; Hu et al., 2024). Such a practical choice not only improves technical knowledge but also fosters creativity and critical thinking because students create technical solutions and find solutions to technical problems (Aravantinos et al., 2024). It starts with the formulation of a central driving question or challenge that is aimed at leading students to definite learning goals (Su & Zhong, 2022). During the project, students are involved in research, planning, and teamwork; they may use a robotics kit, such as LEGO Mindstorms or VEX Robotics, which offer possibilities to easily prototype the ideas of students (Lin et al., 2025). Furthermore, communication proficiency is developed because PBL students are able to present their findings and solutions to other students and educators and discuss their learning process and experience getting feedback (Olari et al., 2021). PBL, due to the inclusion of aspects of robotics and AI, can help an educator build a lively learning experience that will inspire students, develop an interest in STEM-related fields, and provide them with important competencies that will be necessary in their academic and professional endeavors in the future (Sullivan & Strawhacker, 2021).

Collaborative Learning

The potential of integrating robotics and AI in primary education through collaborative learning provides a vibrant method of inculcating team spirit and critical thinking among learners (Naida et al., 2024). This teaching approach motivates students to cooperate in putting together projects on robotics, where other students are allowed to exchange ideas, split tasks, and jointly solve problems (Aravantinos et al., 2024). For example, during the construction of a robot with the help of platforms, such as LEGO Mindstorms or VEX Robotics, students will be able to assume various roles, such as programmer, engineer, and designer, and, as such, will have an opportunity to utilize their unique capabilities based on individual strengths and learn with and about each other (Schafer, 2004; Hu et al., 2024). Not only does this process help them improve their technical knowledge, but it also contributes to communication and interpersonal skills that help them operate in the current interconnected world (Su & Zhong, 2022). Studies have revealed that learners who engage in small school teams experience increased engagement and performance rates than learners who undertake individual programs (Kewalramani et al., 2021). To engage in collaborative learning efficiently in the classroom, a teacher can make use of such robotics-based platforms as LEGO Mindstorms or VEX Robotics, which typically contain collaborative functions and materials that allow students to work in teams (Lin et al., 2025). Moreover, the organization of projects based on actual problems can also encourage students as they will understand the practical connection of their group work (Su & Zhong, 2022). Making students believe that they are part of a team and, in this case, part of managing their learning will not only make them feel committed and eager to complete their learning goals but will also lay the foundation for creating a caring environment to encourage creativity and innovativeness (Olari et al., 2021). To conclude, with the combined features of collaborative learning in teaching robotics, students will not only be able to learn technical aspects but will also gain the necessary life skills that will help them deal with challenges in the future (Sullivan & Strawhacker, 2021).

Inquiry-Based Learning

Inquiry-based learning (IBL) is a student-based strategy that helps develop a responsible attitude and problem-solving skills by tapping into exploration and discovery (Su & Zhong, 2022). Regarding the use of robotics and AI in primary schools, IBL allows learners to create their own questions, conduct research, and solve problems in the form of projects (Olari et al., 2021). Such a pedagogical approach is perfectly intertwined with robotics, as students can explore programmed devices, work with manipulating programs, and observe the consequences of their actions (Lin et al., 2025). For example, students may be asked to design a robot to travel through a maze; therefore, they will ask questions about issues such as sensors, navigation algorithms, and fault-finding techniques (Schafer, 2004). They will converse, form hypotheses, and educate themselves based on the consequences of their experiments as they cooperate to assemble and program their robot, thus reaffirming the iterative quality of the engineering design procedure (Hu et al., 2024). Next, IBL promotes resilience because learners are likely to experience failures and must think innovatively and adapt (Kewalramani et al., 2021). The important role of a teacher in leading an IBL classroom is to moderate conversations, supply materials, and ask specific questions that will help develop further knowledge, but not necessarily indicate an answer (Aravantinos et al., 2024). Robotics not only increases the level of engagement in IBL but also ensures that students are prepared to survive in a technology-driven world, as they will be taught to think critically when dealing with systems (Sullivan & Strawhacker, 2021). Overall, the combination of robotics, AI, and IBL creates a generation of learners that is not only skilled in the use of technology but also prepared to find solutions to problems analytically and hands-on (Naida et al., 2024).

Experiential Learning

Primary school learning, particularly experiential learning via robotics and AI, has a significant impact on learning experiences that can be advantageous to students (Sullivan & Strawhacker, 2021). It can be listed among the main strengths because it encourages active participation, allowing students to immerse themselves in the office of practical work related to the practical use of the material (Hu et al., 2024).

For example, when gaining technical skills in building and programming, students build and learn with a robot kit, such as LEGO Mindstorms and VEX Robotics, and experience a sense of accomplishment and ownership of their work (Schafer, 2004). In addition, experiential learning develops critical thinking and problem-solving skills because students face challenges when constructing or programming (Su & Zhong, 2022). They are motivated to hypothesize, test, and redesign their solutions to achieve successful results, thereby improving their cognitive flexibility (Olari et al., 2021). Such a setting promotes teamwork, as pupils tend to complete their assignments in groups, thus developing communication skills and interpersonal interactions (Naida et al., 2024). The practical application of theoretical lessons strengthens the learning process and enhances memory and effectiveness (Aravantinos et al., 2024). Additionally, as students experience some failures in a non-threatening environment, they also become resilient and learn to think with a solution-based orientation (Kewalramani et al., 2021).

Practical learning is an effective motivator because it enables learners to make, test, and innovate, providing them with a sense of agency in their educational processes (Chen et al., 2024). Working with robots can be interesting and generate enthusiasm in students because they can collaborate in teams, and thus, the educational process is social and interactive (Lin et al., 2025). Having control over physical robotic kits, such as LEGO Mindstorms or VEX Robotics, will enable children to see and touch the parts, which may unlock the mysteries behind complicated concepts and technology, removing barriers to learning (Sullivan & Strawhacker, 2021). Moreover, the gamification of learning activities using robotics is supported by the idea of instilling a spirit of challenges and critical thinking in students who aim to find a solution to design issues or to get a code to work (Sinha et al., 2023). This type of activity is enhanced with the instant feedback that hands-on learning is accompanied with; the student sees their concept brought to life as they gradually perfect their knowledge (Su & Zhong, 2022). The more they troubleshoot and experiment, the more intrinsically motivated they become and the more likely they are to endure in the face of a challenge (Olari et al., 2021). The multiplicity of learning modes that robotics makes accessible (i.e., kinesthetic, visual, and collaborative learning) also satisfies the needs of different learning styles, further boosting motivation (Naida et al., 2024). Students feel a great sense of achievement when they observe the practical results of their work, for example, teaching a robot how to move in a maze or detect obstacles in a crowded room, which contributes to higher confidence and readiness to deal with new challenges (Hu et al., 2024).

Playing with robots does not mean that children are merely passive receivers of facts but must actively follow their projects by designing, completing the programming, and solving issues (Aravantinos et al., 2024). Therefore, it teaches children to think analytically. This practical style enables learners to find solutions, analyze them, and construct good solutions (Su & Zhong, 2022). When robotics students engage in different activities, they are exposed to numerous problems to tackle, including finding ways to make a robot maneuver an obstacle course or writing to make it perform certain acts within limitations (Lin et al., 2025). In every challenge, they are asked to consider various approaches, compare advantages and disadvantages, and test their designs and codes, an activity tantamount to critical thinking (Schafer, 2004). Furthermore, robotics activities encourage students to work as a team and communicate, as learners must share and iron out ideas among each other (Naida et al., 2024). Peer feedback practice also enhances their skills to reevaluate their strategies and introduce the changes required, the key elements of successful problem-solving (Kewalramani et al., 2021). Under favorable conditions of practical work, students understand how to formulate questions, design experiments, use different resources and sources to learn the information, and eventually end up with a powerful toolkit for solving problems in the real world (Olari et al., 2021).

Screen-Free Learning

The importance of screen-free learning in children is multifaceted because screen time has been associated with diverse adverse effects, such as shortened attention spans, sleep impairment, and lack of creativity (Sullivan & Strawhacker, 2021). Practical screen-free activities help children develop greater concentration and improve their cognitive skills, enabling them to solve complicated tasks (Su & Yang, 2022). Through hands-on learning experiences, children acquire critical thinking and analytical skills, which are valued in an increasingly technology-inclined world (Olari et al., 2021). In addition, learning without screens promotes active movement and communication, which are significant for healthy development and emotional well-being (Kewalramani et al., 2021). Block building, role-playing, and nature exploration stimulate a sense of belonging to a stronger world and evoke curiosity and imagination regarding the surrounding reality (Sullivan & Strawhacker, 2021). Furthermore, children can cooperate and share ideas by using robotics-related activities that do not require screens, such as physical basic robotic kits (e.g., LEGO Mindstorms), improving their ability to work as team members (Hu et al., 2024; Naida et al., 2024). Tactile and sensory experiences acquired during screen-free learning may trigger neural pathways vital for development (Su & Zhong, 2022). Studies confirm that children learn more efficiently when actively engaged in the educational process but not when digesting information with the help of a screen (Aravantinos et al., 2024). By focusing on experience-based learning that bypasses digital gadgets, educators and parents can provide children with the basic skills they will require to achieve success in life and further acquire artificial intelligence (Lin et al., 2025). Such adoption is in line with the vision concerning the creation of AI literacy, as it allows children to learn the foundation of AI in an applied form and develop the necessary life skills, which can no longer convey (Sullivan & Strawhacker, 2021).

Programming Concepts for Young Learners

Exposing young learners to programming concepts is essential for instilling rudimentary knowledge that can enable them to navigate an increasingly digitized world (Su & Zhong, 2022). Early exposure to programming enables children to think logically, solve problems, and gain insights into how technology functions (Munusamy et al., 2025). Concepts such as sequences, loops, and conditionals can be explained with persuasive and relevant examples that stimulate astonishment and innovation (Sullivan & Strawhacker, 2021). For example, one can use a relatively easy task, such as a list of instructions for navigating a robot through a maze, to teach children not only the significance of accuracy in coding but also the experience of physically working with a robot (Schafer, 2004). Moreover, the principles of algorithms can be taught, as it may lead to the development of the concept of dividing various responsibilities into smaller, manageable ones (Lin et al., 2025). The given programming concepts can be supplemented with collaborative projects where learners create their own coding tasks and develop teamwork and communication skills (Naida et al., 2024). When incorporated into the curriculum in an entertaining and engaging manner, these basic concepts would help establish the foundation upon which more sophisticated programming and computational thinking strategies would be learned in the future, sparing young learners the role of merely technology users but active users and producers/innovators of a technology-driven world (Kafai & Burke, 2014; Aravantinos et al., 2024).

INTRODUCTION TO PROGRAMMING

In the contemporary digital world, programming is a core skill, and learning about it at a very early stage should be the most significant change, bringing problem-solving and critical-thinking skills to the next level (Munusamy et al., 2025). Fundamentally, programming entails giving a computer machine instruction on what to perform; in the case of young learners, they can start with simplistic commands, for example, sequence, loops, and conditional statements (Su & Zhong, 2022). Robotics in programming enables children to see and touch what their code does in the real world, which in turn gives them a better understanding of abstract concepts (Schafer, 2004). To put it simply, one can teach students to program a robot with basic commands to operate itself to pass through a maze, which would simultaneously help them learn the concept of programming and strengthen their understanding of the need to test and debug and think about algorithms (Lin et al., 2025). In addition, age-specific tools help use programming platforms and tools to complete learning tasks and make the learning experience engaging and user-friendly (Chen et al., 2024). Such sites allow students to learn to code by dragging and dropping the pieces of code into order to form interactive stories, games, and animations, which is easy to begin with coding and encourages creativity and self-efficacy (Kafai & Burke, 2014). These experiential learning activities are then included in the programming projects of robotics solutions, and the peers get to collaborate with their peers and solve issues together and present their programming solutions (Naida et al., 2024). Finally, making students undergo programming-based education starting at a primary level not only supports students in developing the proper technical skills but also inculcates the mindset of innovativeness and persistence that they will be able to use in an increasingly technological world (Aravantinos et al., 2024).

Visual Programming Languages

VPLs provide an attractive and user-friendly approach to learning new coding concepts, particularly suitable for young learners in primary education (Chen et al., 2024). Students can program by placing and manipulating graphical objects instead of typing code, thereby lowering the barrier to entry for new learners (Sullivan & Strawhacker, 2021). Some widely known VPLs, such as Scratch, Blockly, and Tynker, are implemented using a drag-and-drop interface that allows users to assemble blocks to model various programming codes and logical constructions (Munusamy et al., 2025). As shown in Figure 1, the visual design of these platforms not only increases the accessibility of programming but also enhances engagement by allowing children to quickly visualize the results of their efforts, and the feedback they receive helps consolidate knowledge through interaction (Su & Zhong, 2022).

Figure 1. A young learner uses a visual programming language (VPL), such as Scratch, to demonstrate how drag-and-drop blocks make coding concepts accessible and engaging, as discussed in the Visual Programming Languages section.

When used in a classroom setting, VPLs may be combined with educational robotics environments so that students can program robots using the graphical code they write (Lin et al., 2025). This real-life experience stabilizes their knowledge of programming logic and strengthens their critical thinking and problem-solving skills (Schafer, 2004). Moreover, the collaborative nature of VPLs will challenge students to collaborate with each other, exchange ideas, and work out widespread problems, thus strengthening their social and communication abilities (Naida et al., 2024). VPLs provide teachers with the opportunity to support project-based learning, in which students have the opportunity to engage in creative activities in which learning programming concepts can be put into practice in a real-world situation based on their interests (Kafai & Burke, 2014). With the current developments in education, the use of VPLs in primary schools is appropriately placed to enable young students to develop the necessary skills that will serve them in the future, even in a digital world (Aravantinos et al., 2024).

VISUALIZING AI CONCEPTS

It is vital to present AI concepts in visual terms to make them more comprehensible to primary school students, as they are not likely to understand abstract concepts (Su & Zhong, 2022). Diagrams, flowcharts, and infographics can efficiently represent the functioning of AI algorithms and determine how the flow of data works and how the decision-making mechanism is represented (Munusamy et al., 2025). For example, Figure

Figure 2. A simplified visualization of a neural network using diagrams to make complex AI concepts, such as data processing and decision-making, comprehensible for young learners.

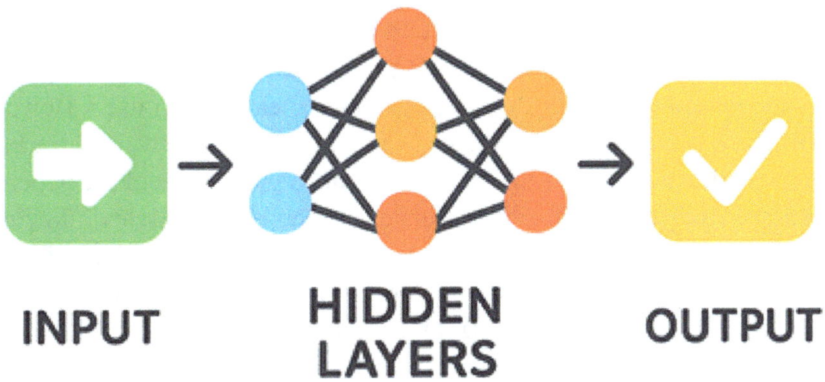

For example, neural networks can be represented using simplified images to illustrate how data on the input turns into output with connected nodes, allowing for a comparison with corresponding data in the brain (Williams et al., 2019). This style demonstrates that AI is no longer a mystery and is becoming more familiar to young learners (Chen et al., 2024). In addition, interactive and colorful materials attract students and increase their interest in learning (Sullivan & Strawhacker, 2021). Another strong device for visualizing AI is an interactive simulation. Simulations enable students to edit AI models and learn how parameter changes impact the results of a machine learning model (Lin et al., 2025). For example, a simulation in which learners manipulate variables to affect the behavior of a virtual robot reinforces algorithmic knowledge and emphasizes the concepts of cause and consequence, which form the core of AI systems (Olari et al., 2021). However, through active learning of a digital nature, students can expand their understanding of AI concepts in addition to refining their critical-thinking and analytical abilities (Aravantinos et al., 2024). Having such practical experiences has been demonstrated to increase the understanding of how AI technologies work in the real world and accelerate the learning process (Su & Zhong, 2022). Overall, the use of such visual aids and interactive simulations can play a critical role in making AI a comprehensible and appealing topic of study among young learners and encouraging them to learn more and become passionate about it (Naida et al., 2024).

Using Visual Aids in Learning

Visual cues are essential for increasing information understanding and memorization, especially when using AI and robotics in primary school (Su & Zhong, 2022). Such media as diagrams, charts, and the use of infographics and interactive multimedia presentations simplify complicated ideas and make learning more interesting (Munusamy et al., 2025). For example, a teacher can use a flowchart to explain the flow of decisions or a video animation to explain how machine learning algorithms work when educating students on the key concepts of AI (Chen et al., 2024). These visual tools do not discriminate between learning styles, allowing each to learn in a desired way, as visual learning provides the opportunity to internalize information, whereas the interactive nature of animations appeals to kinesthetic learners (Sullivan & Strawhacker, 2021). In addition, augmented reality (AR) may further support the learning experience because students would be able to visualize different components of the robots or AI systems in real-time, physically and digitally, and better explore their spatial relationships and functionality (Lin et al., 2025). Moreover, visual aids put the theoretical and practical parts into perspective and create a point of reference that reinforces what is learned (Aravantinos et al., 2024). Visual aids are vital communication tools in group work, where they are used to discuss ideas with peers and explain ideas and provide feedback to others (Naida et al., 2024). This means that the development of a broader range of visual aids in the curriculum not only helps students understand AI and robotics but also makes this process more interactive and inclusive (Olari et al., 2021).

Interactive Simulations

Interactive simulations are an important educational feature of introducing AI and robotics to the primary education curriculum as they generate practical experiences through which students can be involved in the educational process (Lin et al., 2025). Such simulations enable students to see complicated ideas of AI, robotics, and coding in a visceral and interactive context (Su & Zhong, 2022). Students will be able to interact with virtual robots through interactive simulations, work with algorithms, observe the consequences of their actions on robots, and learn faster about the fundamental concepts like sensors, decision-making, and feedback loops (Olari et al., 2021). As an example, the tools, including Scratch, Tinkercad, and Blockly, offer individuals an opportunity to develop simulations that can depict the behavior of self-governing agents under different conditions without the use of tangible products (Chen et al., 2024). Also, using these tools fosters other important competences like problem-solving, critical thinking, and collaboration since it is common to separate students into teams in order to implement their simulations, test them, and iterate (Naida et al., 2024). These simulations are highly accessible, and their interfaces are user-friendly, which makes these simulations particularly efficient in primary education since they are suitable for the needs of learners with different technological expertise (Sullivan & Strawhacker, 2021). Using games and scenarios, which reflect real-life prospects of AI and robotics applications, the educator can help to establish an enriching learning environment, stimulating curiosity and exploration (Aravantinos et al., 2024). Using these interactive simulations, students acquire a practical experience in the implementation of theoretical knowledge and develop a sense of agency in their educational process, which predisposes them to continuing their studies in STEM-related disciplines (Kafai & Burke, 2014). Finally, interactive simulations applied in primary school based on a progressive model of teaching AI and robotics, which provides the potential generation with opportunities to learn about this new world of AI and robotics and understand how to operate and innovate in the more tech-savvy world (Munusamy et al., 2025).

Project Ideas for Primary School

The implementation of robotics and AI in primary education may include various interesting projects aimed at enchanting young minds and helping them better understand technology and its practical applications (Sullivan & Strawhacker, 2021). As one project, it is possible to build an avoidance robot with simple parts such as a microcontroller, motors, and sensors (Lin et al., 2025). Students have the opportunity to program and design their robots, which navigate a maze, and throughout the process, they are introduced to basic engineering and programming concepts (Schafer, 2004). The creation of a virtual assistant program that applies the simplest AI principles is another interesting project. With the help of Scratch or Blockly, students can create a staff that interacts with the user through basic voice commands or questions and become acquainted with the concept of natural language processing in a pleasant situation (Chen et al., 2024; Su & Zhong, 2022). In addition, the experimental application of storytelling to robotics will draw cross-curricular projects with a more seductive appeal; students will have the opportunity to act out scenes from their favorite books with the help of robots or develop new plots to tell, which will increase their creativity and technical skills (Kafai & Burke, 2014). Furthermore, pupils will be able to undertake one coding activity in which they will program a robot to complete a choreographed dance, and participants will be encouraged to participate in activities beyond coding abilities, but also team instigation and innovativeness, as they will choreograph the dance (Naida et al., 2024). Finally, community engagement (as a result of a project that promotes environmental awareness) may be effective. Robotics can be used to solve real problems and fulfill civic duties by having students create robots to clean up a particular space or scan the environment to detect environmental conditions (Aravantinos et al., 2024). All these projects are at an accessible and flexible level, as teachers can adjust them to the different skill levels of their learners, while simultaneously imparting a love of robotics and AI (Olari et al., 2021).

Obstacle-Avoiding Robot

The Obstacle-Avoiding Robot project provides practical experience introducing primary education students to the basics of robotics and programming, where theory and practice are combined (Lin et al., 2025). In this endeavor, students will be taught the importance of creating a robot that can move within a defined space with a series of obstacles, for example, a small maze, to promote the learning process of robotic functioning (Schafer, 2004). This project begins by going through simple robotics concepts, focusing on the use of hardware devices such as microcontrollers, motors, and sensors (Hu et al., 2024). The chosen components are ultrasonic sensors to locate obstacles, servo motors to move around, and a microcontroller board, which is the brain of the robot (Sullivan & Strawhacker, 2021). Collaboration in teams is actively promoted among students, and the processes of communication and project management are also encouraged during the design, building, and programming stages (Naida et al., 2024). In this project, STEM concepts not only feature but also encourage creative problem-solving, where students plan how they want their robot to receive sensory data and alter its course when it hits an obstacle (Aravantinos et al., 2024). The desired effect is to understand robotic operations and acquaint students with the fundamentals of coding, as well as reduce the gap between abstract knowledge and its practical application (Su & Zhong, 2022). Moreover, the repeated cycle of testing and improving the structure and functions of the robot is regarded as training, as students gain the opportunity to see the significance of the debugging process and overcome challenges in the field of engineering through direct experience (Olari et al., 2021). Finally, the overall purpose of the Obstacle-Avoiding Robot project is to provide basic knowledge of robotics and excite students, encouraging them to study more about the use of technologies in their lives (Munusamy et al., 2025).

Components Required

To effectively construct an obstacle-avoiding robot in a primary school, multiple basic elements must be implemented to guarantee functionality and efficacy (Lin et al., 2025). In terms of hardware, the main requirement is a microcontroller (e.g., Arduino or Raspberry Pi), which will act as the robot's brain, processing the inputs and commands (Schafer, 2004; Tariq, 2026). Additionally, obstacle detection relies on sensors; typical types of sensors are ultrasonic or infrared sensors, as they provide data about the distance to the object and allow the robotic device not to crash against the obstacle (Hu et al., 2024). Motor drivers are crucial for controlling the robot's wheel movement to allow for easy and smooth rotation according to the sensor data (Sullivan & Strawhacker, 2021). When it comes to mobility, whether DC or servo motors are used, they provide the necessary torque and precision needed to make movements in narrow passages (Lin et al., 2025). Moreover, there is a structural component of the robot, a chassis kit that is a base constructed using different materials, and, in the majority of cases, wheels or tracks are implemented to allow movement (Hu et al., 2024). To have a reliable source of energy, power management components, such as batteries or power supplies, are important, and jumper wires and breadboards are used to aid in making connections to electronic parts (Schafer, 2004). In addition to hardware, software is also an essential part of the project. The logic that the robot has to follow must be programmed using a suitable programming platform, such as the Arduino IDE or Python (Munusamy et al., 2025). Educational resources such as simulation software, debugging tools, and online forums can be used to improve the learning process by providing students with access to solving problems and collaborating (Chen et al., 2024). When combined, these aspects form a complete set of measures that educators and students can use to learn the interplay between robotics and programming and be creative and critical thinkers in the context of primary school (Aravantinos et al., 2024).

DESIGNING THE ROBOT

Working in teams plays a central role in introducing robotics and AI into primary education, as it provides students with the opportunity to actively participate in a collaborative learning experience (Naida et al., 2024). Team collaboration helps create a team spirit and trains the necessary interpersonal skills among students, including the ability to communicate, negotiate, and resolve conflicts (Aravantinos et al., 2024). Students will need to adequately define roles according to their personal capabilities and preferences as they venture into the project of designing and constructing an obstacle-avoiding robot (Hu et al., 2024). For example, one student can assume the responsibility of creating the program, whereas other students create and test the hardware part of the program, for example, ultrasonic sensors or servo motors (Schafer, 2004). The given division of labor not only makes this project more manageable but also allows more effort to be devoted to it, and every team member will bring a distinct point of view and knowledge to work (Sullivan & Strawhacker, 2021). In addition, teamwork fosters problem-solving; when team members face challenges, they must find a way out creatively together, which is why problem-solving and all-weather character development occur (Su & Zhong, 2022). When it comes to effective teamwork, face-to-face meetings are held to allow students to discuss the progress achieved, the objectives, and provide feedback to their colleagues, hold them accountable, and encourage the development of a team culture (Olari et al., 2021). The integration of collaborative tools, such as a common online venue to manage a project or hold design meetings, would allow for improved interactions, particularly in larger teams (Chen et al., 2024). Finally, the process of collaboratively working on a robotics project prepares students for the future educational and working scenes, where cooperation and teamwork skills are indispensable (Kafai & Burke, 2014). This flexible learning model is consistent with the learning objectives of becoming not only technically competent but also socially competent in the context of a fast-changing technological environment (Munusamy et al., 2025).

Designing the project includes sketching the design, which is an essential part of the robotics project, in the form of a visual blueprint, which is used as a guide to the construction and coding processes of an obstacle-avoiding robot (Hu et al., 2024). Some rough sketches illustrate the arrangement of the robot, chassis, wheels, motors, sensors, and any other features, such as lights and bumpers (Schafer, 2004). Graph paper or computer-aided design software helps with making accurate measurements and scaling, which is critical to component-based integration (Lin et al., 2025). The possible shapes and sizes should be brainstormed by the students using parameters such as stability, weight distribution, and location of the sensors to achieve optimum obstacle detection (Sullivan & Strawhacker, 2021; Tariq, 2026). Playing with various design versions promotes creativity and innovation, and students record the advantages and disadvantages of each (Aravantinos et al., 2024). Team members can critique other ideas through feedback sessions, where the sketches are compared and the ideas are polished, resulting in a more utilitarian final product (Naida et al., 2024). The focus on a user-friendly interface should also be the primary concern, and sketches can feature button locations or communication interfaces to control accessibility (Chen et al., 2024). Such design practice also improves teamwork abilities and helps develop the sense of a cyclical design cycle in which improvements based on critical thinking lead to improved engineering (Olari et al., 2021).

The design must have a physical structure that is safe and convenient for young children to handle, and lightweight yet durable materials, such as plastic or aluminum, should be the material of choice to make the chassis suitable for transportation (Hu et al., 2024).

Figure 3. A student testing a small, wheeled robot that they built, which successfully navigated around a book or cone placed on the floor.

The robot should be equipped with sensors, such as ultrasonic or infrared sensors, placed in a location that can sense most obstacles and allow for a quick response to surrounding objects (Lin et al., 2025). Mobility is important; another consideration is the ease or difficulty of moving along the terrains of a classroom, which depends on the wheels or tracks (Schafer, 2004). The construction must be accessible to all electronics in a ready-to-assemble and maintainable fashion, such as the microcontroller and battery (Sullivan & Strawhacker, 2021). Cognitively, this design also represents an aesthetically effective element that includes playful features that make students more involved and entertained (Kafai & Burke, 2014). It is especially important for educational purposes; modular elements that can be handled by students encourage practical knowledge and learning about robotics (Su

& Zhong, 2022). Placing the design in the context of educational purposes, such as programming instructions or skill optimization in critical thinking, educators would enable people to gain a more profound knowledge of robotics and AI (Munusamy et al., 2025). A mobile application or a simple remote control with a user-friendly interface is a good way to make programming easy to use, even for young learners (Chen et al., 2024). The group project in design improves teamwork, as students will brainstorm, prototype, and make their robot more advanced, thus reinforcing their understanding of the principles of basic engineering and coding (Naida et al., 2024).

Interactive Chatbot Development

Chatbot development in primary education offers an appealing interactive experience in which students learn about artificial intelligence through practical work (Su & Zhong, 2022). Teachers can lead students via websites such as Scratch or Google Teachable Machine to create their own chatbots, as Facebook Messenger chatbots are working examples of natural language processing in practice (Chen et al., 2024). The first process involves installing the environment, during which the students become conversant with the programming interface (Munusamy et al., 2025; Tariq, 2026). In this context, they learn to organize the flows of conversations and specify the interactions between the chatbot and users via different inputs and answers (Williams et al., 2019). This action promotes critical thinking because learners assume the role of users by asking questions to their chatbots and structuring them to deliver the correct answers (Sullivan & Strawhacker, 2021). Once the conversation flows are established, the students can apply natural language processing solutions, which will allow the chatbot to better understand and work with user inputs (Su & Zhong, 2022). It can also entail training the chatbot to identify certain keywords or phrases and provide corresponding answers to develop greater interest in the mechanics of language in young learners (Chen et al., 2024). Students can explore the extensions of introducing more sophisticated features, such as contextual awareness, so that the chatbot can maintain a consistent flow of discussion, spanning a series of interactions (Lin et al., 2025). The entire process is also educational and creative because learners individualize their chatbots with specific themes and features, making learning entertaining and relevant (Kafai & Burke, 2014). Finally, the educational process of interactive chatbot creation enables students to learn the foundations of AI, sharpen their problem-solving skills, and prepare them to face the challenges of technology in the future (Aravantinos et al., 2024).

AI-Based Games and Simulations

Games and simulations using artificial intelligence have become a promising solution to the integration of learning in primary education, with both the fun they provide and their ability to inform (Sinha et al., 2023). Games use artificial intelligence that enables adaptive learning by matching a student with their level of performance (Chen et al., 2024). For example, platforms such as Minecraft: Education Edition use AI to form immersive learning experiences in which students learn mathematical, scientific, and coding concepts (Kafai & Burke, 2014). Problem-solving and critical thinking also develop through these interactive experiences, in which students go through challenges within the game (Su & Zhong, 2022). Moreover, simulations powered by AI reproduce real life, therefore allowing students to conduct experiments with air fracture, feedback, decay, and biology in a controlled, dynamic environment (Lin et al., 2025). As a potential example, virtual science experiments proposed by simulations such as Labster can be used in a regular classroom because they can be either dangerous or rather expensive to implement (Aravantinos et al., 2024). These games provide instant feedback and allow students to process real-time mistakes and learn from them (Olari et al., 2021). Furthermore, most games based on AI introduce group cooperative features, the use of which encourages teamwork and communication skills and forms a community in a classroom (Naida et al., 2024). These games are developed with the use of AI technologies, which render learning exciting and enable students to prepare to fight with a surprise in the future, building their digital literacy and technological proficiency (Munusamy et al., 2025).

Collaborative AI Projects

Participatory AI in primary education promotes cooperation, develops problem-solving abilities, and creativity in primary school children (Naida et al., 2024). Such projects entail the work of small groups of students devoted to the design and implementation of AI-based solutions to certain problems, including enhancements in school sustainability and the creation of simple interactive games (Aravantinos et al., 2024). Tools such as Teachable Machine by Google or Scratch are barrier-free platforms where students can gain practical knowledge of AI by learning about it in detail (Chen et al., 2024). For example, students may develop a machine learning model with environmental sound recognition, promote discussions about data collection, AI ethics, and the societal impact of technologies (Su & Zhong, 2022). By using interdisciplinary strategies, including adding art or storytelling, creativity can be brought into the expression of ideas (Kafai & Burke, 2014), and ensuring that the content is learned. These projects are supported by teachers who provide advice and materials and leave space for development and experimentation (Sullivan & Strawhacker, 2021). Presenting projects to the school-based community or online platforms will allow students to gain experience in presenting concepts and collecting feedback (Olari et al., 2021). By teaching collaboration and ownership through AI-related projects, it is possible to provide students with new skills of learning ownership and a growth mindset, as well as a basis of working knowledge of the concepts that define AI (Munusamy et al., 2025).

CREATING A SUPPORTIVE LEARNING ENVIRONMENT

The establishment of a positive learning environment is indispensable in the development of AI literacy, which directly influences students' involvement in challenging concepts (Su & Zhong, 2022; Tariq, 2026). A positive classroom helps develop confidence and a willingness to take risks to investigate the iterative characteristics of AI (Aravantinos et al., 2024). Emotional safety facilitates a culture of inquiry, which is essential to establish the applications of AI and its ethical aspects (Olari et al., 2021). A patient environment creates a positive experience and boosts engagement, motivation, and knowledge retention because students' contributions are valued (Naida et al., 2024). The combination of classroom spatial, resource, and emotional safety implies a holistic educational system, preparing students to live in an AI-centric world (Sullivan & Strawhacker, 2021).

Such a considerate learning environment can be created by building a physical and emotional area that facilitates safety, exploration, and engagement (Aravantinos et al., 2024; Su & Yang, 2022). An organized classroom must have open access and resources where children can engage in an interactive approach to learning about AI concepts (Lin et al., 2025; Sullivan & Strawhacker, 2021). Creating a day when a part of the time is dedicated to the inquiry-based learning style of learning will lead to the development of a question-asking and researching environment among students (Yang et al., 2024). In addition, flexible seating options can be introduced because this will allow holding meetings and working in groups, which will enable children to complete research projects linked to AI and technology (Hu et al., 2024). In addition to a physical space, it is also important to develop an environment that encourages mistakes to be regarded as learning opportunities (Munusamy et al., 2025). Student willingness to communicate their thoughts and hypotheses can be inspired, even in cases of uncertainty, and confidence instilled in solving problems and critical thinking (Sinha et al., 2023). To even improve this environment, educators should be trained to use effective communication tactics, provide clear instructions, and reassure students through new concepts (Naida et al., 2024).

Designing Physical Spaces

By designing spaces suitable for AI literacy, an atmosphere will be created that will involve the exploration and collaboration of learners (Hu et al., 2024). Classrooms should also be ample and accommodating, such that different seating options can be provided to facilitate group work, discussions, and exploration (Sullivan & Strawhacker, 2021). The arrangement could have groups of desks or tables that encourage interaction and enable students to experience joint projects that have the potential to help them learn AI concepts (Munusamy et al., 2025). Visual access to teaching sites, including whiteboards and screens, is essential to maintain engagement and ensure that every student has the opportunity to be engaged entirely (Lin et al., 2025). Moreover, a combination of different areas in the classroom, such as a tech corner with computers or tablets, a resource area with books and materials on AI, and a relaxed area where students can quietly reflect, should be able to meet different learning styles and needs, leading to a more equally balanced approach to learning (Su & Yang, 2022). Another premise of designing physical spaces regarding AI literacy is the availability of resources (Sinha et al., 2023). Teachers are encouraged to make any materials, whether digital or traditional, accessible to every student, including students with impairments (Chen et al., 2024). This implies arranging tools and materials in an intuitively friendly manner by taking into account different user needs (Naida et al., 2024). It is also imperative to integrate technology; therefore, classrooms must be adapted to include the relevant hardware and software that can facilitate AI learning (Schafer, 2004). Teachers should use learning technology, including smartboards, virtual reality equipment, or educational applications with the use of AI, to make the learning process more engaging and enriched (Olari et al., 2021). Ultimately, the physical learning environment should not only enhance a sense of belonging and participation but also ensure the necessary instruments that enable students to overcome the challenges of AI and build their literacy regarding this essential matter (Yang et al., 2024).

Classroom Layout

Classroom design is an essential factor in creating a positive atmosphere and encouraging AI literacy (Aravantinos et al., 2024). A flexible, accessible, and collaborative classroom layout should be considered the primary design (Sullivan & Strawhacker, 2021). With modular furniture, educators can easily change the exhibit layout of the desks and seats, allowing the formation of groups and interactive discussions that are necessary to explore and develop AI concepts (Lin et al., 2025). For instance, arranging desks in groups can promote teamwork-oriented projects, where learners can interact with their peers, exchange ideas, and discuss the solving of tasks in groups, which is closer to the collaborative spirit of AI in finding solutions to intricate problems (Munusamy et al., 2025). In addition, it is possible to implement a variety of seating options, such as bean bags, standing tables, or even lounges, so that different users feel more comfortable and have distinct learning preferences (Hu et al., 2024).

Another aspect to consider is equipping the classroom with the necessary devices and facilities for AI learning, such as projector devices, whiteboards, and group screens (Sinha et al., 2023). An efficient workspace with as few distractions as possible also ensures the availability of resources and, consequently, an easy transition between different learning activities, such as discussions, practical work, and simulations (Su & Zhong, 2022). In addition, it is possible to set up technology exploration zones where students can focus on writing or robotics, become more interested in the subject, and gain firsthand experience with AI tools (Chen et al., 2024). The layout must support the needs of all students so that they feel welcome and comfortable (Naida et al., 2024). In this case, mobility aids can easily pass through the pathways, materials should be reachable and visible to all students, and the materials should be placed appropriately (Olari et al., 2021). To conclude, smart design is not the only aspect of the classroom setting, as it will contribute to a significant increase in engagement, collaborative work, and the coverage of different learning styles to create a holistic concept of understanding AI literacy (Yang et al., 2024).

Resource Accessibility

The availability of resources plays a critical role in enhancing positive learning experiences with regard to AI literacy development because it provides equal access to the materials and tools required for successful interactions with artificial intelligence concepts to all learners (Hu et al., 2024; Lin et al., 2025). It not only supplies material equipment, such as books, programs, and devices, but also ensures that students have access to digital materials, regardless of their socioeconomic status (Sullivan & Strawhacker, 2021). For example, schools can introduce loaner programs (tablets, laptops, etc.) that support students who do not have access at home (Chen et al., 2024). In addition, one can form a partnership with local libraries or community centers, where learners can access resources beyond school (Munusamy et al., 2025). The variability in the availability of resources is also important; each learning style and capacity can be accommodated by a variety of multimedia elements, including videos, interactive tutorials, and hands-on kits (Sinha et al., 2023). The education of teachers who learn how to find their way around these resources and how to use them is of particular importance because they are the agents of education (Naida et al., 2024). By implementing this strategy, educators can reduce the number of quotas on access to knowledge about AI and better understand its concepts and practical uses (Su & Yang, 2022). In addition, constant reviews of resource situations and their activities should be conducted, and based on them, educators should adjust to the new reality of AI technology evolution and ensure that the given learning resources are up-to-date and helpful to the educational process of these students (Yang et al., 2024).

Creating a Safe Atmosphere

It is also critical to consider that developing a safe environment in the classroom would enable the development of AI literacy, as learners will not be afraid to express themselves (Aravantinos et al., 2024). This consists of introducing ground rules favoring respect, inclusivity, and open communication (Olari et al., 2021). To make learners feel appreciated, educators should adopt and reaffirm positive behavior and suggest empathetic and supportive relationships to their students (Su & Zhong, 2022). This environment can be further promoted by fostering a culture in which the imperfection of mistakes is not considered but rather viewed as a learning experience so that students can practice the concepts of AI without focusing on making perfection (Schafer, 2004). Periodic check-ins and feedback sessions could also be used to estimate the level of emotional well-being of the students so that they would be comfortable sharing their thoughts and concerns (Yang et al., 2024). It is also important to ensure that any bullying or exclusion is handled as quickly as possible because the practice can lead to serious interference with the capacity of a learner to become involved and risk-taking in the development circle of exploration of AI (Munusamy et al., 2025).

REFERENCES

Aravantinos, S., Lavidas, K., Voulgari, I., Papadakis, S., Karalis, T., & Komis, V. (2024). Educational approaches with AI in primary school settings: A systematic review of the literature available in Scopus. *Education Sciences*, *14*(7), 744. DOI: 10.3390/educsci14070744

Chen, L., Xiao, S., Chen, Y., Song, Y., Wu, R., & Sun, L. (2024, May). ChatScratch: An AI-augmented system toward autonomous visual programming learning for children aged 6-12. In *Proceedings of the 2024 CHI Conference on Human Factors in Computing Systems* (pp. 1-19). DOI: 10.1145/3613904.3642229

Hu, C. C., Yang, Y. F., Cheng, Y. W., & Chen, N. S. (2024). Integrating educational robot and low-cost self-made toys to enhance STEM learning performance for primary school students. *Behaviour & Information Technology*, *43*(8), 1614–1635. DOI: 10.1080/0144929X.2023.2222308

Lin, A., Salonen, A., Pope, N., Vartiainen, H., & Tedre, M. (2025, April). A versatile low-cost kit for teaching novice learners ai using robotics components and a no-code development playground. *Proceedings of the AAAI Conference on Artificial Intelligence*, *39*(28), 29162–29170. DOI: 10.1609/aaai.v39i28.35189

Munusamy, P., Sanmugam, M., & Edwards, B. I. (2025). Exploring the World of Coding in Artificial Intelligence: A Guide for Primary School Students. In *Fostering Inclusive Education With AI and Emerging Technologies* (pp. 165-182). IGI Global.

Naida, R., Berezovska, L., Bulgakova, O., Kravets, N., & Savchenkova, M. (2024). Integrating Innovative Pedagogical Technologies Into Early Childhood Education Training Programs: A Comparative Analysis. *Conhecimento & Diversidade*, *16*(41), 568–595. DOI: 10.18316/rcd.v16i41.11551

Olari, V., Cvejoski, K., & Eide, Ø. (2021, May). Introduction to machine learning with robots and playful learning. *Proceedings of the AAAI Conference on Artificial Intelligence*, *35*(17), 15630–15639. DOI: 10.1609/aaai.v35i17.17841

Schafer, J. B. (2004). Hands-on artificial intelligence education using LEGO Mindstorms: Lessons learned. In *Proceedings of the 2004 Midwest Instruction and Computing Symposium.*

Sinha, N., Evans, R. F., & Carbo, M. (2023, May). Hands-on active learning approach to teach artificial intelligence/machine learning to elementary and middle school students. In *2023 32nd wireless and optical communications conference (WOCC)* (pp. 1-6). IEEE.

Su, J., & Yang, W. (2022). Artificial intelligence in early childhood education: A scoping review. *Computers and Education: Artificial Intelligence*, *3*, 100049. DOI: 10.1016/j.caeai.2022.100049

Su, J., & Zhong, Y. (2022). Artificial Intelligence (AI) in early childhood education: Curriculum design and future directions. *Computers and Education: Artificial Intelligence*, *3*, 100072. DOI: 10.1016/j.caeai.2022.100072

Sullivan, A., & Strawhacker, A. (2021). Screen-free STEAM: Low-cost and hands-on approaches to teaching coding and engineering to young children. In *Embedding STEAM in early childhood education and care* (pp. 87–113). Springer International Publishing. DOI: 10.1007/978-3-030-65624-9_5

Tariq, M. U. (2026). Empowering Young Learners: Innovative Strategies for STEM and Literacy in Early Childhood Deaf Education. In Graham, P., & Neild, N. (Eds.), *Early Childhood Deaf Education: Teacher Preparation and Instructional Approaches* (pp. 231–258). IGI Global Scientific Publishing., DOI: 10.4018/979-8-3693-9127-3.ch007

Tariq, M. U. (2026). AI-Powered Assessment Platforms: Transforming Higher Education Evaluation. In Zaky, H. (Ed.), *Innovating Assessment and Evaluation in Higher Education: Inclusive Practices and Technological Advancements* (pp. 117–146). IGI Global Scientific Publishing., DOI: 10.4018/979-8-3373-2130-1.ch004

Tariq, M. U. (2026). Equity-Driven Leadership in Technology Integration for Higher Education. In Areba, G., Gisore, B., Njurai, E., Awuor, F., & Makiya Cyprian, R. (Eds.), *Transformative Leadership and Enhancing Equity in Technological Advancements in Higher Education* (pp. 171–198). IGI Global Scientific Publishing., DOI: 10.4018/979-8-3373-2322-0.ch007

Tariq, M. U. (2026). The Role of AI-Powered Learning Analytics in Enhancing Student Engagement and Performance. In J. Moore, S. Gupta, M. Sharma, A. Garg, & H. Josephine V. L. (Eds.), *Transforming Education With Data Science in the AI Era* (pp. 123-148). IGI Global Scientific Publishing. https://doi.org/DOI: 10.4018/979-8-3373-2185-1.ch005

Yang, W., Hu, X., Yeter, I. H., Su, J., Yang, Y., & Lee, J. C. K. (2024). Artificial intelligence education for young children: A case study of technology-enhanced embodied learning. *Journal of Computer Assisted Learning*, *40*(2), 465–477. DOI: 10.1111/jcal.12892

KEY TERM AND DEFINITIONS

Algorithm: A precise, step-by-step sequence of instructions designed to perform a specific task or solve a problem. In primary education, students learn about algorithms by creating ordered lists of commands, for example, to direct a robot through a simple maze.

Machine Learning: A branch of artificial intelligence (AI) that enables computer systems to learn and improve from data and experience without being explicitly programmed for every scenario. In simple projects, this is demonstrated when students train a model (e.g., using Google's Teachable Machine) to recognize different objects or sounds.

Project-Based Learning (PBL): A dynamic teaching method in which students gain knowledge and skills by working for an extended period to investigate and respond to an authentic, engaging, and complex question, problem, or challenge. In this context, PBL involves students in the end-to-end process of designing, building, and programming a robotics or AI solution.

Sensor: A hardware component that detects and responds to input from the physical environment, such as distance, light, or sound. In educational robotics, sensors (e.g., ultrasonic or infrared) provide the crucial data a robot needs to perceive and interact with its surroundings, such as detecting an obstacle to avoid.

Visual Programming Language (VPL): A programming environment that allows users to create programs by manipulating graphical elements, such as blocks or icons, instead of writing text-based code. This approach eliminates syntax errors and makes foundational programming concepts, such as sequences, loops, and conditionals, accessible and intuitive for young learners. Examples include Scratch and Blockly.

Chapter 8
Designing AI Literacy for Primary Education: A Global Comparative Study of Curriculum Frameworks, Pedagogical Approaches, and Policy Initiatives

Tebogo Lekota
University of Limpopo, South Africa

Oluwatoyin Ayodele Ajani
http://orcid.org/0000-0001-6545-0203
University of KwaZulu-Natal, South Africa

ABSTRACT

The systematic literature review looks into how AI literacy is integrated into primary education through different curriculum frameworks, pedagogical approaches, and policy initiatives across the global arena. Pulling from studies between 2000 and 2025, the review synthesizes research done in advanced and developing countries alike to arrive at overarching trends, challenges, and interesting pedagogies in early AI education: In some countries, AI is placed under computational thinking and digital skills curricula, while in others, isolated modules or interdisciplinary approaches are trialled. Pedagogical approaches range from experiential learning and gamification to project- and inquiry-based learning. While promisingly moving ahead, remaining gaps include teacher readiness, equitable access, and adequately supportive contextualised policies. We call for the evolution of AI literacy initiatives that subscribe to inclusivity, cultural responsiveness, and age-appropriateness, anchored by strong educational frameworks.

DOI: 10.4018/979-8-3373-4893-3.ch008

)27, IGI Global Scientific Publishing. Copying or distributing in print or electronic forms without written permission of IGI Global Scientific Publishing is prohibited. Use of this chapter to
ive artificial intelligence (AI) technologies is expressly prohibited. The publisher reserves all rights to license its use for generative AI training and machine learning model development.

INTRODUCTION

Boden (2018) and Ng et al. (2021a) have observed that the growing ubiquity of AI in daily life has significant implications for education, particularly at the primary level, where interactions with intelligent systems can shape children's cognitive, social, ethical, and emotional development. In response, AI literacy – encompassing the skills and understanding needed to engage with AI technologies, their applications, and their societal impacts – has rapidly emerged as one of the core competencies for the 21st century (Long & Magerko, 2020). AI literacy is increasingly recognized as a critical component of broader digital literacy initiatives, enabling young learners to engage with AI technologies confidently and ethically.

Introducing AI concepts at an early age provides a foundational awareness of areas such as digital thinking, critical thinking, and problem-solving, which complements higher-order skills such as computational thinking and digital citizenship (Wang et al., 2022; Eguchi, 2021). In this way, primary education that prioritizes AI literacy imparts not only core technical skills but also prepares pupils for a future shaped by widespread automation and big data. Equally important, it empowers them to critically navigate AI-driven systems in society, a capacity increasingly seen as crucial for equity and participation in democratic life (Aoun, 2017; Hermann, 2022).

Given its importance, education systems worldwide have begun to integrate AI literacy into primary curricula; however, progress remains uneven across contexts (UNESCO, 2022). For example, China, the United Kingdom (UK), and Finland have introduced national curricula or pilot programmes that embed AI learning objectives in primary education (Zhao et al., 2022; UNESCO, 2022). These initiatives reflect a growing recognition that AI education should begin early and employ pedagogies suitable for young children, covering both technological fluency and ethical understanding (Zhang et al., 2022; Druga et al., 2022). However, approaches to AI literacy in primary education remain fragmented: while some nations have developed comprehensive frameworks and teacher training programmes, others lack a coherent strategy and struggle with issues such as curriculum alignment, digital infrastructure, and teacher professional development (Casal-Otero et al., 2023; Celik, 2023). These disparities raise critical questions about how best to design AI literacy curricula, what instructional practices effectively cultivate AI literacy in young learners, and what policy support is needed to ensure sustainable implementation. To address these challenges, this study undertakes a systematic review of the literature on AI literacy in primary education across global contexts. The review has three primary objectives:

1. Examine and compare curriculum models that introduce AI concepts at the primary level

2. Analysis of pedagogical strategies used to promote AI literacy among young learners
3. Investigate national and regional policies that facilitate or hinder the integration of AI education at the primary level.

By pursuing these objectives, this chapter contributes to the growing body of work on operationalizing AI literacy in diverse educational settings (Ng et al., 2022; Cuomo et al., 2022). This study follows a systematic methodology guided by the PRISMA guidelines for systematic reviews (Moher et al., 2009), ensuring a rigorous and transparent process of identifying, selecting, and synthesising relevant studies published between 2000 and 2025. Comprehensive searches were conducted in major academic databases (Scopus, Web of Science, and ERIC) using keywords related to AI literacy, primary education, curriculum, pedagogy, and policy, supplemented by backward citation tracking and grey literature from organizations such as UNESCO. Sources meeting the inclusion criteria (e.g., a focus on AI literacy in primary and K–12 settings, with empirical findings, curriculum frameworks, or policy analyses) were selected and qualitatively coded in ATLAS.ti to identify key themes. The review emphasizes emerging thematic patterns and trends in the literature, as well as significant gaps that warrant further investigation. A systematic review approach is especially valuable given the rapidly evolving nature of AI in education, as it enables an evidence-based mapping of the field's current state. It provides a robust basis for recommendations to stakeholders, such as educators, curriculum designers, and policymakers, seeking to advance AI literacy in primary education. Furthermore, this comprehensive synthesis offers a foundation for conceptualizing AI literacy in ways that are developmentally appropriate, socially responsive, and pedagogically innovative (Chen et al., 2020; Ranieri et al., 2025).

This chapter is organized into several sections to reflect the multidimensional nature of the topic. This section examines the conceptual underpinnings of AI literacy, drawing on perspectives from computer science, education, and media studies. Subsequent sections present comparative analyses of how different global contexts approach AI literacy through their curriculum frameworks, teaching methodologies, and supporting policies. The chapter concludes with a critical discussion of the key challenges and opportunities identified, offering practical insights for implementation and directions for future research. Taken together, these sections underscore the need for a comprehensive and inclusive approach to AI literacy in primary education, one that combines technological competence with ethical understanding, cultural sensitivity, and equitable access for all learners. By synthesizing insights from diverse contexts, this work aims to catalyze global efforts to prepare young children to actively, knowledgeably, and justly engage in AI-mediated societies.

METHODOLOGY

In our research, we specifically examined the presence of AI literacy in primary curricula in different contexts. This systematic review process was aimed at ensuring that the collection, evaluation, and synthesis of fragmented research findings (Cooper et al., 2019) could be conducted through a well-structured and stringent strategy. The review was conducted in accordance with the Preferred Reporting Items for Systematic Reviews and Meta-Analyses (i.e., PRISMA) to provide a transparent and rigorous description and synthesis of the literature.

Selection Criteria and Screening Process

Studies were included only if they met all of the following requirements:

a) Surveys were conducted from 2000 to 2025.
b) They have focused on AI literacy (or related competencies) in primary education.
c) They contain empirical findings, a curriculum framework, or a policy analysis relevant to AI literacy.
d) In academic peer-reviewed literature (e.g., journal articles or conference publications) or as official policy documents.
e) Studies focusing solely on secondary and higher education were excluded, as were opinion pieces and sources with no transparent research methodology directly linked to the research question.

A multi-stage selection process was undertaken, following the PRISMA guidelines, to obtain the final set of literature. The first stage was a screening process. First, by reviewing titles and abstracts, all duplicates or records that were definitely irrelevant were removed. Second, the full texts were examined according to their level of interest to verify that all those that focused on the material adhered to the guidelines relevant to the inclusion criteria. We also rated each study's quality, relevance to our research question, and findings. Only studies that met all criteria and quality criteria were retained for further analysis.

Sources of Data and Search Strategy

A broad search strategy was employed across multiple sources to gather relevant literature. The search queries were run in Scopus, Web of Science, ERIC, and Google Scholar using Boolean operators and wildcards to link terms such as "AI literacy," "AI education," "primary school," " K–12," and "curriculum, pedagogy, or policy. In addition, backward citation searching was conducted by reviewing the reference lists of seminal papers, and grey literature was searched to identify relevant documents (e.g., UNESCO and OECD reports). Reviews were published no earlier than 2025; unfortunately, they cover only the last 25 years of the open literature because of limitations. This period was selected to capture the advent of AI literacy as an established concept and changing trends in the domain over the last two decades. These significant events, such as China's national AI development (Chinese State Council, 2017) and UNESCO's K–12 AI curriculum mapping initiative (UNESCO, 2022), occurred along the timeline. Being active from the outset meant the review also captured foundational work. However, the surge of interest in introducing AI into primary schools has emerged, leading to a contemporary dataset upon which comparative views can be formed.

Data Extraction and Synthesis

We extracted significant information from each included paper for comparison purposes. For every paper, we noted the year of publication, country or region focused on, target age group of learners, AI-related content or goals, type of pedagogical approach mentioned, and supportive or contextual policy factors, where known. We then conducted inductive coding in ATLAS.ti to develop themes or broader dimensions that capture the combined thematic meaning across all studies. The main contributions of all studies were therefore classified under three major thematic domains that align with our research questions: (1) the structure and content of AI curricula for elementary education; (2) pedagogical methods for teaching AI concepts; and (3) policy initiatives for AI literacy at the elementary level. The thematic synthesis will illuminate common patterns across various contexts without ignoring noteworthy divergences in approach. In the recent literature, these comparative insights help verify this particular observation, indicating that while some general trends linked to AI literacy are visible internationally, there are also significant variations in methods being adopted across regions, more or less, such as the stark contrasts that belong to the local level (Casal-Otero et al., 2023; Druga et al., 2022).

Limitations

Despite the rigorous approach, there are limitations that we must acknowledge in this review:

One is the exclusion of publications in languages other than English that draw on findings from other language-based studies of the exact nature. AI education is advancing rapidly, and a few reform programs may have been overlooked in the present literature, such as initiatives initiated after 2025. Specific grey literature, such as policy whitepapers, was included; however, the same readers must exercise caution as they extend the literature review with insights that are not peer-reviewed.

Our study needs to recognize that these limitations do not distort the broader picture the SLR reveals. This is a comprehensive and up-to-date scan of the status of AI in IT education for primary schools: a valuable platform of facts on which future curricular changes, teacher training initiatives, and policy changes should be judiciously implemented. Moreover, it poignantly illustrates the lacunae in the existing literature, which, in turn, stands as an armature assuring further empirical research in AI education. This is a good platform for further deep qualitative inquiry into AI education progress in different sociocultural settings.

CONCEPTUAL FRAMEWORK

According to Brown et al. (2007), AI literacy has long been defined in terms of technological and pedagogical categories of learning; however, the most innovative teaching involves the generation of ideas for incorporating AI that cater to children's developmental capacities. AI literacy is the understanding of artificial intelligence and the ability to interact effectively with AI systems in real-world contexts, including reflecting on their societal and personal implications. The idea of AI literacy in primary education should be framed in ways that regard reasoning as biological and intuitive, while ethical intuitionality should outweigh mere technical skills. Casal-Otero (2023) emphasizes the importance of developing awareness of AI at an early stage to become a shaping force in decision-making in the real world. Such an approach will change artificial intelligence from being used by children to students questioning, critiquing, and perhaps implicitly or explicitly creating more effective solutions using AI.

From the perspective of many, constructionism in education, as laid out by Seymour Papert, provides a robust philosophical basis for promoting AI literacy among children. This perspective argues that knowledge is more effectively grounded in active participation and in making sense of information about the world. At the same time, people involved create their own hands-on models of AI systems, for example, through project-based learning, resulting in mini-chatbots or simple classification algorithms (Eguchi, 2021). These activities provide children with a real-world walk-through of the underlying principles of computational thinking, that is, the very underpinning skill set that makes problem settings amenable to algorithm-based solutions (Boden, 2018). This implies that AI literacy is connected to positions that are both creative and analytical in the world of digital learning, enabling students to explore the concept of an intelligent system in theory, critique it, and develop essential digital capabilities in reputable classroom and out-of-class activities.

Correspondingly, topics that are frequently characterized as 21st-century skills, including problem-solving, collaboration, digital citizenship, and ethical reasoning, are also directly related to AI literacy. These skills have become more important than ever in understanding and operating technology-dependent societies. The consideration has been made by scholars such as Ng et al. (2022), stressing the fact that AI literacy should not merely lie with the use of AI (operational understandings) but stretch its boundaries in such a way that the individual can present a reasonable critical evaluation of the social, cultural, and ethical implications of AI. Hermann (2022) further argues that learning how to understand and critique how bias eats into AI-mediated communication and personalization is necessary. AI literacy, which emerges as a precursor to digital agency and democratic participation, can serve as a means to promote these.

The curriculum is a keystone for organizing AI literacy in primary education. Curriculum designs for effectiveness should encompass age-appropriate, interdisciplinary, and, above all, culturally responsive learning outcomes (UNESCO, 2022). Competence models that are staged in their comprehension, such as those articulated by Van Brummelen et al. (2021) and Ng et al. (2023), establish a progression from the basic understanding of data and automation as part of their initial phase and finally attempt to understand more challenging concepts, such as machine learning, natural language processing, and algorithmic ethics. Establishing coherence across grade levels not only supports cumulative learning but also benefits teachers, who can develop in turn.

Political frameworks both constrain and support the practical evolution of AI literacy. National strategies might create a broader context within which operations fit, providing a structure, such as mandated provisions and financing, for concrete initiatives in the curriculum, professional development, teacher training, and so on. For instance, the Chinese national 2017 AI plan has brought about several significant changes through curricular reforms and pilot programs in grade schools (Chinese State Council, 2017; Zhao et al., 2022). In the absence of coherent policy guidance, countries often implement fragmented policies through inadequate teacher training and, at times, inappropriate resource distribution (Celik, 2023). The above points indicate a set of policies that could offer equity, sustainability, and context-specific AI education.

In addition, AI literacy should respond to the social and cultural contexts in which learners find themselves. Prior learning, linguistic backgrounds, and socioeconomic outcomes all combine to shape the interpretation and application of AI concepts. A uniform, culturally neutral approach could even amplify inequalities and alienate entire groups (Cardon et al., 2023). Carolus et al. (2023) opt for locally situated AI literacy approaches that tap into the linguistic and cultural specificities of learners' lived experience networks and involve parents or carers, who create an enabling environment for learners to progress AI-related learning beyond the classroom.

It is undeniable that evaluation is a relatively new aspect of AI literacy. A multidimensional approach is used to evaluate the cognitive and affective facets of AI learning. These dimensions include conceptual understanding, ethical reasoning, and learners' confidence when interacting with AI. The development of valid and reliable assessment instruments is critical for monitoring learning outcomes and ensuring curricular and pedagogical improvements.

The role of educators in this process is crucial; teachers' views of AI have influenced how the medium is introduced and framed in classrooms (Zhao et al., 2022; Ng et al., 2022). Effective professional development is needed to equip teachers with the technical understanding and pedagogical skills to adapt and support young learners' engagement with AI. This encompasses initiating services, including professional development, collaborative planning, and access to appropriate teaching guidelines.

AI literacy in elementary education is a significant and complex topic, encompassing intertwined theories, constructive considerations, and socio-constructive considerations. Its intersections with both constructionist and computational paradigms support the fostering of 21st-century skills, curriculum coherence, and supportive policy frameworks. This analysis is grounded in this conceptual framework. Within this framework, AI literacy is not seen only as a technical competence but also as an all-encompassing educational goal that prepares young learners to navigate and shape an AI-driven world.

Figure 1. AI Literacy in the primary education framework

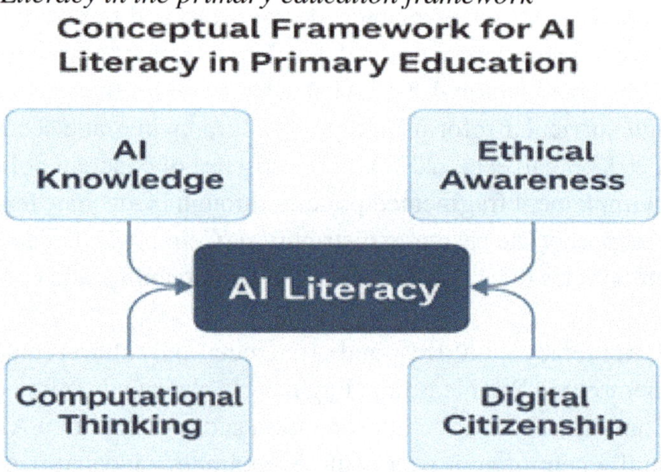

COMPARATIVE CURRICULUM FRAMEWORKS FOR AI LITERACY

The integration of artificial intelligence literacy into primary education has led to diverse starting points and uneven development across cultural and national contexts. This diversity can be attributed to significant variations in political priorities, resource availability, and pedagogical traditions. Consequently, emerging approaches reflect a spectrum of national policy frameworks, industry-driven pilot programs, and fragmented initiatives without comprehensive institutional support.

China provides a prominent example of a policy-driven model, with a national mandate issued in 2017 requiring the introduction of artificial intelligence education at all levels of formal schooling, including primary education (Chinese State Council, 2017; Zhao et al., 2022). The scope and scale of this initiative demonstrate sustained public investment and a strategic commitment to positioning artificial intelligence literacy as a core national competency. In contrast, countries such as the United Kingdom and Finland have embedded artificial intelligence concepts into broader digital skills and computational thinking frameworks. In these contexts, artificial intelligence is not taught as a discrete subject. However, it is incorporated across the curriculum through interdisciplinary activities and thematic modules, supporting a holistic and inclusive approach to digital competence (UNESCO, 2022).

Singapore presents a hybrid model. Through its national digital literacy agenda, the country introduces primary school learners to computational thinking, coding, and data literacy as foundational stepping stones towards later competencies in artificial intelligence (Ng et al., 2022). Finland similarly prioritizes inquiry-based learning and ethical reflection. Here, primary education encourages students to question the role of artificial intelligence systems in society and consider their implications for human agency and fairness (Ng et al., 2021a). South Africa, meanwhile, remains at an emerging stage of implementation. Although the country lacks a systemic framework for artificial intelligence literacy, several industry-supported and non-governmental pilot programmes are underway, and recent curriculum reform advocacy has called for artificial intelligence to be included as a core component of basic education (Casal-Otero et al., 2023).

Taken together, these contrasting models reveal the extent to which national strategies shape curriculum structure and classroom practices. Whether artificial intelligence literacy is taught as a standalone subject or integrated across learning areas reflects deeper values regarding pedagogical purpose and resource allocation. In China and South Korea, artificial intelligence appears as a dedicated subject in the upper primary grades, incorporating early concepts of machine learning, robotics, and algorithmic logic (Zhao et al., 2022). In contrast, in Finland and the United Kingdom, themes of artificial intelligence are distributed across subjects such as mathematics, science, and digital technology (Tomczyk, 2025; UNESCO, 2022). Standalone courses may promote conceptual depth and clarity; however, integrated approaches allow students to situate artificial intelligence within broader knowledge domains. However, integrated models risk being diluted without a coherent national framework or sufficient teacher support.

Curriculum design must also carefully consider developmental appropriateness. Primary-aged learners require instruction that aligns with their cognitive, social, and emotional capacities. Evidence suggests that child-friendly metaphors, visual programming environments, and hands-on exploratory activities are effective for scaffolding complex ideas, such as algorithms, data patterns, and neural networks (Druga et al., 2019; Eguchi, 2021). For example, small educational robots, such as iRobot and Cozmo, have been successfully deployed in early primary classrooms, enabling learners to understand automated systems through concrete problem-solving tasks (Kandlhofer et al., 2016; Tomczyk, 2025). Aligning conceptual learning objectives with age-appropriate pedagogical strategies increases student engagement and supports sustained knowledge development.

Beyond the national context, artificial intelligence literacy is increasingly linked to broader curricular agendas related to STEM and digital competence. By locating artificial intelligence within established digital skills progression frameworks, educators can promote enduring capacity building and foster interdisciplinary transferability. For instance, in Singapore and Finland, artificial intelligence topics are taught alongside computational thinking and problem-solving activities, cultivating transferable skills relevant to subject areas (Ng et al., 2022; Wang et al., 2022).

However, critical challenges persist. Foremost is the lack of global consensus on the core competencies of AI literacy at the primary level. A small but growing body of frameworks highlights competing priorities, with some emphasizing coding and algorithmic logic, others emphasizing ethical literacy, and still others adopting sociocultural approaches (Long & Magerko, 2020; Cuomo et al., 2022; Van Brummelen et al., 2021). This lack of curricular alignment creates difficulties in establishing precise learning trajectories, preparing teachers, and adapting resources to underresourced contexts. In many cases, resource constraints, limited curricular guidance, and lack of access to expertise exacerbate systemic inequalities, particularly in rural and low-income school settings (Chen et al., 2020).

Equity remains a critical concern. Artificial intelligence curricula must proactively address cultural, linguistic, and socioeconomic diversity to avoid reinforcing pre-existing educational inequalities (Carolus et al., 2023; Druga et al., 2022). In many low-income national contexts, infrastructure deficiencies, limited teacher capacity, and fragile policy structures result in artificial intelligence literacy being introduced only in name, with little practical implementation (Casal-Otero et al., 2023; Celik, 2023). Even in technologically advanced nations, children in rural areas or underprivileged communities may lack consistent access to digital tools or qualified instructors. Meaningful artificial intelligence education, therefore, requires teacher training that includes both content knowledge and pedagogical strategies. Research shows that very little professional development in artificial intelligence education currently exists, and where it does, it is often short-term and introductory (Zhao et al., 2022; Ng et al., 2022). National policy support is needed to embed artificial intelligence content into teacher qualification pathways and to foster peer-learning networks and access to teacher resources.

Assessment remains another underdeveloped area within artificial intelligence literacy frameworks. Current assessment tools typically measure proficiency in programming or basic conceptual knowledge but rarely evaluate learners' ethical reasoning, critical thinking, or awareness of AI's social implications (Cuomo et al., 2022; Wang et al., 2022). Holistic assessment strategies that combine formative feedback, project-based activities, and reflective practice are essential for capturing the full spectrum of AI literacy.

In conclusion, a comparative analysis of curriculum models for AI literacy reveals considerable innovation alongside persistent structural disparities. Countries such as China and Singapore illustrate the potential of coordinated, policy-driven approaches, whereas others continue to grapple with fragmented implementation and unequal access. To redress these structural divides, AI curricula must be developmentally informed, interdisciplinary in design, and supported by sustained investment in infrastructure, teacher preparation, and policy alignment. The following section considers pedagogical strategies that operationalize these curriculum choices and examines what it means to embed AI literacy in authentic primary school learning environments.

PEDAGOGICAL APPROACHES AND CLASSROOM IMPLEMENTATION

The pedagogical landscape of artificial intelligence literacy in primary education reflects a dynamic relationship among evolving instructional methods, resource use, teacher training, and inclusive practices. The effective teaching of artificial intelligence requires pedagogical models that support inquiry, creativity, critical thinking, and ethical reasoning while addressing the developmental needs of young learners. Several complementary approaches are emerging that collectively demonstrate the potential of pedagogical innovation to shape early engagement with artificial intelligence concepts.

One prominent pedagogical model is inquiry-based learning. This approach encourages learners to explore artificial intelligence through guided questioning, problem-solving, and application to real-world scenarios. Students are invited to ask how intelligent systems function and why they produce particular outcomes, stimulating curiosity and critical thought while developing an experimental mindset (Eguchi, 2021). These inquiry-based activities embed key aspects of computational thinking and digital engagement by promoting exploration, logical reasoning, and creativity. Such pedagogical aims align with the broader development of 21st-century competencies in young children.

Project-based learning offers another valuable approach for teaching artificial intelligence. In this model, learners work collaboratively to design, prototype, and test solutions to AI-related problems. Examples include designing a model for a smart recycling bin or creating a simple chatbot. By working on concrete tasks, students can explore how algorithms enable machine learning or pattern recognition, grounding abstract concepts in tangible experience (Ng et al., 2023). Through this form of collaboration, students also develop problem-solving and teamwork abilities, gaining confidence in their ability to apply technology to meaningful contexts.

Gamification has emerged as an increasingly popular method for introducing artificial intelligence concepts. Tools such as Cozmo, Minecraft Education, and ScratchJr use game mechanics, including levels, points, and rewards, to maintain students' interest in learning (Kandlhofer et al., 2016; Tomczyk, 2025). These platforms provide opportunities for differentiated instruction, allowing children to learn at varying paces and through diverse learning styles. Gamification is also well aligned with developmental psychology, enabling children to interact intuitively with technology and perceive artificial intelligence not as a remote abstraction but as a system of behaviors they can predict, control, and evaluate.

Digital platforms and instructional tools are increasingly central to AI pedagogy in primary schools. Scratch and ScratchJr provide block-based programming environments that introduce algorithmic logic in visually accessible formats. Meanwhile, Google's Teachable Machine allows learners to create simple ML models using image or sound inputs (Ng et al., 2022). These platforms help teachers scaffold complex ideas, such as pattern recognition, classification, and data representation, in ways that encourage hands-on engagement. The growing availability of AI-focused educational resources, including the AI4K12 initiative, which organizes AI into five central conceptual ideas, enhances educators' capacity to plan structured and engaging classroom projects.

Teachers occupy a central role in the successful delivery of artificial intelligence literacy. They must act as facilitators, co-learners, and ethical guides, helping learners inquire into both the technical and social implications of AI. However, many teachers currently lack confidence and expertise in AI-related content and pedagogy (Zhao et al., 2022). Addressing this gap requires comprehensive teacher development programmes that build an understanding of AI concepts and pedagogical strategies for teaching them. Professional development programmes must include training in adapting teaching materials, lesson planning, ethical instruction, and classroom management in technologically supported environments (Ng et al., 2022). Collaboration, mentoring, and peer support networks further help teachers navigate the unfamiliar terrain of teaching with AI.

An inclusive orientation is central to pedagogical effectiveness. Culturally responsive teaching considers learners' backgrounds and experiences, enabling the teaching of artificial intelligence content through contextually relevant stories, local examples, and indigenous knowledge (Carolus et al., 2023). For instance, discussions of traditional decision-making methods can be used to compare human and machine judgment. Accessibility should extend beyond cultural relevance to include appropriate hardware, language support, and adaptive programs for children with disabilities. Without such support, artificial intelligence education risks reinforcing existing inequities.

Assessment strategies for artificial intelligence literacy remain underdeveloped. Traditional approaches often focus exclusively on technical proficiency, for example, the ability to code or manipulate software. However, artificial intelligence literacy also requires evaluating ethical reasoning, creative design, and critical analysis (Wang et al., 2022). Formative assessment methods that draw on project portfolios, reflective journals, and student presentations support the development of metacognitive awareness and encourage learners to articulate their emerging understanding of artificial intelligence and its social roles. Such approaches align with the goals of ethical and democratic education.

Emerging research indicates that artificial intelligence (AI) education produces significant gains in both cognitive and affective domains. Studies have demonstrated improvements in computational thinking, collaborative problem solving, and creativity among students who participate in AI programmes (Druga et al., 2019; Ng et al., 2022). These learners also exhibit increased awareness of fairness, transparency, and ethical implications, which are essential to their emerging roles as digital citizens. A pedagogical model that integrates inquiry, project-based problem-solving, creative engagement, and ethical awareness has the potential to yield lasting benefits across primary and secondary education.

However, significant challenges remain. Limited time within rigid curricula, insufficient teacher incentives, and irregular access to technological infrastructure often hamper implementation. Furthermore, pedagogies that emphasize technical mastery without engaging ethical reflection risk overlooking important questions about how artificial intelligence shapes social life. Given these challenges, interdisciplinary collaboration remains essential. Effective artificial intelligence education requires engagement among curriculum designers, child development specialists, artificial intelligence researchers, classroom teachers, and policymakers. An iterative design and feedback process is necessary to adapt to advances in artificial intelligence and evolving classroom needs.

Success in artificial intelligence literacy ultimately depends on the strength of its pedagogical ecosystem. Inquiry-based learning, gamified environments, and digital tools can support effective learning; however, thoughtful assessment practices, sustained teacher training, and a commitment to inclusion must underpin them. When these elements are aligned, primary school learners can understand how artificial intelligence works and critically evaluate its use in society and contribute to more equitable and responsible technological futures.

POLICY INITIATIVES AND STRATEGIC INTERVENTIONS

Given the critical role of well-designed policy frameworks, the purpose of this study is to scale AI literacy at the primary level. Nations have already begun to draw up comprehensive plans that position AI at the center of ongoing digital transformations in schools. Regarding emphasis, we can point to a few examples, including China's Next Generation Artificial Intelligence Development Plan, which advocates for early AI literacy in future curriculum reform, and Finland's national roadmap, in which state funding considerably aids curriculum development, teacher training, and the production of educational resources (Chinese State Council, 2017, prepared by Quality Education in the 4th Industrial Revolution, 2019; UNESCO, 2022). There are also commitments within the UK's Artificial Intelligence Sector Deal for digital skills education, albeit with little emphasis on the primary level. Taken together, these policy frameworks capitalize on governments' growing understanding that preparing future citizens to engage with society through technology requires greater AI competencies.

Policy tools are increasingly necessary for collaborative, cross-sector feasibility. A few conventional actors, such as international, research, and civil society organizations, are relevant partners that contribute to resource supply, human capital development, and policy advice. For instance, UNESCO (2022), after a year of field studies, developed a structured approach to allow member states to extract their national curricular essence from standard elements. The OECD (2019) has again presented policy ideas setting out ethical considerations, including confusion, fairness, and lingering surveillance, in the education of artificial intelligence. Organizations such as Code.org and initiatives such as AI4K12 provide ready-made resources to prepare teachers and adapt curricula; thus, the support provides capital for education systems bereft of financial resources and/or relevant expertise in AI-centric tools and structures.

Coordination among ministries of education, curriculum developers, teacher education institutions, and local education authorities is required to scale AI literacy effectively. In some countries, implementation models may be introduced in stages, with small pilot clusters of schools first, only to be standardized nationwide later. The case of the Singaporean model, which is part of a national coding and digital literacy program with an incremental approach, allows for testing, refining, benchmarking, and expanding AI teaching (Ng et al., 2022). In South Africa, community-led initiatives and informal learning hubs have emerged to fill the void left by infrastructure inequalities, thereby supplementing limited formal provision and creating indigenous models of AI education (Casal-Otero et al., 2023).

Hence, funding is one of the basic building blocks of policy. Nations with high levels of public investment in education will be best placed to infuse their primary school systems with the necessary equipment, staff training, and Internet connectivity for artificial intelligence. For low- and middle-income countries, innovative funding mechanisms, such as grants, international aid programs, and public-private partnerships, are key to addressing resource shortages and the humanitarian factors that contribute to sustainable implementation challenges. Equitable allocation of funds is crucial to ensuring that rural and disadvantaged communities are not further excluded from digital transformation.

To make schooling more convenient through technology integration, schools must prioritize infrastructure preparation. In addition to broadband availability and Internet connectivity, learning areas must consider the use of digital resources and ICT devices, consistent servicing, and technical support. Several governments, such as those in Africa, China, Nigeria, South Korea, and Uganda, have begun conducting national digital-readiness audits or creating enabling environments to address basic infrastructure needs. However, implementation has often been impeded by deeply ingrained, long-standing inequalities (Zhao et al., 2022). A clear-cut framework of infrastructure benchmarks with corresponding timelines can significantly strengthen the monitoring of policy formation and responsibility.

Ethical considerations regarding AI literacy policies include addressing concerns about data privacy, surveillance technologies, and algorithmic bias. These considerations necessitate the establishment of frameworks to ensure proper and explicit teaching of ethical reasoning in AI literacy curricula, and that any educational technologies procured for school use undergo ethical review (Adams et al., 2023; Hermann, 2022). Such initiatives aim to protect both learners and teachers from potential damage caused by AI inclusions while laying the foundation for just and inclusive uses of AI.

Monitoring and evaluation mechanisms are necessary to assess the efficacy and fairness of artificial intelligence literacy policies. Some performance indicators could include learner achievement, teacher confidence, infrastructure availability, and regional equity of provision. Evaluation strategies should be transparent, context-sensitive, and collaborative, involving stakeholders across educational, technological, and community sectors (UNESCO, 2022). By ensuring regular feedback and inclusive participation, such mechanisms support policy iteration/improvement and enhanced accountability.

Capacity building for teachers is a crucial policy. Therefore, state standards should integrate artificial intelligence literacy into the teaching certification process, with lifelong learning pathways for both pre-service and in-service educators. This will ensure the sustainability and refreshment of education in the wake of exponential technological advancements. Incentives such as accreditation, micro-credentials, leadership promotions, etc., are needed to spark a sense of vying interest and commitment in teachers' hearts towards not clinging but lifelong learning and embracing the totality of continuously navigating rapid technological changes (Zhao et al., 2022). The best policy for extending pedagogical relevance and novelty is to have teachers contribute to the design and localization of artificial intelligence resources, rather than simply implementing externally imposed materials.

Multisector alignment underpins a broad policy ecosystem concerning AI literacy. Initiatives such as the EU's AI4People and the World Economic Forum's future workforce platforms demonstrate how stakeholders across government, business, and civil society can come together to share experiences, develop open resources, and promote ethical innovation in AI. It provides coherence that should eventually guide policy, where it is less specific, and inform policies that have sometimes been duplicated, thus enabling AI literacy to be rolled out on a more sustainable and equitable basis.

To put it succinctly, strategic policy design is the underpinning of the realisation of artificial intelligence education in primary education. There is no glaring discontinuity between funding for curriculum development, teacher training, and infrastructure preparedness, and the lack of an appropriate ethics component; sustained expenditures, intersectoral coordination, and transparent policy evaluation. By nurturing the pursuit of fairness and allowing for local adaptation, such policies epitomize an effort to unleash the teaching of AI to all young learners: why should education on AI only occur in elite schools when every young learner can, after all, contribute to shaping AI critically or creatively? Continuous policy alignment, guided by collective involvement in governance, has the potential to ensure a fair and efficient integration of AI in schools around the world.

KEY CHALLENGES AND OPPORTUNITIES

The discovery of an opening in artificial intelligence literacy in elementary schooling presents a multitude of challenges to be negotiated, including resistance to constant attention, which, in turn, manifests in vast differences between national infrastructures. In a more luxurious education system, schools start to generate value from steady Internet access, innovative learning environments, and personalized support. In a developing-world setting, as in South Africa, infrastructural snags are common: frequent power cuts, insufficient computer access, and poor telecommunications coverage. Such constraints limit the potential and coherent transmutation of artificial intelligence in the classroom (Zhao et al., 2022; Casal-Otero et al., 2023). Thus, in such circumstances, even the most promising AI teaching frameworks lie dormant in the realm of theory, with no body cast in place.

The lack of teacher training is as significant a barrier to the implementation of AI as any other (Ng et al., 2022). In their profession, most teachers do not possess the requisite digital pedagogical proficiency, nor do they know how to translate artificial intelligence concepts into concrete, meaningful activities. In the worst cases, this has a direct and compelling impact on education in remote rural or low-resourced schools, where heavy administrative workloads weigh down teachers, and multi-grade teaching contexts with sparse training information and very little professional development are not accessible. Most often, teachers do not show any inclination to participate in upskilling programs owing to a lack of institutional incentives, time, and support. Consequently, there are marked disparities in teachers' readiness, leading to a more uneven implementation of AI literacy across classrooms and an aggregated expectation of educational inequalities.

Equitable access to AI literacy is a fundamental concern. Socioeconomic inequalities determine children's ability to engage with and use digital technologies inside and outside of school. In other words, children from wealthy neighborhoods are among the first to use coding programs and AI toys. In contrast, children from poor neighborhoods typically have school as their only resource for such learning experiences (Celik, 2023). A gender perspective complicates this picture because of gendered cultural norms and structural neediness that discourage women from pursuing subjects in science, technology, engineering, and mathematics (STEM) and, by extension, AI education. AI programs must address these disparities in a concerted manner to foster real inclusion.

Pedagogical responsiveness becomes more complex when considering child development. The unique cognitive, socio-emotional, and cultural characteristics of primary-aged children inhibit their ability to operationalize abstract concepts. Therefore, instruction should build on established theories of child development and gradually scaffold materials to avoid overaccessing or skidding (Eguchi, 2021).

Excessive screen time or automated feedback without interactivity or deep reflection will make it harder for children to track their learning progress and may harm their overall well-being.

Eyeing AI in education can raise ethical issues that need attention. AI learning tools often collect sensitive behavioral or biometric data about learners. This raises concerns about privacy, surveillance, and informed consent in the context of ethics. (Adams et, 2023; Hermann, 2022). In another case, algorithms are likely to perpetuate and worsen biases in wider society when used in the classroom, leading to new forms of discrimination. Therefore, AI literacy must be anchored in ethical frameworks that uphold truth, fairness, and the protection of learners' rights.

However, significant opportunities still exist. Modular, open-access AI literacy frameworks are widespread across educational sectors, given their support for training and learning in resource-deprived environments. Initiatives such as AI4K12, AI4People, and national informatics academies are providing highly accessible, evidence-based resources that can contextualize learning across diverse learning environments (Ng et al., 2023; UNESCO, 2022). The rapid outbreak of digital learning amid COVID-19 heightened public and institutional awareness of the need to integrate digital technologies into schools further, opening the door to infusing AI into existing curriculum goals.

International collaboration holds considerable promise for accelerating progress in artificial intelligence literacy. Mechanical research partnerships, multi-country policy frameworks, and regional-level ability-building programs help disseminate best practices, foster local adaptation, and inject much-needed knowledge into policymaking. Entities such as the World Economic Forum and UNESCO play important roles in convening stakeholders worldwide, helping to create space for knowledge exchange and calling for systemic education reform. The concept of artificial intelligence literacy is squarely aligned with broader 21st-century education goals, such as enhancing creativity, collaboration, interdisciplinary learning, and civic engagement. At the same time, digital citizenship and social responsibility are developed in tandem (Long & Magerko, 2020).

There are perceived obstacles to every path of artificial intelligence implementation in basic education. Despite the obstacles of infrastructure, teacher readiness, and ethical uncertainty, the promise of significant transformation remains. By moving forward with responsive policy tools, adaptable partnership strategies, and location-sensitive programme design, the scope for transformation remains large. It is philanthropists who are moving to support a situation of undiluted desecration, flexible regime trials, and evidence-based pilot projects before capacity is present. The process of mutual alliance could begin to generate change. Deficient access to digital opportunities and literacy could be significantly improved at that time, pushing the ministry, academia, industry, and civil society to connect around a shared quest after its closure. Education systems can now equip a whole new generation of ambitious learners to interact with, analyze, and meaningfully transform the AI-injected world, which they will inevitably inherit into regulatory compliance.

STRATEGIES FOR INCLUSIVE, SCALABLE, AND ADAPTABLE AI CURRICULA

Thus, from a design perspective, the artificial intelligence education curriculum for primary-level education must be inclusive, scalable, and adaptable to meet diverse needs and contexts. Effective curricular frameworks should have flexible structures and be responsive to learners' developmental stages. To this end, artificial intelligence curricula must have a modular design that is sensitive to culture, and teachers working with them must appreciate and understand how to serve specific problems and sociocultural realities that shape the classroom environment (Carolus et al., 2023). In addition to technical knowledge, the curriculum should incorporate ethical, social, and cognitive dimensions to foster a holistic understanding of AI for learners, encompassing its technological and societal aspects.

Primary school artificial intelligence literacy should align with experiential and constructivist pedagogy, fostering deep learning. Evidence from established practices in education suggests that approaches to learning, such as inquiry-based, project-based, and gamified learning, offer motivational stimuli, sustain research, deepen understanding, and ensure continuous commitment (Eguchi, 2021; Ng et al., 2022). Therefore, these perspectives should guide educators as they open up all kinds of learning to collaborate and experiment with these approaches, equivalent to the kind of mentorship that leads them toward high-quality openness, along with access to open educational resources and communities of practice that foster and value reflective and collaborative pedagogy. The survival of these pedagogies will therefore entail a system-wide shift that values professional development and peer exchange.

Policy design is essential to guarantee the sensible implementation of artificial intelligence (AI) education. A nonnegotiable priority now is embedding AI as an across-the-board competency in national curricula, rather than as a one-off subject. For such an embedding, there needs to be across-the-board coordination of government ministries, curriculum authorities, and teacher training institutions. The policy framework must also establish accreditation pathways for in-service teachers in AI, develop a system for ongoing ethical oversight, and set digital infrastructure benchmarks for effective classroom deployment (UNESCO, 2022; Zhao et al., 2022). Funding policies must be structured for the long term and sustainability, not temporary pilot projects.

The most basic consideration in launching an artificial intelligence curriculum for all learners is ensuring affordability and equity. Toward that end, resources should be allocated to schools in marginalized communities, including rural districts, low-income areas, and institutions supporting learners with special educational needs. Support includes subsidies for device provisions so that these schools can upgrade themselves in line with current needs, investing in local connectivity, and funding specific workshops and training for school teachers. This was not going to be enough. If international organizations can roll out policies on capacity training for research personnel, it would not only be better but also provide financial support for these positions. UNESCO and the OECD are excellently placed to facilitate further policy dialogue on different projects, expose models of good practice, and support field-based pilot applications that are highly flexible and adaptable to local needs, many of which can, where relevant, be focused on AI in the classroom. Intergovernmental task forces and joint research grant initiatives will greatly complement national capacities to innovate and evaluate AI models.

A functional monitoring and evaluation system is indispensable for guidance and accountability. Such systems should track indicators of teacher preparation, learner achievement, infrastructure management, and regional equity. Subsequent modifications should be evidence-based and formulated based on classroom feed-back, student experiences, and teacher observation. This leads to learner-driven and grounded programs in reality (Ng et al., 2023). Feedback loops must be incorporated into the whole program design and implementation process to promote student-centered innovation.

Dominating teacher education is quintessential for policymaking in terms of attention. In today's world, any teacher training program must include ethics in AI, pedagogical strategies, and digital literacy standards; for this reason, it must be culturally responsive. In-service programs must offer flexible pathways to certification through a range of modalities, including online, blended, and face-to-face. Giving teachers agency in curriculum and pedagogical innovation is crucial, and policy should create incentives that encourage teachers to take leadership roles in co-creating AI literacy resources (Zhao et al., 2022).

In the future, research is needed to understand better how artificial intelligence literacy may set the stage for long-term outcomes. This may involve nurturing student agency, cognitive development, ethical reasoning, and achievement. Cross-cultural investigations could reveal best practices in curriculum models for consistent scaling and applicability. Many areas require further investigation, such as gender dynamics, language inclusion, and disability support within a holistic framework for considerable provisioning. Instead, researchers should place great weight on student voice. This implies students' involvement in co-designing programs to teach AI literacy by using their feedback, youth advisory panels, and peer-teaching projects, which, in turn, promotes youth voice and ensures program relevance.

Approaches to teaching children about AI should be sustainable and keep children's interests, experiences, and identities at the forefront of any intervention. As such, schooling requires curricular, pedagogical, policy, and research interventions. A long-lasting commitment to inclusive, evidence-informed strategies across education systems could ensure that young learners gain and apply foundational technical skills and acquire an awareness of AI that empowers responsible interactions in their lives today and in future societies.

ADVANCING AI LITERACY IN PRIMARY EDUCATION: THEORETICAL FOUNDATIONS, IMPLEMENTATION CASE STUDIES, LEARNER PERSPECTIVES, ASSESSMENT, ETHICS, AND FUTURE DIRECTIONS

Artificial intelligence (AI) literacy has been proposed for primary education. As a contemporary process, curriculum development is being radically affected by the need to include technological, pedagogical, and ethical considerations. Considering the case of its conception and enactment in vastly different global landscapes, the absolute contiguous truth about AI literacy moves toward the very hard questioning of the deep conversations around the implementation processes, learner experiences, types of duties, and various ethical issues that may come as direct fungible thereafter in favor of a research cultural, whereby these implications may stop slowly ridding a few administrations and businesses from more theoretical high-class uses or other viewpoints on whether another warming aid feasibly means or not. This grand overview will provide a rich texture of how artificial intelligence literacy can be effectively embedded in the building blocks of foundational post-elementary education to ensure that students become more capable and aligned with broader social objectives.

There is an educational rationale for AI literacy based on several well-defined learning theories. Constructionism, as derived from Seymour Papert's work, postulates that the active process of "doing while learning" effectively secures knowledge. Consider AI project-based activities in which learners use physical artifacts to build meaningful information—for example, designing algorithms, designing machines, or devising decision-making tools. Vygotsky's sociocultural perspective on collaborative learning environments underscores the role of teachers as scaffolding agents, making concepts accessible to students. Piaget's cognitive development theory, alongside Vygotsky's socio-cultural theory, repeatedly reminds us to be part of the creation of an age-appropriate AI curriculum."-Long and Magerko (2020). Lastly, overlooked yet different aspects of digital literacy must be understood not only in terms of technical aptitude but also in terms of subjective matters of empowerment, agency, and the interrogation of power and ethics within digital systems. A carefully constructed edifice that provides strong theoretical support, suggesting AI literacy in an early education setting, must profoundly consider ways children think, feel, make sense of, and interact with their various social environments.

Examples of worldwide implementation demonstrate the variety of ways in which AI has been actively implemented. China's boot integration of artificial intelligence through a national strategy that inculcates these ideas from primary to higher education levels, along with training large numbers of teachers in AI and demanding updates to curricula. In contrast to China's large-scale model, Finland pursues a distinctly different route; it instead agrees that ethical reasoning and inquiry-based learning practices are key. As reflected in its AI courses, open access for learners of any age allows them to use any user interface. In Singapore, it operates in a phased series that includes introducing computational thinking and coding in primary education and integrating AI into advanced learning. South Africa's experience shows the challenges of implementation in some of the country's most resource-starved environments, where innovation often becomes a joint venture between NGOs and tech companies due to the absence of basic infrastructure and a national policy that would have encouraged it. These contrasting models underscore the importance of considering contextual factors during implementation. A particular curriculum design, when successful in one context, may not necessarily transfer well to another, particularly when resources are unevenly distributed or when a culture of linguistic diversity craves nuanced, adaptive, and local rather than imposed solutions.

Learner perspectives are instructive on pedagogical approaches for artificial intelligence literacy initiatives. Studies have observed that children are more deeply engaged when concepts of artificial intelligence are designed into hands-on activities, storytelling, and game-based learning environments. However, there may be confusion or fear in some other instances when things get too abstract or technical. By anticipating and including learners' voices in the design of educational programs, some of the confusion can be minimised. Participation strategies such as student feedback loops, peer teaching, and collaborative project planning are proposed to improve educational design further and boost student agency and democratic involvement.

Evaluation of artificial intelligence literacy remains a challenge, especially at the primary education level. Existing assessments generally stress technical proficiency or binary indicators of what should be learned, rather than an understanding of the broader AI literacy content domains, skills, and dispositions. This narrow focus does not account for areas such as critical thinking, ethical reasoning, and creative application. A more holistic approach would use formative strategies framed around reflective journals, portfolio-based assessments, and collaborative presentations.

This ecosystem can foster group reflective thinking about how AI is impacting society and elicit individual positions on ethics. These traditions in progressive and constructivist evaluation indeed strike a balance.

Almost everywhere, one of the essential talking points in discussions about artificial intelligence in education has been ethical issues. These may arise regarding privacy, as multiple stakeholders may take it away to collect and process personal information required for active-environment operations. Continuing this guarantee goes way further than that; in more concrete terms, it delves into a more sophisticated and critical stage of informed consent for learners who participate in an intelligence process in which their personal data is all these intelligent algorithms require to know them. The moral significance is further emphasised by the argument from the data and by how far it can reach against the will of a person undergoing its noble scrutiny. Various recent global policies underscore the resulting challenges; for example, universal education guidelines in the U.S. dominate headlines about AI. Meanwhile, to prepare their teaching and learning programs, schools certainly need strong ethical frameworks beyond the methods justified within their own academies. This has also made it so easy to buy into AI ethics and await better times with ethical technology that is just sustainable enough for experiences.

Given a vision for the future, the research on artificial intelligence literacy must focus on assessing the extended scope of a learner's development. The critical question is whether early experiences in AI literacy promote long-term digital agency, academic performance, and ethical awareness. Comparative studies could give reasons for how cultural and institutional contexts mould attitudes, understandings, and capacities of learners. Another area of research is to examine how these considerations influence equitable access to and learning opportunities in AI education. Involving students in program design and evaluation is a positive step toward participatory learning, which may raise the quality and relevance of upcoming AI curricula.

Thus, in summa, the cultivation of artificial intelligence competencies in the primary schools needs to be necessarily multipronged. It cannot afford to be a single-vertical technological juggernaut but must be conceived as an interdisciplinary educational juggernaut instead. It must take into account the unique developmental needs of children, respect teachers as lifelong learners and ethical guides, promote social justice and democratic values, and move forward to integrate that program into the school's curriculum. Established with the view of cooperation, many initiatives in curriculum, policy, pedagogy, and research shall endure to foster an environment that uses AI literacy to extend children's capacity for critical thinking, creative activity, and meaningful participation during times of significant transformation. Only in this overarching, social vision will AI literacy really help prepare children to navigate and shape the technological societies they have been handed.

CONCLUSION

This chapter has undertaken a systematic examination of curriculum frameworks, pedagogical models, and policy initiatives to offer a comprehensive analysis of artificial intelligence literacy in primary education. Against the backdrop of rapid technological change and the expanding influence of artificial intelligence in everyday life and work, the chapter underscores the urgency of introducing artificial intelligence concepts to young learners. Such early education must equip children not only with technical understanding but also with the ethical awareness and critical faculties necessary for responsible participation in digital society.

The chapter demonstrates that while countries around the world share common goals in promoting artificial intelligence literacy, they diverge significantly in terms of implementation strategies, infrastructural readiness, and curricular scope. Artificial intelligence education cannot be approached with a universal model. Instead, context-sensitive solutions are required that take account of children's cognitive development, available resources, and cultural contexts. Effective curricula must therefore balance conceptual rigour with flexibility, enabling educators to adapt content to local needs and realities.

Pedagogical approaches grounded in inquiry, gamification, and project-based learning show particular promise for fostering engagement and deep learning among primary-level students. However, these approaches must be supported by strong systems of in-service teacher education and assessment mechanisms that reflect the multifaceted nature of artificial intelligence literacy. Teachers require not only content knowledge but also pedagogical tools and institutional support to deliver learner-centred, developmentally appropriate instruction in artificial intelligence.

Policy frameworks, both national and international, play an essential role in supporting these efforts. Strategic planning, investment in infrastructure, ethical oversight, and long-term professional development schemes are necessary for artificial intelligence literacy to take root in education systems. Collaboration among governments, international organisations, research institutions, and non-governmental actors can further strengthen the conditions for sustainable implementation. Such coalitions offer opportunities for resource sharing, capacity building, and innovation.

Significant challenges remain. In many contexts, infrastructural deficits, limited teacher capacity, and deep-rooted inequalities hinder equitable access to artificial intelligence education. Ethical questions concerning data privacy, surveillance, and algorithmic bias demand careful attention. Nonetheless, the moment is ripe for action. The increasing emphasis on digital transformation in global education policy, heightened by recent crises and technological acceleration, offers a window of opportunity to embed artificial intelligence literacy within foundational education.

By embracing principles of social justice, child-centred learning, and digital ethics, education systems can harness this momentum with purpose. Open access platforms, modular curriculum frameworks, and international partnerships can all contribute to more equitable and context-appropriate models of artificial intelligence education. However, the success of such efforts depends on sustained involvement from all stakeholders, including teachers, policymakers, researchers, families, and learners themselves.

Artificial intelligence literacy should not be reduced to the accumulation of technical skills. It requires cultivating critical thinking, creativity, ethical reasoning, and civic awareness. With such preparation, young learners can be empowered to interact with artificial intelligence technologies not as passive users but as active, responsible contributors. Meaningful progress in this field offers education systems a pathway to help children navigate, shape, and ultimately thrive in an increasingly complex, AI-infused world.

REFERENCES

Adams, C., Pente, P., Lemermeyer, G., & Rockwell, G. (2023). Ethical principles for artificial intelligence in K-12 education. *Computers and Education: Artificial Intelligence*, *4*, 100131. DOI: 10.1016/j.caeai.2023.100131

Aoun, J. E. (2017). *Robot-proof: Higher education in the age of artificial intelligence*. MIT Press. DOI: 10.7551/mitpress/11456.001.0001

Boden, M. A. (2018). *Artificial intelligence: A very short introduction*. Oxford University Press.

Calvani, A., Fini, A., Ranieri, M., & Picci, P. (2012). Are young generations in secondary school digitally competent? A study on Italian teenagers. *Computers & Education*, *58*(2), 797–807. DOI: 10.1016/j.compedu.2011.10.004

Cardon, P., Fleischmann, C., Artz, J., Logemann, M., & Hedewald, J. (2023). The challenges and opportunities of AI-assisted writing: Developing AI literacy for the AI age. *Business and Professional Communication Quarterly*, *86*(3), 257–295. Advance online publication. DOI: 10.1177/23294906231176517

Carolus, A., Augustin, Y., Markus, A., & Wenrich, C. (2023). Digital interaction literacy model – Conceptualising competences for literate interactions with voice-based AI systems. *Computers and Education: Artificial Intelligence*, *4*, 100114. DOI: 10.1016/j.caeai.2022.100114

Casal-Otero, L., Catala, A., Fernández-Morante, C., Taboada, M., Cebreiro, B., & Barro, S. (2023). AI literacy in K-12: A systematic literature review. *International Journal of STEM Education*, *10*(1), 29. DOI: 10.1186/s40594-023-00418-7

Celik, I. (2023). Exploring the determinants of Artificial Intelligence (AI) literacy: Digital divide, computational thinking, cognitive absorption. *Telematics and Informatics*, *83*, 102026. DOI: 10.1016/j.tele.2023.102026

Chen, L., Chen, P., & Lin, Z. (2020). Artificial intelligence in education: A review. *IEEE Access : Practical Innovations, Open Solutions*, *8*, 75264–75278. DOI: 10.1109/ACCESS.2020.2988510

Chinese State Council. (2017). *Notice of the State Council on issuing the next generation artificial intelligence development plan (Guofa [2017] No. 35)*. https://www.gov.cn/zhengce/content/2017-07/20/content_5211996.htm

Cooper, H., Hedges, L. V., & Valentine, J. C. (Eds.). (2019). *The handbook of research synthesis and meta-analysis* (3rd ed.). Russell Sage Foundation. DOI: 10.7758/9781610448864

Cuomo, S., Bagn, G., & Raneri, M. (2022). *Artificial Intelligence Literacy, che cos'è e come promuoverla. Dall'analisi della letteratura ad una proposta di Framework.* Media Education., DOI: 10.36253/me-13374

Druga, S., Christoph, F. L., & Ko, A. J. (2022). Family as a third space for AI literacies: How do children and parents learn about AI together? In *CHI Conference on Human Factors in Computing Systems* (pp. 1–17). DOI: 10.1145/3491102.3502031

Druga, S., Vu, S. T., Likhtik, E., & Qiu, T. (2019). Inclusive AI literacy for kids around the world. *Proceedings of FabLearn, 2019*, 104–111. DOI: 10.1145/3311890.3311904

Eguchi, A. (2021). AI-Robotics and AI literacy. In Malvezzi, M., Alimisis, D., & Moro, M. (Eds.), *Education in with Robotics to Foster 21st Century Skills* (Vol. 982, pp. 75–85). Springer., DOI: 10.1007/978-3-030-77022-8_7

Hermann, E. (2022). Artificial intelligence and mass personalisation of communication content—An ethical and literacy perspective. *New Media & Society*, *24*(5), 1258–1277. DOI: 10.1177/14614448211022702

Kandlhofer, M., Steinbauer, G., Hirschmugl-Gasch, S., & Huber, P. (2016). Artificial intelligence and computer science in education: From kindergarten to university. In *2016, IEEE Frontiers in Education Conference (FIE)* (pp. 1–9). DOI: 10.1109/FIE.2016.7757570

Long, D., & Magerko, B. (2020). What's AI literacy? Competencies and design considerations. In *Proceedings of the 2020 CHI Conference on Human Factors in Computing Systems* (pp. 1–16). DOI: 10.1145/3313831.3376727

Moher, D., Liberati, A., Tetzlaff, J., & Altman, D. G.The PRISMA Group. (2009). Preferred reporting items for systematic reviews and meta-analyses: The PRISMA statement. *PLoS Medicine*, *6*(7), e1000097. DOI: 10.1371/journal.pmed.1000097

Ng, D. T. K., Leung, J. K. L., Chu, S. K. W., & Qiao, M. S. (2021a). Conceptualising AI literacy: An exploratory review. *Computers and Education: Artificial Intelligence*, *2*, 100041. DOI: 10.1016/j.caeai.2021.100041

Ng, D. T. K., Leung, J. K. L., Su, M. J., Yim, I. H. Y., Qiao, M. S., & Chu, S. K. W. (2022). *AI literacy in K-16 classrooms*. Springer International Publishing., DOI: 10.1007/978-3-031-18880-0

Ng, D. T. K., Luo, W., Chan, H. M. Y., & Chu, S. K. W. (2022). Using digital storytelling as a pedagogy to develop AI literacy among primary students. *Computers and Education: Artificial Intelligence*, *3*, 100054. DOI: 10.1016/j.caeai.2022.100054

Ng, D. T. K., Su, J., & Chu, S. K. W. (2023). Fostering secondary school students' AI literacy through making AI-driven recycling bins. *Education and Information Technologies*. Advance online publication. DOI: 10.1007/s10639-023-12183-9

Ng, D. T. K., Wu, W., Lok Leung, J. K., & Chu, S. K. W. (2023). Artificial Intelligence (AI) literacy questionnaire with confirmatory factor analysis. In *2023 IEEE International Conference on Advanced Learning Technologies (ICALT)* (pp. 233–235). DOI: 10.1109/ICALT58122.2023.00074

OECD. (2019). *Recommendation of the Council on Artificial Intelligence*. OECD Publishing. https://legalinstruments.oecd.org/en/instruments/OECD-LEGAL-0449

Ranieri, M., Biagini, G., & Cuomo, S. (2025). AI Literacy in Higher Education. *International Journal of Digital Literacy and Digital Competence*, *16*(1), 1–25. DOI: 10.4018/IJDLDC.388469

Tomczyk, Ł. (2025). AI in Education - Mapping Theoretical Frameworks for Digital Literacy: DigComp 2.2, AI Literacy Competency Framework, AI Literacy TPACK, the Machine Learning Education Framework, the UNESCO AI Competency Framework for and Teachers and Other Innovative Approaches. New Media Pedagogy: Research Trends, Methodological Challenges, and Successful Implementations, 173–191. DOI: 10.1007/978-3-031-95627-0_12

UNESCO. (2022). *K-12 AI curricula: A mapping of government-endorsed AI curricula*. https://unesdoc.unesco.org/ark:/48223/pf0000380602

Van Brummelen, J., Heng, T., & Tabunshchyk, V. (2021). Teaching tech to talk: K-12 conversational artificial intelligence literacy curriculum and development tools. *Proceedings of the AAAI Conference on Artificial Intelligence*, *35*(17), 15655–15663. DOI: 10.1609/aaai.v35i17.17844

Wang, B., Rau, P. L. P., & Yuan, T. (2022). Measuring user competence in using artificial intelligence: Validity and reliability of artificial intelligence literacy scale. *Behaviour & Information Technology*, •••, 1–14. DOI: 10.1080/0144929X.2022.2072768

World Economic Forum. (2020). *The Future of Jobs Report 2020*. https://www3.weforum.org/docs/WEF_Future_of_Jobs_2020.pdf

Zawacki-Richter, O., Marín, V. I., Bond, M., & Gouverneur, F. (2019). Systematic review of research on artificial intelligence applications in higher education – Where are the educators? *International Journal of Educational Technology in Higher Education, 16*(1), 1–27. DOI: 10.1186/s41239-019-0171-0

Zhang, H., Lee, I., Alshehri, A., D'Paola, D., Cheng, Y., & Breazeal, C. (2022). Integrating ethics and career futures with technical learning to promote AI literacy for middle school students: An exploratory study. *International Journal of Artificial Intelligence in Education*. Advance online publication. DOI: 10.1007/s40593-022-00293-3

Zhao, L., Wu, X., & Luo, H. (2022). Developing AI literacy for primary and middle school teachers in China: Based on a structural equation modeling analysis. *Sustainability (Basel), 14*(21), 14549. DOI: 10.3390/su142114549

KEY TERMS AND DEFINITIONS

AI Literacy: A set of skills and competencies that allow persons to be able to understand, use, and critically engage with AI technologies; this includes technical knowledge, along with awareness about ethical and social implications (Ng et al., 2021a; Bagn et al., 2023).

Artificial Intelligence (AI): A branch of computer science involved with designing intelligent systems, capable of tasks that usually require human intelligence, such as learning, reasoning, general decision-making, and language communication (Boden, 2018).

Computational Thinking: A problem-solving method concerning practices such as decomposition, abstraction, pattern recognition, and algorithmic thinking that are instrumental in understanding and creating AI systems (Long & Magerko, 2020).

Culturally Responsive Pedagogy: An approach that acknowledges the culture of learners when shaping curriculum content, pedagogy, and learning environments in ways that speak to them (Carolus et al., 2023).

Digital Pedagogy: Usage of digital technology and relevant theories to provide support for both teaching and learning processes; importance is given to interaction, student agency, and embedding technology in curriculum design (Calvani et al., 2012).

Ethical AI Education: Teach AI concepts such as fairness, accountability, privacy, and transparency, with a particular focus on protecting children's data and digital rights (Adams et al., 2023; Hermann, 2022).

Project-Based Learning (PBL): An instructional approach where students acquire knowledge and skills working for an extended amount of time to investigate and respond to complex questions or challenges; usually applied in AI education (Eguchi, 2021).

Chapter 9 Developing Critical Thinking: Helping Children Question AI Outputs

Venkatesh Ankarla Sri Ramuloo
http://orcid.org/0009-0007-0837-5914
University of the Cumberlands, USA

ABSTRACT

As artificial intelligence (AI) becomes increasingly embedded in early and primary education through apps, virtual assistants, and adaptive learning tools, fostering critical thinking in children (ages 3–11) is vital for responsible interaction with AI. This chapter, "Developing Critical Thinking: Helping Children Question AI Outputs," explores ways to help young learners evaluate AI-generated content with curiosity and discernment. It introduces AI in the context of children's daily lives and cognitive development, covering bias, reliability, and errors. The chapter offers age-appropriate teaching strategies, classroom activities such as analyzing AI stories, and discussions on fairness. It highlights collaboration with parents and communities to support learning beyond school. By nurturing critical thinking as a foundation of AI literacy, this chapter aims to prepare children to engage with AI ethically, thoughtfully, and confidently in an increasingly digital world.

INTRODUCTION

Artificial intelligence (AI) pervades contemporary learning environments, including educational settings. In this regard, there is a growing emphasis on the need for children to acquire an understanding of AI concepts and principles, and for

DOI: 10.4018/979-8-3373-4893-3.ch009

027, IGI Global Scientific Publishing. Copying or distributing in print or electronic forms without written permission of IGI Global Scientific Publishing is prohibited. Use of this chapter to tive artificial intelligence (AI) technologies is expressly prohibited. The publisher reserves all rights to license its use for generative AI training and machine learning model development.

early exposure before they reach school age (Montenegro et al., 2021). In particular, children with special educational needs (SEN) require even more attention in this area. Moreover, there is an observable trend indicating a growing prevalence of the introduction of AI concepts and principles to children aged 0–8 years. In this light, a research analysis investigating how to introduce AI concepts and principles to children with SEN is warranted, providing insights into the educational environment and AI algorithms appropriate for this age group, the types of cognitive load they may encounter, and the strategies for alleviating difficulties through the cognitive load theory (CLT) lens. CLT offers essential insights into how information is processed and how diverse factors influence the cognitive load of learners, providing valuable references for devising adaptable strategies suited to SEN children (Li et al., 2024).

To provide a comprehensive introduction of AI concepts to SEN children, it is vital to understand the profiles of AI concepts suited for early exposure and to recognize the extraneous cognitive load that children may encounter in such learning. AI deployment encompasses a wide array of methodologies and techniques that are often indistinguishable to children who are innately familiar with the subject. Thus, identifying elements that demand excessive information processing is vital to ensuring that other core AI concepts receive due attention.

This chapter articulates approaches for integrating AI literacy into children's science education. It delineates the prominent components of knowledge, competencies, and related constructs necessary for AI literacy to underpin a systematic approach to educational integration. Furthermore, the framework captures the critical juncture of children's development and societal interaction with AI systems and the ability to engage with scientific inquiry into AI-altered phenomena.

BACKGROUND

Artificial intelligence (AI) will continue to carve an increasingly large space in the lives of children and societies in the future. The need to be literate in the area of AI is increasing, and with it, the skill of critical thinking about AI (Walter, 2024). Critical thinking is reflective, active, and reasonable thinking that aims at decision making, changing what can be believed, and the knowledge-building process (Spector & Ma, 2019). According to Danry (2023), the main elements of critical thinking are to: (1) identify a problem and make a plan on how to deal with it with a commonly posed question; (2) engage skepticism by intelligently doubting the validity of information that one is exposed to; and (3) understand the validity of information by applying a list of clear questions to identify its authenticity (Spector & Ma, 2019). The existence of the same components in the Unite for Literacy site in the Teaching Critical Thinking section, which is also created by educators with references to state and national standards, means that they are relevant in present-day K-12 curriculum design (Spector & Ma, 2019). In addition to specifying the elements of critical thinking, one ought to embrace the aspect of development processes and the consequences of such phases to the way the process of teaching critical thinking talent may vary along the educational lifeline (Adu, 2025).

An important intervention is to provide young children with the tools of critical thinking, specifically, the capacity to perceive and assess the results of AI systems, to produce a sense of agency, ethics in addressing technology, and digital literacy in an AI-augmented world (Su et al., 2023). With the spread of AI-based technologies, such as ChatGPT and DALL-E, to include even the youngest members of society, the need to train all members of society to approach the products produced by AI tools so that they develop new meanings and better comprehend how transformative such systems are will be an essential challenge (Avsheniuk et al., 2024). Critical thinking regarding AI is the ability to see the strengths and flaws in the results of AI systems, which cultivates a culture of curiosity and skepticism that, in turn, leads to the further development of curious minds and their desire to discover and experiment further (Danry, 2023). By providing these kinds of critical thinking skills, students are enhanced to use AI outputs not only as a means of rote production but also as a source of greater comprehension and new idea creation (Rong et al., 2024). Schools, from kindergarten through 12th grade, have either prohibited or limited the use of ChatGPT in schools and school curricula or are trying to find a way to direct the disruptive quality of AI to their benefit (Hsiao et al., 2025). However, the most essential thing to keep in mind is that AI technology already extends to children before they even enter school (Su et al., 2023). To understand how AI has started to be introduced at a young age in terms of learning, one can only look at a very young child telling their voice assistant, which is powered by a type of AI, to do something or asking a question (Su et al., 2023).

Critical thinking is essential because through it, we are able to make rational choices about what we know and what we ought to know (Spector & Ma, 2019). In particular, it is essential when reviewing the results of AI systems (Fabio et al., 2025). Critical thinking is an outcome and a process. It is a process, and in its steps, it can be described as seeking, analyzing, and evaluating information (Matthews & Bartley, 2025). It involves intensive analysis and evaluation of information prior to conclusion-drawing (Matthews & Bartley, 2025). These skills enable one to evaluate the worth of evidence, identify fallacious claims, and have a healthy discussion (Khalabuzar & Shymanovych, 2024). Consequently, the ability to examine and critique ideas or information is a reflection of critical thinking that is commonly applied with ease (Matthews & Bartley, 2025). Issues of the display of these skills differ between adults and early childhood (Adu, 2025).

In the AI, the K-12 Computer Science Framework states, "The evolution of the computational tool no longer being an exclusive item to be utilized by specialists but more of a standard tool to be used by a more universal population is introducing a maturing demand requiring society to acquire a concept of how to utilize the tool with proper care and respect" (Adu, 2025). As a society, we should find a better way to implement critical thinking; however, the masses have been misguided into believing that as long as there is an AI application out there, all one has to do is follow its guidelines because someone, somewhere created and designed it (Walter, 2024). These obstacles show that it is not just AI literacy that should be worked on, but also an essential package of critical thinking skills that enable children (and society as a whole) to develop a sense of agency and ethics (Su et al., 2023).

This chapter serves as a primer and can be used both as a standalone piece and as part of other sections on creating an AI education introduction. It begins by explaining what AI is and subsequently highlights the importance of developing critical thinking. It then elucidates the importance of the critical thinking approach in developing agency, ethics, and digital literacy. Finally, it outlines tactics for assisting young learners in critical thinking.

UNDERSTANDING AI OUTPUTS IN THE CONTEXT OF EARLY EDUCATION

What Are AI Outputs?

Understanding AI outputs is the starting point for delving into AI Advantages for Children. (Walter, 2024). The outputs of the artificial intelligence are the responses or suggestions provided by the artificial intelligence interface (Su et al., 2023). It may even be identified with answers provided by AI in the form of answers given by virtual assistants, sentences created by ChatGPT, and images created by generative AI tools (Avsheniuk et al., 2024). Of concern is the design, application, and impact of AI products (Walter, 2024). As an illustration, the response delivered by a chatbot or virtual assistant is an AI output (Fabio et al., 2025). The next recommendation on how to proceed with learning English via an adaptive app is also the output of AI (Hsiao et al., 2025). Chatbots and virtual assistants are already being used in everyday life, answering questions, offering information, and helping with scheduling (Su et al., 2023). Similar to adults, children can access a virtual assistant like Alexa, Siri, or Google Assistant to play music, games, experience story time, and find information (Su et al., 2023). Undertaking scrolling, typing, spelling, and math can be explored using AI-powered games (Ng et al., 2022). Moreover, content blockers make the Internet safer among children (Walter, 2024). Such examples are clear indications of the central outputs of AI in everyday life (Su et al., 2023).

Children are exposed to AI outputs in their daily lives, such as when they interact with virtual assistants on smart speakers (Su et al., 2023). For instance, a child can request a virtual assistant to play their favorite tune, which it can add to a playlist and play immediately, thereby keeping the child entertained (Su et al., 2023). The numerous ways in which children benefit from AI outputs are as follows (Adu, 2025). AI can encourage children to learn through a new language or through math games (Khalabuzar & Shymanovych, 2024). With the help of AI, language-related tools can provide Spanish-speaking families with access to English-language content (and vice versa), enabling each family member to access these resources (Hsiao et al., 2025). To individualize homework help, a bot would be able to tailor explanations to the learner's understanding level (Hsiao et al., 2025). By accepting content moderation by AI, the content delivered to children will be appropriate and safe, and will also allow families to track their child's inquiry activity (Walter, 2024). Nevertheless, data security and privacy issues should be among the concerns regarding the assessment of AI usage in early learning (Walter, 2024). Evaluating the quality and effects of AI results can ascertain that it provides better learning among young children (Adu, 2025).

How are AI outputs generated ?

AI outputs are products of artificial intelligence decision-making frameworks (Danry, 2023). In order to learn more about how AI outputs, one should learn more about the mechanism of artificial intelligence (Walter, 2024). Artificial intelligence is the intelligence exhibited by machines (Spector & Ma, 2019). Machine learning involves computational algorithms that enable an AI to acquire real-life data and enhance its decisions in the future (Spector & Ma, 2019). AI enables learning that is data-driven (Danry, 2023). Data includes any information utilized either in the training or in generating outcomes, such as pictures, text, voice symbols, Wi-Fi nodes, playing cards, and the hands dealt in a game of UNO (Rong et al., 2024). An AI can only learn the patterns it observes within the data and utterly lacks any external context (Walter, 2024). The AI also does not have human experience in life and cannot question what it comes up with (Spector & Ma, 2019). Such are some of the causes of inaccuracies with the output produced by AI (Walter, 2024). The first occurs when there is bias in the data, that is, the information is biased in one direction, not fairly, for example, not having any data of a particular group (Walter,

2024). One such example is training an AI on facial recognition to work off photos of only a single ethnicity (Walter, 2024).

AI can be said to be good at making decisions, but it all depends on the data given to it when it is making those decisions (Danry, 2023). The data should be considered sets of instructions that define the behavior of an AI and the type of output it produces (Rong et al., 2024). Diversities of data make varieties of impacts on the AI (Rong et al., 2024). Some data allow the AI to understand what it has been requested to do, for example, by creating questions or choosing instructions (Avsheniuk et al., 2024). Other sections of the data provide guidance to the AI on the style or tone that should be used in the response (Avsheniuk et al., 2024). An example is provided that the data may tell the AI to respond succinctly or without bias towards the response (Walter, 2024). The AI will be given different types of output by different instructions, in the form of different data (Rong et al., 2024). To better understand how AI-imagined text is created, simplified explanations are available, especially for teachers who will facilitate children's understanding of AI (Hsiao et al., 2025). With the impressive range of skills that modern AI technologies have, one must not forget that it is still a product developed and delivered by humans first (Spector & Ma, 2019). Therefore, its outputs can only be as good as the instructions and data it has been given (Walter, 2024).

AI in Children's Lives

AI is an extensive technology that now plays a more integrated role in the lives of individuals than ever before (Walter, 2024). Different types of AI serve various purposes; for example, deep learning enables smart devices to hear and respond to voice-based commands; natural language processing enables translation tools to enable individuals to understand and speak other languages; and computer vision enables driverless cars to scan and analyze their surroundings (Spector & Ma, 2019). With these examples, it is easy to identify how new AI-based products and tools have infiltrated our lives (Walter, 2024). Children come into contact with these technologies accidentally, through the content suggested to them by YouTube, which uses machine learning; when playing with smart toys; using educational applications; or talking to virtual assistants (Su et al., 2023). It is essential to understand that such encounters are not necessarily harmless (Walter, 2024). Studies have revealed that AI outputs can influence the intelligence, social life, and emotional well-being of children, establishing in young learners the habit of discerning misinformation, knowing where to turn to, and understanding the rationale behind responses (Ng et al., 2022). Otherwise, the ready solutions of AI may contribute to complacency in their agency (Spector & Ma, 2019). Thus, drawing boundaries, establishing an active identity-and-reflect policy, and making discussions around AI capabilities and limitations open would be a good start (Matthews & Bartley, 2025).

Checking the results of AI is not an easy task, particularly for young learners (Khalabuzar & Shymanovych, 2024). It is recommended that children be taught to uphold the reliability of the source, compare the content with other sources, and discuss suspicions with other adults or professionals (Matthews & Bartley, 2025). Moreover, they must be capable of being on the lookout to be notified of fake, inappropriate, or damaging materials or disinformation, even when it appears through AI, that is, suggestions via YouTube (Walter, 2024). One can also train children on how to detect when the machine is wrong; for example, it will form an incorrect response to a question (Fabio et al., 2025). Efforts should be made to emphasize that it is only when children have specific knowledge of the real world and know the subject matter that it is possible to detect errors (Ng et al., 2022).

DEVELOPMENTAL CONSIDERATIONS FOR TEACHING CRITICAL THINKING

Understanding the cognitive, emotional, and social development of children aged 3–11 years helps to determine the suitability of a given strategy at a particular stage, and this aspect can be applied to how critical thinking skills and AI literacy are taught at a specific age (Adu, 2025). During these years, development can be considered to consist of two stages: preschool (3–6 years) and primary (7–11 years), to reflect the shifts in the peculiarities (Ng et al., 2022). Preschool-aged children are egocentric and inclined towards a process of thinking that is not objective but is focused on what suits them internally (Ng et al., 2022). Children develop an understanding of hypothetical facts by the age of six because children aged three are concrete thinkers who concentrate on what is going on and have limited attention spans; however, at the age of six years, after exposure to one thing, children are able to give extended attention, although not much is made of hypothetical situations (Ng et al., 2022). More advanced preschoolers will develop a sense of their feelings and others and be able to postpone their personal satisfaction and align with the principles (Su et al., 2023). Primary school children exhibit growing independence and the ability to think at a higher level (Adu, 2025). They learn to be empathetic and become aware of how other people perceive a situation and why they are supposed to behave in a certain way in a particular situation (Su et al., 2023). In addition, they are able to adjust to new or demanding circumstances and therefore are able to engage in guided inquiry and test hypothetical solutions (Rong et al., 2024).

Multiple developmental theories of intelligence are useful for understanding a child's development during these ages (Spector & Ma, 2019). This chapter focuses mainly on Piaget and Vygotsky theories and how they can foster AI literacy and critical thinking. The next section explores these theories.

Piaget and AI Literacy

The overview of the stages of cognitive development explained by Piaget forms a theoretical background of understanding AI literacy among children (Ng et al., 2022). Piaget emphasized the role of sensory-motor experiences in early childhood and the process of adapting to novelty through schemas and their transformations, with the help of assimilation, accommodation, and equilibration (Ng et al., 2022). Based on Piaget, cognitive development occurs in four stages: the sensory-motor stage (0–2 years), preoperational stage (2–7 years), concrete operations stage (7–11 years), and formal operations stage (11 years and older) (Ng et al., 2022). The preoperational phase of development is usually unable to answer questions that go beyond that phase of experience, and only when an individual is in the concrete operational stage can they think more about something concrete (Ng et al., 2022; Tariq, 2025). The apparent difficulty in teaching children about AI literacy is that these concepts (bias and reliability of outputs) are too abstract for preoperational thinkers but are better suited to the concrete operational stage (Su et al., 2023). Hence, when examining how AI literacy emerges in young children between the ages of 3 and 11, the following factors should be considered: cognitive abilities relative to their age and the need to question the output of AI as an imperative literacy skill or tool alongside writing and reading (Adu, 2025).

In the preoperational stage (predominantly between the ages of 2 and 7), children can understand and respond to questions about AI; however, they cannot elaborate and explain their answers, and children in the concrete operational stage (approximately between the ages of 7 and 11) are able to grasp the complex aspects of AI and can express their responses by connecting them to their personal experiences (Ng et al., 2022). Young children focus significantly on concrete examples to help them learn new information; this is the principle upon which the gradual acquisition of the ability to ask questions can be said to be founded at these ages (Adu, 2025).

Vygotsky and AI Questioning

Assessing the ways in which children gain the capability of questioning a statement generated by conversational AI would demand an in-depth account of the cognitive complexity of such scenarios (Spector & Ma, 2019). Specifically, concepts related to AI bias and reliability are difficult to comprehend because they are abstract (Walter, 2024). According to Vygotsky's sociocultural theory, social interactions and culture play a prominent role in the cognitive development of children (Spector & Ma, 2019). By scaffolding a child, Vygotsky believed that an adult creates a learning environment that enables the child to take some steps further than their cognitive development (Spector & Ma, 2019). For example, if a child cannot understand what bias is, an adult can engage in a conversation about story bias that is produced by AI to explain the concept to the child, and then the child will be able to identify the bias (Adu, 2025). Vygotsky's approach can also explain what parts of AI need to be studied at different levels of development (Su et al., 2023). As an illustration, children younger than the concrete operational stage, according to Piaget's framework, may not understand bias and reliability because it is an abstract concept; therefore, it would not be the appropriate time to teach these concepts (Ng et al., 2022).

Bloom's Taxonomy and Critical Thinking

Bloom's taxonomy, published in 1956 by Benjamin Bloom, consists of six categories of cognitive processes arranged in a pyramid, beginning with remember, understand, apply, analyze, evaluate, and create at the top (Spector & Ma, 2019).

The taxonomy consists of six cognitive levels arranged in a pyramid structure, as shown below.

Figure 1. Graphical representation of Bloom's Taxonmy-Cognitive Domain

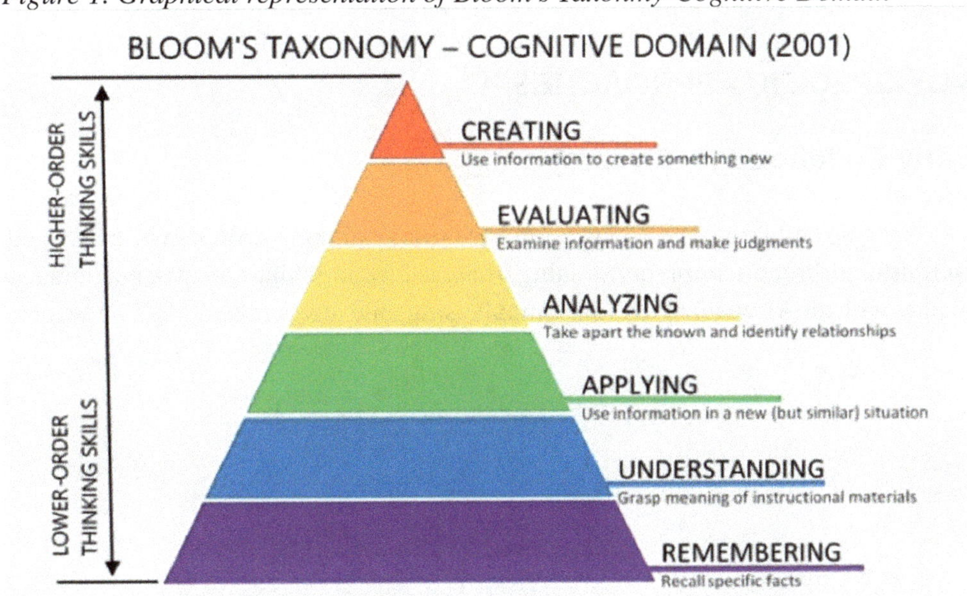

The theory posits that it is natural for all learners to be curious (Rong et al., 2024). Curious people ask questions and desire to know how, why, and what ifs (Rong et al., 2024). The good thing to do as a parent when it comes to a child developing their critical thinking skill is to ensure they are encouraged and supported in being curious and developing inquiry (Adu, 2025). The desire to solve problems independently also boosts these abilities (Danry, 2023). When working with answers produced by ChatGPT and other artificial intelligence applications, one must learn the importance of critical thinking (Avsheniuk et al., 2024).

A learner with critical-thinking skills will learn how to find solutions more frequently than by reading information or being shown answers, and how to remember them (Spector & Ma, 2019). To develop the skills that process entails, an enabling environment needs to be created that encourages students to seek solutions on their own (Adu, 2025). Such learning can be based on questions where learners pose questions to acquire more knowledge, search a topic through following a plan, discover the information or data required, and interpret what the information or data present (Rong et al., 2024). It may refer to researching a field of interest without any preconceived notion of what to do to gain a general understanding (Rong et al., 2024). The brain must be active in one or the other of these ways, and it should be motivated by the desire to find out something of interest in inquiry (Danry, 2023). The ability to evaluate information is a critical thinking skill necessary to make the correct assessments and conclusions (Spector & Ma, 2019).

AGE-SPECIFIC APPROACHES

Early Childhood (3–5 years)

As young children, aged 3–5 years, basic critical thinking skills can be cultivated and nurtured through simple questioning strategies. Young children can be encouraged to play with an AI-enabled toy that can talk, sing, and answer the child's questions.

Figure 2. Child interacting with AI- enabled toy

During free play, the parent or teacher might ask questions such as, "Why did the toy say that?", "How did the toy know that?", or "What do you think would happen if you asked the toy about dinosaurs?" It is important to note that young children's language comprehension might be more advanced than their expressive abilities; therefore, their responses to such questions may be limited to yes/no or one-word answers. The overall strategy, cutting across the age range, is to allow children to challenge the outputs of AI, and the methods for doing so are becoming increasingly complex as children's minds develop. Higher levels of sociocognitive strategies will enable children to judge whether an AI-generated response is trustworthy and to have a discussion centered around the ethical consequences of AI. Strong testimony can be given on the significance of tapping into what excites children most of all, their natural curiosity about how AI generates responses, and challenging children on their ability to question the accuracy, impartiality, and morality of the response, regardless of their age (3, 7, or 11 years).

Middle Childhood (6–8 years)

After the basic "Why did the toy say that?", children should be stimulated to ask a large variety of questions about the toy's reasoning. Additional supporting questions, such as "What else could the toy have responded?" or "Do you think that the toy's response is true?" This will help model the desired behavior of constant critical thinking about AI systems and their outputs.

The idea here is that children can increasingly engage in higher-quality investigations and evaluations. It is hoped that this will provide them with a system that can help them formulate a more probing attitude toward the outputs of AI, as well as help them be aware of the discussions on the dilemmas of the use of AI. It is possible to generalize the critical literacy approach to AI-generated and covert AI operations in everyday life. Children must be able to question how trustworthy the AI is that generated this text, image, video, or idea. They must be educated that AI can occasionally produce information that is unethical or biased, and they need to take that into account when making a judgment on the information. The lack of this judgment has led people to believe in things that are not true and make rash decisions that could damage themselves and others. Children need to ask themselves whether the image or text they are reading is biased or not right so as not to make judgments based on inaccurate or unfair information. The ethics of AI should also be discussed, considering its impact on the world, and the consequences of its use should be discussed at this point.

SOCIAL-EMOTIONAL FRAMEWORK FOR AI CRITICAL THINKING

In the rush to prepare children for the future, many parents attempt to address every fear and anxiety their child expresses through technology (Walter, 2024). Although it would be good, the end result will be a shy child with low confidence when introduced to new technology (Spector & Ma, 2019; Tariq, 2025). In order to make sure that children can go ahead and question what is delivered by AI, it would be essential to make sure that a safe environment is created where all the questions asked by the child can be heard (Adu, 2025). All responses given, whether false, must be encouraged, and in this way, children will become self-confident learners (Rong et al., 2024). Children are adventurous learners most of the time; however, they often feel unprepared and are thus scared of technology (Rong et al., 2024). These children have, however, proven to be very strong (Danry, 2023). By continuing to learn about how technology works, they will be able to live in an AI future without fear (Danry, 2023). It is viable and beneficial to err, which encourages one to constantly learn more about these fears in terms of building on the innate curiosity to gain confidence as a child (Adu, 2025).

It is said that the curious are never bored because curiosity leads to questions and possibilities (Rong et al., 2024). Curiosity compels learners to seek answers and contribute their own perspectives (Danry, 2023). By embracing a spirit of inquiry and treating mistakes as learning opportunities, children can overcome discomfort with uncertainty (Adu, 2025). The myAIguide framework anchors these social-emotional attributes and offers practical suggestions (Hsiao et al., 2025). Encourage questions by linking interests to AI and other technologies, nurturing a non-judgmental mindset towards "incorrect" answers (Rong et al., 2024). Emphasize the exploratory nature of inquiry-based learning and celebrate the value of errors in the educational process (Adu, 2025). Adopt a growth mindset to enhance resilience, understanding that abilities can develop through effort (Danry, 2023). Create a supportive classroom culture that accepts formulating flawed questions as an integral part of learning (Matthews & Bartley, 2025). Finally, involve families in conversations explaining why questions about technology matter, thereby reducing resistance and promoting sustained engagement (Su et al., 2023).

PEDAGOGICAL STRATEGIES FOR FOSTERING CRITICAL THINKING AMONG CHILDREN

In terms of AI literacy, children should comprehend broad definitions of AI, recognize how AI systems perceive the world, explore generative AI systems through open-ended questions, idea generation, and idea elaboration, and conduct inquiry-based explorations into AI and its effects on personal lives and the world (Zhou et al., 2020). However, young children differ markedly from older learners, underscoring the importance of developmentally appropriate approaches to cultivate AI literacy in learners aged 4–8 years. Python programming offers a platform for learning about AI concepts that young children can grasp. The concurrent emergence of K–12 AI curricula necessitates analogous attention to AI-literate children. Piagetian and Vygotskian learning theories emphasize distinct yet complementary cognitive and sociocultural dimensions of early education relevant to AI literacy.

Understanding how children acquire K–12 AI literacy from ages 4 to 8 incorporates these theories. Piaget posits that learners actively construct knowledge through exploration, advancing from concrete to increasingly abstract conceptions in successive stages. At younger ages, children typically transition from Piaget's preoperational to concrete operational stage. Enriching experiences to promote AI literacy may benefit children's understanding of AI and support current K–12 initiatives. Vygotsky emphasizes social interaction and cultural mediation in learning, framing development as a transition from social to individual understanding. Early learning remains oriented around sharing, collaboration, and cultural artifacts, and development occurs within the zone of proximal development (ZPD). The AI landscape is evolving rapidly; however, basic principles, such as concept generation, iteration, and critique, remain consistent. Vygotskian principles continue to guide emerging designs for introductory AI instruction, focusing on collaborative invention and creation, tools and technological practices for knowledge representation, and the formation of expansive, culturally relevant learning ecologies.

A Piagetian perspective on AI learning reveals both a framework for understanding diverse contemporary approaches and practical avenues for enhancing systems based on prevailing paradigms. The active construction of models that incrementally develop in complexity has emerged as an overarching thread linking Piaget-endorsed system designs and contemporary efforts to realize autonomous AI agents. Sensory signals drive learning through cycles of exploration, manipulation of representations, evaluation of fit with experience, and progressive reorganization; these intrinsically motivated flows resonate with Piagetian concepts.

Foundational pedagogical models can guide the integration of critical thinking and AI literacy. Inquiry-, play-, and project-based pedagogies foster the exploration of ideas and practices that initiatives for young learners typically focus on. AI concepts, however, differ fundamentally from early literacy, numeracy, and science, and fully play-based models often provide insufficient instructional support. Inquiry-and structured play approaches that align with project-based pedagogy offer frameworks through which integration can be explored across preschool and primary grades (Zhou et al., 2020; Tariq, 2025).

Young children display the capacity for critical thought; however, observable indicators of such thinking may diverge from established frameworks. Foundational AI literacy complements early critical thinking development by fostering experiential understanding of algorithmic technology, data-related concepts, and cause-and-effect reasoning (Van Brummelen et al., 2021). Pedagogical models for integrating both domains also vary. Inquiry-based, play-based, and project-based approaches can promote critical thinking in preschool and primary-grade settings, whereas a computational thinking project model offers a viable path for introducing AI concepts in grades 1 and 2. The intended goal is to develop integrated curriculum units suitable for preschool through grade 2 that embed both critical thinking and age-appropriate AI literacy.

INTEGRATING CRITICAL THINKING INTO EXISTING CURRICULA

Young learners are increasingly surrounded by AI systems; however, efforts to integrate AI learning into early education remain remarkably scarce. Although foundational "AI literacy" concepts can be introduced to preschool and primary-grade children, they are seldom mentioned in established curriculum guidelines, and related pedagogy is virtually undocumented. Given that numerous AI systems must now be discernibly interrogated and skillfully harnessed, cultivating early comprehension of related AI concepts is increasingly imperative.

Curriculum design considerations include alignment with developmental milestones. Critical thinking emerges in early childhood, progressing in complexity through the preschool years and into primary grades, while the understanding of AI technologies remains rudimentary. Early literacy development, socioemotional factors, and the evolution of executive function further shape curricular decisions. Such considerations suggest complementary learning progressions across grade levels and broader opportunities for cross-disciplinary integration with language arts, mathematics, science, and social studies; the proposal includes exemplar unit threads for the latter subjects. Several strategies can be used to integrate critical thinking into existing curricula. Below is exploration of such strategies.

Hands-On Exploration: Simple AI Models and Simulations

Scientific understanding yields valuable perspectives, enabling young children to grasp basic AI concepts and acquire fundamental AI literacy. Exploring, building, and tinkering with simple AI models, simulations, and applications designed for cognitive development can further broaden their AI literacy. From approximately four years of age, children can actively explore the world by asking questions that influence their natural curiosity. By six years of age, they begin to generate plausible yet imperfect models about how the world works and explore the world to validate these hypotheses, well before they possess the mathematical knowledge to access more formal models. Near the end of primary schooling, children are ready to explore mathematical and logical models (Van Brummelen et al., 2021).

Language trends, as captured by the bestselling "GPT-3" toy, "How do you play with a pet rock?", have witnessed a big shift to younger age groups. This shift indicates the availability of applications and models that greatly reduce the burden on children to demonstrate AI intelligence. Children provided with unfinished everyday applications involving chatbots, image generation, and video simulation can leverage curiosity to extend and complete them independently. Tools that permit broadband exploration of such hybrid "artifacts" allow and stimulate productive questioning, prediction, model building, and knowledge checking. Within a few hours of play, children work forward from simple artifacts to sophisticated validations of core generative probabilities and the accompanying AI hygiene, enhancing both their scientific understanding and AI literacy without undue fatigue (Ali et al., 2023).

Questioning Techniques and Curiosity-Driven Learning

Questioning techniques and curiosity-driven learning are essential for fostering critical thinking and metacognitive strategies in students. These methods help students reevaluate themselves and become autonomous, reflective thinkers. Focusing on concepts such as clarity, accuracy, logic, and depth in specific tasks supports the development of effective questioning skills. Incorporating essential questions and promoting inquiry encourages a deeper understanding and engagement, which are vital for meaningful investigations and learning outcomes (Chalukian, 2015).

Teaching divergent thinking and curiosity can empower children to ask deeper questions about the workings and implications of technology, including AI. A large language model (LLM) trained to act as a pedagogical agent can assist children with expansive question-asking and learning about AI topics. When children interact with the LLM, they answer AI-related questions posed by the agent and ask their own questions. The agent provides targeted feedback and encouragement. The results of a study indicate that the system elicits significantly more divergent questions than before training, with children reporting greater enjoyment of curiosity-focused tasks and enhanced accomplishment in formulating questions (Abdelghani et al., 2022).

Media Literacy and Source Evaluation

Young children are consumed by content, which makes learning to evaluate sources even more important. Educators should introduce students to news, social media, and advertising, emphasizing appropriate sources for different content types. The American Association of School Librarians (2020) foundational standards can guide the selection of media to examine with students.

Educators can draw upon the ALA media literacy framework (American Library Association, 2023), which encourages the critical analysis of content by examining authorship, format, message, intent, and audience. Questions such as "Who created this message?", "What techniques are used to attract my attention?", or "How might different people interpret this message?" can guide discussions.

Reasoning and Argumentation in AI Contexts

Reasoning and argumentation are central components of critical thinking skills and are foundational for effective AI literacy. Therefore, introducing young students to reasoning and argumentation in AI contexts, such as what makes a good AI model and what constitutes intelligent behavior for AI, is essential in promoting the skillful use of AI. Instructional strategies must also remain developmentally appropriate.

Hence, reasoning and argumentation should be embedded in broader, multifaceted activities encompassing exploration, demonstration, and hands-on work with AI.

Young learners can practice argumentation explicitly alongside these activities through reasoning and evidence worksheets. Supplementing a standard three-part structure (claim, reason, evidence) with educator-guided examples related to students' own earlier explorations reinforces engagement. Alternative models featuring an emphasis on values, beliefs, or knowledge can be explored later (Rapanta & Walton, 2016). Further development at earlier primary levels avoids overwhelming students. At later upper-primary levels, delving into more complex models, such as workers involved, facets considered, pros and cons, further information needed, and follow-up questions, enables sophisticated extrapolation from earlier considerations (Antonio Archila et al., 2022).

PRACTICAL ACTIVITIES FOR QUESTIONING AI OUTPUTS

In previous sections, we explored approaches and strategies that can be used to foster AI literacy and critical thinking among children. This section presents four hands-on activities designed to help children in early childhood (ages 3–5) and primary education (ages 6–11) develop critical thinking skills to question AI outputs. Each activity is structured to be engaging, accessible, and adaptable to diverse classroom settings, aligning with developmental stages and fostering curiosity, skepticism, and ethical awareness. The activities encourage children to explore AI responses, identify errors or biases, consider fairness, and create guidelines for responsible AI use.

Activity 1: Exploring AI Responses

Objective: To teach children to compare AI outputs with human knowledge and encourage them to question the accuracy and clarity of AI-generated information.

Rationale: Young children frequently encounter AI outputs through voice assistants, educational applications, and online content. This activity introduces the concept that AI responses are not always definitive, prompting children to verify information using their own knowledge or trusted sources.

Target age group: Ages 4–11 (adaptable for early childhood and primary learners).

Materials:

- A voice assistant device or application (e.g., Siri, Google Assistant, or Alexa), or a teacher-moderated AI chatbot.
- Whiteboard or chart paper for group discussions

- Simple question cards with prompts such as "What is a dinosaur?", "What do birds eat?", or "Why is the sky blue?".
- Access to age-appropriate reference materials (e.g., picture books, classroom posters, or library corners).

Steps:

1. **Introduction (5–10 minutes)**: Begin with a brief discussion about AI, using simple language: "AI is like a smart computer that tries to answer our questions, but sometimes it's not perfect." Explain that the class will ask an AI a question and check whether its answer makes sense.
2. **Asking the AI (10–15 minutes)**: Select a question from the prompt cards (e.g., "What is a dinosaur?"). For younger children (ages 4–6), use concrete, familiar topics such as animals or weather. For older children (ages 7–11), include slightly more complex questions such as "Why do stars shine?". Have a volunteer ask the question to the voice assistant or type it into a chatbot (with teacher supervision). Write down or display the AI's response for the class to see.
3. **Comparing with Human Knowledge (15–20 minutes)**: Divide the class into small groups or pairs. Provide each group with a reference source (e.g., a picture book about dinosaurs or a classroom poster). Ask them to compare the AI's answer with the information in the source. Guide them with questions such as, "Does the AI's answer match the book?", "Is anything missing?", or "Does it sound clear?". For younger learners, focus on simple comparisons (e.g., "The AI said dinosaurs are big. Does the book say that too?"). For older learners, encourage deeper analysis (e.g., "Did the AI explain why dinosaurs went extinct?").
4. **Class Discussion (10–15 minutes)**: Bring the groups together to share the findings. Write key points on the whiteboard, such as "The AI was right about dinosaurs being reptiles" or "The AI didn't mention that some dinosaurs had feathers." Discuss why the AI might have missed details or provided unclear answers, introducing the idea that AI relies on data and may not always be complete.
5. **Reflection (5–10 minutes)**: Ask children to reflect: "Can we always trust the AI's answer?", "What should we do if we're not sure?" Encourage responses like "Check a book" or "Ask a teacher." For older children, introduce the concept of "reliable sources" (e.g., books vs. random websites).

Adaptations:

- For early childhood (ages 3–5): Use visual aids, such as drawings, to compare AI answers with known facts. Keep questions simple and concrete.
- For primary learners (ages 6–11): Encourage independent research using classroom resources to verify AI responses.
- For diverse learners: Provide translated question cards or visual prompts for multilingual or neurodiverse students.

Outcomes: Children learn to question AI outputs by comparing them with trusted sources and build confidence in their ability to evaluate information critically.

Activity 2: Spotting AI Mistakes

Objective: To enable children to identify errors or biases in AI outputs and foster skepticism and analytical skills.

Rationale: AI outputs can contain inaccuracies or reflect biases from training data, such as stereotypical representations. This activity helps children recognize these flaws in a safe, guided context and encourages them to challenge AI reliability.

Target age group: 6–11 years (best suited for primary learners with basic analytical skills).

Materials:

- AI image generators (e.g., teacher-moderated tools such as DALL·E or Stable Diffusion) or pre-generated AI images.
- A projector or printed images for display.
- Discussion prompts (e.g., "What looks wrong in this picture?", "Does this seem fair or realistic?").
- Paper and crayons for younger children to draw comparisons

Steps:

1. **Introduction (5–10 minutes)**: Explain that AI can create pictures or stories; however, it may sometimes make mistakes or show things unfairly. Use a simple example: "If we ask AI to draw a scientist, it might only show men, even though women are scientists too."
2. **Generating AI Images (10–15 minutes)**: Show the class an AI-generated image based on a prompt like "Draw a doctor" or "Show a family." Alternatively, pre-generated images can be used to save time or ensure age-appropriate content.

Ensure that the images are simple and non-controversial but may contain subtle errors or biases (e.g., all doctors wearing white coats or families depicted in a stereotypical way).

3. **Analyzing the Output (15–20 minutes)**: In small groups, ask children to examine the image and discuss: "Does this look real?", "Is anything strange or missing?", "Does it show everyone fairly?" For example, if the AI depicts all doctors as men, ask, "Are all doctors men? Why might the AI show it this way?" For younger children (ages 6–8), focus on visual errors (e.g., "The dog has three legs!"). For older children (ages 9–11), introduce bias (e.g., "Why are all the people in this picture the same?").
4. **Class Sharing (10–15 min)**: Each group shares one observation about the AI image. Write findings on a chart, categorizing them as "Mistakes" (e.g., unrealistic details) or "Unfairness" (e.g., stereotypes). Discuss why AI might make these mistakes, using simple terms: "AI learns from pictures it's seen, but it might not have enough different ones."
5. **Reflection (5–10 minutes)**: Ask: "What should we do if AI shows something wrong or unfair?" Encourage answers like "Tell a teacher" or "Look for better pictures." For older learners, we discuss how biases in AI can affect their feelings or decisions.

Adaptations:

- For younger learners (ages 6–8), Use AI-generated stories instead of images and focus on factual errors (e.g., "The AI said the moon is made of cheese!").
- For diverse learners: Provide verbal prompts or tactile materials (e.g., 3D models) for visually impaired students.
- For advanced learners: Research real-world examples of AI bias (e.g., in media or advertising) with teacher guidance.

Outcomes: Children develop skills to identify inaccuracies and biases in AI outputs, fostering critical evaluation and awareness of fairness.

Activity 3: Role-Playing AI Scenarios

Objective: To encourage empathy and ethical reasoning by having children role-play as AI systems and humans interacting with them.

Rationale: Role-playing helps children understand AI decision-making processes and their ethical implications, such as fairness in recommendations or responses, in a relatable and imaginative manner.

Target age group: 5–11 years (adaptable for both early childhood and primary learners).

Materials:

- Scenario cards with prompts (e.g., "You're an AI recommending games for kids" or "You're an AI answering questions about animals").
- Props (for example, a "computer" made from a cardboard box for younger children).
- Whiteboard to record discussion points

Steps:

1. **Introduction (5–10 minutes)**: Explain that AI makes decisions based on rules or data; however, these decisions may not always be fair or correct. Say, "Today, we'll pretend to be AI and humans to see how AI thinks."
2. **Role-Playing Setup (10–15 minutes)**: Divide the class into pairs or small groups. Assign roles: one child (or group) is the "AI," and the other is the "human" asking questions or requesting recommendations. Provide a scenario card, such as "The human asks the AI to recommend games for boys and girls." For younger children, simplify the scenario (e.g., "What toy should I play with?").
3. **Role-Play Activity (15–20 minutes)**: The "human" asks the question, and the "AI" responds based on imaginary "data." For example, the AI might say, "Boys should play with trucks, and girls should play with dolls." After the response, pause to discuss: "Was that fair?", "Why did the AI say that?", "What would happen if the AI only suggests certain toys?" For younger learners, keep responses simple and focus on fairness (e.g., "Everyone should get to choose their toy!"). For older learners, explore deeper implications (e.g., "What if the AI's data only had boys playing with trucks?").
4. **Class Discussion (10–15 minutes)**: Gather the class to share their role-play experiences. Write down key points, such as "The AI wasn't fair because it left out some kids" or "The AI didn't know enough about everyone." Discuss how AI decisions affect people and why it is important to question them.
5. **Reflection (5–10 minutes)**: Ask: "How did it feel to be the AI?", "What would you change about the AI's answers?" Encourage empathy-focused responses, like "I'd make the AI suggest toys for everyone."

Adaptations:

- For early childhood (ages 3–5): Use props such as a toy computer and focus on simple scenarios (e.g., choosing snacks).
- For primary learners (ages 6–11): Introduce more complex scenarios, such as AI filtering content for a school project.
- For diverse learners, use visual scenario cards or role-play scripts for students with language or cognitive differences.

Outcomes: Children gain empathy for how AI decisions impact others and practice ethical reasoning by questioning their fairness.

ETHICAL RISKS AND DATA SECURITY

AI literacy programs for young learners should embrace ethical principles grounded in beneficence and non-maleficence while also respecting learners' autonomy. The similar but more general aims of beneficence and non-maleficence underlie most child protection standards. Beneficence aims to confer tangible benefits directly to the learner, especially to foster individual and collective growth (Yu & Yu, 2023). Non-maleficence establishes a moral threshold against actions that harm learners physically, financially, or socially (Lakkaraju et al., 2024). Children should not be exposed to experiences that cause serious cognitional and affective harm or threaten their subsistence. Early-childhood and primary-aged learners readily identify extreme situations; however, they may struggle to articulate less visible risks associated with learning analytics and self-disclosure in intelligent tools (Nguyen et al., 2023).

Respecting autonomy remains a paramount consideration. Educators should promote agency and co-agency, even when full autonomy remains impractical. Young learners can engage in platform use, content exploration, and learning-style choices; however, consent dynamics require clarification. Children cannot legally consent because of the complexity and range of agreements. Assent constitutes a more appropriate, refined, and widely accepted approach from both moral and operational viewpoints. Converging on a definition remains challenging, particularly in classrooms subject to external mandates. Nevertheless, educators can encourage the exploration of topics, modalities, and styles that resonate with distinct preferences.

Successful integration of AI literacy with strong data safeguards

While the promotion of AI literacy for early years education is frequently coupled with regulatory or ethical warnings around data protection, it is feasible to adopt a dual approach that prioritizes both ethical safeguards and the exploration of AI systems. In the French-speaking community of Belgium, educators of students aged 9 to 12 have integrated AI literacy into the curriculum while also implementing robust safeguards around data protection. The 2023 AI framework of the French-speaking Community of Belgium addresses the ethical use of AI in primary education and encourages teachers and learners to experiment with AI systems (Zhou et al., 2020). Concurrently, the use of the free online ChatGPT platform is restricted within these classrooms, due to both the storage of conversational data and the potential for inappropriate responses to basic prompts such as "Tell me a joke," prompting educators to consider how learners might interact with larger chat models at home (Xu, 2024).

CONCLUSION

The development of critical thinking ability in young people to assess the outputs produced by AI is a necessary step towards ensuring that children are equipped to cope with a world that is becoming increasingly built on the use of AI. By integrating AI literacy into other curricula, including reading, writing, science, and social studies, teachers will enable young students to challenge the accuracy, reliability, and ethical design of AI-based content. This methodology not only improves students' awareness of AI technologies but also fosters autonomy, interest, and a sense of accountability in communicating with these technologies (Su et al., 2023). The initiative to encourage students to use problem-solving to process information with the help of scaffolded questioning and project-based learning will allow children to become aware of misinformation and biases in the future, fostering knowledge and ethics as users of modern technology (Matthews & Bartley, 2025).

The combination of AI literacy and critical thinking helps children solve the problems presented by AI to society, such as loss of privacy, data discrimination, and misinformation. The use of developmental theories, such as Piaget's stages, Vygotsky's sociocultural theory, and Bloom's taxonomy, allows teachers to adjust their practices to the cognitive and emotional level of the child and instill a lifetime routine of asking questions and thinking about them (Ng et al., 2022; Spector & Ma, 2019). By equipping children with the ability to interrogate what AI outputs, they will be able to leverage the potential of the technology and mitigate the risks of its applications in a potential future where technology is used to benefit the common good (Walter, 2024).

REFERENCES

Abdelghani, R., Wang, Y. H., Yuan, X., Wang, T., Sauzéon, H., & Oudeyer, P. Y. (2022). GPT-3-driven pedagogical agents for training children's curious question-asking skills. ArXiv. *preprint arXiv, 2211.*

Adu, I. E. (2025). Integrating computational thinking and AI in early childhood education using holistic stem framework. In *Empowering early education with computational thinking, AI, and STEM* (pp. 65-96). IGI Global Scientific Publishing. DOI: DOI: 10.4018/979-8-3693-6210-5.ch003

Ali, S., Kumar, V., & Breazeal, C. (2023). AI audit: A card game to reflect on everyday AI systems. *Proceedings of the AAAI Conference on Artificial Intelligence, 37*(13), 15981–15989. DOI: 10.1609/aaai.v37i13.26897

Archila, P. A., Molina, J., Danies, G., Truscott de Mejía, A. M., & Restrepo, S. (2022). Using the controversy over human race to introduce students to the identification and the evaluation of arguments. *Science & Education, 31*(4), 861–892. DOI: 10.1007/s11191-021-00299-8 PMID: 34803229

Avsheniuk, N., Lutsenko, O., Svyrydiuk, T., & Seminikhyna, N. (2024). Empowering language learners' critical thinking: Evaluating ChatGPT's role in english course implementation. *Arab World English Journal (AWEJ) Special Issue on ChatGPT.* https://ssrn.com/abstract=4814724

Chalukian, M. (2015). Pedagogy of Curiosity: Initial Explorations of Instructional Practice in a Critical Thinking and Curious Classroom. https://scholarworks.umb.edu/cct_capstone/340/

Danry, V. M. (2023). *AI enhanced reasoning: Augmenting human critical thinking with AI systems.* Massachusetts Institute of Technology.

Fabio, R. A., Plebe, A., & Suriano, R. (2025). AI-based chatbot interactions and critical thinking skills: An exploratory study. *Current Psychology, 44*(9), 8082–8095. DOI: 10.1007/s12144-024-06795-8

Hsiao, W., Yeh, C. J., Lin, P. Y., & Cavalcanti, A. (2025, March). Enhancing Critical Thinking for Teaching through AI. In *Society for Information Technology & Teacher Education International Conference* (pp. 2169-2173). Association for the Advancement of Computing in Education (AACE). https://www.learntechlib.org/primary/p/226026/

Khalabuzar, O., & Shymanovych, I. (2024). Developing critical thinking skills through artificial intelligence and language learning. *Modern educational strategies under the influence of the development of the information society and European integration*. DOI:DOI: 10.30525/978-9934-26-405-4-26

Lakkaraju, K., Khandelwal, V., Srivastava, B., Agostinelli, F., Tang, H., Singh, P., . . . Kundu, A. (2024). Trust and ethical considerations in a multi-modal, explainable AI-driven chatbot tutoring system: The case of collaboratively solving Rubik's Cube. *arXiv preprint arXiv:2402.01760.*

Li, G., Zarei, M. A., Alibakhshi, G., & Labbafi, A. (2024). Teachers and educators' experiences and perceptions of artificial-powered interventions for autism groups. *BMC Psychology*, *12*(1), 199. DOI: 10.1186/s40359-024-01664-2 PMID: 38605422

Matthews, A. S., & Bartley, B. (2025). Pay attention to the chatbot behind the curtain when AI 'is no place like home': A framework and toolkit for integrating critical thinking and information literacy in educational and professional settings. *Advances in Online Education: A Peer-Reviewed Journal, 3*(3), 247-273. DOI: 10.69554/FMAI7138

Montenegro, R., Corona, E., Badillo-Perez, D., Mandujano, A., Vazquez, L., Cruz, D., & Xochicale, M. (2021). AIR4Children: Artificial Intelligence and Robotics for Children. *arXiv preprint arXiv:2103.07637.*

Ng, D. T. K., Luo, W., Chan, H. M. Y., & Chu, S. K. W. (2022). Using digital story writing as a pedagogy to develop AI literacy among primary students. *Computers and Education: Artificial Intelligence*, *3*, 100054. DOI: 10.1016/j.caeai.2022.100054

Nguyen, A., Ngo, H. N., Hong, Y., Dang, B., & Nguyen, B. P. T. (2023). Ethical principles for artificial intelligence in education. *Education and Information Technologies*, *28*(4), 4221–4241. DOI: 10.1007/s10639-022-11316-w PMID: 36254344

Rapanta, C., & Walton, D. (2016). The use of argument maps as an assessment tool in higher education. *International Journal of Educational Research*, *79*, 211–221. DOI: 10.1016/j.ijer.2016.03.002

Rong, J., Terzidis, K., & Ding, J. (2024). Kids AI design thinking education for creativity development. *Archives of Design Research*, *37*(3), 119–133. DOI: 10.15187/adr.2024.07.37.3.119

Spector, J. M., & Ma, S. (2019). Inquiry and critical thinking skills for the next generation: From artificial intelligence back to human intelligence. *Smart Learning Environments*, *6*(1), 1–11. DOI: 10.1186/s40561-019-0088-z

Su, J., Ng, D. T. K., & Chu, S. K. W. (2023). Artificial intelligence (AI) literacy in early childhood education: The challenges and opportunities. *Computers and Education: Artificial Intelligence*, *4*, 100124. DOI: 10.1016/j.caeai.2023.100124

Tariq, M. (Ed.). (2025). *Merging Artificial Intelligence With the Internet of Things*. IGI Global., DOI: 10.4018/979-8-3693-8547-0

Tariq, M. (Ed.). (2025). *Emerging Multisector Applications of AI and IoT*. IGI Global., DOI: 10.4018/979-8-3373-4332-7

Tariq, M. U. (2025). *AI-Driven Learning and Engagement in Higher Education*. IGI Global., DOI: 10.4018/979-8-3693-4074-5

Van Brummelen, J., Heng, T., & Tabunshchyk, V. (2021, May). Teaching tech to talk: K-12 conversational artificial intelligence literacy curriculum and development tools. *Proceedings of the AAAI Conference on Artificial Intelligence*, *35*(17), 15655–15663. DOI: 10.1609/aaai.v35i17.17844

Walter, Y. (2024). Embracing the future of artificial intelligence in the classroom: The relevance of AI literacy, prompt engineering, and critical thinking in modern education. *International Journal of Educational Technology in Higher Education*, *21*(1), 15. DOI: 10.1186/s41239-024-00448-3

Xu, Y. '. (2024). The Double-Edged Sword of AI Writing Tools. https://osf.io/preprints/socarxiv/wnpd5 DOI: 10.31235/osf.io/wnpd5

Yu, L., & Yu, Z. (2023). Qualitative and quantitative analyses of artificial intelligence ethics in education using VOSviewer and CitNetExplorer. *Frontiers in Psychology*, *14*, 1061778. DOI: 10.3389/fpsyg.2023.1061778 PMID: 36968737

Zhou, X., Van Brummelen, J., & Lin, P. (2020). Designing AI learning experiences for K-12: Emerging works, future opportunities and a design framework. *arXiv preprint arXiv:2009.10228*.

KEY TERMS AND DEFINITIONS

AI Literacy: The ability to comprehend basic AI concepts, recognize AI systems in everyday life, and critically engage with AI technologies, including understanding their capabilities, limitations, and ethical implications, particularly in educational contexts for young children.

AI Outputs: The responses, suggestions, or generated content produced by AI systems, such as answers from virtual assistants, text from chatbots, or images from generative tools, which rely on data and algorithms but may contain inaccuracies or biases.

Bias in AI: Systematic errors or unfair representations in AI outputs resulting from skewed training data, leading to inaccurate or discriminatory results, such as facial recognition failing for certain ethnicities, which children must learn to identify and question.

Cognitive Load Theory (CLT): A framework explaining how information processing affects learning, highlighting the need to manage cognitive demands, especially extraneous loads, when introducing complex AI concepts to children with special educational needs to enhance comprehension and reduce difficulties.

Critical Thinking: A reflective, active, and reasonable process involving identifying problems, engaging in skepticism, evaluating information validity, and making informed decisions, essential for assessing AI outputs and fostering curiosity and agency in learners.

Compilation of References

Abdelghani, R., Wang, Y. H., Yuan, X., Wang, T., Sauzéon, H., & Oudeyer, P. Y. (2022). GPT-3-driven pedagogical agents for training children's curious question-asking skills. ArXiv. *preprint arXiv, 2211.*

Adams, C., Pente, P., Lemermeyer, G., & Rockwell, G. (2023). Ethical principles for artificial intelligence in K-12 education. *Computers and Education: Artificial Intelligence*, *4*, 100131. DOI: 10.1016/j.caeai.2023.100131

Adom, D., Yeboah, A., & Ankrah, A. (2016). Constructivism philosophical paradigm: Implications for research, teaching and learning. *Global Journal of Arts. Humanities and Social Sciences*, *4*(10), 1–9.

Adu, I. E. (2025). Integrating computational thinking and AI in early childhood education using holistic stem framework. In *Empowering early education with computational thinking, AI, and STEM* (pp. 65-96). IGI Global Scientific Publishing. DOI: DOI: 10.4018/979-8-3693-6210-5.ch003

Aghaziarati, A., Nejatifar, S., & Abedi, A. (2023). Artificial intelligence in education: Investigating teacher attitudes. *AITECHBESOSCI*, *1*(1), 35–42. DOI: 10.61838/kman.aitech.1.1.6

Ahmad, I. (2024). *Factors Affecting High Attrition Rate of MOOCs and Its Prediction Using Machine Learning Techniques* [Uttaranchal University]. http://hdl.handle.net/10603/543480

Ahmad, I., Jasola, S., Ahmad, S., & Sharma, S. (2020). Technology Enabled Learning in Higher Education: A Case Study. *Xplore The Xavier's Research Journal, 11*(1), 68–73. https://9dec1e70-3d6c-406f-960b-920f18cdab25.filesusr.com/ugd/03b37e_0a4fe5f7f9764c23a239c95f05ae24fc.pdf

Ahmad, I., Sharma, S., Chaubey, M. K., Dhyani, S., Ahmad, S., & Kumar, A. (2023). SWAYAM MOOC Reviews: Assessing Acceptability through Sentiment Analysis using Machine Learning. *2023 14th International Conference on Computing Communication and Networking Technologies (ICCCNT)*, 1–5. DOI: 10.1109/ICCCNT56998.2023.10306960

Ahmad, I., Sharma, S., Kumar, R., Dhyani, S., & Dumka, A. (2023). Data Analytics of Online Education during Pandemic Health Crisis: A Case Study. *2023 2nd Edition of IEEE Delhi Section Flagship Conference (DELCON)*, 1–6. DOI: 10.1109/DELCON57910.2023.10127423

Ahmad, I., Sharma, S., Kurubacak, G., Kumar, A., Kumar, R., & Ahmad, S. (2022). Artificial Intelligence in MOOCs: A Bibliometric Perspective. In Singh, R., Gehlot, A., & Buddhi, D. (Eds.), *Intelligent Systems - Proceedings of ICIS-2022* (pp. 38–47). River Publishers., https://www.riverpublishers.com/research_article_details.php?book_id=1004&cid=6

Ahmad, I., Sharma, S., Leal-Saballos, C., Kumar, M., Kumar, A., & Ahmad, S. (2025). *Predicting Early Dropouts in SWAYAM MOOCs Using Machine Learning Techniques: A Comparative Analysis*., DOI: 10.1007/978-3-031-80778-7_18

Ahmad, I., Sharma, S., Singh, R., Gehlot, A., Gupta, L. R., Thakur, A. K., Priyadarshi, N., & Twala, B. (2024). Inclusive learning using industry 4.0 technologies: Addressing student diversity in modern education. *Cogent Education, 11*(1), 2330235. Advance online publication. DOI: 10.1080/2331186X.2024.2330235

Ahmad, I., Sharma, S., Singh, R., Gehlot, A., Priyadarshi, N., & Twala, B. (2022). MOOC 5.0: A Roadmap to the Future of Learning. *Sustainability (Basel), 14*(18), 11199. DOI: 10.3390/su141811199

Akavova, A., Temirkhanova, Z., & Lorsanova, Z. (2023). Adaptive learning and artificial intelligence in the educational space. *E3S Web of Conferences, 451*, 06011. https://doi.org/DOI: 10.1051/e3sconf/202345106011

Akgun, S., & Greenhow, C. (2022). Artificial intelligence in education: Addressing ethical challenges in K-12 settings. *AI and Ethics*, *2*(3), 431–440. DOI: 10.1007/s43681-021-00096-7 PMID: 34790956

Alade, T. T., Opele, J. K., Adeyeye, O. O., & Balogun, B. N. (2024). A Desk Review of the Impact of Open Access and Open Data on Research Productivity of Lecturers in Developing Countries. *Journal of Education in Developing Areas, 31*(5), 186–195.

AlAli, R., & Wardat, Y. (2024). Opportunities and challenges of integrating generative artificial intelligence in education. *International Journal of Religion*, *5*(7), 784–793. DOI: 10.61707/8y29gv34

Alanazi, A. (2016). A critical review of constructivist theory and the emergence of constructionism. *American Research Journal of Humanities and Social Sciences*, *2*, 1–8.

Ali, S., Kumar, V., & Breazeal, C. (2023). AI audit: A card game to reflect on everyday AI systems. *Proceedings of the AAAI Conference on Artificial Intelligence*, *37*(13), 15981–15989. DOI: 10.1609/aaai.v37i13.26897

Allen, A. (2022). An introduction to curriculum development: Its theoretical roots and impact on contemporary education. *Journal of Learning Design and Leadership*, *1*(1), 1–11.

Allen, L. K., & Kendeou, P. (2024). ED-AI Lit: An Interdisciplinary Framework for AI Literacy in Education. *Policy Insights from the Behavioral and Brain Sciences*, *11*(1), 3–10. DOI: 10.1177/23727322231220339

Alrayes, A., Henari, T., & Ahmed, D. (2024). ChatGPT in education: Understanding the Bahraini academics' perspective. *Electronic Journal of e-Learning*, *22*(2), 112–134. DOI: 10.34190/ejel.22.2.3250

Alsohaimi, M., Albahiri, M., & Alhaj, A. (2025). Addressing and managing artificial intelligence challenges and opportunities in elementary education in Saudi Arabia: An in-depth consideration. *Educational Process: International Journal*, 1–33.

al-Zyoud, H. M. M. (2020). The Role of Artificial Intelligence in Teacher Professional Development. *Universal Journal of Educational Research*, *8*(11B), 6263–6272. DOI: 10.13189/ujer.2020.082265

Aoun, J. E. (2017). *Robot-proof: Higher education in the age of artificial intelligence*. MIT Press. DOI: 10.7551/mitpress/11456.001.0001

Aravantinos, S., Lavidas, K., Voulgari, I., Papadakis, S., Karalis, T., & Komis, V. (2024). Educational approaches with AI in primary school settings: A systematic review of the literature available in Scopus. *Education Sciences*, *14*(7), 744. DOI: 10.3390/educsci14070744

Archila, P. A., Molina, J., Danies, G., Truscott de Mejía, A. M., & Restrepo, S. (2022). Using the controversy over human race to introduce students to the identification and the evaluation of arguments. *Science & Education*, *31*(4), 861–892. DOI: 10.1007/s11191-021-00299-8 PMID: 34803229

Arvin, N., Hoseinabady, M., Bayat, B., & Zahmatkesh, E. (2023). Teacher experiences with AI-based educational tools. *AITECHBESOSCI, 1*(2), 26–32. DOI: 10.61838/kman.aitech.1.2.5

Assaraf, O. B.-Z., & Orion, N. (2010). Development of system thinking skills in the context of Earth system education. *Journal of Research in Science Teaching, 47*(5), 540–563. DOI: 10.1002/tea.20351

Australian Government Department of Education. (2025). *China's approach to AI education in schools*. Department of Education.

Avsheniuk, N., Lutsenko, O., Svyrydiuk, T., & Seminikhyna, N. (2024). Empowering language learners' critical thinking: Evaluating ChatGPT's role in english course implementation. *Arab World English Journal (AWEJ) Special Issue on ChatGPT*. https://ssrn.com/abstract=4814724

Azhimia, F., & Parnawati, T. (2023). The contribution of language input, conducive learning environment, and motivation toward students' speaking proficiency. *Journal of Language Intelligence and Culture, 5*(1), 33–44. DOI: 10.35719/jlic.v5i1.122

Baghiro, R. N., Rahmawati, Y., & Sam, T. T. A. (2025). Coding Learning to Stimulate Early Childhood Computational Thinking. *International Journal of Computational and Experimental Science and Engineering, 11*(2). Advance online publication. DOI: 10.22399/ijcesen.1824

Baldwin, J. R., Pingault, J. B., Schoeler, T., Sallis, H. M., & Munafò, M. R. (2022). Protecting against researcher bias in secondary data analysis: Challenges and potential solutions. *European Journal of Epidemiology, 37*(1), 1–10. DOI: 10.1007/s10654-021-00839-0 PMID: 35025022

Barua, P., Vicnesh, J., Gururajan, R., Oh, S., Palmer, E., Azizan, M., & Acharya, U. (2022). Artificial intelligence enabled personalised assistive tools to enhance education of children with neurodevelopmental disorders: A review. *International Journal of Environmental Research and Public Health, 19*(3), 1192. DOI: 10.3390/ijerph19031192 PMID: 35162220

Baştürk, S. (2016). Primary pre-service teachers' perspectives on constructivism and its implementation in schools. *Universal Journal of Educational Research, 4*(4), 904–912. DOI: 10.13189/ujer.2016.040428

Belda-Medina, J., & Goddard, M. (2024). AI-driven digital storytelling: A strategy for creating English as a foreign language (EFL) materials. *International Journal of Linguistics Studies, 4*(1), 40–49. DOI: 10.32996/ijls.2024.4.1.4

Bhose, M. (2024, October 2). What are the ethical challenges in AI-driven assessments? Retrieved from https://elearningindustry.com/what-are-the-ethical-challenges-in-ai-driven-assessments

Biagini, G. (2025). Towards an AI-Literate Future: A systematic literature review exploring education, ethics, and applications. *International Journal of Artificial Intelligence in Education, 35*(4), 1–51. DOI: 10.1007/s40593-025-00466-w

Bialystok, E. (2011). Reshaping the mind: The benefits of bilingualism. *Canadian Journal of Experimental Psychology = Revue Canadienne de Psychologie Expérimentale, 65*(4), 229–235. DOI: 10.1037/a0025406 PMID: 21910523

Bialystok, E. (2017). The bilingual adaptation: How minds accommodate experience. *Psychological Bulletin, 143*(3), 233–262. DOI: 10.1037/bul0000099 PMID: 28230411

Biggs, J., Kember, D., & Leung, D. (2001). The revised two-factor study process questionnaire: R-SPQ-2F. *The British Journal of Educational Psychology, 71*(1), 133–149. DOI: 10.1348/000709901158433 PMID: 11307705

Black, N. B., George, S., Eguchi, A., Dempsey, J. C., Langran, E., Fraga, L., & Howard, N. (2024, March). A framework for approaching AI education in educator preparation programs. *Proceedings of the AAAI Conference on Artificial Intelligence, 38*(21), 23069–23077. DOI: 10.1609/aaai.v38i21.30351

Blair, C., & Raver, C. C. (2015). School readiness and self-regulation: A developmental psychobiological approach. *Annual Review of Psychology, 66*(1), 711–731. DOI: 10.1146/annurev-psych-010814-015221 PMID: 25148852

Boden, M. A. (2018). *Artificial intelligence: A very short introduction.* Oxford University Press.

Bórquez Morales, L. S., & Hernández Alvarado, M. G. (2021). Exposición, Producción e Internalización: Input, Output, and Intake: Role and Relevance in Second Language Learning. *Edähi Boletín Científico de Ciencias Sociales y Humanidades del ICSHu, 10*(19). https://repository.uaeh.edu.mx/revistas/index.php/icshu/article/view/7869

Brokensha, S., Kotzé, E., & Senekal, B. A. (2023). *AI in and for Africa: A Humanistic Perspective.* Chapman and Hall/CRC. DOI: 10.1201/9781003276135

Bronfenbrenner, U. (1979). *The ecology of human development: Experiments by nature and design.* Harvard University Press. DOI: 10.4159/9780674028845

Bruner, J. (1990). Culture and human development: A new look. *Human development, 33*(6), 344–355.

Calvani, A., Fini, A., Ranieri, M., & Picci, P. (2012). Are young generations in secondary school digitally competent? A study on Italian teenagers. *Computers & Education, 58*(2), 797–807. DOI: 10.1016/j.compedu.2011.10.004

Calvo, R. A., & D'Mello, S. K. (2010). Affective computing: An overview. In *Handbook of research on computational arts and creative informatics* (pp. 23–44). IGI global.

Capital Technology University. (2023, May 30). *The ethical considerations of artificial intelligence*. Retrieved from https://www.captechu.edu/blog/ethical-considerations-of-artificial-intelligence

Capra, F., & Luisi, P. L. (2014). *The systems view of life: A unifying vision*. Cambridge University Press. DOI: 10.1017/CBO9780511895555

Cardon, P., Fleischmann, C., Artz, J., Logemann, M., & Hedewald, J. (2023). The challenges and opportunities of AI-assisted writing: Developing AI literacy for the AI age. *Business and Professional Communication Quarterly, 86*(3), 257–295. Advance online publication. DOI: 10.1177/23294906231176517

Carolus, A., Augustin, Y., Markus, A., & Wenrich, C. (2023). Digital interaction literacy model – Conceptualising competences for literate interactions with voice-based AI systems. *Computers and Education: Artificial Intelligence, 4*, 100114. DOI: 10.1016/j.caeai.2022.100114

Casal-Otero, L., Catala, A., Fernández-Morante, C., Taboada, M., Cebreiro, B., & Barro, S. (2023). AI literacy in K-12: A systematic literature review. *International Journal of STEM Education, 10*(1), 29. DOI: 10.1186/s40594-023-00418-7

Castro, D., Hammer, C., Franco, X., Cycyk, L., Scarpino, S., & Burchinal, M. (2020). Documenting bilingual experiences in the early years: Using the CECER-DLL child and family and teacher questionnaires. *Bilingualism: Language and Cognition, 23*(5), 958–963. DOI: 10.1017/S1366728920000401

Celik, I. (2023). Exploring the determinants of Artificial Intelligence (AI) literacy: Digital divide, computational thinking, cognitive absorption. *Telematics and Informatics, 83*, 102026. DOI: 10.1016/j.tele.2023.102026

Chakabwata, W. (2022). Digital-based assessments for higher-order and critical thinking in higher education. In Keengwe, J. (Ed.), *Digital-based assessments for innovative practices in education* (pp. 228–246). IGI Global. DOI: 10.4018/978-1-6684-2468-1.ch012

Chakabwata, W. (2023). Using an eclectic approach to design curriculum instruction in an online environment. In Walters, K. (Ed.), *Dynamic curriculum development and design strategies for effective online learning in higher education* (pp. 96–115). IGI Global. DOI: 10.4018/978-1-6684-8646-7.ch006

Chakabwata, W. (2023). Using technology to enhance student engagement in STEM subjects in higher education. In Martin, C., Miller, B., & Polly, D. (Eds.), *Technology integration and transformation in STEM classrooms* (pp. 165–183). IGI Global.

Chakabwata, W., & Hategekimana, E. (2024). Using project-based pedagogies in African higher education. In Keengwe, J. (Ed.), *Handbook of research on transformative and innovative pedagogies in education* (pp. 55–75). IGI Global.

Chalukian, M. (2015). Pedagogy of Curiosity: Initial Explorations of Instructional Practice in a Critical Thinking and Curious Classroom. https://scholarworks.umb.edu/cct_capstone/340/

Chandio, D. T., Pandhiani, S., & Iqbal, R. (2016). Bloom's taxonomy: Improving assessment and teaching-learning processes. *Journal of Education and Educational Development, 3*(2), 203–221. DOI: 10.22555/joeed.v3i2.1034

Chauhan, S. A. K., & Ahmad, I. (2024). The Attitude of Experts in Higher Education Towards New NEP-2020. In *Virtual Lifelong Learning: Educating Society with Modern Communication Technologies* (pp. 26–36). BENTHAM SCIENCE PUBLISHERS. DOI: 10.2174/97898151965661240l0005

Chee, H., Ahn, S., & Lee, J. (2025). A Competency Framework for AI Literacy: Variations by Different Learner Groups and an Implied Learning Pathway. *British Journal of Educational Technology, 56*(5), 2146–2182. DOI: 10.1111/bjet.13556

Chen, L., Chen, P., & Lin, Z. (2020). Artificial intelligence in education: A review. *IEEE Access : Practical Innovations, Open Solutions, 8*, 75264–75278. DOI: 10.1109/ACCESS.2020.2988510

Chen, L., Xiao, S., Chen, Y., Song, Y., Wu, R., & Sun, L. (2024, May). ChatScratch: An AI-augmented system toward autonomous visual programming learning for children aged 6-12. In *Proceedings of the 2024 CHI Conference on Human Factors in Computing Systems* (pp. 1-19). DOI: 10.1145/3613904.3642229

Chen, X., Lee, M. K., & Razi, A. (2022). How does affective computing bias hiring? A user study on the impact of emotion analysis on hiring decisions. In *Proceedings of the 2022 ACM Conference on Fairness, Accountability, and Transparency* (pp. 1152-1163).

Chinese State Council. (2017). *Notice of the State Council on issuing the next generation artificial intelligence development plan (Guofa [2017] No. 35).* https://www.gov.cn/zhengce/content/2017-07/20/content_5211996.htm

Chinta, S. V., Wang, Z., Yin, Z., Hoang, N., Gonzalez, M., Le Quy, T., & Zhang, W. (2024). *FairAIED: Navigating Fairness.* Bias, and Ethics in Educational AI Applications.

Chiu, T. K. F. (2025). AI literacy and competency: Definitions, frameworks, development and future research directions. *Interactive Learning Environments, 33*(5), 3225–3229. DOI: 10.1080/10494820.2025.2514372

Chiu, T. K. F., Ahmad, Z., Ismailov, M., & Sanusi, I. T. (2024). What are artificial intelligence literacy and competency? A comprehensive framework to support them. *Computers and Education Open, 6*, 100171. DOI: 10.1016/j.caeo.2024.100171

Chiu, T. K., Ahmad, Z., & Çoban, M. (2025). Development and validation of teacher artificial intelligence (AI) competence self-efficacy (TAICS) scale. *Education and Information Technologies, 30*(5), 6667–6685. DOI: 10.1007/s10639-024-13094-z

Cohen, S., Mompelat, L., Mann, A., & Connors, L. (2024). The linguistic leap: Understanding, evaluating, and integrating AI in language education. *Tydskrif vir Taalonderrig, 4*(2), 23–31. DOI: 10.54475/jlt.2024.012

Cooper, H., Hedges, L. V., & Valentine, J. C. (Eds.). (2019). *The handbook of research synthesis and meta-analysis* (3rd ed.). Russell Sage Foundation. DOI: 10.7758/9781610448864

Cuomo, S., Bagn, G., & Raneri, M. (2022). *Artificial Intelligence Literacy, che cos'è e come promuoverla. Dall'analisi della letteratura ad una proposta di Framework.* Media Education., DOI: 10.36253/me-13374

D'Alessandro, W., & D'Alessandro, M. (2025). Deontology and safe artificial intelligence. *Philosophical Studies, 182*(7), 1681–1704. DOI: 10.1007/s11098-024-02174-y

Dale, A., Arber, S., & Procter, M. (2025). *Doing secondary analysis.* Taylor & Francis. DOI: 10.4324/9781003632467

Danry, V. M. (2023). *AI enhanced reasoning: Augmenting human critical thinking with AI systems.* Massachusetts Institute of Technology.

Dasen, P. R. (1972). Cross-cultural Piagetian research: A summary. *Journal of Cross-Cultural Psychology, 3*(1), 23–40. DOI: 10.1177/002202217200300102

Davoodifard, M., & Eskin, D. (2024). Exploring the role of generative AI in second language education: Insights for instruction, learning, and assessment. *Studies in Applied Linguistics and TESOL, 24*(1). Advance online publication. DOI: 10.52214/salt.v24i1.12863

Dennis, L., & Whalon, K. (2020). Effects of teacher- versus application-delivered instruction on the expressive vocabulary of at-risk preschool children. *Remedial and Special Education, 42*(4), 195–206. DOI: 10.1177/0741932519900991

Diamond, A. (2013). Executive functions. *Annual Review of Psychology, 64*(1), 135–168. DOI: 10.1146/annurev-psych-113011-143750 PMID: 23020641

Dogan, S., Nalbantoglu, U. Y., Celik, I., & Agacli Dogan, N. (2025). Artificial intelligence professional development: A systematic review of TPACK, designs, and effects for teacher learning. *Professional Development in Education, 51*(3), 519–546. DOI: 10.1080/19415257.2025.2454457

Druga, S., Christoph, F. L., & Ko, A. J. (2022). Family as a third space for AI literacies: How do children and parents learn about AI together? In *CHI Conference on Human Factors in Computing Systems* (pp. 1–17). DOI: 10.1145/3491102.3502031

Druga, S., Otero, N., & Ko, A. J. (2022, July). The landscape of teaching resources for AI education. In *Proceedings of the 27th ACM Conference on on Innovation and Technology in Computer Science Education* Vol. 1 (pp. 96-102). DOI: 10.1145/3502718.3524782

Druga, S., Vu, S. T., Likhtik, E., & Qiu, T. (2019). Inclusive AI literacy for kids around the world. *Proceedings of FabLearn, 2019*, 104–111. DOI: 10.1145/3311890.3311904

Dube, A., & Chisaka, B. (2021). Challenges militating against primary school learners' maximum access to e-education programmes in Goromonzi District of Zimbabwe. *International Journal of Research Studies in Computer Science and Engineering, 8*(1), 31–42.

Durand-López, E. (2020). A bilingual advantage in memory capacity: Assessing the roles of proficiency, number of languages acquired and age of acquisition. *The International Journal of Bilingualism, 25*(3), 606–621. DOI: 10.1177/1367006920965714

Dusenbury, L., Dermody, C., & Weissberg, R. P. (2023). *State scorecard scan: Social and emotional learning assessment and accountability*. Collaborative for Academic, Social, and Emotional Learning.

Eguchi, A. (2021). AI-Robotics and AI literacy. In Malvezzi, M., Alimisis, D., & Moro, M. (Eds.), *Education in with Robotics to Foster 21st Century Skills* (Vol. 982, pp. 75–85). Springer., DOI: 10.1007/978-3-030-77022-8_7

Entwistle, N., McCune, V., & Hounsell, J. (2003). Investigating ways of enhancing university teaching-learning environments. In De Corte, E. (Eds.), *Unravelling basic components and dimensions of powerful learning environments* (pp. 89–107). Elsevier.

Epley, N., Waytz, A., & Cacioppo, J. T. (2007). On seeing human: A three-factor theory of anthropomorphism. *Psychological Review*, *114*(4), 864–886. DOI: 10.1037/0033-295X.114.4.864 PMID: 17907867

European Commission. (2021). *Digital Education Action Plan 2021-2027: Resetting education and training for the digital age*. European Commission.

Eyal, L. (2025). Rethinking artificial-intelligence literacy through the lens of teacher educators: The adaptive AI model. *Computers and Education Open*, *9*, 100291. DOI: 10.1016/j.caeo.2025.100291

Fabio, R. A., Plebe, A., & Suriano, R. (2025). AI-based chatbot interactions and critical thinking skills: An exploratory study. *Current Psychology*, *44*(9), 8082–8095. DOI: 10.1007/s12144-024-06795-8

Fergencs, T., Pilawka, O., Broholm, R., & Magnussen, R. (2020, October). Barriers to implementing technology-enhanced learning in south african primary schools. In *Proceedings of the European Conference on e-Learning* (pp. 182-189).

Fırat, M. (2023). What ChatGPT means for universities: Perceptions of scholars and students. *Journal of Applied Learning & Teaching*, *6*(1). Advance online publication. DOI: 10.37074/jalt.2023.6.1.22

Flavell, J. H. (1979). Metacognition and cognitive monitoring: A new area of cognitive–developmental inquiry. *The American Psychologist*, *34*(10), 906–911. DOI: 10.1037/0003-066X.34.10.906

Forero-Corba, W., & Bennasar, F. (2024). Techniques and applications of machine learning and artificial intelligence in education: A systematic review. *RIED – Revista Iberoamericana de Educación a Distancia, 27*(1).

Fountoulakis, M. (2024). Evaluating the impact of AI tools on language proficiency and intercultural communication in second language education. *International Journal of Second and Foreign Language Education*, *3*(1), 12–26. DOI: 10.33422/ijsfle.v3i1.768

Freire, P. (2005). Education for critical consciousness. *Continuum.*

Freire, P. (2012). Pedagogy of the oppressed. *Continuum.*

Fullan, M. (2022). *The new meaning of educational change* (6th ed.). Teachers College Press.

Fundi, M., Sanusi, I. T., Oyelere, S. S., & Ayere, M. (2024). Advancing AI education: Assessing Kenyan in-service teachers' preparedness for integrating artificial intelligence in competence-based curriculum. *Computers in Human Behavior Reports*, *14*, 100412. DOI: 10.1016/j.chbr.2024.100412

Gardner, J., O'Leary, M., & Yuan, L. (2021). Artificial intelligence in educational assessment: Breakthrough or buncombe and bullyhoo? *Journal of Computer Assisted Learning*, *37*(5), 1207–1216. DOI: 10.1111/jcal.12577

Gatrell, A. C. (2020). 14. Using and analysing secondary data. *Handbook of Theory and Methods in Applied Health Research: Questions, Methods and Choices*, 268.

Gay, G. (2018). *Culturally responsive teaching: Theory, research, and practice* (3rd ed.). Teachers College Press.

Gentner, D., & Holyoak, K. J. (1997). Reasoning and learning by analogy: Introduction. *The American Psychologist*, *52*(1), 32–34. DOI: 10.1037/0003-066X.52.1.32 PMID: 9017930

Gentner, D., & Smith, L. (2012). Analogical reasoning. In Ramachandran, V. S. (Ed.), *Encyclopedia of Human Behavior* (2nd ed., pp. 130–136). Elsevier. DOI: 10.1016/B978-0-12-375000-6.00022-7

George, A. S. (2023). Preparing students for an AI-driven world: Rethinking curriculum and pedagogy in the age of artificial intelligence. *Partners Universal Innovative Research Publication*, *1*(2), 112–136.

Geurts, S., Koning, I., Vossen, H., & Van den Eijnden, R. (2021). A qualitative study on children's digital media use and parents' self-interest. *Journal of Child and Family Studies*, *31*(7), 2015–2026. DOI: 10.1007/s10826-021-02074-3 PMID: 34580571

Ghotbi, N. (2023). The Ethics of Emotional Artificial Intelligence: A Mixed Method Analysis. *Asian Bioethics Review*, *15*(4), 417–430. DOI: 10.1007/s41649-022-00237-y PMID: 37808444

Göçen, A., & Aydemir, F. (2020). Artificial intelligence in education and schools. *Research on Education and Media*, *12*(1), 13–21. DOI: 10.2478/rem-2020-0003

Goleman, D. (2005). *Emotional intelligence: Why it can matter more than IQ*. Bantam Books.

Gopnik, A. (2020). Childhood as a solution to explore–exploit tensions. *Philosophical Transactions of the Royal Society B*, *375*(1803), 20190502.

Gopnik, A., Meltzoff, A. N., & Kuhl, P. K. (2004). *The scientist in the crib: What early learning tells us about the mind*. HarperCollins.

Gopnik, A., & Schulz, L. (2007). *Causal learning: Psychology, philosophy, and computation*. Oxford University Press. DOI: 10.1093/acprof:oso/9780195176803.001.0001

Gopnik, A., & Wellman, H. M. (2012). Reconstructing constructivism: Causal models, Bayesian learning mechanisms, and the theory theory. *Psychological Bulletin*, *138*(6), 1085–1108. DOI: 10.1037/a0028044 PMID: 22582739

Granström, M., & Oppi, P. (2025). Assessing teachers' readiness and perceived usefulness of AI in education: An Estonian perspective. *Frontiers in Education*, *10*, 1622240. Advance online publication. DOI: 10.3389/feduc.2025.1622240

Guan, L., Zhang, Y., & Gu, M. M. (2025). Pre-service teachers preparedness for AI-integrated education: An investigation from perceptions, capabilities, and teachers' identity changes. *Computers and Education: Artificial Intelligence*, *8*, 100341. DOI: 10.1016/j.caeai.2024.100341

Guo, Y., & Kühler, M. (2025). History, AI and utilitarianism. *AI and Ethics*, *5*(3), 2903–2917. DOI: 10.1007/s43681-024-00581-9

Gutiérrez, L. (2023). Artificial intelligence in language education: Navigating the potential and challenges of chatbots and NLP. *RSELTL*, *1*(3), 180–191. DOI: 10.62583/rseltl.v1i3.44

Gu, X., & Ericson, B. J. (2025). AI Literacy in K-12 and Higher Education in the Wake of Generative AI. *Integral Review*, 125–140. Advance online publication. DOI: 10.1145/3702652.3744217

Hackman, D. A., & Farah, M. J. (2009). Socioeconomic status and the developing brain. *Trends in Cognitive Sciences*, *13*(2), 65–73. DOI: 10.1016/j.tics.2008.11.003 PMID: 19135405

Harrison, R., Jones, B., Gardner, P., & Lawton, R. (2021). Quality assessment with diverse studies (QuADS): An appraisal tool for methodological and reporting quality in systematic reviews of mixed-or multi-method studies. *BMC Health Services Research*, *21*(1), 144. DOI: 10.1186/s12913-021-06122-y PMID: 33588842

Heckman, J. J. (2011). The economics of inequality: The value of early childhood education. *American Educator*, *35*(1), 31–47.

Herlinawati, H., Marwa, M., Ishmael, N., Junaidi, L. L., & Situmorang, D. O. (2024). Integration of 21st-century skills in the education curriculum. *Heliyon*, •••, 11. DOI: 10.1016/j.heliyon.2024.e35148 PMID: 39170322

Hermann, E. (2022). Artificial intelligence and mass personalisation of communication content—An ethical and literacy perspective. *New Media & Society*, *24*(5), 1258–1277. DOI: 10.1177/14614448211022702

Hirsh-Pasek, K. (2009). A mandate for playful learning in preschool: Applying the scientific evidence.

Hmelo-Silver, C. E., Marathe, S., & Liu, L. (2017). Fish swim, rocks sit, and lungs breathe: Leveraging everyday experiences to teach complex systems thinking. *Educational Psychology Review*, *29*, 1–23.

Holmes, W., Bektik, D., & Woolf, B. (2018). Ethics in artificial intelligence in education. In *Artificial Intelligence in Education* (pp. 551–553). Springer.

Holstein, K., Aleven, V., & Rummel, N. (2020, June). A conceptual framework for human–AI hybrid adaptivity in education. In *International conference on artificial intelligence in education* (pp. 240-254). Cham: Springer International Publishing. DOI: 10.1007/978-3-030-52237-7_20

Hsiao, W., Yeh, C. J., Lin, P. Y., & Cavalcanti, A. (2025, March). Enhancing Critical Thinking for Teaching through AI. In *Society for Information Technology & Teacher Education International Conference* (pp. 2169-2173). Association for the Advancement of Computing in Education (AACE). https://www.learntechlib.org/primary/p/226026/

Hu, C. C., Yang, Y. F., Cheng, Y. W., & Chen, N. S. (2024). Integrating educational robot and low-cost self-made toys to enhance STEM learning performance for primary school students. *Behaviour & Information Technology*, *43*(8), 1614–1635. DOI: 10.1080/0144929X.2023.2222308

Hwang, W., Nurtantyana, R., Purba, S., Hariyanti, U., Indrihapsari, Y., & Surjono, H. (2023). AI and recognition technologies to facilitate EFL writing. *Journal of Educational Computing Research*, *61*(5), 1008–1035. DOI: 10.1177/07356331221137253

Idham, A., Rauf, W., & Rajab, A. (2024). Navigating the transformative impact of AI on English language teaching. *JES*, *4*(1), 8–14. DOI: 10.56185/jes.v4i1.620

Immordino-Yang, M. H. (2015). *Emotions, learning, and the brain: Exploring the educational implications of affective neuroscience*. W. W. Norton & Company.

Inagaki, K., & Hatano, Y. (2002). *Young children's naive thinking about the biological world*. Psychology Press.

Independent Commission on Assessment in Primary Education (ICAPE). (2022). *ICAPE report*. ICAPE.

Ismail, A., Aliu, A., Ibrahim, M., & Sulaiman, A. (2024). Preparing teachers of the future in the era of artificial intelligence. *Journal of Artificial Intelligence. Machine Learning and Neural Network, 44*, 31–41.

Jaakkola, E. (2020). Designing conceptual articles: Four approaches. *AMS Review, 10*(1-2), 18–26. DOI: 10.1007/s13162-020-00161-0

Jacobson, M. J., & Wilensky, U. (2006). Complex systems in education: Scientific and educational importance. *Educational Researcher, 35*(7), 3–12. DOI: 10.3102/0013189X035007003

Kachergis, G., Marchman, V., & Frank, M. (2021). Toward a "standard model" of early language learning. *Current Directions in Psychological Science, 31*(1), 20–27. DOI: 10.1177/09637214211057836

Kandlhofer, M., Steinbauer, G., Hirschmugl-Gasch, S., & Huber, P. (2016). Artificial intelligence and computer science in education: From kindergarten to university. In *2016, IEEE Frontiers in Education Conference (FIE)* (pp. 1–9). DOI: 10.1109/FIE.2016.7757570

Kayal, A. (2024). Transformative pedagogy: A comprehensive framework for AI integration in education. In *Explainable AI for education: Recent trends and challenges* (pp. 247–270). Springer Nature Switzerland. DOI: 10.1007/978-3-031-72410-7_14

Kementerian Pendidikan Malaysia. (2020). *Curriculum guidelines for preschool education in Malaysia*. Ministry of Education.

Kemp, S. (2024). *Digital 2024: Zimbabwe*. DataReportal. Retrieved from https://datareportal.com

Keshishi, N., & Hack, D. S. (2023). Emotional Intelligence in the Digital Age: Harnessing AI for Students' Inner Development. *Journal of Perspectives in Applied Academic Practice, 11*(3). Advance online publication. DOI: 10.56433/jpaap.v11i3.579

Khalabuzar, O., & Shymanovych, I. (2024). Developing critical thinking skills through artificial intelligence and language learning. *Modern educational strategies under the influence of the development of the information society and European integration*. DOI:DOI: 10.30525/978-9934-26-405-4-26

Kim, Y. J., Kim, G., & Stoiber, A. (2025). Playful design for AI Literacy: Creating inclusive learning and assessment opportunities. *International Journal of Human-Computer Studies, 199*, 103508. DOI: 10.1016/j.ijhcs.2025.103508

Klingefjord, O., Lowe, R., & Edelman, J. (2024). *What are human values, and how do we align AI to them?* Konstantina, L., & Stamatios, P. (2024). Enhancing computational thinking in early childhood education through ScratchJr integration. *Heliyon, 10*(10), e30482. DOI: 10.1016/j.heliyon.2024.e30482 PMID: 38778958

Kołak, J., Monaghan, P., & Taylor, G. (2022). Language in educational apps for pre-schoolers. *Journal of Child Language, 50*(4), 895–921. DOI: 10.1017/S0305000922000198 PMID: 35481491

Kotsidis, K., & Dima, A. (2025). Integrating AI Tools and Drama Pedagogy in Digital Classrooms to Foster Critical Thinking and Inclusion in Primary Education. *Advances in Mobile Learning Educational Research, 5*(2), 1524–1535. DOI: 10.25082/AMLER.2025.02.008

Krahenbuhl, K. (2016). Student-centred education and constructivism: Challenges and clarity for teachers. *The Clearing House: A Journal of Educational Strategies, Issues and Ideas, 89*(3), 97–105. DOI: 10.1080/00098655.2016.1191311

Kroll, J. F., & Bialystok, E. (2013). Understanding the consequences of bilingualism for language processing and cognition. *Journal of Cognitive Psychology, 25*(5), 497–514. DOI: 10.1080/20445911.2013.799170 PMID: 24223260

Küçük, T. (2023). AI integrated grammar teaching in language preparatory school. *International Journal of Social Sciences and Educational Studies, 11*(1). Advance online publication. DOI: 10.23918/ijsses.v11i1p1

Kuhn, D. (2010). Teaching and learning science as argument. *Science Education, 94*(5), 810–824. DOI: 10.1002/sce.20395

Kumar, S. (2019). Effective constructivist teaching learning in the classroom. *International Journal of Research and Analytical Reviews, 7*(4).

Lakkaraju, K., Khandelwal, V., Srivastava, B., Agostinelli, F., Tang, H., Singh, P., . . . Kundu, A. (2024). Trust and ethical considerations in a multi-modal, explainable AI-driven chatbot tutoring system: The case of collaboratively solving Rubik's Cube. *arXiv preprint arXiv:2402.01760.*

Langeveldt, D. C., Pietersen, D., & van Wyk, A. (2023). South African legal framework to prepare pre-service teacher education programmes: A Freirean approach. *Research in Educational Policy and Management, 5*(3), 95–107. DOI: 10.46303/repam.2023.25

Lehrer, R., & Schauble, L. (2015). Modeling and modeling practices in the development of scientific thinking. *Journal of the Learning Sciences, 24*(2), 133–174.

Leung, S., Perry, C., Guy, J., Loats, D., Highfield, K., & Kaufman, J. (2025). Short-term exposure to second language apps modulates brain responses in preschoolers. *Infant and Child Development, 34*(3), e70015. Advance online publication. DOI: 10.1002/icd.70015

Lewis, C., & Hurd, J. (2023). *Lesson study step by step: How teacher learning communities improve instruction*. Heinemann.

Lewis, C., Koyasu, M., Oh, S., Ogawa, A., Short, B., & Huang, Z. (2009). Culture, executive function, and social understanding. *New Directions for Child and Adolescent Development, 2009*(123), 69–85. DOI: 10.1002/cd.236 PMID: 19306275

Li, X., & Kangas, M. (2024). A systematic literature review of playful learning in primary education: teachers' pedagogical activities. *Education 3-13*, 1–16. DOI: 10.1080/03004279.2024.2416954

Li, G., Zarei, M. A., Alibakhshi, G., & Labbafi, A. (2024). Teachers and educators' experiences and perceptions of artificial-powered interventions for autism groups. *BMC Psychology, 12*(1), 199. DOI: 10.1186/s40359-024-01664-2 PMID: 38605422

Li, L., Wang, C., Chen, J., Sun, H., & Zhang, H. (2024). Artificial Intelligence Education Policy Analysis From International Perspective. *Proceedings of the 2024 7th International Conference on Educational Technology Management*, 264–270. DOI: 10.1145/3711403.3711448

Lin, A., Salonen, A., Pope, N., Vartiainen, H., & Tedre, M. (2025, April). A versatile low-cost kit for teaching novice learners ai using robotics components and a no-code development playground. *Proceedings of the AAAI Conference on Artificial Intelligence, 39*(28), 29162–29170. DOI: 10.1609/aaai.v39i28.35189

Linnemann, G. A., & Reimann, L. E. (2024). Artificial Intelligence as a New Field of Activity for Applied Social Psychology–A Reasoning for Broadening the Scope.

Liu, M. (2023). Exploring the application of artificial intelligence in foreign language teaching. *SHS Web of Conferences, 168*, 03025. https://doi.org/DOI: 10.1051/shsconf/202316803025

Long, D., & Magerko, B. (2020). What is AI Literacy? Competencies and Design Considerations. *Proceedings of the 2020 CHI Conference on Human Factors in Computing Systems*, 1–16. DOI: 10.1145/3313831.3376727

Loukatou, G., Scaff, C., Demuth, K., Cristià, A., & Havron, N. (2021). Child-directed and overheard input from different speakers. *Journal of Child Language, 49*(6), 1173–1192. DOI: 10.1017/S0305000921000623 PMID: 34663486

Lucas, M., Bem-haja, P., Zhang, Y., Llorente-Cejudo, C., & Palacios-Rodríguez, A. (2025). A comparative analysis of pre-service teachers' readiness for AI integration. *Computers and Education: Artificial Intelligence*, *8*, 100396. DOI: 10.1016/j.caeai.2025.100396

Lundgren, B., Catena, E., Robertson, I., Hellrigel-Holderbaum, M., Jaja, I. R., & Dung, L. (2024). On the need for a global AI ethics. *Journal of Global Ethics*, *20*(3), 330–342. DOI: 10.1080/17449626.2024.2425366

MacCallum, K., Parsons, D., & Mohaghegh, M. (2023). Identifying the components of foundational Artificial Intelligence (AI) literacy-Early results from a Delphi study. *ASCILITE Publications*, 157-166.

Mahesh, B. (2020). Machine learning algorithms: A review. *International Journal of Scientific Research*, *9*(1), 381–385.

Makeleni, S., Mutongoza, B., & Linake, M. (2023). Language education and artificial intelligence. *Journal of Culture and Values in Education*, *6*(2), 158–171. DOI: 10.46303/jcve.2023.14

Maponga, M. (2024). The penetration of mobile technology in schools: A case of selected schools in Mazowe District. *IRASS Journal of Multidisciplinary Studies*, *1*(3), 25–36.

Marino, C., Bernard, C., & Gervain, J. (2020). Word frequency is a cue to lexical category for infants. *Current Biology : CB*, *30*(8), 1380–1386.e3. DOI: 10.1016/j.cub.2020.01.070 PMID: 32169213

Marino, M., Vasquez, E., Dieker, L., Basham, J., & Blackorby, J. (2023). The future of artificial intelligence in special education technology. *Journal of Special Education Technology*, *38*(3), 404–416. DOI: 10.1177/01626434231165977

Martinez-Comsaria, M., Rigueira-Díaz, X., Larranaga-Janeira, A., Martinez-Torres, J., Ocarranza-Prado, I., & Keribel, D. (2023). Impact of artificial intelligence on assessment methods in primary and secondary education: A systematic review. *Revista de Psicodidáctica*, *28*(2).

Marton, F., & Säljö, R. (1976). On qualitative differences in learning: Outcome and process. *The British Journal of Educational Psychology*, *46*(1), 4–11. DOI: 10.1111/j.2044-8279.1976.tb02980.x

Mathebula, N. Z., Moila, O., Maile, S., & Mnisi, S. (2025). Inadequate Teacher Training as a Barrier to ICT Integration in Early Childhood Education: A Case of Selected Primary Schools in Tshwane West District Circuit 4. *International Journal of Learning. Teaching and Educational Research, 24*(3), 55–74. DOI: 10.26803/ijlter.24.3.3

Matsumoto, D., Yoo, S. H., & Nakagawa, S. (2008). Culture, emotion regulation, and adjustment. *Journal of Personality and Social Psychology, 94*(6), 925–937. DOI: 10.1037/0022-3514.94.6.925 PMID: 18505309

Matthews, A. S., & Bartley, B. (2025). Pay attention to the chatbot behind the curtain when AI 'is no place like home': A framework and toolkit for integrating critical thinking and information literacy in educational and professional settings. *Advances in Online Education: A Peer-Reviewed Journal, 3*(3), 247-273. DOI: 10.69554/FMAI7138

McKay, V. (2018). Literacy, lifelong learning and sustainable development. *Australian Journal of Adult Learning, 58*(3), 390–425.

McKinsey Global Institute. (2023). *The future of work in America: People and places, today and tomorrow*. McKinsey & Company.

McLeod, S. (2025). Piaget's Theory and Stages of Cognitive Development. Simply Psychology. https://www.simplypsychology.org/piaget.html

Melaku, T., & Wudu, M. (2022). Primary school teachers' conceptions and practice of assessment and their relationships. *Cogent Education*.

Miao, F. H. W. R. H. H. Z. (2021). *AI and education: guidance for policy-makers*. UNESCO., DOI: 10.54675/PCSP7350

Miao, F., & Cukurova, M. (2024). *AI competency framework for teachers*. UNESCO., DOI: 10.54675/ZJTE2084

Miao, F., Shiohira, K., & Lao, N. (2024). AI competency framework for students. In *AI competency framework for students*. UNESCO., DOI: 10.54675/JKJB9835

Ministry of Education Malaysia. (2017). *National preschool standard curriculum*. Kurikulum Standard Prasekolah Kebangsaan.

Ministry of Education Malaysia. (2022). *Early childhood education statistics report*.

Ministry of Education of the People's Republic of China. (2024). *Guidance on teaching AI in primary and middle schools*. Retrieved from http://en.moe.gov.cn

Miyake, A., & Friedman, N. P. (2012). The nature and organization of individual differences in executive functions. *Current Directions in Psychological Science*, *21*(1), 8–14. DOI: 10.1177/0963721411429458 PMID: 22773897

Moher, D., Liberati, A., Tetzlaff, J., & Altman, D. G.The PRISMA Group. (2009). Preferred reporting items for systematic reviews and meta-analyses: The PRISMA statement. *PLoS Medicine*, *6*(7), e1000097. DOI: 10.1371/journal.pmed.1000097

Montenegro, R., Corona, E., Badillo-Perez, D., Mandujano, A., Vazquez, L., Cruz, D., & Xochicale, M. (2021). AIR4Children: Artificial Intelligence and Robotics for Children. *arXiv preprint arXiv:2103.07637.*

Moybeka, A. M., Syariatin, N., Tatipang, D. P., Mushthoza, D. A., Dewi, N. P. J. L., & Tineh, S. (2023). Artificial Intelligence and English classroom: The implications of AI toward EFL students' motivation. *Edumaspul: Jurnal Pendidikan*, *7*(2), 2444–2454. DOI: 10.33487/edumaspul.v7i2.6669

Munusamy, P., Sanmugam, M., & Edwards, B. I. (2025). Exploring the World of Coding in Artificial Intelligence: A Guide for Primary School Students. In *Fostering Inclusive Education With AI and Emerging Technologies* (pp. 165-182). IGI Global.

Mwembe, D., & Moyo, H. (2024). Implementing continuous assessment learning activities in Zimbabwe's Education 5.0 system. *Educational Point, 1*(2).

Naida, R., Berezovska, L., Bulgakova, O., Kravets, N., & Savchenkova, M. (2024). Integrating Innovative Pedagogical Technologies Into Early Childhood Education Training Programs: A Comparative Analysis. *Conhecimento & Diversidade*, *16*(41), 568–595. DOI: 10.18316/rcd.v16i41.11551

Ng, D. T. K., Leung, J. K. L., Chu, S. K. W., & Qiao, M. S. (2021). Conceptualizing AI literacy: An exploratory review. *Computers and Education: Artificial Intelligence*, *2*, 100041.

Ng, D. T. K., Leung, J. K. L., Chu, S. K. W., & Qiao, M. S. (2021a). Conceptualising AI literacy: An exploratory review. *Computers and Education: Artificial Intelligence*, *2*, 100041. DOI: 10.1016/j.caeai.2021.100041

Ng, D. T. K., Leung, J. K. L., Su, J., Ng, R. C. W., & Chu, S. K. W. (2023). Teachers' AI digital competencies and twenty-first century skills in the post-pandemic world. *Educational Technology Research and Development*, *71*(1), 137–161. DOI: 10.1007/s11423-023-10203-6 PMID: 36844361

Ng, D. T. K., Leung, J. K. L., Su, M. J., Yim, I. H. Y., Qiao, M. S., & Chu, S. K. W. (2022). *AI literacy in K-16 classrooms*. Springer International Publishing., DOI: 10.1007/978-3-031-18880-0

Ng, D. T. K., Luo, W., Chan, H. M. Y., & Chu, S. K. W. (2022). Using digital storytelling as a pedagogy to develop AI literacy among primary students. *Computers and Education: Artificial Intelligence*, *3*, 100054. DOI: 10.1016/j.caeai.2022.100054

Ng, D. T. K., Su, J., & Chu, S. K. W. (2023). Fostering secondary school students' AI literacy through making AI-driven recycling bins. *Education and Information Technologies*. Advance online publication. DOI: 10.1007/s10639-023-12183-9

Ng, D. T. K., Wu, W., Lok Leung, J. K., & Chu, S. K. W. (2023). Artificial Intelligence (AI) literacy questionnaire with confirmatory factor analysis. In *2023 IEEE International Conference on Advanced Learning Technologies (ICALT)* (pp. 233–235). DOI: 10.1109/ICALT58122.2023.00074

Ngoveni, M. (2025). Bridging the AI Knowledge Gap: The Urgent Need for AI Literacy and Institutional Support. *International Journal of Technologies in Learning*, *32*(2), 83–100. DOI: 10.18848/2327-0144/CGP/v32i02/83-100

Ng, T., Wu, W., Leung, J., & Chiu, T. (2023). Design and validation of the AI literacy questionnaire. *British Journal of Educational Technology*.

Nguyen, A., Ngo, H. N., Hong, Y., Dang, B., & Nguyen, B.-P. T. (2023). Ethical principles for artificial intelligence in education. *Education and Information Technologies*, *28*(4), 4221–4241. DOI: 10.1007/s10639-022-11316-w PMID: 36254344

Nisbett, R. E. (2003). *The Geography of Thought: How Asians and Westerners Think Differently... and Why*. Free Press.

Nisbett, R. E., Peng, K., Choi, I., & Norenzayan, A. (2001). Culture and systems of thought: Holistic versus analytic cognition. *Psychological Review*, *108*(2), 291–310. DOI: 10.1037/0033-295X.108.2.291 PMID: 11381831

Noble, S. U. (2018). *Algorithms of oppression: How search engines reinforce racism*. NYU Press. DOI: 10.18574/nyu/9781479833641.001.0001

Nsamenang, A. B. (2008). Culture and human development. *International Journal of Psychology : Journal International de Psychologie*, *43*(2), 73–77. DOI: 10.1080/00207590701859093 PMID: 22023601

Nziramasanga, C. (1999). *Report of the Presidential Commission of Inquiry into Education*. Government of Zimbabwe.

OECD. (2019). *Recommendation of the Council on Artificial Intelligence*. OECD Publishing. https://legalinstruments.oecd.org/en/instruments/OECD-LEGAL-0449

Okada, A., Sherborne, T., Panselinas, G., & Kolionis, G. (2025). Fostering transversal skills through open schooling supported by the CARE-KNOW-DO pedagogical model and the UNESCO AI competencies framework. *International Journal of Artificial Intelligence in Education, 35*(4), 1–46. DOI: 10.1007/s40593-025-00458-w

Olari, V., Cvejoski, K., & Eide, Ø. (2021, May). Introduction to machine learning with robots and playful learning. *Proceedings of the AAAI Conference on Artificial Intelligence, 35*(17), 15630–15639. DOI: 10.1609/aaai.v35i17.17841

Oloyede, J. (2025). Artificial Intelligence in Education: Building Ethical and Inclusive Smart Learning Ecosystems in the UAE. SSRN *Electronic Journal.* DOI: 10.2139/ssrn.5405420

Omar, A. S., Mgala, M., & Mwakondo, F. (2025). AI-Driven Visual Scaffolding in Education: A Comprehensive Literature Review. *International Journal of Innovation and Scientific Research, XII*(III), 740–750. DOI: 10.51244/IJRSI.2025.12030055

Opesemowo, O. A. G., & Adekomaya, V. (2024). Harnessing artificial intelligence for advancing sustainable development goals in South Africa's higher education system: A qualitative study. *International Journal of Learning. Teaching and Educational Research, 23*(3), 67–86. DOI: 10.26803/ijlter.23.3.4

Ornstein, A. C., & Hunkins, F. (2018). *Curriculum: Foundations, principles, and issues* (7th ed.). Pearson.

Ozturk, E. (2025). Artificial Intelligence in Early Childhood STEM Education: A Review of Pedagogical Paradigms, Ethical Issues, and Socio-Political Implications. *Journal of Education in Science, Environment and Health, 11*(2), 108–125. DOI: 10.55549/jeseh.800

Pack, A., & Maloney, J. (2024). Using artificial intelligence in TESOL. *TESOL Quarterly, 58*(2), 1007–1018. DOI: 10.1002/tesq.3320

Park, W., & Kwon, H. (2023). Implementing AI education in Korea. *International Journal of Technology and Design Education, 34*(1), 109–135. DOI: 10.1007/s10798-023-09812-2 PMID: 36844448

Patel, S., & Ragolane, M. (2024). The implementation of artificial intelligence in South African higher education institutions: Opportunities and challenges. *Technium Education and Humanities, 9*, 51–65. DOI: 10.47577/teh.v9i.11452

Pedro, F., Subosa, M., Rivas, A., & Valverde, P. (2019). Artificial intelligence in education: Challenges and opportunities for sustainable development.

Pew Research Center. (2023). *Parenting children in the age of screens*. Pew Research Center.

Picard, R. W. (1997). *Affective computing*. MIT Press. DOI: 10.7551/mitpress/1140.001.0001

Qayyum, A., Rafique, Z., Shah, S. S. W. A., Ahmad, S., & Haider, Z. (2025). Artificial intelligence (AI)-driven curriculum development in early childhood education: Educators' insights, barriers, and policy pathways. *Research Journal of Psychology*, *3*(1), 713–733. DOI: 10.59075/rjs.v3i1.102

Ranieri, M., Biagini, G., & Cuomo, S. (2025). AI Literacy in Higher Education. *International Journal of Digital Literacy and Digital Competence*, *16*(1), 1–25. DOI: 10.4018/IJDLDC.388469

Rapanta, C., & Walton, D. (2016). The use of argument maps as an assessment tool in higher education. *International Journal of Educational Research*, *79*, 211–221. DOI: 10.1016/j.ijer.2016.03.002

Resnick, L. B. (1994). *Developing mathematical knowledge*. Lawrence Erlbaum.

Rogoff, B. (2003). *The cultural nature of human development*. Oxford university press.

Rogoff, B. (2023). Mutually constituting, fractal: Individual and cultural aspects of holistic process. *Review of Research in Education*, *47*(1), 60–83. DOI: 10.3102/0091732X231224666

Rong, J., Terzidis, K., & Ding, J. (2024). Kids AI design thinking education for creativity development. *Archives of Design Research*, *37*(3), 119–133. DOI: 10.15187/adr.2024.07.37.3.119

Rosmayanti, V., Noni, N., & Patak, A. (2022). Students' acceptance of technology in learning English pharmacy. *International Journal of Language Education*, *6*(3), 314–331. DOI: 10.26858/ijole.v6i3.24144

Roumeliotis, K., & Tselikas, N. (2023). ChatGPT and OpenAI models: A preliminary review. *Future Internet*, *15*(6), 192. DOI: 10.3390/fi15060192

Ruan, S., Jiang, L., Xu, Q., Liu, Z., Davis, G. M., Brunskill, E., & Landay, J. A. (2021, April). Englishbot: An ai-powered conversational system for second language learning. In *Proceedings of the 26th international conference on intelligent user interfaces* (pp. 434-444). DOI: 10.1145/3397481.3450648

Rusmiyanto, R., Huriati, N., Fitriani, N., Tyas, N. K., Rofi'i, A., & Sari, M. N. (2023). The role of Artificial Intelligence (AI) in developing English language learner's communication skills. *Journal of Education*, *6*(1), 750–757. DOI: 10.31004/joe.v6i1.2990

Saal, P. E., Chetty, K., Ntshayintshayi, N., Moosa, T., & Masuku, N. (2025). A scoping review of the integration of artificial intelligence in primary and secondary schools from 2020 to 2024: Policy implications for South Africa. *Journal of Education (University of KwaZulu-Natal)*, (98), 62-85.

Saffran, J. R., Aslin, R. N., & Newport, E. L. (1996). Statistical learning by 8-month-old infants. *science, 274*(5294), 1926-1928.

Santos, O., Rodrigo, M., Cukurova, M., Bittencourt, I., & Koedinger, K. (2021). Ethics of AI in education: Towards a community-wide framework. *International Journal of Artificial Intelligence in Education.*

Sapci, A., & Sapci, H. (2020). Artificial intelligence education in health informatics. *JMIR Medical Education, 6*(1), e19285. DOI: 10.2196/19285 PMID: 32602844

Schafer, J. B. (2004). Hands-on artificial intelligence education using LEGO Mindstorms: Lessons learned. In *Proceedings of the 2004 Midwest Instruction and Computing Symposium.*

Schön, D. A. (1983). *The reflective practitioner: How professionals think in action.* Basic Books.

Shi, L. (2024). AI-enabled emotion detection and adaptive learning systems. *Journal of Educational Computing Research, 63*(1), 173–201. DOI: 10.1177/07356331241296890

Siegler, R. S. (2016). Continuity and change in the field of cognitive development and in the perspectives of one cognitive developmentalist. *Child Development Perspectives, 10*(2), 128–133. DOI: 10.1111/cdep.12173

Sikhakhane, M., Govender, S., & Maphalala, M. C. (2021). The extent of South African schools' preparedness to counteract 4IR challenges: learners' perspectives. *Journal of e-learning and knowledge society, 17*(1), 1-9.

Sileyew, K. J. (2019). Research design and methodology. In *Cyberspace.* IntechOpen.

Simpson, T. L. (2002). Dare I oppose constructivist theory? *The Educational Forum, 66*(4), 347–354. DOI: 10.1080/00131720208984854

Simuţ, R., Simuţ, C., Badulescu, D., & Badulescu, A. (2024). Artificial intelligence and the modelling of teachers' competencies. *Amfiteatru Economic, 26*(65), 181–200. DOI: 10.24818/EA/2024/65/181

Sinha, N., Evans, R. F., & Carbo, M. (2023, May). Hands-on active learning approach to teach artificial intelligence/machine learning to elementary and middle school students. In *2023 32nd wireless and optical communications conference (WOCC)* (pp. 1-6). IEEE.

Song, Y., Weisberg, L. R., Zhang, S., Tian, X., Boyer, K. E., & Israel, M. (2024). A framework for inclusive AI learning design for diverse learners. *Computers and Education: Artificial Intelligence*, *6*, 100212. DOI: 10.1016/j.caeai.2024.100212

Southworth, J., Migliaccio, K., Glover, J., Glover, J., Reed, D., McCarty, C., Brendemuhl, J., & Thomas, A. (2023). Developing a model for AI Across the curriculum: Transforming the higher education landscape via innovation in AI literacy. *Computers and Education: Artificial Intelligence*, *4*, 100127. DOI: 10.1016/j.caeai.2023.100127

Spector, J. M., & Ma, S. (2019). Inquiry and critical thinking skills for the next generation: From artificial intelligence back to human intelligence. *Smart Learning Environments*, *6*(1), 1–11. DOI: 10.1186/s40561-019-0088-z

Srinivasan, R., & San Miguel González, B. (2022). The role of empathy for artificial intelligence accountability. *Journal of Responsible Technology*, *9*, 100021. DOI: 10.1016/j.jrt.2021.100021

Sterman, J. D. (2000). *Business dynamics: Systems thinking and modeling for a complex world*. Irwin/McGraw-Hill.

Su, J., Ng, D. T. K., & Chu, S. K. W. (2023). Artificial Intelligence (AI) Literacy in Early Childhood Education: The Challenges and Opportunities. *Computers and Education: Artificial Intelligence*, *4*, 100124. DOI: 10.1016/j.caeai.2023.100124

Su, J., & Yang, W. (2022). Artificial intelligence in early childhood education: A scoping review. *Computers and Education: Artificial Intelligence*, *3*, 100049. DOI: 10.1016/j.caeai.2022.100049

Su, J., & Zhong, Y. (2022). Artificial Intelligence (AI) in early childhood education: Curriculum design and future directions. *Computers and Education: Artificial Intelligence*, *3*, 100072. DOI: 10.1016/j.caeai.2022.100072

Sullivan, A., & Strawhacker, A. (2021). Screen-free STEAM: Low-cost and hands-on approaches to teaching coding and engineering to young children. In *Embedding STEAM in early childhood education and care* (pp. 87–113). Springer International Publishing. DOI: 10.1007/978-3-030-65624-9_5

Sutton-Smith, B. (1997). *The ambiguity of play*. Harvard University Press.

Tan, C. (2018). *Comparing high-performing education systems: understanding Singapore, Shanghai, and Hong Kong*. Routledge. DOI: 10.4324/9781351238724

Tang, X., Ding, X., Ma, X., Zhang, S., & Diao, J. (2024). *An Exploration of Project-Based Learning Supported by Artificial Intelligence*., DOI: 10.2991/978-94-6463-417-4_20

Tan, S., & Neo, M. (2022). Digital literacy in early childhood education: Systems reasoning and engagement. *Asia Pacific Journal of Education*, *42*(3), 375–391. DOI: 10.53797/icccmjssh.v4i1.6.2025

Tan, X., Cheng, G., & Ling, M. H. (2025). Artificial intelligence in teaching and teacher professional development: A systematic review. *Computers and Education: Artificial Intelligence*, *8*, 100355. DOI: 10.1016/j.caeai.2024.100355

Tariq, M. U. (2026). The Role of AI-Powered Learning Analytics in Enhancing Student Engagement and Performance. In J. Moore, S. Gupta, M. Sharma, A. Garg, & H. Josephine V. L. (Eds.), *Transforming Education With Data Science in the AI Era* (pp. 123-148). IGI Global Scientific Publishing. https://doi.org/DOI: 10.4018/979-8-3373-2185-1.ch005

Tariq, M. (Ed.). (2025). *Emerging Multisector Applications of AI and IoT*. IGI Global., DOI: 10.4018/979-8-3373-4332-7

Tariq, M. (Ed.). (2025). *Merging Artificial Intelligence With the Internet of Things*. IGI Global., DOI: 10.4018/979-8-3693-8547-0

Tariq, M. U. (2025). *AI-Driven Learning and Engagement in Higher Education*. IGI Global., DOI: 10.4018/979-8-3693-4074-5

Tariq, M. U. (2025). AI-Driven Personalized Learning: Revolutionizing Student Engagement and Teacher Efficiency in Education 5.0. In Mobo, F. (Ed.), *AI and Emerging Technologies for Emergency Response and Smart Cities* (pp. 75–96). IGI Global Scientific Publishing., DOI: 10.4018/979-8-3693-9770-1.ch004

Tariq, M. U. (2025). Bridging Home and Classroom: Harnessing Cultural and Ecological Wisdom in Teacher Education. In Liu, L., Mohamed, N., Lin, C., Bauler, C., & Kapur, K. (Eds.), *Funds of Knowledge in Teacher Education: Sustaining Local Diversity Amidst Global Standards* (pp. 405–424). IGI Global Scientific Publishing., DOI: 10.4018/979-8-3693-8094-9.ch018

Tariq, M. U. (2026). AI-Driven Curriculum Design in Higher Education: Frameworks for Future-Ready Learning Ecosystems. In Abdelaal, R., & Kayyali, M. (Eds.), *AI Education Strategies for Future-Proofing Curriculum Design* (pp. 21–46). IGI Global Scientific Publishing., DOI: 10.4018/979-8-3373-2752-5.ch002

Tariq, M. U. (2026). AI-Powered Assessment Platforms: Transforming Higher Education Evaluation. In Zaky, H. (Ed.), *Innovating Assessment and Evaluation in Higher Education: Inclusive Practices and Technological Advancements* (pp. 117–146). IGI Global Scientific Publishing., DOI: 10.4018/979-8-3373-2130-1.ch004

Tariq, M. U. (2026). AI-Powered Sustainability in Airline Operations: Digital Innovation as a Strategic Driver for Decarbonization and Efficiency. In Mizrak, F., & Rodoplu, D. (Eds.), *Strategic Innovation for Sustainable Aviation Management* (pp. 291–316). IGI Global Scientific Publishing., DOI: 10.4018/979-8-3373-4992-3.ch010

Tariq, M. U. (2026). Algorithmic Nudging for Eco-Friendly Fashion: A Framework for Ethical AI Interventions. In Arantes, L. (Ed.), *Promoting Sustainable Consumption in Fashion With AI* (pp. 89–112). IGI Global Scientific Publishing., DOI: 10.4018/979-8-3373-5525-2.ch003

Tariq, M. U. (2026). Empowering Young Learners: Innovative Strategies for STEM and Literacy in Early Childhood Deaf Education. In Graham, P., & Neild, N. (Eds.), *Early Childhood Deaf Education: Teacher Preparation and Instructional Approaches* (pp. 231–258). IGI Global Scientific Publishing., DOI: 10.4018/979-8-3693-9127-3.ch007

Tariq, M. U. (2026). Equity-Driven Leadership in Technology Integration for Higher Education. In Areba, G., Gisore, B., Njurai, E., Awuor, F., & Makiya Cyprian, R. (Eds.), *Transformative Leadership and Enhancing Equity in Technological Advancements in Higher Education* (pp. 171–198). IGI Global Scientific Publishing., DOI: 10.4018/979-8-3373-2322-0.ch007

Tariq, M. U. (2026). Innovation and Agility-Adapting Business Strategies for Sustainable Growth in Dynamic Markets. In Ananthan, S., Kohli, A., Manickam, T., & Dhanabalan, T. (Eds.), *New Business Development Strategies for Achieving Sustainable Growth* (pp. 113–140). IGI Global Scientific Publishing., DOI: 10.4018/979-8-3373-2048-9.ch005

Tariq, M. U. (2026). Micro-Credentials for Workforce Development: Addressing Skills Gaps in High-Demand Industries. In Maming, J. (Ed.), *Transforming the Workforce With Microcredentials* (pp. 99–126). IGI Global Scientific Publishing., DOI: 10.4018/979-8-3373-2257-5.ch004

Tariq, M. U. (2026). Revolutionizing Educator Preparation: Exploring the Efficacy of Grow Your Own Models. In Sande, B., & Marvel, A. (Eds.), *Enhancing Educational Access Through Innovative Educator Preparation Pathways* (pp. 75–100). IGI Global Scientific Publishing., DOI: 10.4018/979-8-3693-7337-8.ch004

Tarisayi, K. (2024). Preparing for AI's transformational potential: Rethinking teacher education in South Africa. *International Education Trend Issues*, *2*(1), 31–40. DOI: 10.56442/ieti.v2i1.364

Tjano, R. N., & Mphahlele, R. (2025). Cultivating cognitive justice in AI-enhanced education: Harnessing intelligent tutoring systems and navigating ethical horizons. In *Artificial Intelligence and Human Agency in Education: Volume One* (pp. 45–68). Springer. DOI: 10.1007/978-981-96-7937-9_3

Tomczyk, Ł. (2025). AI in Education - Mapping Theoretical Frameworks for Digital Literacy: DigComp 2.2, AI Literacy Competency Framework, AI Literacy TPACK, the Machine Learning Education Framework, the UNESCO AI Competency Framework for and Teachers and Other Innovative Approaches. New Media Pedagogy: Research Trends, Methodological Challenges, and Successful Implementations, 173–191. DOI: 10.1007/978-3-031-95627-0_12

Touretzky, D., Gardner-McCune, C., Martin, F., & Seehorn, D. (2019). Envisioning AI for K-12: What should every child know about AI? In *Proceedings of the AAAI Conference on Artificial Intelligence*. DOI: 10.1609/aaai.v33i01.33019795

Touretzky, D., Gardner-McCune, C., & Seehorn, D. (2023). Machine Learning and the Five Big Ideas in AI. *International Journal of Artificial Intelligence in Education*, *33*(2), 233–266. DOI: 10.1007/s40593-022-00314-1

Turkle, S. (2007). *Evocative objects: Things we think with*. MIT Press.

Turkle, S. (2011). *Alone together: Why we expect more from technology and less from each other*. Basic Books.

U.S. Department of Education, O. of E. T. (2023). *Artificial Intelligence and Future of Teaching and Learning: Insights and Recommendations*.

UNESCO. (2022). *Early childhood care and education (ECCE) global monitoring report 2022*. https://www.unesco.org

UNESCO. (2022). *K-12 AI curricula: A mapping of government-endorsed AI curricula*. https://unesdoc.unesco.org/ark:/48223/pf0000380602

UNESCO. (2023). *Global Education Monitoring Report 2023: Technology in education—A tool on whose terms?* UNESCO.

UNESCO. (2025). *Recommendation on the ethics of artificial intelligence*. UNESCO.

UNICEF Regional Office for East Asia and the Pacific. (2021). *Early learning and development in Southeast Asia*.

United Nations. (2025). *Sustainable Development Goal 4: Quality education*. United Nations.

Van Brummelen, J., Heng, T., & Tabunshchyk, V. (2021). Teaching tech to talk: K-12 conversational artificial intelligence literacy curriculum and development tools. *Proceedings of the AAAI Conference on Artificial Intelligence*, *35*(17), 15655–15663. DOI: 10.1609/aaai.v35i17.17844

Van Wyk, B. (2024). Exploring the philosophy and practice of AI literacy in higher education in the Global South: A scoping review. *Cybrarians Journal*, (73), 1–21. DOI: 10.70000/cj.2024.73.601

Vygotsky, L. S. (1978). *Mind in society: The development of higher psychological processes*. Harvard University Press.

Walliman, N. (2021). *Research methods: The basics*. Routledge. DOI: 10.4324/9781003141693

Walter, Y. (2024). Embracing the future of artificial intelligence in the classroom: The relevance of AI literacy, prompt engineering, and critical thinking in modern education. *International Journal of Educational Technology in Higher Education*, *21*(1), 15. DOI: 10.1186/s41239-024-00448-3

Wang, B., Rau, P. L. P., & Yuan, T. (2022). Measuring user competence in using artificial intelligence: Validity and reliability of artificial intelligence literacy scale. *Behaviour & Information Technology*, •••, 1–14. DOI: 10.1080/0144929X.2022.2072768

Wang, X., Li, L., Tan, S. C., Yang, L., & Lei, J. (2023). Preparing for AI-enhanced education: Conceptualizing and empirically examining teachers' AI readiness. *Computers in Human Behavior*, *146*, 107798. DOI: 10.1016/j.chb.2023.107798

Wellman, H. M. (2014). *Making minds: How theory of mind develops*. Oxford University Press. DOI: 10.1093/acprof:oso/9780199334919.001.0001

Wiese, L. J., Patil, I., Schiff, D. S., & Magana, A. J. (2025). AI ethics education: A systematic literature review. *Computers and Education: Artificial Intelligence*, *8*, 100405. DOI: 10.1016/j.caeai.2025.100405

Wiggill, C. R. (2023). *South African Teachers' Perceptions of the Adoption of Artificial Intelligence in the Classroom* (Master's thesis, University of Johannesburg (South Africa)).

World Economic Forum. (2020). *The Future of Jobs Report 2020*. https://www3.weforum.org/docs/WEF_Future_of_Jobs_2020.pdf

World Economic Forum. (2023). *The Future of Jobs Report 2023*. World Economic Forum.

Wu, D., Chen, M., Chen, X., & Liu, X. (2024). Analyzing K-12 AI education: A large language model study of classroom instruction on learning theories, pedagogy, tools, and AI literacy. *Computers and Education: Artificial Intelligence*, *7*, 100295. DOI: 10.1016/j.caeai.2024.100295

Xatamova, N., & Ashurov, J. (2024). The future of legal English learning: Integrating AI into ESP education. SPAST Reports, 1(7).

Xu, Y. '. (2024). The Double-Edged Sword of AI Writing Tools. https://osf.io/preprints/socarxiv/wnpd5 DOI: 10.31235/osf.io/wnpd5

Yahaya, A. A., Rasheed, F., Muaz, B. S., Haruna, U., Sani, A., Yahaya, I. A., & Ahmad, B. M. (2024). Application of machine learning in education: Recent trends challenges and future perspective. *Información Tecnológica*, *7*(3), 118–131.

Yang, H. C. S. (2025). *Promoting AI Literacy in K-12: Components*. Challenges, and Opportunities.

Yang, W., Hu, X., Yeter, I. H., Su, J., Yang, Y., & Lee, J. C. K. (2024). Artificial intelligence education for young children: A case study of technology-enhanced embodied learning. *Journal of Computer Assisted Learning*, *40*(2), 465–477. DOI: 10.1111/jcal.12892

Yan, Y., & Liu, H. (2024). Ethical framework for AI education based on large language models. *Education and Information Technologies*.

Yim, I. H. Y. (2024). A critical review of teaching and learning artificial intelligence (AI) literacy: Developing an intelligence-based AI literacy framework for primary school education. *Computers and Education: Artificial Intelligence*, *7*, 100319. DOI: 10.1016/j.caeai.2024.100319

Yim, I. H. Y. (2024). Artificial intelligence literacy in primary education: An arts-based approach to overcoming age and gender barriers. *Computers and Education: Artificial Intelligence*, *7*, 100321. DOI: 10.1016/j.caeai.2024.100321

Yim, I., & Su, J. (2025). Artificial intelligence literacy in primary schools: A review. *International Journal of Technology and Design Education*, *35*(5), 2175–2204. DOI: 10.1007/s10798-025-09979-w

Yin, Y., Jia, N., & Wakslak, C. (2024). AI can help people feel heard. *Proceedings of the National Academy of Sciences of the United States of America, 121*(14), e2319112121. Advance online publication. DOI: 10.1073/pnas.2319112121 PMID: 38551835

Yue, M., Jong, M. S. Y., & Ng, D. T. K. (2024). Understanding K–12 teachers' technological pedagogical content knowledge readiness and attitudes toward artificial intelligence education. *Education and Information Technologies, 29*(15), 19505–19536. DOI: 10.1007/s10639-024-12621-2

Yue, M., Jong, M. S.-Y., Dai, Y., & Lau, W. W.-F. (2025a). Students as AI literate designers: A pedagogical framework for learning and teaching AI literacy in elementary education. *Journal of Research on Technology in Education*, •••, 1–22. DOI: 10.1080/15391523.2025.2449942

Yuen, C., & Schlote, N. (2024). Learner experiences of AI-supported language learning. *Journal of Educational Technology Systems, 52*(4), 507–525. DOI: 10.1177/00472395241238693

Yu, L., & Yu, Z. (2023). Qualitative and quantitative analyses of artificial intelligence ethics in education using VOSviewer and CitNetExplorer. *Frontiers in Psychology, 14*, 1061778. DOI: 10.3389/fpsyg.2023.1061778 PMID: 36968737

Yunina, O. (2023). Artificial intelligence tools in foreign language teaching in higher education institutions. *The modern higher education review*, (8), 77-90.

Zawacki-Richter, O., Marín, V. I., Bond, M., & Gouverneur, F. (2019). Systematic review of research on artificial intelligence applications in higher education – Where are the educators? *International Journal of Educational Technology in Higher Education, 16*(1), 1–27. DOI: 10.1186/s41239-019-0171-0

Zelazo, P. D. (2015). Executive function: Reflection, iterative reprocessing, complexity, and the developing brain. *Developmental Review, 38*, 55–68. DOI: 10.1016/j.dr.2015.07.001

Zhang, H., Lee, I., Alshehri, A., D'Paola, D., Cheng, Y., & Breazeal, C. (2022). Integrating ethics and career futures with technical learning to promote AI literacy for middle school students: An exploratory study. *International Journal of Artificial Intelligence in Education*. Advance online publication. DOI: 10.1007/s40593-022-00293-3

Zhang, K., & Dede, C. (2023). Assessing AI literacy in K-12: A comprehensive framework and assessment tool. *Computers & Education: Artificial Intelligence, 4*, 100142.

Zhao, H.-G., Li, X.-Z., & Kang, X. (2024). Development of an artificial intelligence curriculum design for children in Taiwan and its impact on learning outcomes. *Humanities & Social Sciences Communications*, *11*(1), 1339. DOI: 10.1057/s41599-024-03839-z

Zhao, L., Wu, X., & Luo, H. (2022). Developing AI Literacy for Primary and Middle School Teachers in China: Based on a Structural Equation Modeling Analysis. *Sustainability (Basel)*, *14*(21), 14549. DOI: 10.3390/su142114549

Zhou, X., Van Brummelen, J., & Lin, P. (2020). Designing AI learning experiences for K-12: Emerging works, future opportunities and a design framework. *arXiv preprint arXiv:2009.10228.*

Zhou, X., Li, Y., Chai, C. S., & Chiu, T. K. F. (2025). Defining, enhancing, and assessing artificial intelligence literacy and competency in K-12 education from a systematic review. *Interactive Learning Environments*, *33*(10), 1–23. DOI: 10.1080/10494820.2025.2487538

Zou, B., Du, Y., Wang, Z., Chen, J., & Zhang, W. (2023). AI speech evaluation programs in EFL. *SAGE Open*, *13*(3). Advance online publication. DOI: 10.1177/21582440231193818

Zou, B., Guan, X., Shao, Y., & Chen, P. (2023). Social network-based AI-assisted language learning. *Sustainability*, *15*(4), 2872. DOI: 10.3390/su15042872

Zou, D., Xie, H., & Kohnke, L. (2025). Navigating the Future: Establishing a Framework for Educators' Pedagogic Artificial Intelligence Competence. *European Journal of Education*, *60*(2), e70117. DOI: 10.1111/ejed.70117

Zuboff, S. (2019). *The age of surveillance capitalism: The fight for a human future at the new frontier of power*. PublicAffairs.

About the Contributors

Muhammad Usman Tariq has more than 17+ year's experience in industry and academia. He has authored more than 300+ research articles/book chapters/case studies and 4 patents. He is founder and CEO of The Case HQ, a unique repository for courses and teaching case studies. His work has encompassed sectors in aviation, manufacturing, food, hospitality, education, operations, software and suppl chain. He has diverse and significant experience working with accreditation agencies of ABET, ACBSP, AACSB, WASC, CAA, EFQM and NCEAC. He is Certified Higher Education Teacher from Harvard University, USA, Certified Online Educator from HMBSU, Certified Six Sigma Master Black Belt, Lead Auditor ISO 9001 Certified, ISO 14001, IOSH MS, OSHA 30, and OSHA 48. He has been awarded Principal Fellowship from Advance HE UK, Chartered Fellowship of CIPD UK, and Certified business and management educator recognition.

***

Ishteyaaq Ahmad is an academician at University of Petroleum & Energy Studies, Dehradun, India, with over two decades of experience in teaching and research. Specializing in Artificial Intelligence, Machine Learning, and Online Education, his work focuses on leveraging technology to create inclusive and innovative learning environments. Dr. Ahmad holds a Ph.D. in Computer Applications, with his research centered on predicting and mitigating high attrition rates in MOOCs using Machine Learning. He has authored extensively in SCI and SCOPUS-indexed journals and conferences and has developed a top-rated MOOC on the SWAYAM platform, recognized by ClassCentral as one of the Top 100 free courses of all time. Additionally, he has created Open Educational Resources for the Commonwealth of Learning (COL), and has mentored MOOC development for Open Education for a Better World (OE4BW) program of University of Nova Gorica, Slovenia. As a sought-after Resource Person, Dr. Ahmad has contributed to institutions like NCERT, SCERT Uttarakhand, and Allahabad University. He is a recipient of the Young Scientist Award and a Professional Research Grant from the Department of Science & Technology, Government of India. He is also a Fellow of the India School on Internet Governance (inSIG2017). Dr. Ahmad is passionate about advancing education through technology and fostering impactful learning experiences globally.

Oluwatoyin Ayodele Ajani is a distinguished scholar and Senior Lecturer in Curriculum Studies at the University of KwaZulu-Natal, Edgewood Campus, South Africa. With a strong academic background in teacher education, curriculum development, and the sociology of education, Dr. Ajani brings a wealth of experience to the field of educational research and practice. He holds a PhD in Curriculum Studies and has served as a postdoctoral research fellow at North-West University, as well as a research fellow at Durban University of Technology. He was also a lecturer at the University of Zululand, South Africa, where his research contributions won him the institution's prestigious Vice Chancellor's Award in 2022 and 2024. Dr. Ajani's scholarly work focuses on teacher professional development, decolonisation of education, and the integration of technology in curriculum delivery, particularly within the African context. His research has been widely published in peer-reviewed journals and has significantly contributed to understanding the challenges and innovations in teacher education across rural and urban settings. He is especially known for his work on narrative pedagogy.

Venkatesh Ankarla Sri Ramuloo is a Distinguished Industry Leader (Gulf HE) and Test Automation Engineer. With over a decade of experience spanning the healthcare, retail, and insurance sectors, he brings deep expertise in engineering leadership, data governance, data science, artificial intelligence, quantum computing, machine learning, the Internet of Things (IoT), blockchain, and cybersecurity. Dr. Ramuloo has led numerous enterprise-level initiatives focused on sustainable development, driving innovation in software testing, CI/CD pipeline integration, and Agile team collaboration. His work is grounded in building scalable, high-quality solutions across a wide range of platforms and technology stacks. Academically, he holds a Ph.D. in Information Technology and an M.S. in Computer Science. He is an active contributor to the scholarly community through his research publications and peer-reviewed work for reputable journals. As a committed IEEE Senior member, he actively promotes professional development and cross-disciplinary collaboration within the global tech community. Dr. Ramuloo is recognized for his balanced blend of technical rigor, academic excellence, and dedication to advancing both industry practices and IT education.

Sumanth Banakar holds a Ph.D. in Information Technology from the University of the Cumberlands, Kentucky (2023), a Master of Science in Information Technology Management from Campbellsville University, Kentucky (2019), and a Master of Science in Computer Science from Silicon Valley University, California (2016). With over six years of professional experience as a Software Engineer, he has worked across diverse domains including healthcare, banking, finance, retail, and insurance. Sumanth brings a strong academic foundation and practical expertise in designing and implementing technology solutions that drive business outcomes.

WilliamChakabwata holds a PhD in Curriculum and Instruction obtained from University of South Africa on 27 September 2023.He also holds a master degree in Curriculum and arts education which he earned from University of Zimbabwe. He has taught at Midlands State University in Namibia and also at Namibia University of Science and Technology(NUST). He may be contacted at williechaka@gmail.com

Tebogo Lekota is a seasoned academic development officer with the University of Limpopo, South Africa.

Jabulisiwe Mamba is a PhD candidate in Educational Psychology with 35+ years as a primary school educator. Master of Education in Educational Psychology. Former, Head of Department, Deputy Principal, and acting Principal at Crovoca Primary School.

Sithokozile Mamba is a PhD candidate in Management. Master of Commerce in Management. Multiple academic publications.

Vivit Rosmayanti, S.Pd.I., M.Pd was born in Botta on June 26, 1987. She has over 10 years of experience teaching at the University. She obtained a bachelor's degree in English Education from Alauddin State Islamic University. She completed her master's and doctoral degrees in English Education from Makassar State University. She is currently a lecturer in the Post Graduate Program, Department of English Education at Makassar State University, South Sulawesi, Indonesia. She is also actively writing research articles to be published in nationally and internationally accredited journals. She has written in some chapter books, monographs, and reference books. She is interested in teaching methods for teaching English. Her research interests include language teaching methodology, ICT instruction, and ESP teaching. She can be contacted at email: rosmayantivivit@gmail.com

Bellona Mardhatillah Sabillah, S.Pd., M.Pd., is a passionate and inspiring lecturer in the Primary School Teacher Education Program at Universitas Megarezky. Born in Malang on March 22, 1990, Bellona's academic journey began with a Bachelor's degree in Primary School Teacher Education from Universitas Muhammadiyah Makassar, followed by a Master's degree in the same field from Universitas Negeri Makassar. Today, as a dedicated educator, she is shaping the next generation of teachers, empowering them with the knowledge and skills to create impactful learning experiences in primary schools.

Wahyu Muh. Syata, S.E., M.Pd., is a dedicated lecturer at Universitas Halu Oleo Kendari, with a passion for education and management. Born in Balusu on January 1, 1989, Wahyu began his academic journey with a Bachelor's degree in Management from Universitas Muslim Indonesia. Building on his expertise, he further pursued a Master's degree in Economic Education at Universitas Negeri Makassar. Now, as a faculty member, Wahyu is committed to shaping future leaders and inspiring his students to excel in the fields of education and management, preparing them for success in a dynamic world.

Index

Symbols

A

B

C

D

E

F

H

L

M

N

O

P

R

S

T

V

www.ingramcontent.com/pod-product-compliance
Lightning Source LLC
LaVergne TN
LVHW080858300926
849162LV00003B/471
* 9 7 9 8 3 3 7 3 4 8 9 3 3 *